Myths and Border Conflicts in Greece

Andrew A. Rosenthal

Contents

Introduction: Old Wars between Neighbors 1

1. Fighting over an Egyptian bean............1

2. Performing identity in the borderlands............5

3. The shared values of "Mursiness:" confrontation as cooperation............15

4. *Agôn* and carnage............22

5. Bottom-up and top-down: synchrony, diachrony, history............33

6. The outline of the argument............38

PART I: The Lelantine War

Chapter 1: The Bronze Generation and the Generation of Bronze............44

1. A war in search of an identity............44

2. Thucydides' logic............47

3. The poetry of the Lelantine Plain............51

4. Amphidamas of Chalcis and the Bronze Generation............60

5. Metals and war............73

6. Leaving the Golden Age at Pithecusae..85

7. The lost Euboea..88

Chapter 2. Tresses, Pastures and Vineyards..94

1. Archilochus or Strabo?..94

2. The lords of Euboea and the future battle..100

3. The reenactment..108

4. Allies and pillars..115

5. Warriors with bangs..127

6. Riders on the earth..137

7. Theognis' stanza..142

8. Earwax and the end of the Lelantine war..150

PART II: The Confrontation between Argos and Sparta over the Thyreatis

Chapter 3: Three Hundred Men from Each Side..162

1. The Argive proposal..162

2. Was there a war?..167

3. To flee or not to flee..176

4. What Herodotus has joined together...185

5. Beautiful death in the Thyreatis..191

6. The ritual battle..197

7. Fighting at the Gymnopaediae...203

8. Border games...212

9. Apollo Pythaeus..216

10. The transformation of the *hippeis*..224

Chapter 4: City of Women: Democratic Argos and the Battle of Sepeia...237

1. Harnessing the energy of the myth..237

2. Cleomenes' ruses...239

3. Women and slaves disentangled: varieties of inversion............................245

4. Liberating the Pamphyliacum..251

5. The bearded bride..259

6. Women in arms: the glory, the farce and the permanent changes............266

7. The Hybristica and the democratic dissolution..278

8. The Sepeia oracle: an immodest proposal...284

Chapter 5. Cobwebs on Shields: Scenes from the Argive Synoecism 296

1. The demise of the seventh 296

2. The curious incident of the missing conquest 301

3. The *Hyrnathioi* and other migrants 309

4. Slaves and other villains 316

5. The shields of Archinus 325

6. A farewell to arms and the moveable Apollo Pythaeus 333

7. Writing on the shield 341

Chapter 6: As They Did in the Past: The Dispute over the Thyreatis in Argive Politics of 421–417 BC 356

1. The ritual battle as an oligarchic motion 356

2. The versatile Thousand 359

3. Apollo Pythaeus: a democratic move 366

4. Heroic and unscathed at Mantinea 369

5. Apollo Pythaeus: a countermove 374

6. Waiting for the Gymnopaediae 380

7. Bryas, *hubris*, and memories of the past 386

Conclusion: Border Between Myth and Ritual 389

1. Old frontiers 389

2. The rest of the Greeks 394

Introduction

Old Wars between Neighbors

> *I realized that the history of culture is a chain of equations in images, sequentially pairing an unknown with the known, so that the known, the constant for the whole series, is the myth set in the foundation of the tradition, while the unknown, every time new, is the pressing moment of the current culture.*
> Boris Pasternak, *Safe Conduct*[1]

1. Fighting over an Egyptian bean

The boundaries are arbitrary. The planet is real. Spaceflight, therefore, is subversive. If they are fortunate enough to find themselves in Earth orbit, most people, after a little meditation, have similar thoughts. The nations that had instituted spaceflight had done so largely for nationalistic reasons; it was a small irony that almost everyone who entered space received a startling glimpse of a transnational perspective, of the Earth as one world.[2]

Eighteen centuries before Carl Sagan wrote these words, another flight, no less subversive — a flight of fancy — resulted in a similar insight about the preposterousness of boundary-lines.

---

[1] Я понял, что история культуры есть цепь уравнений в образах, попарно связывающих очередное неизвестное с известным, причем этим известным, постоянным для всего ряда, является легенда, заложенная в основание традиции, неизвестным же, каждый раз новым – актуальный момент текущей культуры.

[2] Sagan 1986, 278–279.

Thus speaks Menippus, Lucian's character, who flew to the Moon and gazed at the Earth from there:

> Μάλιστα δὲ ἐπ' ἐκείνοις ἐπῄει μοι γελᾶν τοῖς περὶ γῆς ὅρων ἐρίζουσι [...]. ἀποβλέψας δὲ δὴ καὶ ἐς τὴν Πελοπόννησον, εἶτα τὴν Κυνουρίαν γῆν ἰδὼν ἀνεμνήσθην περὶ ὅσου χωρίου, κατ' οὐδὲν Αἰγυπτίου φακοῦ πλατυτέρου, τοσοῦτοι ἔπεσον Ἀργείων καὶ Λακεδαιμονίων μιᾶς ἡμέρας.
>
> I was especially inclined to laugh at the people who quarreled about boundary-lines… And when I looked toward the Peloponnese and caught sight of Cynuria, I noted what a tiny region, no bigger in any way than an Egyptian bean, had caused so many Argives and Spartans to fall in a single day.[3]

A boundary, somehow, invites a look from above. It also apparently invites to be fought over. This dissertation explores the subject of ancient border wars in Greece. I argue that while these border wars were perceived as archetypal occasions for bloodshed, as early as in the Archaic period stories of these wars served to motivate unity and peace between the opposing cities. Paradoxically, Argives and Spartans may have received "a startling glimpse of a transnational perspective" while locked in fight over the region of Cynuria.

*

---

[3] Lucian, *Icaromenippus* 18.1–2, 11–16. Trans. A. M. Harmon.

Border conflicts constituted the main type of Archaic warfare.[4] Modern scholars are increasingly in agreement with Thucydides' perception of a stark contrast between the Peloponnesian wars and the earlier Greek wars (Thucydides 1.15.2):

> κατὰ γῆν δὲ πόλεμος, ὅθεν τις καὶ δύναμις παρεγένετο, οὐδεὶς ξυνέστη· πάντες δὲ ἦσαν, ὅσοι καὶ ἐγένοντο, πρὸς ὁμόρους τοὺς σφετέρους ἑκάστοις, καὶ ἐκδήμους στρατείας πολὺ ἀπὸ τῆς ἑαυτῶν ἐπ' ἄλλων καταστροφῇ οὐκ ἐξῇσαν οἱ Ἕλληνες. οὐ γὰρ ξυνειστήκεσαν πρὸς τὰς μεγίστας πόλεις ὑπήκοοι, οὐδ' αὖ αὐτοὶ ἀπὸ τῆς ἴσης κοινὰς στρατείας ἐποιοῦντο, κατ' ἀλλήλους δὲ μᾶλλον ὡς ἕκαστοι οἱ ἀστυγείτονες ἐπολέμουν.

> Wars by land there were none, none at least by which power was acquired; we have the usual border contests, but of distant expeditions with conquest for object we hear nothing among the Hellenes. There was no union of subject cities round a great state, no spontaneous combination of equals for confederate expeditions; what fighting there was consisted merely of local warfare between rival neighbors.

The wars between Eretria and Chalcis over the Lelantine Plain and between Argos and Sparta over Cynuria are the main subject of my investigation. These two wars stand in the context of a longer list of confrontations between the neighboring city-states over a contested border territory, a list that includes a mythical war between Athens and Eleusis,[5] as well as wars

---

[4] Hall 2007a, 90; Singor 2009, 595-599; van Wees 2004, 28; De Ste. Croix 1972, 218-220.
[5] Thucydides 2.15.1; Pausanias 1.5.2, 1.27.4, 1.36.4, 1.38.3; Apollodorus 3.15.4(203). According to the tradition, the fighting took place in Sciron, the ancient border district between Athens and Eleusis, and the site of the temple of Athena Sciras. The myth of the war between Athens and Eleusis is also connected with the festival of *Skira*. Burkert 1983, 147-148 and n52 with further references. On the tradition of fighting between Athens and Eleusis, as reflected in Herodotus 1.30.4, see Chapter 3, Section 4.

and/or disputes between Sparta and Tegea,[6] Samos and Priene,[7] Corinth and Megara,[8] Thebes and Orchomenus,[9] Athens and Megara,[10] Athens and Boeotia.[11] Different as the respective details are, these conflicts share some broad characteristic features. They typically concern a relatively modest border territory, they are portrayed in our sources as long-running and ancient, and they are often associated with myths, cults and rituals. The intensity and length of these confrontations seem disproportionate to the value of the disputed land. How do we explain this apparent incongruity? What factors led to the ancient perception of these strips of borderland as the foci of incessant military strife? When did this perception emerge? And what is the relation between the ancient narratives of border conflicts and the historical reality of the interstate dealings on these borders?

The ubiquity of border conflicts in the Archaic period means that any progress in our understanding of the historical reality and ideology of these conflicts has important

---

[6] Herodotus 1.66–68; Pausanias 8.47–48; Deinias *FrGrHist* 306 F4. Daverio Rocchi 1988, 199–201. See Chapter 4, Section 6.
[7] On the war between Samos and Priene over the aria called Batinetis ("The Brambles") see Thonemann 2011, 27–30; Daverio Rocchi 1988, 170–177; see also Conclusion.
[8] De Polignac 1995, 51–52.
[9] Pausanias 10.37.1. De Polignac 1995, 50.
[10] On *hiera orgas*, see Papazarkadas 2011, 244–259 with further references; Daverio Rocchi 1988, 186–194.
[11] There was a long-running dispute between Athens and Boeotia over Oropus, as well as over the territory around Oenoe and Panactum (associated with the myth of the duel between Xanthus and Melanthus). Vidal-Naquet 1986, 106–128; Daverio Rocchi 1988, 180–186; de Polignac 1995, 56–57. See Chapter 2, Section 3, and Chapter 6, Section 5.

implications for our general understanding of the nature of Archaic warfare. Such progress, in turn, may result in new insights concerning inter-polis relations, and intra-polis power dynamics between the elites and the rest of the inhabitants. The inextricable connection between borders conflicts and myths about the past makes the stories of these conflicts rich sites for exploring the ideological construction and reconstruction of the past.

2. Performing identity in the borderlands

One of the most striking characteristics of borders in Greece is that till late in the Hellenistic period, and even later, they were not strictly defined.[12] They can be often characterized as border zones (frontiers) rather than borderlines.[13] These borderlands were frequently (although not exclusively) located in mountainous areas.[14] When we encounter borderlands in Hellenistic and Roman inscriptions, the picture that emerges is one of largely uninhabited "déserts-frontières."[15] Denis Rousset, who has analyzed a large corpus of inscriptions concerning disputes between *poleis* over border territories, comments about the

---

[12] Tréheux 1979, 34, Rousset 1994, 122.
[13] Daverio Rocchi 1988, 131–177.
[14] Rousset 1994, 117–119; Penttinen 2005, 98.
[15] Rousset 1994, 119.

scarcity of public property in these areas.[16] The borderlands seem to have been mainly public lands, belonging to the *polis*.[17] Military forts were located at the margins of the border zone, in the frontiers patrolled by *peripoloi* and *(h)orophylakes*.[18] Sanctuaries constituted the most prominent signs of the sparse human presence in the border areas: Rousset observes that references to sanctuaries account for more than half of all references to man-made structures in his corpus of inscriptions.[19] We will return to the prominence of sanctuaries in the borderlands and the question of their possible roles there.

Important steps in assessing the ideological significance of these border areas have been taken by Pierre Vidal-Naquet and François de Polignac. Both scholars understand the border regions, *eschatiai*, as a polar opposite of the cultivated and civilized center of the *polis*, its *chôra*. On this logic, the wilderness of the *eschatiai* is a place outside culture, a locus of non-normative behaviors.[20] Vidal-Naquet has argued that from the Archaic period onward the *eschatiai* were the setting of the initiatory ephebeia, that provided an experience of exclusion

---

[16] Most of the inscriptions analyzed by Rousset are Hellenistic.
[17] Rousset 1994, 123.
[18] Rousset 1994, 122; on *(h)orophylakes*, see *ibid.*, 98n4; Robert and Robert 1983, 101–109.
[19] Rousset 1994, 121.
[20] Similarly, Ellinger 1993, 2–3; differently, Rousset 1994, 125–6, who emphasizes that the *eschatiai* are part of the *polis*.

and reversal of values which, paradoxically, contributed to preparing an ephebe to become a hoplite.[21]

De Polignac accepts this model.[22] His focus of interest is the establishment of sanctuaries on the borders of the *polis'* territory in the early stages of the development of the *polis*. He has argued that these extra-urban sanctuaries unified the emerging *polis* and helped to construct its identity. According to de Polignac, the establishment of a connection between the center of the *polis* and a sanctuary on its periphery, often prominently enacted by means of a procession, is the focus of numerous rituals of integrative character, including rites of passage, incorporating young people into the citizen body,[23] or rites emphasizing cohesion between constituent communities of the *polis*.[24]

Vidal-Naquet and de Polignac have made major progress in the understanding of the border areas, drawing attention to their potential ideological significance. However, a recent critical appraisal of these scholars' ideas has revealed some problematic aspects of their arguments. Let us start from Vidal-Naquet. First, in Athens the institution of ephebeia is not attested in the Archaic period. More importantly, Irene Polinskaya has pointed out that Vidal-

---

[21] Vidal-Naquet 1986, 106–128. See also Osborne 1987, 146-9. The posting of the ephebes on the Attic frontiers is attested by Aristotle (*Athenian Constitution* 42.3-4).
[22] De Polignac 1995, 57.
[23] *Ibid.*, 60–64.
[24] *Ibid.*, 65–81.

Naquet's visualization of the Athenian *eschatiai* as wild and isolated frontier regions where the ephebes resided is not literally true. The frontiers of Attica often were not "wild";[25] further, we have evidence that the ephebes frequently did not remain in the frontier areas but moved around, patrolling the Attic countryside.[26] Finally, the word *eschatiai* does not necessarily refer to the land located on the frontiers of a polis.[27] The word denotes marginal land, often hilly, more suitable for grazing than agriculture.[28] (Nikolaos Papazarkadas comments that Attic *eschatiai* typically were on the borders between the Athenian demes).[29] Further, David Leitao's analysis of some literary representations of the ephebic stage (in a broad sense) suggests that this stage can be better described not as a reversal of rules but rather (following van Gennep's tripartite model) as phases of separation and integration of young men into society. Leitao stresses that the adult warriors' protection of the *polis* was also taking place in the frontier areas.[30]

---

[25] Polinskaya 2003, 93–96.
[26] *Ibid.*, 101.
[27] *Ibid.*, 96–97.
[28] Robert 1960a, 304–306; Lewis 1973, 210–12; Lambert 1997, 225–9; Jameson 2002; Krasilnikoff 2008, 45–8; Papazarkadas 2011, 134.
[29] Papazarkadas 2011, 159–160.
[30] Leitao 1999, 270–271. For further constructive critique of Vidal-Naquet's concept of initiation, see Dodd 2003, and a discussion of marginality and initiation in Versnel 1993, 60–74.

Polinskaya's reflection that Vidal-Naquet's model of initiation is based on a metaphoric, not literal, understanding of the Athenian frontiers[31] leads me to point out the culturally constructed nature of the concept of wilderness. We can fine-tune Vidal-Naquet's distinction between "wild frontiers" and "civilized center" by observing that in the opposition 'wild/civilized,' the "wild" is as culturally constructed as the "civilized." That is to say, the borderlands are as much part of *polis* identity as its center.[32] This cultural construction of wild(er)ness as a composite part of civilization is evident in the figure of Artemis, whose cults are frequently located in the borderlands.[33] Pierre Ellinger observes an association between Artemis and conflicts that he describes as wars of total annihilation, that is, confrontations that endanger the survival of the whole community.[34] On the basis of Ellinger's research and his own investigation, Jean-Pierre Vernant states that Artemis is concerned with "the uncertain boundary between savagery and civilization, the boundary whose fragility is marked by both war and the hunt."[35] The appearance of Artemis' sanctuaries in the borderlands is part

---

[31] Polinskaya 2003, 91–93.

[32] Compare Nagy's observation that in myths "the opposition of disorder and order [...] serves to achieve an overall concept of *order*." Nagy 1990a, 8. Cole (2004, 82) remarks concerning the Athenian ephebeia that "[t]he oath of the ephebes, sworn at the sanctuary of Aglauros on the east slope of the *acropolis*, tied the ephebe to the city's ritual core and at the same time bound him to her territory and external borders." Cf. Freitag 2007.

[33] Cole 1998, 27–28; 2004, 184–188.

[34] Ellinger 1993, 335–338.

[35] Vernant 1991, 247. See pp. 244–260; Ellinger 1993; Cole 2000.

of the cultural construction of wilderness: the association between Artemis and marginality is bi-directional, so that Artemis' presence makes the borders "wilder."[36]

Let us now return to de Polignac's model of extra-urban sanctuaries as foci of community integration. The difficulty with de Polignac's suggestion is that it tends to overstate the capacity of urban centers in the early Archaic period to gain exclusive control over the sanctuaries on their borders. Jonathan Hall has demonstrated that the Heraion of Argos, which serves as a central example in de Polignac's argument,[37] did not become Argive until the fifth century.[38] Thus, de Polignac's model, according to which the early *poleis* claimed possession of their limits through their control of extra-urban sanctuaries, needs to be adjusted. Indeed, recent research shows that the borderlands between *poleis* often were neutral, or common, territory.[39] Particularly interesting are the cases where the borderland between two cities was defined as sacred and left uncultivated:[40] *hiera orgas* between Athens and Megara, and the area around Panactum, between the Athenian and Boeotian territories,

---

[36] Further on the construction of wilderness at the borderlands see McInerney 2006.
[37] De Polignac 1995, 41-42.
[38] Hall 1995.
[39] Howe 2008 stresses the importance of the common grazing territories; Chandezon 2003, 351-389, for a discussion of *epinomia* decrees; Daverio Rocchi 1988, 31-40; Sartre 1979; Tréheux 1979, 34.
[40] See Horden and Purcell 2000, 453 for typological parallels.

are well-known instances.[41] Angelos Chaniotis' exploration of inter-polis relationships on Crete during the Hellenistic period provides similar examples of a sacred 'Niemandsland' there.[42] Jeremy McInerney concludes his overview of the cultic and economic aspects of borderlands by suggesting that "rather than [...] seeing extra-mural sanctuaries as the penetration of the hinterland by the *astu*, as does de Polignac, we should see border sanctuaries and their territories as playing a critical role in modulating conflict at the edge of cultivated territory and allowing for the incorporation of wilderness and hinterland into the world of the *polis*."[43] The border sanctuaries, thus, can be viewed as a particular case of a broader phenomenon, described by Jonathan Hall, on the basis of George Forrest's earlier suggestion, as "a neutral space for competitive interaction, free from the control of any single state, in which states could forge and define their identities, interests and achievements."[44]

A clear-cut example of a sanctuary in *eschatiai* that functioned as a locus for the competitive interaction of different *poleis* is the sanctuary of Messon on Lesbos. The very name of the sanctuary means 'midpoint;' as for its location in *eschatiai*, we have the authority of Alcaeus (F 130.9). Messon was situated in the island's most isolated area, its middle; the

---

[41] McInerney 2006, 50–52, also mentioning the sanctuary of Artemis Limnatis between Sparta and Messenia; Cole 2004, 77–78; Tréheux 1979, 36.
[42] Chaniotis 1988; 2006.
[43] McInerney 2006, 56.
[44] Hall 2007b, 100 (citing Forrest 2000, 284), on regionally based leagues of *poleis*.

location of the sacred middle-point on the outskirts of the Lesbian *poleis* demonstrates how the same site can be represented as both peripheral and central.[45] The sanctuary served as "a place for shared festivals in times of peace, for negotiations in times of stress."[46] Importantly, the relationship between the Lesbian *poleis* was highly competitive. Nigel Spencer has analyzed a group of nineteen large towers on Lesbos, constructed in the distinctive Lesbian style of polygonal masonry; Spencer tentatively dates the towers to the Archaic period.[47] These towers are all situated in marginal locations, at the edges of the plains where the Lesbian *poleis* were located, or above routes connecting these plains; there are no signs of any functional installations such as wells, presses, cisterns or threshing floors.[48] Spencer provides the following summary of his analysis of these polysemic structures:

> ...the functions performed by all these rural structures are quite complex, and [...] at different times they served a whole range of purposes if one examines them on various levels. One can see them as manifestations of peer competition and emulation among the élites; a symbolic way in which the upper orders of society tried to distinguish themselves above the lower members by conspicuous display of consumable wealth; also, on a wider scale, in times of tension between the states, the structures could have served as symbols of possession at the outer limits of a city's 'territory.' In the latter scenario, the substantially built towers and enclosures (many at strategic locations) were suitable also to act as foci for defense of border areas at a time when sought-after natural

---

[45] Cole 2004, 78n81 cites an example from scholia for Aeschines 1.97, describing Delphi as *eschatê gê*.
[46] *Ibid*. On the cult of Alcaeus at Messon, see Nagy 1993; 2007, 214.
[47] Spencer 1995, 32–33.
[48] *Ibid*., 33.

resources and/or territory may have been in dispute.[49]

Spencer's analysis provides a fascinating example of multiple and mutable meanings associated with marginal structures in Greece; I find particularly interesting the interplay between the competition in tower constructions among the elites of the same or different *poleis*, and the possible confrontations between these *poleis*. The towers on the margins of the Lesbian cities seem to be implicated in the creation of a number of identities for different social groups.[50]

Let us now return to the question of the long-standing border conflicts in Greece. The preceding discussion demonstrates the significance of border areas in constructing the *polis'* identity. Let us consider Archaic wars over border territories in this light. On one level, a fight between two neighboring city-states over border territory is a zero-sum game:[51] there is a winner and a loser in the competition. However, the struggle also has another consequence: the identities of the contestants are redefined through the confrontation. The fight for the border territory performs the borders of the two communities.[52] In the most literal terms, we can think of two phalanx lines meeting on a plain: each line constitutes the moving border of a

---

[49] Spencer 2000, 73.
[50] For a case-study of the role of Arcadian border regions in the formation of ethnic identities, see Cardete del Olmo 2005.
[51] Hall 2007a, 88.
[52] On the performative aspect of borders, see Green 2010, 261, and 273n2 with further references.

city. Sparta and Argos, Eretria and Chalcis become themselves through their oppositions. The acquisition of an identity, as opposed to the acquisition of the territory, is not a zero-sum game. Argos can be Argos, and Sparta can be Sparta, as long as the fight concerns only the border territory and there is no attempt to annihilate the opponent. As I am going to argue, the definition of the participants' identities through their opposition has a potential of becoming, under certain conditions, a factor unifying the two sides.

Another important aspect of the border confrontations in Greece is their alleged long duration and antiquity: these conflicts are often characterized by the ancient sources as "old wars."[53] Thus, in these cases the contested spatial division of the territory also entails a particular demarcation of the past.[54] When two *poleis* have a tradition of ancient confrontation at their common border, they share, at least in part, a vision of the past. The disputed borderland therefore does not only separate but also unites the contending city-states.[55]

---

[53] For example, Thucydides 1.15.3 (the war between Eretria and Chalcis); 5.42.1 (the dispute over the territory around Panactum); Herodotus 5.81 (an old enmity between Athens and Aegina).

[54] In thinking about the nexus of the representation of space and historical time in a landscape, I am inspired by Ferrari 1999. See also Mitchell 1994, 1–34; Bender 2002; Zhurzhenko 2011 (on borders and memory).

[55] Compare Vernant's description of archaic warfare, in which cities "in their very confrontation with one another were brought together in a community united by language, religions, customs, forms of social life, and ways of thought." Vernant 1988, 41.

3. The shared values of "Mursiness:" confrontation as cooperation

I will start with an example from a different culture. The Mursi are the people occupying the Lower Omo Valley in southwestern Ethiopia. They number about 6000. They subsist on herding and cultivation, and move seasonally in a highly predictable pattern over a limited territory. Mursi are divided into five local groups (*buranyoga*, sg. *buran*); the cooperation between these groups is crucial for the survival of the people as a whole.[56] What makes the Mursi interesting for our purposes is an existence of ritual duelling between these local groups.

David Turton gives a detailed account of this practice. The Mursi structure their society according to an age grade system; the junior grade of adult men is *rora* (warriors). The intervals between initiations into this group can be long (the last one was thirty years); thus, the biological ages of men in this grade vary greatly. However, the idealized expectation is that the *rora* will be unmarried but mature men playing the social role of warriors. It is the unmarried *rora* who are expected to be particularly active in duelling events.[57] Such duelling events between two *buranyoga* are carefully planned in advance, and involve men of one *buran* travelling into the territory of another. The duels take place inside a tight circle of spectators,

---
[56] Turton 2002, 175.
[57] *Ibid.*, 178–179.

one at a time, on a specially prepared duelling ground. The weapons are six feet long poles; during the duel, two opponents deliver and parry blows, aiming to knock the adversary over. The duels are controlled by referees, who separate the contestants when the fight does not end in a clear victory (i.e. the fall of one of the participants). Turton reports that none of the duels that he witnessed lasted longer than 40 seconds; duelling bouts between different participants occurred in rapid succession.[58]

Cases of homicide during the duels are rare, but occasionally they do occur.[59] Turton reports that the duelling event that he attended was preceded by a ritual aimed to insure that no fatal injuries would be suffered by either side.[60] According to Turton's informants, the concern about a possible fatal injury lies at the foundation of an important rule of duelling: the duelling opponents never belong to the same clan. Mursi clans are exogamous; the only way to reestablish peace between the families of killer and victim is through marriage; thus, "a man only duels [...] with men whose "sisters" [women of the same clan] he can marry."[61]

The duels are taken with "utmost seriousness."[62] They are often described metaphorically as war (*kaman*), the same word that refers to lethal attacks between the Mursi

---

[58] Turton 2002, 179–180.
[59] *Ibid.*, 181n9.
[60] *Ibid.*, 184.
[61] *Ibid.*, 181.
[62] *Ibid.*

and non-Mursi. Most importantly, the duels are perceived as belonging to long-running conflicts between the *buranyoga*:

> ...duelling contests are not seen as isolated or "one off" events. They are seen as part of a continuing relationship of antagonism between the groups in question, in which each "side" takes it in turn to visit the other side's "home ground," at intervals of up to a year, to "exchange" or "take revenge for," their "wounds" (*chacha muloi*). Each duelling event, then, looks back to a previous one and anticipates a future one.[63]

Turton provides a highly relevant analysis of Mursi duelling practices. First, he notes the performative role of the duelling: it brings about differences between the local groups (*buranyoga*).[64] However, in addition to the local loyalties, separating between the *buranyoga*, there are also relations of kinship connecting the participants across different *buranyoga*. Turton observes concerning the audience's moral support of the contestants during the duels that "local loyalties were cross-cut by, and systematically subordinated to, loyalties based on kinship."[65] He concludes:

> Duelling [...] asserts an overall Mursi political identity, or "context," even while it distinguishes and sets against each other different political "sub-groups" of Mursi; it asserts the shared values of "Mursiness," embodied most notably in the institutions of clanship, marriage, priesthood and the age organization. It does this most obviously through the rules and conventions which govern the conduct of individual bouts and the planning and organization of duelling events.[66]

---

[63] Turton 2002, 181–182.
[64] *Ibid.*, 173.
[65] *Ibid.*, 186.
[66] *Ibid.*, 187. Ritual battles between different communities are also attested elsewhere. The Andean tradition of *tinku* is one example. Mendizábal Nuñez et al., 1997; de Munter and Note

The mentality of Mursi duelling, as analyzed by Turton, is close to what Gregory Nagy observes concerning the choral competition in Greece: "the ritual essence of the choral lyric performance is that it is *constitutive* of society in the very process of *dividing it*."[67] The phenomenon of constitution through division, and, more particularly, constitution through confrontation, is well attested on the level of the communities comprising Greek *poleis*. Ephebic ball games in Sparta, in which competing teams represented five *ôbai* (the ancient constituent villages of Sparta) provide a good example.[68] Another instance is the Athenian *anthippasia*, an equestrian military contest in which two regiments, representing different Athenian tribes, pursued each other.[69] Plutarch provides an especially relevant example concerning confrontations between the villages that comprised the polis of Megara (*Greek questions* 295b–c):[70]

'Τίς ὁ δορύξενος;' τὸ παλαιὸν ἡ Μεγαρὶς ᾠκεῖτο κατὰ κώμας, εἰς πέντε μέρη νενεμημένων τῶν πολιτῶν. ἐκαλοῦντο δ' Ἡραεῖς καὶ Πιραεῖς καὶ Μεγαρεῖς καὶ

2009, 94. For a possible attestation of a ritual battle between communities at a Hittite festival, see van den Hout 1991. A Roman equestrian contest called Troy is attested in Virgil *Aeneid* 5.545–603; Suetonius, *Julius Caesar* 39.2, *Augustus* 43.2, *Tiberius* 6.4, *Nero* 7.1; Plutarch, *Cato the Younger* 3.1. See also Zotz 2002 on medieval tournaments, Shelton 2002 on the Aztec ball game, and Knauft 2002 on Melanesian contests.

[67] Nagy 1990a, 367.

[68] See Chapter 3, Section 8. Compare also the aetiological myth about the strife between four Spartan villages in the cult of Artemis Orthia (Pausanias 3.16.9-10). De Polignac 1995, 67–68.

[69] Xenophon *On the Cavalry Commander* 3.10-13; Vanderpool 1974.

[70] Mentioned in Singor 2009, 597.

Κυνοσουρεῖς καὶ Τριποδίσκιοι. τῶν δὲ Κορινθίων πόλεμον αὐτοῖς ἐξεργασαμένων πρὸς ἀλλήλους (ἀεὶ γὰρ ἐπεβούλευον ὑφ' αὑτοῖς ποιήσασθαι τὴν Μεγαρικήν), ὅμως δι'ἐπιείκειαν ἡμέρως ἐπολέμουν καὶ συγγενικῶς. τοὺς μὲν γὰρ γεωργοῦντας οὐδεὶς ἠδίκει τὸ παράπων, τοὺς δ' ἁλισκομένους λύτρον τι τεταγμένον ἔδει καταβαλεῖν, καὶ τοῦτ' ἐλάμβανον ἀφέντες. πρότερον δ' οὐκ εἰσέπραττον, ἀλλ' ὁ λαβὼν αἰχμάλωτον ἀπῆγεν οἴκαδε, καὶ μεταδοὺς ἁλῶν καὶ τραπέζης ἀπέπεμπεν οἴκαδε. ὁ μὲν οὖν τὰ λύτρα κομίσας ἐπηνεῖτο καὶ φίλος ἀεὶ διετέλει τοῦ λαβόντος ἐκ δορυαλώτου 'δορύξενος' προσαγορευόμενος· ὁ δ' ἀποστερήσας οὐ μόνον παρὰ τοῖς πολεμίοις ἀλλὰ καὶ παρὰ τοῖς πολίταις ὡς ἄδικος καὶ ἄπιστος ἡδόξει.

What is the "spear-friend"? In days of old the Megarid used to be settled in village communities with the citizens divided into five groups. They were called Heraeïs, Piraeïs, Megareis, Cynosureis, and Tripodiscioi. Although the Corinthians brought about a civil war among them, for the Corinthians were ever plotting to get Megara under their control, none the less, because of their fair-mindedness, they conducted their wars in a civilized and a kinsmanly way. For no one did any harm at all to the men working in the fields, and when anyone was captured, he but needed to pay a certain specified ransom; this his captors received after they had set him free, and did not collect it earlier; but he who took a prisoner conducted the man to his house and, after sharing with him salt and food, sent him home. He, accordingly, who brought his ransom, was highly regarded and continued thenceforward to be a friend of his captor; and, as a consequence of his capture by the spear, he was now called "spear-friend." But anyone who failed to pay the ransom was held in disrepute as dishonest and faithless, not only among his enemies, but also among his fellow-citizens.

In this dissertation, I propose that in the Archaic period similar ritual confrontations took place between combatants from neighboring cities. We can view the border territories that were continually fought over as special cases of the shared sacred borderlands between two *poleis*. The border territory fought over in ritual battles can be construed as a sacred common space, which provided the fighting sides with a paradoxical unity in confrontation.

I submit that traces of this attitude, according to which two cities involved in a long-standing confrontation over a border territory are at the same time being unified by this confrontation, are discernible in the repeated description of conflicts over border territory as *polemoi* (or *machai*) between *astugeitones* (Thucydides 1.15.3; Herodotus 1.30; Aristotle *Politics* 1289b38–39). *Geitôn* is a term implying communal values. Suffice it to recall Hesiod's description of the reliance on neighbors (*Works and Days* 344–51). Interestingly, Plutarch describes "neighborly wars" (αἱ πολέμοις ἀστυγειτονικοῖς) as promoting a city-state's wellbeing (*How to Profit by One's Enemies* 87e):

> καθάπερ γὰρ αἱ πολέμοις ἀστυγειτονικοῖς καὶ στρατείαις ἐνδελεχέσι σωφρονιζόμεναι πόλεις εὐνομίαν καὶ πολιτείαν ὑγιαίνουσαν ἠγάπησαν...
>
> For just as states which are chastened by border warfare and continual campaigning become well content with good order and a sound government...

This description portrays war against neighbors as a good *eris*, in Hesiodic terms. We will repeatedly return to the Hesiodic distinction between good and bad *eris* over the course of the following chapters' exploration.

Let me explain what I mean by inter-polis "ritual battle." I envisage fighting between groups representing two (or more) city-states as taking place under the condition of an existing peace agreement between the opponent city-states, over a possession of a limited border territory. The condition of a peace agreement is crucial in my definition of the ritual battle for distinguishing between this phenomenon and "real" warfare, which can also be strongly ritualized.[71] The difference between real and ritual battle is, in my view, the isolation of the latter from the military struggle for dominance between the city-states. The outcome of a ritual battle concerns solely the control of a border territory, without affecting the balance of power between the opponent city-states. I would expect such ritual fighting to have a periodic recurrent character, similar to the yearly cyclical pattern of festivals, or the slower rhythms of the stephanitic games.

The affinity between the militarily contested territory and the sacred borderlands between *poleis* further suggests, as I have already noted, that the contested territory should be also perceived as sacred. That is, we may expect that the ritual battles were fought in a cultic framework, such as a common border cult.

I have identified the main characteristics that in my view define a battle over a border territory as a ritual one: the cultic framework and the peace agreement between the participating city-states. There is also an important feature of restricted violence, which I discuss in the next section. However, if the information about one (or more) of these key characteristics is lacking, what other elements can serve as indications that a border conflict described in our sources featured, at some point, a practice of ritual battles? While the absence

---

[71] Adcock 1957, 7; Snodgrass 1986, 51; Connor 1988.

of information concerning one of the main criteria makes the inference more tentative, the following features of the descriptions suggest to me the ritual character of the confrontation.

- The sources portray the conflict as lasting for centuries, without giving specific reasons for single instances of fighting.
- The outcome of the fighting is described vaguely, without specifying who of the opponents won.
- The future fighting is envisaged as continuing perpetually without reaching a final territorial resolution.

In short, the emphasis in the sources on the perpetuity of the conflict, combined with the indeterminacy concerning the outcome of the fighting, signal the possibility that the portrayed fighting was a recurrent ritual.

4. *Agôn* and carnage

Let us assume, for the sake of the argument, that long-term confrontations over a contested borderland may indeed have featured ritual battles for the disputed territory. If so, how could we situate these ritual confrontations in the broader context of current research on Greek warfare?

Let us start from the character of the border conflicts, so widespread in the Archaic period. I have tentatively suggested an affinity between the perpetually contested borderlands and the uncultivated sacred territories on the borders between *poleis*. This understanding not only removes the contested borderlands from the power struggles between the adjacent *poleis*; it also supposes that the contested territory was not used for agriculture. My hypothesis sharply contrasts with a widespread approach associating border conflicts with the mounting population pressure of the early Archaic period. According to this interpretation, the population growth resulted in land scarcity, which triggered increasingly fierce conflicts between the neighboring city-states for the agricultural lands on their frontiers. As the competition over the land intensified, more and more people needed to be drawn into the military action; moreover, the farmers were particularly interested in participating in the armed conflicts in order to protect their own fields. This trend eventually resulted in the development of a hoplite phalanx (and a simultaneous enfranchisement of small land-owners).[72]

An initial observation casting some suspicion on the applicability of this scenario for understanding ancient border conflicts is that the famous confrontations between Sparta and Argos concerned the possession of the territory of Cynuria, a rugged mountainous frontier

---

[72] A few selected references are Detienne 1968, 120; Bowden 1993, 48; de Polignac 1995, 49; Hanson 1999, 239. For a recent critique of this view, see Hall 2007a, 161–170.

land. Admittedly, the confrontation was focused on the plain of Thyreatis, a subpart of Cynuria; however, the agricultural value of the Thyreatis pales in comparison with the rich resources of arable land under Sparta's control.[73] More generally, recent research suggests a lack of interest in territorial expansion during the Archaic period; apparently, the efforts of the city-states were rather aimed at the exploitation of adjacent smaller communities.[74] Between city-states of comparable size, prominent motifs for conflicts were retaliation and honor.[75] Destructive war, seeking the obliteration of the adversary's *polis* and the appropriation of its territory, was relatively rare.[76]

Another point requiring discussion is the ritualized character of Greek warfare vis-à-vis the ritual battles. Greek battles had some clear ritual constituents: the advance of the infantry into the battle was immediately preceded by blood-letting sacrifices (*sphagia*) and taking of divinatory signs;[77] as the phalanx marched forward to meet the enemy line, a *paian* was chanted;[78] the triumphant side erected a trophy and performed thanksgiving and victory sacrifices;[79] the losing side in admission of a defeat asked for a truce through a herald in order

---

[73] Brelich 1961, 22; Kelly 1970a, 980; van Wees 2004, 28.
[74] Hall 2007a, 170–176; van Wees 2004, 28–32.
[75] Van Wees 2004, 22–26.
[76] Connor 1988, 6–8; Singor 2009, 586–587 with further references.
[77] Jameson 1991, 204–209, 220–221; Connor 1988, 22–23; Pritchett 1971, 109–115.
[78] Pritchett 1971, 105–108.
[79] Jackson 1991; Pritchett 1974, 246–275.

to recover the bodies of the fallen soldiers.[80] In addition, it has been observed that there was "a considerable overlap in terminology and spirit between sports and hoplite warfare" in the late Archaic and early Classical periods;[81] moreover, significant correlations exist between the structures of ritual sacrifice and warfare.[82]

However, these ritual features of Greek battles do not preclude a vital distinction between the usual hoplite battles and more heavily ritualized confrontations. According to Stanley Tambiah's observation, is may be impossible to separate between rituals and non-rituals in an absolute way; however, one can draw "relative contrastive distinctions" between more or less ritualized actions. He further speaks of "typical or focal examples of 'ritual' events."[83] Ritual battles for a limited territory, happening in the framework of a particular cult, seem to be more focal examples of ritual than regular battles. Yet, this distinction begins to look blurred in the light of scholarly discussions of agonistic warfare. The following description of hoplite battles by T. J. Cornell is a good illustration:

> The ferocity of the battles should not be allowed to conceal the ludic character of hoplite warfare. In effect they were ritual wars staged in artificial conditions which ensured that a fair fight would take place between equals.

---

[80] Pritchett 1985, 246–249.
[81] Singor 2009, 598.
[82] Connor 1988, 22.
[83] Tambiah 1979, 116.

Cornell adds that the use of missile weapons, light-armed troops and cavalry in hoplite battles was restricted.[84] The only distinction between this representation of hoplite warfare and what I have called "ritual battles" is the level of lethality. When I speak of the ritual battles, I visualize a situation close to that of Mursi duels, in which the casualties sporadically occur but are an exception rather than the rule.

However, the applicability of the concept of agonistic warfare to the Greek evidence is a hotly discussed and controversial topic. An important trend in the discussion of Greek agonism, relevant to the present discussion, is that the proponents of the existence of agonistic warfare often cite the Lelantine War and the war between Sparta and Argos over the Thyreatis as characteristic examples of Greek warfare.[85] The opponents of agonism, in contrast, emphasize the exceptional nature of these two wars (and, in addition, are likely to

---

[84] Cornell 2002, 45. See also Singor 2009, 596–7; Del Corno 2002. The restricted conditions (such as flat ground) required for the hoplite phalanx suggest to some scholars an artificial and ritualized character of hoplite warfare. Bowden (1993, 49), drawing on the work of Detienne and de Polignac, asserts that "the hoplite phalanx was a basic feature of the polis from the beginning" and that "hoplite warfare only makes sense in the context of the polis." However, Luraghi (2006a) has demonstrated that Greek hoplites served as mercenaries in the Near East already in the Archaic period; thus, the hoplite phalanx was capable of operating effectively in relatively non-ritualized conditions when fighting with non-Greeks. On the emergence of the phalanx see a recent treatment by Schwartz 2009.

[85] Cornell's description of hoplite warfare that I have quoted is typical in this respect, referring to the Lelantine War right after the end of the quoted text. Cornell 2002, 45. Similarly, Connor 1988, 9, 20, 21; Singor 2009, 596–7.

cite epic and fifth-century examples as their evidence).[86] Thus, the concept of agonism, or of a "hoplite ideal," is heavily dependent on the evidence derived from the confrontations that constitute the subject of my exploration. Accordingly, I leave the question of the agonistic character of the Greek warfare temporarily open so as to address it in the light of my study's conclusions.[87]

A study that has exerted a major influence on the present exploration is *Guerre, agoni e culti nella Grecia arcaica* by Angelo Brelich. Brelich's examination differs from the more general discussions of the agonistic character of Greek fighting inasmuch as Brelich does not extrapolate the results of his several case studies to all Greek warfare. The focus of Brelich's investigation, the Argive-Spartan dispute over the Thyreatis and the war between Eretria and Chalcis over the Lelantine plain, coincides with the subjects of my exploration. My concept of ritual battles also owes much to Brelich's work, with some important differences.

Brelich's study emphasizes the repeated appearance of regulations, mitigating the magnitude of the fighting in several border conflicts. Brelich notices several features of border conflicts that I have already mentioned above: their long duration, the reports of their inception in legendary antiquity, and the incommensurability between the value of the

---

[86] Krentz 2002, 29; Dayton 2006, 30–36.
[87] Wheeler 2007, 189 and Cornell 2002, 45 emphasize that the concept of limited warfare is an ideal; the question is at what occasions was this ideal embodied in reality.

disputed territory and the scale of the conflict. He also observes the frequent cultic and ritual associations of these confrontations, and especially the links with initiations of young men into adulthood.[88] Brelich concludes that the border conflicts originated as ritual combats for border territory, serving as rites of transition into adult status for the combats' participants. Over time, these ritual combats were transformed into real wars, leaving only traces of ritual associations.[89]

The reception of the notion of ritual combat in recent scholarship has been mixed. Michael Sage includes a discussion of the "agonal or ritual battle" in his sourcebook on Greek warfare. Such battles, according to his description, are

> often manifested in the form of *monomachia* or duel between selected individuals or groups. [...] This sort of battle is in later times closely connected with border disputes over territory whose acquisition bears little proportion to the expenditure of effort and loss of life involved. The engagement was delimited by a set of rules designed to confine the destructive effects to both sides.[90]

However, Sage remarks that "[t]he functions of such fighting are difficult to discern." He mentions the possible link between ritual battles and rites of initiation, but points out that the attested border confrontations are too irregular to be functioning as such rites.[91] Hans van Wees expresses even graver doubts concerning the appropriateness of the term 'ritual' for the

---

[88] Brelich 1961, 80–84.
[89] *Ibid.*, 83–84.
[90] Sage 1996, 73.
[91] *Ibid.*

border wars, and concerning the claim that the chief function of such confrontations was the initiation of the young man into warrior status. He notes that the border confrontations "were not as a rule fought subject to any special restrictions, let alone confined to the youngest age classes."[92] Indeed, the lack of consistency in the appearance of fighting regulations had already perplexed Brelich himself, who noted cases in which the apparently ritual limitation of violence was combined with severe bloodshed (we will return to this subject).[93]

I would like to examine some problems in previous interpretations construing the border conflicts as ritual battles. This undertaking is crucial to my investigation, since I hope that the model of the ritual battle that I offer avoids the methodological shortcomings of the line of inquiry that Brelich has launched, while nevertheless building on the valuable insights derived from his research.

The first problematic assumption is that the border conflicts must have had only *one* function in the societies participating in these confrontations. This function is believed to be initiatory and is presumed to persist throughout the attested history of border conflicts. Notably, even Sage's and van Wees' critique of the idea of ritual battles is underlined by the assumption that if there existed a connection between initiation and border conflicts, such a connection would be diachronically consistent. Both scholars interpret the sporadic nature of

---

[92] Van Wees 2004, 261n43.
[93] Brelich 1961, 79.

attestations of fighting regulations in border conflicts as an argument against *any* association between initiation practices and border confrontations.

A variant assumption, adopted by Brelich, is to assert that the initiation of the young men into adulthood was the main function of the border conflicts at their inception; these ritual confrontations were later transformed into political conflicts, but retained a certain ritual "aura."[94]

Both of these ideas, that the function of border conflicts remained rigidly unchanged throughout their history, and, conversely, that the border conflicts could lose their initiatory role but retain vague ritual associations, underestimate the dynamic nature and diachronic

---

[94] Brelich 1961, 82-84. Similarly, Garlan 1975, 29, 31. Another problematic tendency involves pushing the genesis of the ritual border battles into the Greek Dark Ages. Brelich 1961, 84; Garlan 1975, 29-30; Sage 1996, 73. This idea is unverifiable, since we lack any contemporary accounts from that period. Moreover, this suggestion can be explained as a result of a methodological fault in the interpretation of the ancient sources. These sources, indeed, often depict the border fighting as originating in the most ancient past. However, such a depiction does not warrant the inference that the border battles really are traceable to the beginning of Greek history: to claim this is to confuse the ancient Greeks' ideas about their past with historical reality. An example demonstrating the dangers of such an approach comes from Garlan's discussion of the war between Eretria and Chalcis over the Lelantine plain: "In mythical times this plain had been the object of a battle between the Abantes [...] and the Kouretes [...]. *Later* [italics mine], between the eighth and sixth centuries, the Eretrian and Chalcidians suspended their friendly collaboration from time to time for a little honest fighting over the frontier areas." Garlan 1975, 29. In this description, the mythical past of the Curetes seamlessly blends with the modern historical concept of the eighth century BC.

variability of the functioning of such social phenomena.[95] Border conflicts could have been perpetuated for very different reasons in different historical periods, losing and then regaining their link to initiation rites. We can expect, however, that at any given moment of their existence, border conflicts played specific roles in the communities who took part in the fighting. We can hope to uncover these roles and factors only through an investigation that embeds specific border conflicts in the synchronic and specific historical circumstances of the given period.

I will have more to say about the historical reconstruction of border conflicts in the next section; however, before that I would like to discuss another study that has deeply influenced my analysis. The study in question is the exploration of the phenomenon of wars of total annihilation by Pierre Ellinger. In his study Ellinger demonstrates that there existed a recurrent story-pattern portraying certain conflicts as total wars, unlimited by any rules, threatening the survival of the whole community.[96] As Ellinger observes at the end of his analysis, the war of total destruction is the eternal shadow of the hoplite ideal: "ideal hoplitique et contre-idéal de la guerre d'anéantissement ont constamment coexisté, l'un étant comme l'ombre de l'autre."[97] The fascinating fact is that images characteristic of wars of total

---

[95] See Kowalzig 2007a, 34 on the dynamism and adaptability of rituals.
[96] Ellinger 1993.
[97] Ellinger 1993, 337.

destruction appear in the narratives related to perpetual border conflicts nearly as persistently as do agonistic regulations (the death of all but three participants in the battle of Champions provides one example).[98] Both Brelich's *agôn* and Ellinger's carnage are present in the borderlands.

The exploration of relations between the instances of limited and total warfare in borderland conflicts is one of the important themes of my dissertations. As a preliminary comment I would like to point out that ritualized (controlled) violence has a strong propensity to be converted into uncontrolled violence under various circumstances.[99] An example, discussed at length by Michael Nagler, is the transition in the *Odyssey* between the bow contest and the killing of the suitors (*Odyssey* 22.5-7). Nagler notes that the contrast between contest and combat has a parallel in the *Iliad* (22.159-166): at the climactic moment of Achilles' pursuit of Hector, the narrative includes images of athletic contests, which serve as a foil for the real violence.[100] Nagler connects his exploration to the question of the ritual battles:

> Ritual combat has received, deservedly, much attention of late because of its highly ambiguous relationship to violence. As a symbolic representation of violence it is dangerous by nature, even though or perhaps precisely because it can be construed as

---

[98] The difference between the behavior of Cleomenes (Herodotus 6.78-81) and Polydorus (Plutarch *Saying of Spartans* 231e) toward the Argives is another illustration.
[99] Turton (2002, 185) notes this about Mursi duelling events.
[100] Nagler 1990, 349-350, citing Redfield 1975, 183. See also Forsdyke 2005a (analyzing transitions from revel to riot in ancient Megara) and Detienne 1989.

the "good" kind of violence in opposition to unregulated conflict.[101]

Thus, in life and in myth, controlled ritual violence may swiftly turn into an unrestrained violence. The difference between them, and the point of transition are what is all-important.

5. Bottom-up and top-down: synchrony, diachrony, history

My study includes an in-depth analysis of the two most famous ancient border conflicts, the Lelantine war and the Argive-Spartan struggles over the Thyreatis. The restricted scope is determined by my objective to produce a historically sensitive analysis; this aim necessitates more detailed investigations of separate cases but also limits the exploration to those border conflicts about which we have a relatively higher amount of information, allowing a perception of temporal change.

The initial step in the investigation of these border confrontations is the reconstruction of the ancient perceptions of these conflicts. Rather than attempting directly to extract from the sources information about the "historical core" of the described events, I aim first to

---

[101] Nagler 1990, 354; see also Kertzer 1988, 126–130.

recover the ideologies underlying the narratives of border confrontations, i.e. the myths about these conflicts.[102]

My emphasis on the sharp distinction between actual historical events and ancient representations of the past derives from the character of the most important sources concerning the border conflicts, which are informed by oral traditions. These sources are Archaic poetry and traditional narratives transmitted by ancient historians, most prominently by Herodotus.[103] It has been recognized that the image of the past constructed by an oral tradition is deeply informed by the changing ideals and norms of the society perpetuating the tradition; the past events reported by an oral tradition must be relevant to the society's present.[104] In the words of Rosalind Thomas, "[t]he character, content, and rate of change of oral tradition are [...] intimately related to the society transmitting them, as they are constantly refined, honed or 'deformed' by the beliefs, needs, and values of the society."[105] Thus, if the stories of the Lelantine war and of the Argive-Spartan enmity were worthy of

---

[102] The connection between myth and ideology is succinctly expressed in Bruce Lincoln's definition of the myth as "ideology in narrative form." Lincoln 1999, 147. Similarly, Nagy 1990a, 436.
[103] On the traditional oral nature of archaic Greek poetry see Nagy 1990a, especially 18-29, 51, 53-55, 79, 82-85; on the oral traditions in Herodotus see Griffiths 2006, 136-140; Luraghi 2006b, 80-85; Murray 2001a, 2001b.
[104] Vansina 1985, 31-32, 118-119.
[105] Thomas 1992, 109. See also the classic discussion by Vansina 1985, 118-119.

transmission by the oral tradition(s), they must have had important ideological content throughout the existence of the tradition.

The idea of reconstructing the ideologies of the border conflicts immediately leads to a further concern: whose ideologies were those? What were the societies transmitting the narratives of the border conflicts? It is reasonable to assume that the city-states that are portrayed by the traditions as key participants in the border confrontations were also the loci of the perpetuation of these traditions. However, it is clear that in addition to examining the role of local traditions, one also needs to consider the Panhellenic components in the narratives of border conflicts: the presence of a Panhellenic aspect is apparent from the mention of local border conflicts in the poetry of such Panhellenic figures as Theognis, Archilochus and Hesiod.[106] Moreover, it is an oversimplification to assume that only one vision of the past could originate from one city-state: it is possible that separate social groups in the same city would perpetuate different versions of border conflict narratives both in terms of form and of ideological content. Finally, in addition to the potential geographical and social variability in narratives about border conflicts, there is also a temporal aspect: both the details of the narrative and its ideological functioning could change diachronically.

---

[106] On the pan-Hellenic character of these poetic figures, see Nagy 1985; 1990a, 53, 67, 79–81, 84, 434–436; 1990b, 48–52.

Differentiating between narratives of the same conflict stemming from different *poleis*, social groups and historical periods is going to be one of my central concerns. Another crucial concern is distinguishing between the traces of the oral traditions, and the modifications and elaborations that the traditional narratives acquired at the hands of later writers. I will attempt to understand the agendas of these writers and their rationales for reporting the stories of the border conflicts.

Two fundamental assumptions which I hold are first, the traditionality of myths and rituals and second, their adaptability. I will start from the latter, quoting Jonathan Hall's observation:

> Since myths are cognitive artifacts in currency among social groups, the passage of historical time with its concomitant restructuring of social relationships will inevitably affect the form and content of mythical episodes. Secondly, there is a tendency for structuralist approaches to neglect the *sociological contexts* of myths. In short, both historical positivism and structuralism leave little room for knowledgeable social actors through their concentration on the passive character of myth...[107]

The traditionality, characterizing myths and rituals, is succinctly expressed by Stanley Tambiah: "Emergent meanings ride on the already existing grids of symbolic and indexical meanings, while also displaying new resonances.[108]" Thus, historical reconstruction of myths and rituals requires attention to both their traditional and innovative aspects. Accordingly, my

---

[107] Hall 1997, 86.
[108] Tambiah 1979, 160. See also Versnel 1993, 89–135; Nagy 1996, 56; Yatromanolakis and Roilos 2004, 19–20.

methodology can be described as following: I first reconstruct the general contours of a tradition, its stable elements, appearing in multiple sources. This task has been already largely accomplished by Angelo Brelich, to whose work my analysis repeatedly refers. However, after reconstructing the general contours of the tradition, the next crucial step is to examine the constitutive pieces of evidence again and to establish more precisely their relation with the rest of the tradition. This stage allows us to detect the peculiarities of individual ancient references, resulting in the recognition of different strands in the tradition. The exploration of the "distinctive slant" of a given source often involves its thematic analysis: I attempt to identify broader patterns affecting the source's presentation of the relevant evidence. Finally, the analysis of the source's rhetoric is followed by an attempt to situate it in a specific historical context. This often leads to a more precise reconstruction of other elements of the overarching tradition. The process can be expressed as constantly shifting between synthesis and analysis, or, in other terms, between bottom-up and top-down strategies of information processing. I hope that the result is a sensitive historical reconstruction of the changing myths and rituals associated with border confrontations.

6. The outline of the argument

Let me start from the title. In choosing the phrase "pushing the boundaries of myth," I have three different meanings in mind. The first is the most literal: I think about the *othismos* of a hoplite battle. The boundary across which the hoplites are pushing each other is a "boundary of myth" inasmuch as the ritual battles, which I reconstruct, are reenactments of ancient mythical conflicts. The second sense of "pushing the boundaries of myth" refers to another theme important in my exploration, namely, the modifications and renovations that are introduced into the myths that I study by different social groups throughout the Archaic and Classical periods. The boundaries of myths, particularly the boundaries between myths and associated rituals, are continually pushed and adjusted by different social actors. Finally, the third sense of pushing the boundaries of myth pertains to my own efforts: in this investigation, I repeatedly attempt to redefine events that have been previously considered historical as myths.

The first part of my analysis concerns the war between Eretria and Chalcis over the Lelantine Plain. Chapter 1 starts from an observation that the current research on the Lelantine war fails to produce a coherent reconstruction of the war's historical core. An analysis of Thucydides' famous reference to the war as an occasion on which the Greek world took sides in a conflict helps to establish that in Thucydides' time there was a Panhellenic tradition of the old war between Eretria and Chalcis. This tradition can be perceived as a myth of the Lelantine War. The chapter proceeds to reconstruct features of this myth. The myth of the Lelantine War turns out to have structural affinities with Hesiod's description of the Bronze Generation. An examination of local Euboean traditions reveals a rich variety of myths concerning the production and invention of bronze. The first wearers of bronze armor are the local Curetes. The Curetes are also portrayed as the first combatants in the war for the Lelantine Plain. The primeval war fought by the Curetes results in the destruction of the mythical city of Chalcis by an earthquake.

Chapter 2 reconstructs the ritual counterpart of the myth of the Lelantine War. Archilochus' and Strabo's references to hostilities on Euboea portray the fighting as a replica of a heroic style of combat characteristic for the Abantes. This leads to a suggestion that in the Archaic period there were ritual battles for the Lelantine Plain between Eretria and Chalcis, in which the participants reenacted the strife between the legendary Curetes/Abantes (synonymous in the Euboean context). The participants were the elites of Eretria and Chalcis, the *Hippeis* and the *Hippobotai*. The territory fought over by them is likely to be identifiable with the location of the destroyed mythical city of Chalcis in the Lelantine Plain; it was a common sacred ground for the two cities, which simultaneously constituted a pasture for the horses of their elites. The last part of the chapter proposes a new interpretation of a poem by Theognis, depicting a devastation of the Lelantine Plain. The poem refers to the Athenian takeover of the Lelantine Plain after Athens defeated Chalcis in 506 BC, which put an end to the ritual battles.

The second and longer part of the investigation examines the legacies associated with the traditional enmity between Argos and Sparta. The subject of contention between Argos and Sparta was the plain of Thyreatis in the border territory of Cynuria. Chapter 3 takes as its starting point Thucydides' report of the eccentric terms of a peace treaty presented by the Argives to the Spartans in 420 BC, which proposed replaying an ancient battle for Cynuria. The tradition of this battle is reflected in Herodotus' famous description of the battle of Champions, in which three hundred Argives and three hundred Spartans fought for the possession of the Thyreatis. An analysis of Herodotus' account and other representations of fighting over the Thyreatis shows that the myth of the ancient battle for the Thyreatis, in which all the participants die, expressed the Spartan ideal of the beautiful death and served as an *aition* of the festival of Gymnopaediae. Taken together, Thucydides' and Herodotus' accounts lead to a reconstruction of ritual battles between Argos and Sparta for the territory of Thyreatis before the middle of the sixth century BC. The battles reenacted the mythical lethal confrontation over the Thyreatis and were overseen by Apollo Pythaeus, who was also the deity uniting Sparta, Argos and Epidaurus in a league with a center in Asine. The Spartan participants in the ritual battles belonged to the aristocratic class of *hippeis*, later transformed into an elite corps.

Chapter 4 investigates how the ideological significance of the confrontation with Sparta changed in Argos after the Spartan annexation of Cynuria (occurring in the middle of the sixth century) and the battle of Sepeia. The battle of Sepeia became a foundational event for the Argive democracy of the 460s BC: the heroic defense of Argos by the Argive women, and the subsequent marriage between Argive women and *perioikoi* is a democratic myth motivating the establishment of the democratic regime and the unification of the Argive Plain. An analysis of stories about armed participation of women in other military conflicts highlights the ambivalent status of the female power in the *polis*: women were perceived to be capable of producing irreversible historical changes, and therefore their agency needed to be confined to the past. The Argive cross-dressing festival of Hybristica, associated with both tragic and comic versions of the myth of defense of Argos by women, presented a safe space of ritual where the normative gender roles were challenged but ultimately reinforced.

Chapter 5 explores contradictory representations of the Argive synoecism and the establishment of democracy by different Argive social groups. The first case in point is an account of the enfranchisement of the Argive *perioikoi* after the battle of Sepeia. The rhetoric of this democratic myth elides the violence of the conquest of the Argive Plain by Argos, and amalgamates synoecism and democratization. On the other hand, Herodotus' story of the rule of slaves in Argos after the battle of Sepeia derives from a contrasting representation of Argive history promoted by the Argive oligarchic aristocracy, a social class that was greatly affected by Cleomenes' attack at Sepeia. The historical referent of the story of the slaves' rule is the struggle between the Argive democratic and oligarchic factions in the period between the battle of Sepeia and 450 BC. This interpretation is supported by a consideration of another closely comparable and equally hostile account of the Argive synoecism and democratization, deriving from the same oligarchic milieu. An additional component of the democratic renovation of the myths and rituals associated with the confrontation between Argos and Sparta was the appropriation of the figure of Apollo Pythaeus by the Argive democracy of the 460s BC. The chapter concludes by an examination of a Spartan myth, proclaiming Sparta's rights over the Thyreatis, which probably derives from the period after the Spartan annexation of the Thyreatis/Cynuria.

Chapter 6 finally returns to the Argive proposal to the Spartans in 420 BC to fight over the territory of Thyreatis in the framework of a peace treaty. The proposal is placed in the context of contemporaneous internal Argive affairs. The suggestion of reviving the ritual battles is interpreted as an initiative of the Argive oligarchic faction, aimed at achieving the military backing of an elite corps intended to participate in the ritual battle, along with a greater rhetorical maneuverability. The chapter reconstructs an ideological competition transpiring in the period of 421–417 BC between the Argive oligarchic and democratic factions over the possession of the myths associated with the ancient war for the Thyreatis, and over the figure of Apollo Pythaeus, the deity who presided over the Archaic ritual battles.

PART I: The Lelantine War

Chapter 1

The Bronze Generation and the Generation of Bronze

> *Unfortunately, the Island of Euboea has recently been overrun by Nefarious Hyenas for a reason that nobody is quite sure of yet.*[1]

1. A war in search of an identity

To introduce the subject of the war between Eretria and Chalcis over the Lelantine Plain,[2] it seems apt to recall a short story by the Russian absurdist writer Daniil Kharms: "There lived a redheaded man who had no eyes and no ears. He didn't even have hair so that he was called redheaded only as a figure of speech..." In the next few lines, it turns out that the man also lacked nose, legs and the rest of his body. The story concludes: "He didn't have

---

[1] "The Battle of Lelantine Farm," GodsWar Online, http://gw.igg.com/guide/guide.php?acid=185

[2] In the following exposition, I use "the Lelantine War" as shorthand for "the war between Eretria and Chalcis for the Lelantine Plain." The expression "the Lelantine War" is a modern construction (on the origin of the term, see Bakhuizen 1976, 36n144), however, it effectively reflects the centrality of the Lelantine Plain in the ancient narratives describing the confrontation between the two cities (see the discussion below).

anything! So that it's unclear who it is we're talking about. In fact, we better change the subject now."[3]

Little is undisputed about the Lelantine War.[4] The proposed dates of the war range over nearly two hundred years, between the last third of the eighth century and the first half of the sixth.[5] Some scholars insist that the war was fought exclusively for the possession of the Lelantine Plain;[6] others connect it with issues of colonization and trade.[7] In addition to Eretria and Chalcis, the powers involved in the war may have included Samos, Miletus, Erythrae, Chios, Corinth, Megara, Thessaly, Paros, Naxos, Sparta, Messenia, and more[8] — or none of the above. Conceivably, the war became "the origin of certain stable alignments that were destined to have a considerable influence on the subsequent course of Greek history at home

---

[3] Daniil Kharms, *The Blue Notebook No. 10*.
[4] Tausend (1987, 501-508) gives a concise summary and a critical evaluation of the previous literature on the subject, including proposed dates and duration of the war, possible allies, and grounds of the war, in particular the economic factors; Parker 1997 also includes a comprehensive discussion of the proposed dates, allies, military techniques, causes of the war, and its possible archaeological correlatives.
[5] See Hall 2002, 233-234 for the list of the suggested dates; Tausend (1987, 501), Parker (1997, 59) and Brelich (1961, 15) also review dates and opinions on the war. Parker (1997, 59-93) argues for continuous hostilities from 710 to 650 BC; van der Vliet (2001, 117) has "serious doubts on the extremely long duration" of war, suggested by Parker. Recently, Walker (2004, 156) has suggested that the war continued until 506 BC.
[6] Parker 1997, 153-160; Tausend 1987, 510; Coldstream 2003 (1977), 201; Brelich 1961, 21; for other scholars who consider the possession of the Plain as the main motive of hostilities, see Tausend 1987, 503, and nn36-38.
[7] Burn 1929; Bradeen 1947; Forrest 1957; hesitantly, Boardman 1957, 27-29.
[8] Burn 1929; Bradeen 1947; Forrest 1957; see discussion in Parker 1997, 119-152.

and abroad;"[9] or perhaps, it had "keinerlei überregionale oder politische Bedeutung."[10] We do not know whether the war was "a brief but severe struggle, or rather a prolonged series of wars and border raids that spanned more than one generation."[11] It has been construed as an aristocratic martial engagement, led according to the rules of chivalry;[12] it has been also described as a "particularly savage and unremitting conflict."[13] The war between Eretria and Chalcis is mentioned once by Herodotus and once by Thucydides, although it is not certain that the two passages refer to the same conflict. Reviewing the rest of the ancient sources on the war, S. C. Bakhuizen has come to the following conclusion: "Nothing can be deduced from them about the beginning of the war, the main issue, its immediate cause, its course, its chronology, its duration, its end, or the consequences of the conflict."[14] Accordingly, he suggests: "To avoid further confusion I recommend to dismiss the term 'the Lelantine War' in historical and archaeological treatises…"[15] Recently, Jonathan Hall's examination of the textual

---

[9] Ridgway 1992, 20. On the causes and consequences of the war, see Burn 1929; Bradeen 1947; Forrest 1957; Boardman 1957, 27–29; Murray [1978] 1993, 76–77.

[10] Tausend 1987, 510.

[11] Janko 1982, 94. Parker (1997, 59–93) argues that the war lasted for sixty years.

[12] Gardner 1920, 91; cf. Brelich 1961, 9–21. See Donlan 1970, 133–4n5 for a bibliography of the early interpretations of the Lelantine War as a contest conducted according to the rules of chivalry. Dayton 2006, 7–29 is a historiographic overview of the literature on agonistic warfare in Greece, with references to the Lelantine War *passim*.

[13] Donlan 1970, 139; in pp. 133–142 Donlan critiques the chivalrous interpretation.

[14] Bakhuizen 1976, 36. Similarly, Lambert 1982; Tausend 1987, 510.

[15] Bakhuizen 1976, 34n139.

and archaeological data associated with the war has reached a similar conclusion: "In short, we do not know when — or even whether — the Lelantine War occurred."[16]

2. Thucydides' logic

Thus, similarly to Kharms' redheaded man, the Lelantine War has been "deconstructed."[17] Should we then change the subject? Not yet, I propose. Among the ruins of the untrustworthy primary sources (analyzed in detail below), a single reference in Thucydides remains standing. This difficult passage is our only explicit evidence of the war's allegedly great scope, and a source of the conflicting perceptions of the war between Chalcis and Eretria as either a pan-Hellenic confrontation or a chronic quarrel between neighboring states.

Thucydides famously opens his work with an assertion that the war between the Peloponnesians and the Athenians is the greatest war ever experienced by the Greek world (1.1). Subsequently, he explains why the wars of the past were less significant: long-distance campaigns with the aim of subjugating the enemy did not exist. There were neither coalitions

---

[16] Hall 2007a, 8.
[17] *Ibid.*, 4.

of subject cities headed by the great city-states, nor joint campaigns of equal partners.[18] Wars amounted only to border conflicts between neighbors (1.15.2). Then comes the thorny sentence (1.15.3):

> μάλιστα δὲ ἐς τὸν πάλαι ποτὲ γενόμενον πόλεμον Χαλκιδέων καὶ Ἐρετριῶν καὶ τὸ ἄλλο Ἑλληνικὸν ἐς ξυμμαχίαν ἑκατέρων διέστη.
>
> At the most, in the once-upon-a-time war between the Chalcidians and Eretrians, the rest of the Greeks also separated into alliances with one or the other party.

Chalcis and Eretria are neighbors, and later sources report that they fought over the Lelantine Plain, situated between them.[19] Thus, the war between Eretria and Chalcis seems to be a quintessential border war. And yet, Thucydides claims that the war caused the Hellenic world to divide into two camps. This turn of phrase strikingly parallels an expression in the first sentence of *The Peloponnesian War*, where Thucydides relates his reasons for believing from the very start of the war in its unmatched greatness: he perceived the Athenians and the Peloponnesians to be at the peak of their powers, and saw "the rest of the Greeks uniting under one or the other party" (καὶ τὸ ἄλλο Ἑλληνικὸν [...] ξυνιστάμενον πρὸς ἑκατέρους,

---

[18] οὐ γὰρ ξυνειστήκεσαν πρὸς τὰς μεγίστας πόλεις ὑπήκοοι, οὐδ' αὖ αὐτοὶ ἀπὸ τῆς ἴσης κοινὰς στρατείας ἐποιοῦντο, κατ' ἀλλήλους δὲ μᾶλλον ὡς ἕκαστοι οἱ ἀστυγείτονες ἐπολέμουν. "There was no union of subject cities round a great state, no spontaneous combination of equals for confederate expeditions." Trans. by Richard Crawley.
[19] Plutarch, *Banquet of the Seven Sages* 10 = *Moralia* 153f; Strabo 10.1.12; scholia ABGc$_2$ for Thucydides 1.15.3; scholia for *Works and Days* 650–662 = Plutarch F 84 Sandbach.

1.1.1). The old war between Eretria and Chalcis and the supposedly incomparable Peloponnesian war are described in very similar terms.

What is the role of Thucydides' remark about the war between Eretria and Chalcis in the overall rhetoric of his argument in Book 1? Does it support his thesis about the unprecedented scope of the Peloponnesian wars, or does it contradict it?[20] On the face of it, the war between Eretria and Chalcis does look like a pointed exception to Thucydides' claim about the lack of significant alliances before the Peloponnesian war. And yet, this impression is belied by the casualness with which the reference to the old war is made. As S. D. Lambert comments in his analysis of the convoluted logic of this sentence of Thucydides, "it does not seem that he or his readers can have thought it was much of an exception to his general rule that τὰ πρὸ αὐτῶν [the previous wars, Thucydides 1.1.3] were οὐ μεγάλα or that it had any serious claim to challenge the Peloponnesian war in μέγεθος."[21] For some reason, the war between Eretria and Chalcis is still no match for the Peloponnesian war, despite the broad alliances that it is said to have elicited.

What were Thucydides' reasons for including the reference to the pan-Hellenic character of the war in his treatise? As I have already mentioned, he is the only author that

---

[20] Lambert 1982, 217. Cf. Tausend 1987, 511–2. Van der Vliet (2001, 115) comments: "Thucydides' words [...] seem to resist interpretation: on the one side he suggests a division of 'the rest of Greece' in two alliances, but 'μάλιστα' seems to detract from the implications."
[21] Lambert 1982, 217.

portrays the war in such terms. Brief references to the war between Chalcis and Eretria in Herodotus and Aristotle do not foster an impression of a pan-Hellenic breadth. Herodotus (5.99.1) remarks that when the Athenians sent ships to aid Miletus, the Eretrians participated in the campaign because they were repaying the Milesians for the help against Chalcis, on an occasion when the Chalcidians were supported by the Samians. Aristotle refers to the Eretrians and Chalcidians as an example of the use of horses in wars between neighbors (*Politics* 1289b). The local character of the conflict in Aristotle and its limited scope in Herodotus make Thucydides' mention of the division of the Greeks into two camps even more surprising. Jonathan Hall invokes considerations of symmetry as an explanation. The war between Eretria and Chalcis "stands in the same relationship to the Peloponnesian War as the Trojan War does to the Persian War: the former are wars among Greeks while the latter are wars between Greeks and their eastern neighbors, but in each set the more recent war is greater in scope that the former."[22] Significantly, as Hall himself recognizes, this attractive scheme could be rhetorically effective only if the story of the war between Eretria and Chalcis, supported by numerous allies, was familiar in Thucydides' time.[23]

What do we gain from the examination of Thucydides' reference to the war between Eretria and Chalcis? First, that the tradition of the Panhellenic character of that war was

---

[22] Hall 2007a, 5.
[23] *Ibid.*

current in Thucydides' time. Second, that the war was perceived as one of the most important confrontations of the past. Third, that despite the apparent parallelism between the old and the new war, Thucydides' audience probably felt that the alliances of the Greeks cities around Eretria and Chalcis were somehow obviously and qualitatively different from the alliances in the Peloponnesian war.

These inferences produce more questions. What exactly did Thucydides and his audience know about the war between Eretria and Chalcis? Why was that war perceived to be so different from the Peloponnesian war, despite its supposedly great scope? What traditions about the war explain the peculiar mixture of Panhellenic and local, of prominence and obscurity, in Thucydides' brief mention of it?

3. The poetry of the Lelantine Plain

Thucydides' wording provides the first hint of an answer. Thucydides describes the war between Eretria and Chalcis as τὸν πάλαι ποτὲ γενόμενον πόλεμον. I quote S. D. Lambert's note on this expression:

> ποτὲ either merely emphasizes πάλαι thus suggesting the mists of antiquity, or it invests whatever πάλαι is describing with a sort of legendary quality, equally misty (*cf.*

'once upon a time'). [...] There is here, [...] I think, a suggestion of either the great amount of time since the war or its rather mythical character.[24]

Lambert further suggests that the memory of the war was perhaps "kept alive through poetry."[25]

Indeed, poetry and stories of mythical character constitute the bulk of references to the war between Eretria and Chalcis. We find mentions of fighting on Euboea in Archilochus (F 3 West), Theognis (891-894), and in an anonymous elegiac fragment (*Adespota elegiaca* 62 West = *P. Oxy.* 2508).[26] Moreover, Plutarch transmits a tradition that Amphidamas of Chalcis, at the funeral games in whose honor Hesiod won a tripod (*Works and Days* 654-57), fell in a battle for the Lelantine Plain (*Banquet of the Seven Sages* 10 = *Moralia* 153f). Elsewhere, Plutarch narrates a story of the Thessalian Cleomachus, who came to aid the Chalcidians against the Eretrians and heroically died in battle; Plutarch portrays Cleomachus' death as the *aition* of the Chalcidian acceptance of pederasty (*Dialogue on Love* 17 = *Moralia* 760e-761b). Strabo, citing Archemachus of Euboea, reports that Curetes fought continually for the Lelantine Plain (Strabo 10.3.6).

Strabo's description of the Lelantine Plain (10.1.9), in general, is full of extraordinary details: Strabo reports that there were disease-curing fountains of hot water in the Plain, used

---

[24] Lambert 1982, 218-219n27. I will have more to say about Thucydides' πάλαι ποτὲ in the next chapter.
[25] Lambert 1982, 220; also 217n9, 219n27.
[26] On *P. Oxy.* 2508 and its connection to the Lelantine War, see Walker 2004, 124, 138n250, 139; Drews 1972, 141-2; Donlan 1970, 136; Podlecki 1969, 75-76.

by Cornelius Sulla. He also states that the Plain once had a remarkable (θαυμαστὸν) mine that contained both copper and iron, a phenomenon that to Strabo's knowledge does not occur anywhere else; Strabo adds that by his time both metals had already run out. Finally, he says that the whole Euboea in general is seismically active, and the area around the strait of the Euripus particularly so, so that an earlier city called Euboea was swallowed up by an earthquake.

Surprisingly, apparently all of these statements can be shown not to correspond to reality, or contain errors: Sulla was bathing in the hot springs in Aedepsus, not in the Lelantine Plain;[27] there is absolutely no evidence of a mine combining copper and iron in the vicinity of the Plain;[28] Strabo adduces a seemingly unrelated quote from Aeschylus as evidence for the destroyed city of Euboea.[29] As Mervyn Popham notes, "Strabo's account of Euboea is unusually long, detailed and seemingly well-informed despite several obvious errors and confusions: the surviving work of a local historian is likely to have been his prime source."[30] It seems that the Lelantine Plain in Strabo's account magnetically attracts unusual details, including those belonging to other places on the island. This suggests that Strabo and/or the local historians on whose accounts Strabo relied viewed the Lelantine Plain in a heavy emanation of legendary

---

[27] Bakhuizen 1976, 83.
[28] *Ibid.*, 48–49.
[29] *Ibid.*, 11–12.
[30] Popham 1980, 423.

associations. The mention of the Plain in the *Homeric Hymn to Apollo* (line 220) as a locale considered by Apollo for his temple, as well as in Callimachus' *Hymn to Delos* (288-89) as a stop in the itinerary of the Hyperboreans' offerings to Delian Apollo, demonstrate the cultic prominence of the Plain.[31]

The legendary quality of the traditions connected with the war between Eretria and Chalcis for the Lelantine Plain has been noted before. Angelo Brelich commented about "un rilievo mitico" of the war;[32] Klaus Tausend called the war "ein[en] Mythos."[33] But what is meant by "myth"? For Tausend, using this term is essentially a way to describe a process of accretion of unrelated stories into one conglomerate, glued together by epic poetry. According to Tausend, Amphidamas, whose funeral was commemorated by Hesiod, became a legendary figure; then the figure of Amphidamas, for an unclear reason, got attached to the tradition of the war between Eretria and Chalcis. Gradually, a local conflict between Eretria and Chalcis transformed into a Panhellenic war mentioned by Thucydides.[34] In this scenario, the word "myth" masks our lack of understanding of how various narrative elements associated with the Lelantine War fit together, and of what is the historical context of their creation.

---

[31] Brelich 1961, 17-18. Aelian (*Varia Historia* 6.1) also reports that the Athenians made a temple to Athena in the Lelantine Plain after defeating the Chalcidians (in 506 BC).
[32] Brelich 1961, 18.
[33] Tausend 1987.
[34] *Ibid.*, 1987, 513-14; cf. Fehling 1979, 199-210.

Jonathan Hall argues that the Lelantine War is not an ancient but, ironically, a modern myth. For Hall, a synthesizing historical reconstruction of the Lelantine War, assembled from the literary references and archaeological findings, is "probably little more than a modern historian's fantasy, cobbled together from isolated pieces of information that, both singly and in combination, command little confidence."[35] Hall's deconstructionist approach exposes numerous weak links in the modern arguments concerning the war. And yet, it seems to me that the problems with the modern reconstructions of the war stem not only, and perhaps not even chiefly, from cobbling together unrelated pieces, but, paradoxically, from failing to analyze the literary evidence — particularly the archaic poetry — more cohesively. Let us return to Thucydides' passage. As we have seen, we can be fairly certain that Thucydides and his audience were familiar with a story of the war between Eretria and Chalcis that had a Panhellenic scope. Thucydides' passage also shows that this war was perceived as one of the most prominent wars of the past. This information can be rephrased as follows: in Thucydides' times, there existed a tradition of the old war between Eretria and Chalcis, and this tradition had a Panhellenic status. Now, we have references to fighting on Euboea in Archilochus and Theognis. Both of these poets were figures of Panhellenic standing.[36] That is to say, their

---

[35] Hall 2007a, 4.
[36] On Panhellenism and poetic authorship, see Nagy 1990a, 52-115. A concise representation of Nagy's views is given in Forsdyke 2005b, 32-34. The view adopted in this exploration is that

poetry transcended concerns limited to local communities, and featured themes and events that could be understood and embraced by Greeks across different *poleis*. It appears reasonable that Panhellenic poets and Panhellenic traditions should go together. Therefore, I believe that when we encounter a detail (a mention of fighting on Euboea) resembling a known Panhellenic tradition (the war between Eretria and Chalcis) in the poetry of Panhellenic scope, we can expect that the particular Panhellenic tradition is in some way relevant to the poem.[37] That is to say, a poem about fighting on Euboea is not necessarily set in the time of the Lelantine War, but the subject of the Lelantine War is extremely likely to be evoked in the poem.

The disinclination of modern scholars to accept that the Lelantine War was evoked in the compositions of all three poets — Hesiod, Archilochus and Theognis —stems to a large extent from chronological considerations.[38] The logic runs as follows. If we accept the dates

---

poetic figures such as Hesiod, Archilochus and Theognis are not historical people but embodiments of particular poetic traditions; see Introduction.

[37] This reasoning can be contrasted with Boardman's comment that Archilochus F 3 West cannot be used as a "chronological pointer" for the dating of the Lelantine War, since "we cannot be sure that he is referring to the 'Lelantine War' rather than some skirmish." Boardman 1957, 29. Similarly, Forrest cites with approval "Wade-Gery's suggestion that 'Theognis' refers merely to some minor interference." Forrest 1957, 162, referring to Wade-Gery 1952, 61n1.

[38] Numerous studies attempt to date the Lelantine War on the basis of synchronisms with these poets.
Burn 1929, 34; Bradeen 1947, 227, 229; Tausend 1987, 504; Parker 1997, 59-88 is a discussion of Archilochus' date as a key to the dating of the Lelantine War. See Parker 1997, 90n395 for references to scholars dating the war on the basis of Hesiod's date.

conventionally ascribed to these poets, and if all three of them referred to the Lelantine War as a contemporary event, then the war stretches enormously from the late eighth century to the beginning of the sixth.[39] Therefore, scholars frequently reject the relevance of one or another of these poets to the war.[40] This primacy of chronological concerns over thematic analysis is precisely what I mean when I speak about the failure of the scholarship to analyze the literary evidence cohesively. Before dating the war, we need to understand it better.

Studies of the Lelantine War typically attempt to reach the historical core of the events by paring away layers of poetic and mythical traditions, perceived as irrelevant.[41] The outcome of this exercise is disappointing: the historical kernel is not to be found. I suggest that a different procedure may give better results: we can use poetry, as well as prose evidence, previously discarded as patently mythologizing, for reconstructing not the historical core of the war, but the ancient perception of the war. This objective presents us with a different set of topics to explore. The war between Eretria and Chalcis over the Lelantine Plain was a

---

[39] Noted in Hall 2007a, 7–8.
[40] Thus, Bradeen (1947, 230) eliminates Theognis 891-94 on the basis of chronological considerations, and dates the war between 720 and 660 BC; similarly, Burn 1929, 34. Forrest (1957, 163-64) rejects the idea that Archilochus F 3 West is an eye-witness account of the Lelantine War, and proposes that in the poem Archilochus looks back at the war.
[41] The analysis of the Lelantine War by Angelo Brelich (1961, 9-12), to which I will be repeatedly returning below, is a major exception; however, even Brelich, whose study is highly sensitive to the ritual and mythical overtones of the Lelantine War, does not attempt to reconstruct the myths associated with the war in any detail.

Panhellenic tradition: can we reconstruct the contours of this tradition in more detail? What was the thematic significance of this tradition? Why was the war between the two neighboring cities felt to be of interest to audiences throughout Greece? I will approach these questions through literary analysis of the sources, looking for recurrent motifs and overarching themes. This reconstruction of the myths of the Lelantine War will eventually bring us back to history: as I hope to demonstrate, in some cases it is possible to reconstruct fairly definitely the historical circumstances in which a particular reference to the Lelantine War was made, and the ideological subtext of such a reference.

I do not expect the ancient mythological tradition about the war to be uniform: obviously, there can be multiple versions, challenging each other.[42] However, our conjectures about the existence of rival versions should derive from the differences between the ancient sources, and not be superimposed onto them on the basis of extrinsic concern with the war's chronology.

A further issue needs to be addressed. I have been using "the war" throughout my discussion: but is the definite article adequate? Were there perhaps many wars between Eretria and Chalcis? Since what I am exploring is the ancient perception of the war, the answer to this question should be sought in the ancient references to the war. The evidence is

---

[42] Lambert 1982, 217n9.

somewhat ambiguous: Plutarch, for example, speaks of ταῖς περὶ Ληλάντου μάχαις (*Banquet of the Seven Sages* 10 = *Moralia* 153f), while Strabo tells that Curetes fought for the Lelantine Plain συνεχῶς 'continuously' (Strabo 10.3.6). Thus, Strabo's and Plutarch's descriptions give an impression of a prolonged war with many battles. However, both Thucydides (1.15.3) and Herodotus (5.99.1) use the definite article for the war; they clearly think there was a single one.[43] Plutarch similarly uses the definite article referring to the battles for the Plain: thus, he also visualizes a well-defined occasion. The extended nature of fighting in Plutarch and Strabo is interesting and will be discussed below; however, it seems that on balance the ancient traditions portray the hostilities between Eretria and Chalcis as a coherent whole, and not as multiple wars.

I also believe that we can safely assume that in all of the versions of the war the subject of contention between Eretria and Chalcis is the Lelantine Plain. The possession of the Plain is the only objective of the conflict that is ever mentioned. Admittedly, it is attested only in the later sources (Plutarch, *Banquet of the Seven Sages* 10 = *Moralia* 153f; Strabo 10.1.12; scholia ABGc₂ for Thucydides 1.15.3; scholia for *Works and Days* 650–662 = Plutarch F 84 Sandbach); as we have seen, Herodotus and Thucydides simply speak about the war between Eretria and Chalcis. However, to argue that for these authors the war between the two *poleis* had a different cause

---

[43] Lambert 1982, 218n23.

is an argument from silence. The unanimity of the later sources, in combination with the parallel case of the Argive-Spartan enmity over the territory of Thyreatis/Cynuria, explicitly mentioned both by Herodotus (1.82) and Thucydides (5.41), as well as Thucydides' emphasis on the prevalence of border conflicts in earlier Greece (1.15.2), make it extremely likely that the tradition of the fighting over the Lelantine Plain was already present in the fifth century and earlier.

Thus, while for different ancient authors "the Lelantine War" may potentially mean different things, I think it is a good working hypothesis that each source refers to *a* version of *the* war for the Lelantine Plain. Below I hope to show that that the story of the war between Chalcis and Eretria is neither a construction by modern historians, nor an ancient medley of disjoined historical events in a poetic sauce, but a deeply traditional and thematically rich subject, going back as far as Hesiod.

4. Amphidamas of Chalcis and the Bronze Generation

In the *Works and Days* (654–657), Hesiod declares that he travelled to Chalcis and won a poetic contest there at the funeral games in honor of Amphidamas:

ἔνθα δ' ἐγὼν ἐπ' ἄεθλα δαΐφρονος Ἀμφιδάμαντος
Χαλκίδα [τ'] εἰσεπέρησα· τὰ δὲ προπεφραδμένα πολλὰ

ἄεθλ' ἔθεσαν παῖδες μεγαλήτορος· ἔνθα μέ φημι
ὕμνῳ νικήσαντα φέρειν τρίποδ' ὠτώεντα.

It was there that I, heading for the funeral games of warlike Amphidamas, crossed over to Chalcis. And there were many games and prizes arranged in advance by the sons of the great-hearted one. And I say solemnly that it was there that I won a contest in song and that I carried off as a victory prize a tripod with handles on it.[44]

In the *Banquet of the Seven Sages* (=Moralia 153f), Plutarch ascribes the following speech to Periander of Corinth, the party's host:

ἀκούομεν γὰρ ὅτι καὶ πρὸς τὰς Ἀμφιδάμαντος ταφὰς εἰς Χαλκίδα τῶν τότε σοφῶν οἱ δοκιμώτατοι ποιηταὶ συνῆλθον· ἦν δ' ὁ Ἀμφιδάμας ἀνὴρ πολεμικός, καὶ πολλὰ πράγματα παρασχὼν Ἐρετριεῦσιν ἐν ταῖς περὶ Ληλάντου μάχαις ἔπεσεν.

For we have the story that the most famous poets among the wise men of that time gathered at Chalcis to attend the funeral of Amphidamas. Now Amphidamas was a warrior who had given much trouble to the Eretrians, and had fallen in one of the battles for the possession of the Lelantine Plain.

Periander further states that the contestants were Hesiod and Homer (*Moralia* 153f–154a).

How should we regard this account? The question is important both practically and methodologically. Practically, do we accept that Amphidamas fell in the Lelantine War? Methodologically, how do we decide that the information provided by the later author is relevant for our understanding of the *Works and Days*?

---

[44] All translations from the *Works and Days* are by Gregory Nagy (with some modifications).

To complicate the matter, Plutarch, our source for Amphidamas' participation in the Lelantine War, apparently did not subscribe to this tradition himself. The information comes from a Hesiodic scholion (scholia for *Works and Days* 650-662 = Plutarch F 84 Sandbach):

> Ταῦτα πάντα περὶ τῆς Χαλκίδος τοῦ Ἀμφιδάμαντος, καὶ τοῦ ἄθλου, καὶ τοῦ τρίποδος, ἐμβεβλῆσθαι φησιν ὁ Πλούταρχος οὐδὲν ἔχοντα χρηστόν. Τὸν μὲν οὖν Ἀμφιδάμαντα ναυμαχοῦντα πρὸς Ἐρετριέας ὑπὲρ τοῦ Ληλάντου ἀποθανεῖν· ἆθλα δὲ ἐπ' αὐτῷ καὶ ἀγῶνες ἐγένοντο τελευτήσαντος παρὰ τῶν ἑαυτοῦ παίδων· νικῆσαι δὲ ἀγωνιζόμενον τὸν Ἡσίοδον, καὶ ἆθλον μουσικὸν τρίποδα λαβεῖν, καὶ ἀναθεῖναι τοῦτον ἐν τῷ Ἑλικῶνι, ὅπου καὶ κάτοχος ἐγεγόνει ταῖς Μούσαις, καὶ ἐπίγραμμα ἐπὶ τούτῳ θρυλλοῦσι. Πάντα οὖν ταῦτα ληρώδη λέγων ἐκεῖνος ἀπ' αὐτῶν ἄρχεται τῶν εἰς τὸν καιρὸν τοῦ πλοῦ συντεινόντων, ἤματα πεντήκοντα λέγων.

> Plutarch says that all this about Chalcis, Amphidamas, the games, and the tripod has been interpolated, and contains nothing of value. The story is that Amphidamas died in a naval battle with the Eretrians over the Lelantine Plain; contests and games for the dead man were held by his sons; Hesiod competed and won, and received, as a prize for poetry, a tripod which he dedicated on Helicon, where he had been possessed by the Muses; the inscription is constantly quoted. Plutarch says that all this is silly stuff, and begins with the lines concerned with the right season for navigation, "Fifty days, etc."

The scope of Plutarch's skepticism is not clear from this summary: did Plutarch deny Amphidamas' participation in the Lelantine War, or even his existence? Or did he just think that Amphidamas had nothing to do with Hesiod?[45] We cannot tell, and must proceed in our exploration under the shadow of Plutarch's disparagement.

---

[45] In another passage, Plutarch calls the tradition of a contest between Homer and Hesiod on the occasion of Amphidamas' funeral "the hackneyed lore of the literary scholars" (τῷ διατεθρυλῆσθαι πάνθ' ὑπὸ τῶν γραμματικῶν, *Table-Talk* 5.2 = *Moralia* 675a).

The modern scholars accept Amphidamas' participation in the Lelantine War more readily than the idea that in Chalcis Hesiod competed with Homer. Martin West, for example, accepts the former and rejects the latter.[46] I suspect that the widespread acceptance of Amphidamas' participation in the war has to do with the usefulness of the synchronism with the war for dating Hesiod.[47] Plutarch's information is equally appealing to those who wish to date the war from its synchronism with Hesiod.[48] Both directions of dating are common, and, as Richard Janko notes, "[t]here seems to be a widespread unawareness of the circularity of this argument."[49] The issue of dating brings me to my methodological question: what are the grounds for believing that Plutarch's information is relevant? West notes that Amphidamas' epithets in the *Works and Days* (654, 656) are characteristic of a warrior.[50] Apart from this thematic observation, discussions typically focus on the compatibility of the dates for Hesiod and the Lelantine War.[51] However, as we have seen, the proposed dates for the Lelantine War range from the eighth to the sixth century: how valuable is such a broad chronological

---

[46] West 1978, 319–321.
[47] See, for example, Tedeschi 1975.
[48] See Parker 1997, 90n395 for references to scholars dating the war on the basis of Hesiod's date, and vice versa. For dating Hesiod as a historical figure see also Kõiv 2011 with further references.
[49] Janko 1982, 95. Janko (1982, 94-98) then reviews the historical information relevant for the date of the war, independently of Hesiod's date.
[50] West 1978, 320.
[51] West 1978, 321; Debiasi 2012, 486.

correspondence with Hesiod? Are there any other grounds, apart from the chronological, on which we can evaluate the information provided by Plutarch?

At this point we need to discuss some basic assumptions. The "practical" question that I have posited, concerning our acceptance or rejection of Plutarch's information that Amphidamas fell in the Lelantine War, implicitly assumes the historicity of Amphidamas, Hesiod and the Lelantine War. Only if Hesiod's attendance of Amphidamas' funeral is a fact, and the Lelantine War is a historical reality, can the truth-value of Amphidamas' participation in the war be potentially established.

Indeed, the historical and autobiographical quality of Hesiod's reference to Amphidamas is a conviction strongly held by some scholars in the field. As Martin West expresses it, "no one will suppose Hesiod's Amphidamas to be a fiction."[52] The following passage from a recent publication is representative of the reasoning that ties together the historicity of the war and of Hesiod:

> A crucial historical reference in Hesiod's work, that members of the oral formulaic school pass over in silence, is to the so-called Lelantine War. Because it refers to a historical fact, this reference in *Works and Days* (654–659) not only enables us to establish *terminus post quem* for Hesiod's poetic activity, but it also suggests Hesiod may have composed with the aide of writing.[53]

---

[52] West 1978, 321. Recently, Debiasi 2012, 486 and n94 with further references.
[53] Naddaf 2005, 44.

Here the participation of Amphidamas in the Lelantine War is declared to be history, which is used to make further inferences about the nature of the *Works and Days* as composed in writing.

The emphasis on the episode of Amphidamas' funeral as a stronghold of Hesiod's historical veracity is a reaction to a steady advance of thematic studies into the previously autobiographic territory of the *Works and Days*. At the current stage of research nearly all details, previously thought to preserve personal information about Hesiod's life, such as Hesiod's conflict with his brother Perses, his father's journey from Aeolian Cyme to Ascra, even the very names of Ascra and Perses, have been shown to feature themes structurally important in the overarching design of the *Works and Days*.[54] The logical next step is to explore the thematic importance of the funeral of Amphidamas.

The work of Gregory Nagy demonstrates that Hesiodic poetry, along with Homeric poetry, is a product of a long tradition of oral composition and transmission, and Panhellenic propagation.[55] If we recognize the *Works and Days*' long period of oral development and dissemination, we have to abandon such notions as the autobiographical realism of the Hesiodic poetry, or the possibility of dating an event on the basis of its mention in the poem.

---

[54] Nagy 1990b, 74–75. On the thematic importance of Hesiod's name, see Nagy 1990b, 47–48; [1979] 1999, 296–297; see Rosen 1990 on the theme of sailing and poetic self-referentiality in the *Works and Days*.

[55] Nagy 2009, 273–274; 1990b, 38–47; cf. Most 2006, xix–xx. Stoddard 2004, 1–33 is a good overview of the literature on the subject.

Moreover, we have to leave behind the idea of a single stable text of the poem. Oral poetry is fundamentally multiform,[56] and this multiformity is still reflected in the variants preserved in the textual traditions of the *Works and Days* available to us,[57] or in the ancient testimonies about the existence of significantly different versions.[58] The oral development of the poem also excludes a rigid distinction between the stages of formation and reception of the poetry. New interpretations were integrated into the poetry through the constant process of recomposition-in-performance.

The perception of the *Works and Days* as a product of a long history of oral development views the poem as a multi-vocal, multi-layered, diachronic structure, incorporating tensions between rival traditions;[59] this variability co-exists with a high level of thematic unity and an extremely prominent Panhellenic tendency. Let us see how this understanding of the poem changes our interpretation of Plutarch's reference to Amphidamas' death in the Lelantine War.

Periander's speech in Plutarch's *Banquet* and the Hesiodic scholion for *Works and Days* 650–662 show that, at least in Plutarch's time, the tradition of Amphidamas' participation in the Lelantine War was widely known. The same Hesiodic scholion, reporting Plutarch's

---

[56] Lord [1960] 2000, 100; 1995, 23; Nagy 2001a; 1996, 107–152.
[57] I analyze one such variant in Bershadsky 2011, 31–34. Another notable variant is a line ὕμνῳ νικήσαντ' ἐν Χαλκίδι θεῖον Ὅμηρον (scholia for *Works and Days* 657a).
[58] Pausanias' mention of the text of the *Works and Days* without the first ten lines (the *prooimion* to Zeus), preserved on Helicon (Pausanias 9.31.4), is a good example.
[59] Examples in Bershadsky 2011.

athetesis of Hesiod's travel to Chalcis, also demonstrates that this tradition was not uniformly accepted.[60] How do we determine the value of this contested tradition? Plutarch describes the story of the competition between Homer and Hesiod in Chalcis as "the hackneyed lore of the literary scholars" (*Table-Talk* 5.2 = *Moralia* 675a). Can Amphidamas' participation in the Lelantine War be merely an innovation of an ancient commentator? On the other hand, the Panhellenic quality of the tradition of the Lelantine War makes it potentially highly suitable material for Hesiod's Panhellenic poetry. How do we decide how closely this tradition is related to the *Works and Days*?

If the allusion to the Lelantine War is indeed built into the poetry of the *Works and Days*, the themes related to the war will "reverberate" in the poem.[61] This is particularly true about the immediate context of the potential reference to the Lelantine War, the passage describing

---

[60] We also know of an altogether different rival tradition, proposing Delos as a location of the contest between Homer and Hesiod. Hesiod F 357 M-W. See Nagy 2010, 336-340; 2011a, 295-304.

[61] My thinking about the function of allusions in traditional poetry, and, in particular, my use of the term "reverberation," is informed by the work of Slatkin 1991, 107-122. I quote Slatkin's formulation: "allusions, both abbreviated and extended in lengthy digressions, are highly charged and repay scrutiny for the myths whose resonance or "reverberation" they carry into the narrative as a whole, signaling a constellation of themes that establish bearings for the poem as it unfolds and linking it continually to other traditions and paradigms and to a wider mythological terrain." Slatkin 1991, 108. She continues further on: "Allusions form a system of evocation in which each reference produces not a single meaning but a sequence of overlapping significations — as with echoes, in which it is not the original sound but each subsequent iteration that is picked up and relayed." Slatkin 1991, 109-110.

Amphidamas' funeral. If the information about Amphidamas that Plutarch and the scholion give is really relevant for the poem, we can expect that plugging this information in will amplify the underlying themes of the Hesiodic passage. Thus, exploring the fit between the information about Amphidamas' participation in the Lelantine War and the underlying themes of Amphidamas' funeral in the *Works and Days* will allow us to evaluate how deeply the tradition about the Lelantine War is embedded in the *Works and Days*. The first step in this procedure, of course, is to trace the network of associations of Amphidamas' funeral in the *Works and Days*.

A passage that exhibits lexical ties to the portrayal of Amphidamas is the depiction of the Bronze Generation (*Works and Days* 143-155). Chalcis, the Bronze City (655), finds a counterpart in the bronze armor, houses and implements of the Bronze Generation (150-151). In addition, Ἀμφιδάμαντος (654) resonates with two phrases, describing the Bronze Men's ruthlessness and their self-destruction: ἀδάμαντος ἔχον κρατερόφρονα θυμόν, "they had harsh temper of adamant" (147), and χείρεσσιν ὑπὸ σφετέρῃσι δαμέντες, "having been overcome by the violence of their own hands" (152). The verb δαμάζω appears only one more time in the *Works and Days*, in the form δεδμημένοι (116), very different phonetically.

Taken by themselves, these verbal correspondences provide no more than a hint of direction. Are the two passages connected on a thematic level? The men of the Bronze

Generation are warriors, characterized by *hubris*: οἷσιν Ἄρηος |ἔργ' ἔμελε στονόεντα καὶ ὕβριες "they cared mostly for the lamentable works of Ares and for acts of *hubris*" (146). Amphidamas' heroic epithets δαΐφρων 'warlike' and μεγαλήτωρ 'great-hearted' suggest that he also was a warrior.[62] Further, the epithet μεγαλήτωρ also appears to be connected with the quality of *biê*, in its negative incarnation of savage brutality.[63]

The possibility that the *Works and Days* envisages Amphidamas as a warrior is particularly remarkable when viewed in the light of a powerfully negative general attitude to war in the poem. War is a prime expression of a bad *eris* (*Works and Days* 13-14). The City of *Dikê* does not have war at all (*Works and Days* 228-29):

εἰρήνη δ' ἀνὰ γῆν κουροτρόφος, οὐδέ ποτ' αὐτοῖς
ἀργαλέον πόλεμον τεκμαίρεται εὐρύοπα Ζεύς·

Peace, the nurturer of the young men, ranges about the land, and never do they have wretched war manifested for them by Zeus who sees far and wide.

Conversely, the City of *Hubris* suffers from war (*Works and Days* 244–45):

ἢ τῶν γε στρατὸν εὐρὺν ἀπώλεσεν ἢ ὅ γε τεῖχος
ἢ νέας ἐν πόντῳ Κρονίδης ἀποτείνυται αὐτῶν.

---

[62] West 1978, 320. Δαΐφρων can also mean 'wise.'
[63] Nagy [1979] 1999, 321 and §4n8. Nagy notes that the Cyclops (*Odyssey* 10.200), Achilles at the height of his rage (*Iliad* 9.629) and the fierce warriors Phlegues (*Iliad* 13.302) are all given this epithet.

> There will be a time when Zeus will destroy their vast host of fighting men, or he can exact retribution against them by destroying their city-walls or their ships sailing over the sea.

Finally, as we have already noted, war and *hubris* are the Bronze Men's chief interests (145–146). Thus, in the *Works and Days* war is an expression of the bad *eris* and a correlative of *hubris*.

The verbal correspondences with the description of the Bronze Generation, as well as the epithets, alluding to Amphidamas' warlike disposition, can be construed as subtle but coherent cues of a negative characterization of Amphidamas in the *Works and Days*. How does a portrayal of Amphidamas outside of the *Works and Days* match his negative evaluation internal to the poem? The answer is that the external representations perfectly match the internal point of view: the image of Amphidamas that they produce casts him as a highly problematic figure from the standpoint of the *Works and Days*. It is as if the information about Amphidamas supplied by the external traditions confirmed the poem's "worst suspicions" about the hero.

Let us start from Amphidamas' description in Plutarch's *Banquet*. The detail that Amphidamas was ἀνὴρ πολεμικός, a warrior, makes him a representative of the bad *eris*. The tradition that Amphidamas died in a war between Eretria and Chalcis, close neighbors, brings us back to the motif of the Bronze Generation's self-destruction (χείρεσσιν ὑπὸ σφετέρῃσι δαμέντες,[64] "overcome by the violence of their own hands," *Works and Days* 152). Further, the

---

[64] The link between Amphidamas' name and this particular formula is noteworthy.

Hesiodic scholion, quoted above, reports that Amphidamas died in a sea battle: ναυμαχοῦντα πρὸς Ἐρετριέας ὑπὲρ τοῦ Ληλάντου, "in a naval battle with the Eretrians over the Lelantine Plain" (scholia for *Works and Days* 654-656 = Plutarch F 84 Sandbach). Such an end recalls the assertion in the *Works and Days* 244-45, already cited, that Zeus destroys ships and armies in retribution for men's *hubris*.[65]

The war between Eretria and Chalcis, a quintessential bad *eris*, contrasts with a prototypical good *eris* of the poetic contest (*Works and Days* 24-26), won by Hesiod.[66] Amphidamas' life and death, from the standpoint of the *Works and Days*, are redolent of *hubris*;[67]

---

[65] A statement that the people of the City of *Dikê* do not ever travel on ships (*Works and Days* 235-6) sharply contrasts with traditions of the Euboean seafaring and colonizing activities, on which see Antonelli 1995, 11-24; Huber 2003, 66 with n198 with further references to early representations of ships on Euboea. See also discussion below. On ships as emblems of the Eretrian identity on tombs of the captive Eretrians in Cissia (Persia), see Philostratus, *Life of Apollonius of Tyana* 1.24.

[66] Cf. Debiasi 2012, 487.

[67] Interestingly, in Hesiod's biographic tradition, as reflected by the *Contest of Homer and Hesiod*, the visit to Chalcis is thematically associated with Hesiod's death. The name of the contest organizer, Amphidamas' son Ganyctor (*Contest of Homer and Hesiod* 63 Allen) curiously coincides with the name of one of Hesiod's murderers (Amphiphanes and Ganyctor, two brothers, who suspected that Hesiod dishonored their sister). *Contest of Homer and Hesiod* 14.227 Allen; the same names of Hesiod's murderers are found also in Aristotle F 565 Rose = Tzetzes, *Vita Hesiodi* line 51 Allen = Hesiod T 2 p. 160 Most. Ganyctor's name recurs, this time as the name of the father of Hesiod's murderers, in a variant account of Hesiod's death given in Eratosthenes' *Hesiod*. *Contest of Homer and Hesiod* 14.241 Allen; Plutarch *On the Cleverness of Animals*, *Moralia* 969e; Pausanias 9.31.6. Debiasi 2012, 484. It is tempting to view Hesiod's participation in the contest at Chalcis, on the very un-Hesiodic occasion of a warrior's funeral, as a point when Hesiod becomes metonymically affected by *hubris*, leading to his death. On the subject of

Hesiod, of course, is an exponent of *dikê*.⁶⁸ Hesiod seems to have an ameliorating influence on the posthumous destiny of Amphidamas: his poetic voice saves Amphidamas from the anonymity of the Bronze Men (νώνυμνοι, *Works and Days* 154).⁶⁹

Thus, there is a remarkable thematic agreement between the implicitly negative attitude to Amphidamas in the *Works and Days* and the figure of Amphidamas as a hero of the Lelantine War, attested elsewhere. The network of associations linking the Amphidamas of the Lelantine War with key motifs and themes of the *Works and Days*, such as the Bronze Generation or *eris*, suggests that the connection between the Hesiodic Amphidamas and the war is deeply embedded in the structure of the *Works and Days*. Such an organic connection is very unlikely to be an artificial construction by an ancient scholar.

However, we have further means of ascertaining the traditionality of the connection between the Hesiodic Amphidamas and the Lelantine War. We have seen that there are some formal lexical ties between Amphidamas and the Bronze Generation in the *Works and Days*. If

---

Hesiod's *hubris*, some traditions asserted that he did seduce Ganyctor's sister, naming Stesichorus as his son. Aristotle F 565 Rose = Tzetzes, *Vita Hesiodi* line 51 Allen = Hesiod T 2 p. 160 Most; also Scholia for *Works and Days* 271a = Hesiod T 19 p. 172; cf. Cicero *De republica* 2.20 = Hesiod T 20 p. 172 Most.

⁶⁸ Nagy 1990b, 63–79.

⁶⁹ Hesiod's mention essentially transforms Amphidamas into a figure of the Fourth Generation. On the Third and Fourth Generations (the Bronze Men and the heroes) as dark and light sides of the epic hero, see Nagy [1979] 1999, 155–173. On Hesiod in the *Works and Days* as an agent of temporary transformation of the Iron Age into the Golden Age, see Bershadsky 2011, 24–25.

we are able to show that motifs associated with Hesiod's Bronze Generation recur in the descriptions of the ancient Euboea, Chalcis and, in particular, of the Lelantine War, the 'bronze reverberations' of Amphidamas will be substantiated on a deeper thematic level. What we are ultimately looking for is a representation of the Lelantine War as belonging to the Age of Bronze.

5. Metals and war

Hesiodic Bronze Men are warriors and bronze workers.[70] A nexus of war and metals (especially bronze) is featured in a rich assortment of Euboean traditions displaying a strikingly fabulous quality. Motifs range from mining to creation of the first arms and armor.

Let us start from seemingly the most realistic realms, mining and the production of weapons. I have already mentioned Strabo's report of a wonderful mine in the Lelantine Plain, uniquely combining copper and iron (10.1.9). Strabo notes that the mine did not yield metals in his time; however, it is very unlikely that the mine ever existed, since geological conditions in

---

[70] *Works and Days* 145-146, 151. On the key themes and motifs of the myth of the Bronze Generation (war, *hubris*, ash-trees, bronze), and their expressions in associated traditions, see Vernant [1965] 2006, 35-40; Vian 1968, 59-64; Nagy [1979] 1999, 156-9.

the vicinity of the Plain appear to exclude copper.[71] Plutarch (*On the Failure of Oracles* 434a) also mentions a depletion of a Euboean copper mine as an illustration of the impermanence of earthly phenomena; as for the objects that used to be produced from the mine's copper, he cites a line from Aeschylus (F 703 Mette):

λαβὼν γὰρ αὐτόθηκτον Εὐβοικὸν ξίφος

...for, taking a self-sharpened Euboean sword...

The adjective αὐτόθηκτον 'self-sharpened' endows the sword with a magical quality, resembling the automata such as Hephaestus' tripods in the *Iliad* 18.373-77.

Stephanus of Byzantium also mentions a mine combining copper and iron in Aedepsos; perhaps this notice resulted from a transfer of Strabo's mine in the Lelantine Plain to Aedepsos. Apropos the mine, Stephanus quotes Callimachus (F 701 Pfeiffer):

δέδαεν δὲ λαχαινέμεν ἔργα σιδήρου

...he taught to dig iron mines...

While we know neither the teacher nor the student in Callimachus' fragment, it probably refers to mythical times of acquisition of cultural skills. A little further on in the same entry on Aedepsus, Stephanus quotes Callimachus again (from *Hecale*, F 236 Pfeiffer):

ἄρκιος ἢ χείρεσσιν ἑλὼν Αἰδήψιον ἄορ

---

[71] Bakhuizen 1976, 49; cf. Boardman 1957, 27; Davies 1935, 244.

taking into his hands a reliable Aedepsian sword...

This time, we do know who is supposed to wield the Aedepsian sword: it is Theseus, and the sword, along with sandals, serve as Theseus' tokens of recognition by his father.

Finally, Chalcidian swords (Χαλκίδικαι σπάθαι) appear in Alcaeus F 357 L-P (= 140 Campbell) with its magnificent catalogue of heroic arms and armor, permeated by the gleam of bronze. It has been recognized that the poem "surely shows a romanticized appreciation of the equipment and the heroic status it implies."[72]

A peculiar pattern emerges, in which the mines are doubtful and the swords are poetic. Apparently, the Euboean metals and weapons were traditional accoutrements of poetry. The abundance of poetic and legendary associations indicates that Euboean metalworking belonged to the realm of mythological discourse.

The story of the mice from Elymnium is relevant to the subject of metal and myth. Elymnium is a Euboean island,[73] whose mice were famous for gnawing through iron.[74] Iron-

---

[72] Morgan 2001, 24, with further references.
[73] Herodian 3.1.364, s.v. Ἐλύμνιον; Stephanus of Byzantium 269.19-20, s.v. Ἐλύμνιον; Hesychius s.v. Ἐλύμνιον; Heraclides Lembus *Excerpta politiarum* F 62 Dilts = Aristotle F 611.314-316 Rose; Scholia for Aristophanes *Peace* 1126; Bakhuizen 1976, 49-50 with n28.
[74] Heraclides Lembus *Excerpta politiarum* F 62 Dilts = Aristotle F 611.314-316 Rose; Bakhuizen 1976, 49-51.

gnawing mice are a wide-spread topos;[75] the underlying image is that of everything remotely edible having been consumed by the rodents, with only iron being left for them to nibble on.[76] Several Latin sources attest to a belief that mice gnawing on metals predict war.[77] It seems that exactly the same idea underlies Aristophanes' reference to Elymnium in *Peace* 1126. At the point of Trygaeus' joyful sacrifice to Peace, he is accosted by Hierocles, "the oracle monger from Oreus" (*Peace* 1047), delivering prophecies of war (1063-1086).[78] Hierocles then starts to demand a share of the sacrificial meat (1105-1118). Trygaeus and his slave beat the seer away, and the slave's parting words to Hierocles are: "Won't you, this instant, fly off to Elymnium?" (Οὐκ ἀποπετήσει θᾶττον εἰς Ἐλύμνιον; *Peace* 1126). The mention of flying is a carry-over from a comparison of Hierocles to a raven in the preceding line (1125); however, Elymnium as a destination in which the gluttonous warmongering seer is sent off seems uniquely suitable if Elymnium was an abode of voracious mice who portended war through gnawing on iron.[79]

---

[75] Aelian *On the Nature of Animals* 5.15; Aristotle *On Marvellous Things Heard* 25–26, 832a22; Theophrastus F 174 Wimmer; Herodas 3.74–76; Antigonus of Carystus *Mirabilia* 18 ap. Stephanus of Byzantium 213.19–20, s.v. Γύαρος; Tacitus *Annals* 7.1; Pliny *Natural History* 8.222; Marcovich 1988, 47–51; Bakhuizen 1976, 50.

[76] Marcovich 1988, 49.

[77] Cicero *Concerning Divination* 2.59; Pliny *Natural History* 8.221; Livy 30.2.10; Marcovich 1988, 50.

[78] Hierocles' real-life counterpart was a religious expert who assisted the Athenians in their dealings with the Euboean Chalcis in 446 BC, and was apparently granted land in Oreus, confiscated from the Euboeans after Pericles' military campaign of 445 BC, as a reward. Flower 2008, 62 and nn108, 109 with further references.

[79] For the correlation between war and hunger, see *Works and Days* 243–247.

Commentaries on this line of Aristophanes in the scholia preserve a very different tradition related to Elymnium. We learn that Elymnium had a temple on a spot of Zeus' intercourse with Hera.[80] In the *Iliad*, Zeus' and Hera's lovemaking brings about a delightful lushness of the earth, sprouting grass and flowers under a cover of a golden cloud (*Iliad* 14.346-51).[81] It is probable that a similar tradition was associated also with the Elymnian temple. What we have, then, is a striking contrast, in which the same Euboean locale is connected with two very different visions: the blissfully thriving land and the nightmare of a barren terrain with only iron remaining unconsumed by mice. We will encounter elsewhere in Euboean tradition a similar contrast between a paradisiacal abundance and a total devastation, associated with war.

Euboea, and Chalcis in particular, are named in the ancient sources as places where χαλκός 'copper/bronze' was first discovered. In our sources, this innovation is tied together with the discovery of copper mines and the invention of bronze arms and armor. There are different traditions concerning the agents of the discovery. The first tradition reports that weapons of war were originally made by the Cyclopes in the Euboaen cave called Teuchion.[82] A

---

[80] Scholia for Aristophanes *Peace* 1126, citing Apollonius and Sophocles (F 437, 888 Radt).
[81] On the association of Zeus' and Hera' intercourse with the terrestrial fertility, see Janko 1992, 171-72, 206.
[82] P. Oxy. 1241 iv 12-14; Scholia A for *Iliad* 10.439; Eustathius 3.107.7-12 on *Iliad* 10.439. The scholia and Eusthatius name Istrus as a source of this information.

fascinating note by Hesychius (s.v. χαλκιδικὸς λειμών) provides further evidence of the Cyclopes' presence in the myth-ritual landscape of Chalcis:[83]

> χαλκιδικὸς λειμών· οἱ μὲν τὴν Κυκλωπίαν κώμην. οἱ δὲ Κυκλωπι...λίμνη
>
> Chalcidian meadow. Some say that it is a village of the Cyclopes, others that it is ...of the Cyclopes ... marsh.

Another tradition that probably also derives from Euboea identifies Briareus as the first figure to employ armor.[84] Briareus and his double Aegaeon have a well-attested cultic presence on Euboea. We learn from Solinus 11.16 that Briareus had a cult in Carystus, and Aegaeon in Chalcis; other sources associate Aegaeon also with Carystus, referring to him as Carystus' ruler, and reporting that Carystus was called Aegaea after him.[85] Hesychius also calls Euboea a daughter of Briareus.[86] The Panhellenic Briareus-Aegaeon of the *Iliad* (1.402-6) and the *Theogony* (147-153, 669-678, 713-719) is a Hundred-Hander, characterized by a surpassing *biê*, which in both poems is instrumental for defending the rule of Zeus.[87] Despite these positive associations of Briareus' *biê*, there are notable parallels between the description of the Bronze

---

[83] See Mele 1981, 24.
[84] P. Oxy. 1241 iv 15–17. My discussion below is indebted to Mele 1981, 19–20. See also Debiasi 2004, 83–84; Antonelli 1997, 64–66, and 64n82 with further references.
[85] Stephanus of Byzantium 363.1 s.v. Κάρυστος; scholia for Apollonius Rhodius 1.1165; Eustathius 1.432.7-8 on *Iliad* 2.539.
[86] Hesychius s.v. τιτανίδα.
[87] On Briareus-Aegaeon as an exponent of *biê*, see Nagy [1979] 1999, 346-347; Vernant [1965] 2006, 41.

Generation in the *Works and Days* and of the Hundred-Handers in the *Theogony*: both groups are ὄβριμοι 'mighty' (*Theogony* 148, *Works and Days* 145), and they share a formula ἐξ ὤμων ἐπέφυκον ἐπὶ στιβαροῖσι μέλεσσιν 'grew out of their shoulders over powerful limbs' (*Theogony* 152, 673 = *Works and Days* 149). The Hundred-Handers are also οὐκ ὀνομαστοί (*Theogony* 148), in parallel to the νώνυμνοι Bronze Men (*Works and Days* 154).[88] Returning to the Euboean context, we learn that Aegaeon, according to Archemachus of Euboea, was the first to sail "in a long vessel" (or "in a warship," *longa nave*, ap. Pliny *Natural History* 7.207). A historicizing version portrays Briareus-Aegaeon, a child of Earth and Sky, using Euboea as a base for naval operations and subduing the Cyclades, so that the sea becomes known as Aegean in his honor (Arrian F 35 Roos ap. Eustathius 1.190.37-39 on *Iliad* 1.401-4). Further, we can infer that when Briareus-Aegaeon sailed on ships, he went very far indeed, since a tradition traceable to Euphorion of Chalcis called the pillar of Heracles "pillars of Briareus" or "pillars of Aegaeon:"[89] what we apparently face is a local Euboean toponymic tradition for the limits of the inhabited world.

---

[88] Briareus was identified as a Cyclops by Demetrius of Callatis, *FGrH*, 85 F 4; see Mele 1981, 13, 19; in the *Theogony* the birth of the Hundred-Handers immediately follows the birth of the Cyclopes (*Theogony* 139-146).

[89] Euphorion F 169 Lightfoot, ap. Scholia for Dionysius Periegetes 64, *Geographi graeci minores* ii. p.434[b]4 Müller; Scholia for Pindar *Nemean* 3.40, iii. p. 48.10 Drachmann; Lightfoot 2009, 394-395. See also Debiasi 2008, 121n76 with further references, and Antonelli 1995, 21-23.

Briareus-Aegaeon of the Euboean tradition, with his connection to war and ships,[90] is a cosmic parallel for the figure of Amphidamas. It is instructive to observe the clash of values between the *Works and Days*, with its disapproval of war and sailing, and the local Euboean myths, in which Briareus is a culture hero.

I have saved the most relevant tradition for last. Several sources connect the name of the Euboean Chalcis with the discovery of copper/bronze.[91] The explicit etymological quality does not make the tradition less significant. Moreover, as I have already mentioned, copper is geologically improbable in the vicinity of Chalcis; thus, the traditions associating the invention of bronze with Chalcis cannot be explained as a mythologizing dressing-up of the reality.

This tradition introduces new actors: the Curetes[92] and their mother Combe.[93] The Curetes are said to be the first wearers of bronze armor,[94] while Combe is credited with the creation of bronze, for which she is nicknamed Chalcis.[95] Here is an account by Zenobius (6.50):

---

[90] The motifs of armor and ships, associated with Briareus, parallel Chalcis, the Bronze City, and Eretria, the City of Rowers.

[91] Herodian *De prosodia catholica* 3.1.88; Zenobius 6.50; Strabo 10.3.19; Solinus 11.15; Pliny *Natural History* 4.64; Stephanus of Byzantium 45.17–19, s.v. Αἴδηψος; 683.12–13, s.v. Χαλκίς; Eustathius 1.428.10–13 on *Iliad* 2.537.

[92] On a possible connection between the Cyclopes and Curetes on Euboea, see Mele 1981, 23–24.

[93] Hesychius s.v. Κόμβη· Κουρήτων μήτηρ.

[94] καὶ πρῶτοι χαλκὸν ἐκεῖ ἐνεδύσαντο οἱ Κούρητες "and the first ones there to put on bronze armor were the Curetes." Epaphroditus ap. Herodian *De prosodia catholica* 3.1.88; Strabo 10.3.19; Stephanus of Byzantium s.v. Αἴδηψος.

[95] P. Oxy. 1241 iv 26–29 ascribes the invention of bronze to the Curetes themselves.

Ὥσπερ Χαλκιδικὴ τέτοκεν ἡμῖν ἡ γυνή· ταύτης Πολύζηλος μέμνηται ἐν Μουσῶν γοναῖς, ἐπί τινος πολλὰς θυγατέρας ἀπογεννώσης· ἐπειδὴ Χαλκίδα τῆς Εὐβοίας πόλιν φασὶ ποτὲ ἀνθῆσαι δόρασί τε καὶ πλήθει τετρώρων ἁρμάτων. Οἱ δὲ φασὶν οὐ τὴν πόλιν, ἀλλὰ τὴν ἡρωΐδα Χαλκίδα εἰρῆσθαι. Κόμβην γὰρ φασὶ, τὴν ἐπικληθεῖσαν Χαλκίδα, ἐπειδὴ ὅπλα χαλκᾶ ἐποιήσατο, πρώτην συνοικήσασαν ἀνδρὶ ἑκατὸν παίδων γενέσθαι μητέρα, ὡς ἱστοροῦσιν οἱ τὰ Εὐβοϊκὰ συγγράψαντες καὶ Ἄριστος ὁ Σαλαμίνιος.

"The woman has born us children like the Chalcidian one:" Polyzelos mentions this in *The Birth of the Muses*, about somebody who bears many daughters. For they say that the Euboean city Chalcis once blossomed with spears and a multitude of four-horse chariots. But others say that it is not the city but the heroine Chalcis who is talked about. For they say that Combe, who was called Chalcis because she created bronze weapons, became the mother of a hundred children, after having been the first woman to live with a man, as record those who write about the Euboean affairs, and Aristus the Salaminian.

In this passage, Combe, the eponymous heroine of Chalcis, seems to be presented as a progenitor of the human race: she is the first woman to live together with a man, giving birth to a hundred children, the Curetes. Combe's ability to create bronze weapons suggests her visualization as the Chalcidian earth. Another hint in the same direction is provided by a parallel tradition, attested in the Euboean context, which describes the Curetes as earth-born.[96] Thus, the Curetes can be alternatively imagined as having a nymph Chalcis as a mother, or as sprung from the earth. In this context, it becomes appealing to understand "blossomed with spears and a multitude of four-horse chariots" (ἀνθῆσαι δόρασί τε καὶ πλήθει τετρώρων

---

[96] Nonnus 13.154–5; compare Strabo 10.3.19. Blakely 2006, 18.

ἁρμάτων) not metaphorically, but literally: perhaps what is described is the Chalcidian earth generating not only copper but also spears and chariots.[97]

The duality of the human genesis from the local nymph or from the earth finds an exact parallel in an Aeginetan tradition, reflected in a fragment from the Hesiodic *Catalogue of Women* (Hesiod F 205 = scholia for Pindar *Nemean* 3.21). The fragment contains two birth stories, imagined to happen consecutively. According to the first narrative, the most important Aeginetan cult-hero Aeacus was born from the nymph Aegina, a daughter of river Asopus.[98] According to the second narrative, the people of Aegina were created by Zeus from ants. Gregory Nagy analyses the rhetorics of this passage:

> As we take a closer look at the Hesiodic narrative, we can see two levels of anthropogony. On one level, the hero Aiakos originates from Aigina the nymph, who is his mother. On another level, the people of this hero's native land originate from Aigina the island, which is their Mother Earth. ... The identity of Aigina as a nymph converges with the identity of Aigina as a land that becomes the localized Mother Earth of the native population.[99]

In a precise parallel to the Curetes who become the first wearers of bronze armor, the people

---

[97] Compare Apollonius Rhodius' description of the emergence of warriors from dragon's teeth, sown by Jason in Colchis (*Argonautica* 3.1354–7): οἱ δ' ἤδη κατὰ πᾶσαν ἀνασταχύεσκον ἄρουραν| γηγενέες· φρίξεν δὲ περὶ στιβαροῖς σακέεσσιν| δούρασί τ' ἀμφιγύοις κορύθεσσί τε λαμπομένῃσιν| Ἄρηος τέμενος φθισιμβρότου "By now the earthborn men were springing up over all the field; and the plot of Ares, the death-dealer, bristled with sturdy shields and double-pointed spears and shining helmets..." See discussion in Vernant ([1965] 2006, 38) of the affinities between this passage and the myth of the Bronze Generation.
[98] Combe-Chalcis is also Asopus' daughter.
[99] Nagy 2011b, 46–47.

of Aegina, upon their transformation from ants, become the first builders of ships:

οἳ δή τοι πρῶτοι ζεῦξαν νέας ἀμφιελίσσας

and these humans, I can now say, were the first to fit together ships, which are curved at both ends...[100]

The numerous similarities between the Hesiodic fragment and the story of Combe, transmitted by Zenobius, highlight a deeply traditional character of the Chalcidian narrative, which may go all the way back to the Archaic period.

A different version of the tradition about the Chalcidian Curetes portrays them as coming to Chalcis from Crete. Logically, this variant excludes the Chalcididan autochthony and Combe's motherhood, although our sources report this version along with the mention of Combe-Chalcis (Herodian *De prosodia catholica* 3.1.88).

The last account of the Curetes in Chalcis that I am going to discuss depicts them settling (συνοικῆσαι) in that city and fighting for the Lelantine Plain:

Ἀρχέμαχος δ' ὁ Εὐβοεύς φησι τοὺς Κουρῆτας ἐν Χαλκίδι συνοικῆσαι, συνεχῶς δὲ περὶ τοῦ Ληλάντου πεδίου πολεμοῦντας, ἐπειδὴ οἱ πολέμιοι τῆς κόμης ἐδράτ-τοντο τῆς ἔμπροσθεν καὶ κατέσπων αὐτούς, ὄπισθεν κομῶντας γενέσθαι, τὰ δ' ἔμπροσθεν κείρεσθαι· διὸ καὶ Κουρῆτας ἀπὸ τῆς κουρᾶς κληθῆναι·

Archemachus the Euboean says that the Curetes settled at Chalcis, but since they were continually at war for the Lelantine Plain and the enemy would catch them by the front hair and drag them down, they let their hair grow long behind but cut short the part in front, and because of this they were called "Curetes," from the cut of their hair...

---

[100] Trans. Nagy 2011b, 46.

Strabo 10.3.6[101]

As a next step in their itinerary, the Curetes move to Aetolia and call their neighbors with unshorn (ἀκούρους) hair Acarnanians (Strabo 10.3.6).

While the Curetes of Archemachus' story are imported into Chalcis (from an undetermined location), the narrative about cutting hair in order not to be dragged down by the enemy is a local Euboean tradition: as we will see, Plutarch (*Theseus* 5.4) narrates the same story about the Abantes. I believe that the narrative elements set in Chalcis, that is, the birth of the Curetes from Combe and their fighting for the Lelantine Plain, belong to an earlier stage of the tradition than the migrations from Crete and to Aetolia. The ancient traditions concerning the Curetes were extraordinarily varied and multi-local: suffice it to say that their discussion takes up twenty-three sections of Strabo's *Geography* (10.3.1–23). It is probable that different local versions were joined at assorted points of the tradition's development, resulting in numerous references to the Curetes' migrations from one region to another.[102] While the reasons for such joining of the local traditions into more complicated patterns are worth exploring in every given case, it seems to me that the local version in which the Curetes are autochthonous should predate the itinerant variants.

---

[101] Trans. by Horace Leonard Jones.
[102] Compare Nagy 2011b.

Thus, I reconstruct the following local story of the Curetes: as soon as Combe the Nymph gives birth to them as the first inhabitants of Chalcis, they don bronze armor and start to fight for the Lelantine Plain. (The enemies that the Curetes fight with remain unspecified). What happens next, as a result of the non-stop (συνεχῶς) fighting? I will attempt to give an answer at the end of the chapter.

The search for the Euboean traditions similar to the motifs associated with the Bronze Generation brings abundant results. Euboea, providing heroes with swords from fabulous mines, the island whose residents were taught to sail by Briareus, and especially the city of Chalcis, with its Cyclopes in residence and the bronze-clad Curetes, fighting for the Lelantine Plain, have a pronounced Bronze Generation atmosphere.[103]

6. Leaving the Golden Age at Pithecusae

There is one more ostensibly historical tradition about Eretria and Chalcis, reporting that these cities founded together Cymae and Pithecusae.[104] The story of the joint colonization of Pithecusae is presented by Strabo (5.4.9). I am going to show that Strabo's account follows a mythical pattern in which the conflict between Eretria and Chalcis leads to a disastrous

---

[103] Cf. Bakhuizen 1981, 167–169.
[104] The joint foundation of Cymae: *Dionysius of Halicarnassus Roman Antiquities 7.3.1.*

transition from an era of prosperity and abundance to times of cataclysmic strife. In Hesiodic terms, such a transition can be viewed as a switch from the way of life of the Golden Generation to that of the Bronze Men.

Strabo (5.4.9) narrates that a happy existence of the Chalcidians and Eretrians at Pithecusae came to an end because of stasis:

> Πιθηκούσσας δ' Ἐρετριεῖς ᾤκισαν καὶ Χαλκιδεῖς, εὐτυχήσαντες [δὲ] δι' **εὐκαρπίαν** καὶ διὰ τὰ **χρυσεῖα** ἐξέλιπον τὴν νῆσον κατὰ **στάσιν**, ὕστερον δὲ καὶ ὑπὸ σεισμῶν ἐξελαθέντες καὶ ἀναφυσημάτων πυρὸς καὶ θαλάττης καὶ θερμῶν ὑδάτων·
>
> Pithecusae was once settled by Eretrians and also Chalcidians, who, although they had prospered there owing to the <u>fertility of the crops</u> and the <u>gold mines</u>, abandoned the island as the result of a stasis; later on they were also driven out of the island by earthquakes, and by eruptions of fire, sea, and hot waters; ...[105]

The mythical pattern is transparent: first, there was a period of a blissful existence, rich in gold and fruitful. Then a bad *eris*, a *stasis* between the previously cooperative neighbors ended the idyllic life, and the colonists needed to abandon the island.[106] Strabo continues by saying that the colonists were driven out by earthquakes and eruptions of fire and sea. Superficially, the account is confused: Strabo seems to give two versions of the expulsion.[107] However,

---

[105] Trans. by Horace Leonard Jones, modified.
[106] Bakhuizen (1976, 20) calls the story a "romantic conception."
[107] *Ibid.*, 22 n93; see also Parker 1997, 52–53.

conceptually, the two explanations are perfectly in tune and complementary: the *stasis* between people parallels natural disaster.[108]

The impression that Strabo portrays a fabulous prosperity, and not just an everyday affluence, is supported by an examination of another instance of co-occurrence of words from the roots *chrus-* and *eukarp-* in Strabo (7a.1.33):

> εἰσὶ δὲ περὶ τὸν Στρυμονικὸν κόλπον πόλεις
> καὶ ἕτεραι, οἷον Μύρκινος Ἄργιλος Δραβῆσκος Δάτον,
> ὅπερ καὶ ἀρίστην ἔχει χώραν καὶ **εὔκαρπον** καὶ ναυ-
> πήγια καὶ **χρυσοῦ μέταλλα**· ἀφ' οὗ καὶ παροιμία „Δά-
> τον ἀγαθῶν," ὡς καὶ „ἀγαθῶν ἀγαθῖδας."
>
> There are about the Strymonic Gulf other cities also, as Myrcinus, Argilus, Drabescus, and Datum, which has an excellent and <u>most productive</u> soil, dock-yards for ship-building, and <u>gold mines</u>; whence the proverb, "A Datum of good things," like to the proverb, "Piles of plenty."[109]

Thus, the combination of gold mines and fruitful land amounts to a proverbial good fortune.

The interpretation of Strabo's account of the colonization of Pithecusae as based on a mythical perception of the past helps to explain an otherwise perplexing unrealism of the Pithecusan *chruseia*. It has been observed that gold mines are geologically impossible on

---

[108] See Nagy 1985, 62 on the image of a ship in a storm as a basic metaphor for a city-state affected by *stasis*.
[109] Trans. by H.C. Hamilton and W. Falconer.

Ischia.[110] *Chruseia*, therefore, is sometimes translated as 'gold-workshops,' or 'gold jewelry.'[111] However, as Coldstream notes, "[s]o far, the gold ornaments from the site are few and unimpressive,"[112] an unlikely situation if gold-working was a prominent industry at Pithecusae. The gold of Pithecusae seems to be mined in the same place as the copper of Chalcis: in the realm of the imaginary past.[113]

7. The lost Euboea

If we return to Euboea now, we will notice interesting parallels between Strabo's account of the colonization of Pithecusae and some details that Strabo reports about the Lelantine Plain. Similarly to Pithecusae's gold mine, the Plain used to boast a remarkable copper-iron mine. Further, there was once a great earthquake on Euboea that swallowed up a city of the same name (Strabo 10.1.9):

---

[110] Coldstream 2003 (1977), 243 n11 (on p. 226 Coldstream calls Strabo's two sources of Pithecusae's prosperity "rather puzzling"); Walker 2004, 146, 173n48, citing Ridgway 1992, 34; Parker 1997, 52.
[111] Bakhuizen 1976, 85; Coldstream 2003 (1977), 226; Walker 2004, 173n49 with further references.
[112] Coldstream 2003 (1977), 226. According to Walker, not a single gold object was found in Pithecusae. Walker 2004, 146–47; cf. Ridgway 1992, 75, 95.
[113] Strabo's *eukarpia* is also not quite accurate in application to Pithecusae: the island's soil is indeed productive, but only for growing of grapes. Coldstream 2003 (1977), 226; Walker 2004, 146.

ἔστι δὲ καὶ ἅπασα μὲν ἡ Εὔβοια εὔσειστος, μάλιστα δ' ἡ περὶ τὸν πορθμόν, καὶ δεχομένη πνευμάτων ὑποφοράς [...]. ὑπὸ τοιοῦδε πάθους καὶ ἡ ὁμώνυμος τῇ νήσῳ πόλις καταποθῆναι λέγεται...

The whole of Euboea is much subject to earthquakes, but particularly the part near the strait, which is also subject to blasts through subterranean passages [...]. And it is said that the city which bore the same name as the island was swallowed up by reason of a disturbance of this kind...

The parallels with the Pithecusan story make it appealing to connect the destruction of Euboea the city to the war for the Lelantine Plain: the earthquake swallowing the city can be understood as a cosmic response to the war. Hecataeus' statement that Chalcis was previously called Euboea[114] supports this suggestion: the destroyed Euboea is the city of Chalcis, perennially fighting in the Lelantine War. However, Strabo's testimony complicates the picture. There is an ambiguity in Strabo's text concerning the location of Euboea the city: while the immediate subject of Strabo is the Lelantine Plain, and while Strabo has been speaking about the Euripus strait (τὸν πορθμόν) in the preceding sentence, a quotation from Aeschylus' *Glaucus Pontius* that Strabo adduces as a reference to the city of Euboea is set in the north of the island, near Cape Cenaeum: Εὐβοΐδα καμπτὴν ἀμφὶ Κηναίου Διὸς| ἀκτήν, translated by H. L. Jones as "Euboeïs, about the bending shore of Zeus Cenaeus." I follow S. C. Bakhuizen's suggestion that Strabo inserted a wrong quote into his account of the Lelantine

---

[114] Ἑκαταῖος Εὐρώπῃ «Χαλκὶς πόλις ἐστίν, ἣ πρότερον Εὔβοια προσηγορεύετο». "Hecataeus in Europe: 'Chalcis is a city, which was previously called Euboea.' " Herodian *De prosodia catholica* 3.1.88; Stephanus of Byzantium 683.9–10, s.v. Χαλκίς.

Plain, which does not in fact refer to the city of Euboea: as Bakhuizen notes, the line can be construed as "round Cape Cenaeum, where Euboea curves."[115]

If we disregard Strabo's reference to Cape Cenaeum as mistaken, the conclusion based on the rest of Strabo's passage is that the destroyed city of Euboea was imagined to have been located in the Lelantine Plain. Strabo's emphasis on the intense seismic activity in the Lelantine Plain (Strabo 1.3.16) strengthens the idea that he believed that the lost city used to be there.

How do we bring together the tradition about the destroyed Euboea in the Lelantine Plain and Hecataeus' claim that Chalcis was once called Euboea? The answer offered by Bakhuizen is historical: he suggests that the archaeological site of Lefkandi-Xeropolis in the Lelantine Plain must have been an earlier location of the city of Chalcis; the Chalcidians later

---

[115] Bakhuizen 1976, 12. Sommerstein (2008, 29) translates these lines as "rounding the extremity of Euboea like a four-horse chariot, off the shore sacred to Zeus Cenaeus..." I should note, however, that there is a persistent sharing of mythical traditions between Chalcis and the North Euboea, especially Aedepsus. First, Strabo (10.1.9) places the hot springs of Aedepsus in the Lelantine Plain. Second, the tradition of the lost Euboea-city can be compared with the report that the Lichadian islands and a part of Cape Cenaeum were submerged by an earthquake. Demetrius of Callatis ap. Strabo 1.3.20. Third, in the same passage Strabo further relates that an earthquake suppressed the hot springs of Aedepsus for three days; he mentions an earthquake-induced obstruction of the spring in Chalcis in 1.3.16. Finally, Stephanus of Byzantium s.v. Αἴδηψος contains a quote from Epaphroditus (concerning the Curetes as first wearers of bronze armor) that is taken to refer to Chalcis by Herodian *De prosodia catholica* 3.1.88; Stephanus' passage also mentions an iron-copper mine in Aedepsus. See Bakhuizen 1976, 10n17, 12n31, 44, 48, 83. The recurrent confusion between Chalcis and Aedepsus requires further research.

abandoned this city and moved away because of the threat from the Eretrians.[116] Since I am concerned in this exploration with the reconstruction of ancient traditions, not of historical events, I would like to provide a different solution.

The city of Euboea, destroyed by an earthquake in the aftermath of the Lelantine War, belongs to the realm of the myth. This myth fits very well with the tradition that I have reconstructed, according to which the Curetes, Chalcis' primordial inhabitants, continually fought for the Lelantine Plain. I suggest that Chalcis called Euboea is the Chalcis of the fighting Curetes, the city where the bronze armor was invented and copper was discovered. This Bronze City of perpetual strife, located in the Lelantine Plain, was believed to be destroyed by an earthquake.[117] The destruction of Chalcis-Euboea finds an exact parallel in the fate of the hybristic warriors Phlegyae, who were "completely overthrown by the god with continual thunderbolts and violent earthquakes" (τὸ μὲν δὴ Φλεγυῶν γένος ἀνέτρεψεν ἐκ βάθρων ὁ θεὸς κεραυνοῖς συνεχέσι καὶ ἰσχυροῖς σεισμοῖς, Paus. 9.36.3). Another version of the Phlegyae's story

---

[116] Bakhuizen 1976, 9.

[117] It is obviously tempting to suggest that the destroyed mythical Euboea was anciently believed to be located at the site of Xeropolis/Lefkandi, but more research on the subject is required. I note with interest that the old war between Eretria and Chalcis for the Lelantine Plain is reenacted in the modern archaeological dispute concerning the identification of Lefkandi as the Old Chalcis or Old Eretria. For a review of opinions, see Knoepfler 1981, 309–312.

that we have derives from Euphorion of Chalcis (Euphorion F 105 Lightfoot = Servius on Vergil *Aeneid* 6.618):

> hi *[Phlegyae] namque secundum Euphorionem populi insulani fuerunt, satis in deos impii et sacrilegi; unde iratus Neptunus percussit tridenti eam partem insulae quam Phlegyae tenebant, et omnes obruit.*
>
> They (the Phlegyae) according to Euphorion were island people, impious towards the gods and sacrilegious to a degree; with the result that Neptune grew angry with them and struck the part of the island in which they lived with a trident, and sank the lot of them.[118]

This version provides a perfect parallel for the destruction of Euboea; perhaps more than a parallel, even, with its reference to an island, given Euphorion's Euboean provenience. As we will see, the Euboean Curetes can be also identified as Abantes or Corybantes; it is possible that Phlegyae is another way to describe these insatiable warriors.

The myth about the Curetes, fighting in the Lelantine War, and the destruction of their city by an earthquake, is more than a local lore of the city of Chalcis: the name of the destroyed city, Euboea, suggests that we are dealing with a pan-Euboean myth. Pliny, citing Callidemus, reports that the island of Euboea used to be called Chalcis, since copper was discovered there (Pliny *Natural History* 4.64). Thus, the metonymy between the island and the Bronze City works in both directions. The myth of the destroyed city of Chalcis-Euboea, which, like the Bronze Generation, springs up solely to devastate and to be devastated, serves as an example of the

---

[118] Trans. Lightfoot 2009, 337.

disastrous effects of a bad *eris* for all Euboean cities. In the next chapter we will investigate how the real ancient cities of Chalcis and Eretria dealt with that mythical lesson.

Chapter 2

Tresses, Horses and Vineyards

> *I said: the vineyard lives like an ancient battle,*
> *Where wavy-haired horsemen fight in a curly order...*
> Osip Mandelstam[1]

1. Archilochus or Strabo?

The starting point of inquiry in the previous chapter was an exploration of the resonances of Hesiod's Amphidamas. The process resulted in the reconstruction of the myth about the obliteration of Chalcis, the Bronze City of the continuous war for the Lelantine Plain. Let us now proceed in investigation of other sources associated with the Lelantine War.

Two ancient references to fighting on Euboea are commonly discussed together: Archilochus F 3 West and Strabo 10.1.12. Strabo speaks about the general accord between Eretria and Chalcis, and gives evidence of a regulation applied to the fighting for the Lelantine Plain:

> Τὸ μὲν οὖν πλέον ὡμολόγουν ἀλλήλαις αἱ πόλεις αὖται, περὶ δὲ Ληλάντου διενεχθεῖσαι ... οὐδ' οὕτω τελέως ἐπαύσαντο ... ὥστ' ἐν τῷ πολέμῳ κατὰ αὐθάδειαν δρᾶν ἕκαστα,

---

[1] Я сказал: виноград, как старинная битва, живет,
Где курчавые всадники бьются в кудрявом порядке...

ἀλλὰ συνέθεντο ἐφ' οἷς συστήσονται τὸν ἀγῶνα. δηλοῖ δὲ καὶ τοῦτο ἐν τῷ Ἀμαρυνθίῳ στήλη τις φράζουσα μὴ χρῆσθαι τηλεβόλοις.

Now in general these cities were in accord with one another, and when differences arose concerning the Lelantine plain they did not so completely break off relations as to wage their wars in all respects according to the will of each, but they came to an agreement as to the conditions under which they were to conduct the fight. This fact, among others, is disclosed by a certain pillar in the Amarynthium, which forbids the use of the long-distance missiles.[2]

The tone of Archilochus' poem, which speaks of a battle on Euboea, is much more somber:

οὔτοι πόλλ' ἐπὶ τόξα τανύσσεται, οὐδὲ θαμειαὶ
 σφενδόναι, εὖτ' ἂν δὴ μῶλον Ἄρης συνάγηι
ἐν πεδίωι· ξιφέων δὲ πολύστονον ἔσσεται ἔργον·
 ταύτης γὰρ κεῖνοι δάμονές εἰσι μάχης
δεσπόται Εὐβοίης δουρικλυτοί.

Not many bows will be stretched, neither slings
plentiful, when Ares joins the throng
in the plain. It will be the grievous work of the swords.
For of this kind of battle those ones are masters,
the lords of Euboea famed for their spears.

Both Archilochus and Strabo associate the fighting on Euboea with the absence of long-distance missiles. A number of scholars accept the connection between the two references, and use Archilochus to date the Lelantine war.[3] However, the precise relationship between the two descriptions, as well as their historical import, prove to be quite elusive. The difficulty stems

---

[2] Cf. Polybius 13.3.4.
[3] For example, Burn 1929, 33; Bradeen 1947, 227; Janko 1982, 95–96; Parker 1997, 59–60. Some scholars dispute the relevance of Archilochus' poem to the war between Eretria and Chalcis. Wheeler 1987, 160–61 and n21 for earlier references.

from the drastically different attitudes of Archilochus' poem and Strabo's account. While both sources seem to converge technically, pointing toward the prominence of close fighting on Euboea, Archilochus stresses the violence of the fighting, while Strabo stresses the fighting regulations; Archilochus seems to present a descriptive view of the hostilities, while Strabo reports a prescriptive agreement. The difference between the sources translates into the difference of the modern researchers' opinions. Some prefer to interpret the absence of long-distance missiles as a ceremonial measure, and accordingly argue for the agonistic character of the war.[4] Strabo's passage is a cornerstone for these interpretations.[5] Others view the disappearance of long-distance missiles as a byproduct of a historical development of fighting techniques, and assert that Archilochus' poem is a testimony of the emergence of the hoplite phalanx.[6] The first line of reasoning has difficulty accommodating the grim brutality of Archilochus' poem;[7] the second one, the regulatory tenor of Strabo's testimony.

The validity of Strabo's report and its connection with Archilochus' poem have been pelted with the following objections. One reason to divorce Strabo's and Archilochus' accounts

---

[4] This point of view was more common in the earlier scholarship. The classic expression is Gardner 1920, 91 (cited in Bradeen 1947, 223n2, Brelich 1961, 16, Donlan 1970, 140n27, Walker 2004, 178n154, Dayton 2006, 47), describing the war as "a kind of fighting-match or ordeal by combat, [...] which taught the cities to respect one another, but left little rancour." See Donlan 1970, 133n5 and Brelich 1961, 16 for references to other proponents of this view.
[5] Walker 2004, 157.
[6] Principally, Forrest 1957 and Donlan 1970.
[7] Archilochus' poem is not mentioned by Gardner 1920.

is that the stele's total ban on the long-distance missiles clashes with Archilochus' description, which only says that there will be "not many" bows and slings, not that they will be completely absent.[8] Further, the proponents of the view that Archilochus' lines refer to the introduction of the hoplite phalanx[9] argue that the hoplite equipment made the participants much less vulnerable to the long-range missiles, which led to a drop in the missiles' use:[10] if this is true, it is not clear what is gained from the prohibition of already disappearing weapons. Finally, the protective value of the prohibition of the long-distance missiles is questionable, since close fight is supposed to be a far more destructive mode of fighting.[11] George Forrest comments acerbically:

> At the end of the eighth and beginnings of the seventh century the new hoplite technique of warfare was appearing in Greece. We are asked to believe that some years after its introduction the δουρικλυτοί δεσπόται of Euboea solemnly agreed to ban obsolete methods and use only the newest weapons, to ban pikes and stick to gunpowder. It is difficult to believe that any competent δουρικλυτὸς δεσπότης needed a compact to persuade him to make any change.[12]

---

[8] Donlan 1970, 134; Wheeler 1987, 161.
[9] Forrest 1957, 164; Donlan 1970, 138–9.
[10] Donlan 1970, 137 with n19, citing Snodgrass 1967, 60; Anderson 1991, 21.
[11] Forrest 1957, 163, Donlan 1970, 140. However, Greenhalgh (1973, 92, 136-7), Boardman (1982, 761) and Walker (2004, 159) suggest that the ban of the long-distance missiles was meant to protect the horses. Wheeler (1987, 173n70) criticizes this idea. Wheeler's study includes a critical assessment of arguments for and against the historicity of the treaty, described by Strabo; however, the usefulness of Wheeler's analysis for clarifying the connection between Strabo 10.1.12, Archilochus F 3 West and the Lelantine War is impaired by his assumption that the war dates *ca* 700 BC (Wheeler 1987, 160).
[12] Forrest 1957, 164.

Accordingly, Strabo's treaty is considered to be a later misinterpretation of the military changes witnessed by Archilochus. Forrest suggests: "Later Euboeans ... who did not know about the introduction of hoplite warfare might well be puzzled by Archilochus' lines and so invented the story of the compact to account for them."[13] Forrest also comments on the scarcity of seventh-century inscriptions, and doubts that "Strabo would have been epigraphist enough to read" such an early specimen.[14] Donlan agrees with Forrest's point concerning Strabo's epigraphic inadequacy, and proposes a compound scenario: the original stele memorialized not a treaty but a factual halt in the employment of missiles. For some reason, "the seventh century Euboeans had recorded a noteworthy event, the transition from long-range to close combat."[15] "To later generations the momentousness of the change would have become unclear, and it is reasonable to conjecture that the stele seen by Strabo was a later copy in which the original message had been misinterpreted."[16]

Donlan and Forrest exaggerate the correlation between the phalanx and the lack of missiles. The presence of long-range missiles does not exclude hoplite fighting. For example,

---

[13] Forrest 1957, 164.
[14] Forrest 1957, 163. Cf. Wheeler 1987, 168–169.
[15] Donlan 1970, 140.
[16] Donlan 1970, 141.

Tyrtaeus' famous poem (F 11), described as a "first sure literary testimony"[17] of the hoplite phalanx, ends with the following injunction to the light-armed soldiers: "And you, o light-armed fighters crouching behind the shields on either side, hurl your great boulders."[18] The missiles apparently were to some extent effective even when used against a hoplite phalanx.[19] Further, a recent reexamination of the history of hoplite fighting by Adam Schwartz convincingly argues that phalanx fighting did not significantly change from c. 750 to c. 320 BC.[20] Thus, it is inherently unlikely that Archilochus' poem describes a transition to a new mode of fighting. What does it describe?

---

[17] Sage 1996, 28.

[18] Translation from Sage 1996, 29. See the discussion of Tyrtaeus F 11 in Lorimer 1947, 126-8 and van Wees 2004, 172-4. Hall 2007a, 167-168 notes that Tyrtaeus' portrayal of fighting is quite similar to the Classical period representations, the main difference being in the position of the light-armed soldiers closer or among the hoplites in the Archaic period; similarly, Schwartz 2009, 121-122.

[19] Lorimer 1947, 126-8; Snodgrass 1964, 156; Snodgrass 1965, 110-114; Snodgrass 1967, 56; van Wees 2004, 172-4; Wheeler 1987, 171-2.

[20] Schwartz 2009, 143-146, 226-230. Schwartz' methodology (pp. 22-24) seems to me particularly sound: he draws principally on testimonies of Classical authors and archaeologically attested hoplite weapons, exercising caution in the use of the Homeric poems and the vase painting.

2. The lords of Euboea and the future battle

I shall endeavor to arrive at an interpretation that makes room both for Strabo's account of the fighting regulations and for Archilochus' fierce battle. Let us start by exploring the associations that Archilochus' poem evokes. An obvious first observation is that the fighting in Archilochus' poem resembles epic combats on the levels of both form and content. The poem's diction exhibits numerous similarities to Homeric language.[21] The combination of spear and sword, conjured up in the poem (ξιφέων, δουρικλυτοί), is also the standard equipment of the Homeric heroes.[22] Moreover, numerous scholars have remarked that *Iliad* 2.543–544 describes the Euboean Abantes as close fighters.[23] This point brings us to the question of the interpretation of the poem's final lines. Who are δεσπόται Εὐβοίης δουρικλυτοί? Forrest and Donlan assume that they are Euboean war-lords contemporary with

---

[21] See Tarditi 1968, 61 for the list of parallels.

[22] Renehan 1983, 2. While the fighting in the poem is consistent with the Homeric pattern, it also conforms to the hoplite mode of fighting. The prominence of the swords is sometimes taken as a sign that the poem refers to a pre-hoplite or non-hoplite battle (Boardman 1982, 761; Anderson 1991, 17–18); however, a sword was the hoplite's standard equipment. Boardman 1957, 29; Anderson 1991, 25–27; Parker 1997, 118; differently, van der Vliet 2001, 117.

[23] Donlan 1970, 133, Bradeen 1947, 227, Boardman 1957, 29, Bérard 1970, 32, Walker 2004, 158 all discuss the relation between the close-fighting style of the Abantes and the poem of Archilochus.

Archilochus.[24] However, Plutarch, our source for Archilochus' poem (*Theseus* 5.3), cites it as an illustration of the fact that the Abantes were "war-like men and close fighters" (πολεμικοὶ καὶ ἀγχέμαχοι, *Theseus* 5.2). Therefore, for Plutarch the poem's lords of Euboea are the Abantes. The epithet δουρικλυτοί, characterizing the lords of Euboea in the poem, "is not a general epic epithet but a specific allusion to the Homeric account of the Abantes."[25]

In modern scholarship the legendary Abantes and the historical Euboean aristocrats of the Archaic period are frequently telescoped into one entity.[26] However, in the poem there are two distinct temporal realms: the heroic past of the Abantes and the future battle in the plain. This battle will be fought in a style characteristic of the Abantes, but it will not be fought by the Abantes themselves. We will take up the question of the future battle and its participants in the next section; for now, let us keep looking into the past.

The Abantes, evoked by Archilochus' poem, display distinct similarities with the men of Hesiod's Bronze Generation in the Homeric Catalogue of Ships (*Iliad* 540–544):

---

[24] Forrest 1957, 163–164; Donlan 1970, 134 directly equates the "lords of Euboea" with the Chalcidian *Hippobotai*.

[25] Renehan 1983, 2.

[26] For example, Jeffery (1976, 65) rephrases the poem in the following way: "The lord of Euboea, he [Archilochus] says, when they fight on the plain, will do it in the way wherein they excel, with swords at close quarters, not with bows and slings. The lords of Euboea were traditionally descendants of the Abantes with their thrusting-spears..." Thus, in Jeffery's rendition, the "lords of Euboea," appearing in the fifth line of the poem, are made to participate in the future battle, described in the first three lines.

> τῶν αὖθ' ἡγεμόνευ' Ἐλεφήνωρ ὄζος Ἄρηος
> Χαλκωδοντιάδης μεγαθύμων ἀρχὸς Ἀβάντων.
> τῷ δ' ἄμ' Ἄβαντες ἕποντο θοοὶ ὄπιθεν κομόωντες
> αἰχμηταὶ μεμαῶτες ὀρεκτῇσιν μελίῃσι
> θώρηκας ῥήξειν δηΐων ἀμφὶ στήθεσσι·

> Elephenor, scion of Ares, was in command of these —
> Chalcodon's son, the leader of the great-hearted Abantes.
> With him the Abantes followed, swift, wearing their hair long behind,
> spearmen, striving with their outstretched ash spears
> to break through the corselets on their enemies' breasts.

The motifs of war and bronze are sounded in the description of the Abantes' leader, Elephenor, who is a scion of Ares and a son of Chalcodon.[27] Further, In the *Iliad* the Abantes are the only group carrying ash spears (the only individual who has *meliê* in the *Iliad* is Achilles).[28] One can compare this characterization of the Abantes with ἐκ μελιᾶν "out of ash-trees," describing the genesis of the Bronze Generation in the *Works and Days* (145).[29]

The association between the Homeric Abantes and the Hesiodic Bronze Men brings us back to the myth of the bronze-armed Curetes, fighting for the Lelantine Plain. As I have already noted (and as we will discuss in detail below), the Euboean Curetes share the same hair-style with the Abantes (ὄπιθεν κομόωντες, *Iliad* 2.541, and Plutarch *Theseus* 5.4). We can

---

[27] On the traditions associated with the figure of Chalcodon, see Mele 1981, 25–32, especially pp. 31–32 on Chalcodon's link with the working of bronze.
[28] For discussion of Achilles' ash spear as an expression of an affinity between Achilles and the men of the Bronze Generation, see Nagy [1979] 1999, 157–159.
[29] On the motif of ash-trees in the Bronze Generation myth and the associated traditions, see Vernant [1965] 2006, 36–37, 39; Nagy [1979] 1999, 156.

posit an equivalence between the Abantes and the Curetes on Euboea. It appears that the Homeric poetry in the Catalogue of Ships is attuned to the local Euboean tradition, presenting the Curetes-Abantes as the primeval Bronze Men.

In the context of the Abantes' link to the Bronze Generation, it is interesting to note the prominence of the swords in Archilochus' poem. Robert Renehan notes concerning this detail that Euboea was renowned for its swords.[30] As we have seen in the previous chapter, the Euboean swords have legendary overtones, thematically related to the motif of the Age of Bronze.

The understanding of δεσπόται Εὐβοίης δουρικλυτοί as the Abantes elucidates the variant δαίμονες (instead of δάμονες) in the manuscripts.[31] The characterization of the Abantes as δαίμονες portrays them as local cult heroes, a role that is fitting for them *qua* mythical ancestors of the Euboeans.[32] The suggestion that the Abantes were honored as cult heroes on Euboea finds confirmation in Hesychius' gloss: Ἄβαντες· Εὐβοεῖς καὶ κολοσσοί, νεκροί. The

---

[30] Renehan 1983, 2.
[31] Another attested variant is δαήμονες, 'knowledgeable.'
[32] On δαίμων as referring to a hero in his cultic afterlife, see Nagy [1979] 1999, 191. The men of the Golden Generation are described as δαίμονες after their death in *Works and Days* 122. The Curetes, associated with the Abantes on Euboea, are often called δαίμονες (for example, Strabo 10.3.7).

description of the Abantes as dead and as statues (very likely, colossal statues)[33] implicitly suggests that they were perceived as dead heroes.[34]

The relationship between the past of the dead heroes and the future battle is established by the interplay of the pronouns ταύτης and κεῖνοι in Archilochus' poem:

ταύτης γὰρ **κεῖνοι** δάμονές εἰσι μάχης
δεσπόται Εὐβοίης δουρικλυτοί.

For <u>of this kind</u> of battle <u>those ones</u> are masters,
the lords of Euboea famed for their spears.

Anna Bonifazi shows by pragmatic analysis of (ἐ)κεῖνος in the *Odyssey* that (ἐ)κεῖνος is connected with the perception of distance and proximity. Bonifazi describes the cognitive processes associated with the use of (ἐ)κεῖνος thus: "The (ἐ)κεῖνος-subject is initially far away or absent or unseen, and through the utterance (ἐ)κεῖνος that subject becomes — all of a sudden — close or present to the speaking "I" 's vision."[35] This dynamic fusion of absence and presence makes (ἐ)κεῖνος uniquely suitable for narratives of epiphanies.[36] Bonifazi observes that (ἐ)κεῖνος can be also used for dead people and heroes; in such cases, the use of the

---

[33] On cult heroes imagined to be gigantic, see Asheri, Lloyd, and Corcella 2007, 130–131; Nagy 2012, 50 with nn104, 105; Brelich 1958, 233–234.
[34] On statues of cult heroes, see Ekroth 2002, 149; Currie 2005, 143–144.
[35] Bonifazi 2012, 56.
[36] Bonifazi 2012, 54–55.

pronoun "conveys not only the tragic distance that separates the living from the dead, but also the impetus to establish contact with the dead, at least on the imaginative level."[37]

The statement that κεῖνοι are masters of *this* battle goes beyond the observation of similarity of the fighting style.[38] It literally resurrects the dead Abantes, transporting them from the remote antiquity of the myth all the way into the immediacy of the present. We can note how "of this … battle" frames "those ones are masters:" the present iconically contains the past; however, it is the past which is described as the master of the present. The Abantes still rule Euboea.

Let us now consider Strabo's account. There is a beautiful correspondence between Plutarch's and Strabo's patterns of thinking. Plutarch moves from the discussion of the Abantic hairstyle, as reflected in the Homeric ὄπιθεν κομόωντες (*Iliad* 2.542, *Theseus* 5.1), to Archilochus' poem (*Theseus* 5.1). Similarly, Strabo moves from the report of the prohibition of

---

[37] Bonifazi 2012, 58.
[38] Compare Mimnermus F 14 with its juxtaposition of κείνου (line 1) and τοῖον (line 2); the poem has been tentatively interpreted by Nagy (1990a, 200-201 with n10) as describing an epiphany of a hero. See also Nagy's discussion of Aristotle's famous οὗτος ἐκεῖνος (*Poetics* 1448b17) and its connection with the mentality of a ritual reenactment of myth. Nagy 1990a, 44.

the missiles (10.1.12) into a discussion of the Abantes and their superiority in close fighting (10.1.13), quoting the same Iliadic lines (2.543-4) that we have discussed:[39]

> οἱ δ' Εὐβοεῖς ἀγαθοὶ πρὸς μάχην ὑπῆρξαν τὴν σταδίαν, ἣ καὶ συστάδην λέγεται καὶ ἐκ χειρός. δόρασι δ' ἐχρῶντο τοῖς ὀρεκτοῖς, ὥς φησιν ὁ ποιητής
> αἰχμηταὶ μεμαῶτες ὀρεκτῇσι μελίῃσι
> θώρηκας ῥήσσειν.

> The Euboeans excelled in standing fight, which was also called close fight, and fight hand to hand. They used spears extended at length according to the words of the poet:
> spearmen, striving with their outstretched ash spears
> to break through corselets...

Thus, the treaty and Archilochus' poem converge not only in the motif of the lack (or scarcity) of the long-range missiles. If we trust the testimonies of Plutarch and Strabo, the poem and the treaty share an association with the heroic past of the Abantes. Moreover, both the poem and the treaty, through different methods, establish a resemblance between the present (or future) and the heroic past: the poem proclaims that the future battle will be fought in the manner of the Abantes, while the treaty prohibits the long-range missiles, making the fighting resemble the old model.

It has been argued by Wheeler that if the treaty about the prohibition of the missiles ever existed, it was probably set up in the Amarynthium in the fourth century.[40] The fourth

---

[39] Lorimer (1947, 114) notes that this description of the Abantes in the *Iliad* 2.543-4 suggests hoplitic fighting with a thrusting-spear. Similarly, Boardman 1957, 29.
[40] Wheeler 1987, 166, 177.

century date seems likely to me: there was a major reorganization of a festival in honor of Artemis of Amarynthus in 340 BC, and we have an important inscription commemorating the reorganization of the musical competitions (IG XII 9 189).[41] However, the comparatively late date of the inscription does not remove its validity as a thematic parallel to Archilochus' poem. While the historical circumstances that led to the erection of the stele with the treaty in the Amarynthium need further research, it is clear that the poem and the inscription belong to the same tradition, which shows a remarkable continuity through time. This tradition insists on the similarity between the present/future and the past. In the case of the treaty, it actively shapes the present in the mold of the past. But what about Archilochus' poem? Why is there certainty that something that happened to heroes in the distant past is going to take place again?[42]

---

[41] Strabo's other reference to a stele in the Amarynthium (Strabo 10.1.10) reports a grand procession, including hoplites, horsemen and chariots. It is unclear whether the two notices belong to the same inscription. Walker (2004, 123), who think that both the treaty and the procession are parts of the same inscription, proposes a sixth century date for the stele on the basis of the large number (600) of hoplites participating in the procession in Strabo's report (10.1.10). Van Wees (2004, 287) notes that the treaty is unlikely to date much before 550 BC, when the earliest inscribed treaties are attested. Tausend (1987, 510) also dates it to the sixth century.

[42] Forrest (1957, 164) reads the future tense as a warning based on a painful past experience: "like anyone to-day who fears a future war because he remembers Hiroshima, Archilochus looked back and was afraid." Donlan (1970, 136n11) thinks that the poem refers to a "coming battle in a continuing war." Murray ([1978] 1993, 79) takes it to be a reminiscence of the past.

3. The reenactment

This question can be tackled by turning to Angelo Brelich's proposition that the Lelantine War had a ritual and recurrent nature.[43] Brelich notes persistent mythical and cultic connotations of the Lelantine War, as well as its fighting regulations, and proposes tentatively that the war was waged for centuries in a comparatively restrained manner, and was associated with the festival of Artemis Amarynthia.[44] On this reasoning, Archilochus' future battle can be the next installment of the Lelantine War series.

Such a recurrent ritual battle resembles the Eleusinian festival Βαλλητύς, to which, as it has been argued, the *Homeric Hymn to Demeter* 265-67 refers:[45]

ὥρῃσιν δ' ἄρα τῷ γε περιπλομένων ἐνιαυτῶν
παῖδες Ἐλευσινίων πόλεμον καὶ φύλοπιν αἰνὴν
αἰὲν ἐν ἀλλήλοισι συνάξουσ' ἤματα πάντα.

At the right season, every year, as the years go round, the sons of the Eleusinians will join against each other in war and terrible din of battle, for all days to come.

Βαλλητύς honored the baby hero Demophon. Little is known about the battle, but apparently the opposing sides were pelting each other with stones.[46] As Nicholas Richardson observes

---

[43] Brelich 1961, 9–21.
[44] Brelich 1961, 21.
[45] Richardson 1974, 245–246, with earlier references. Athenaeus *Deipnosophistae* 406d, Hesychius s.v. Βαλλητύς.

concerning the expression πόλεμον καὶ φύλοπιν αἰνὴν, "such mock battles can be very fierce, and may lead to bloodshed and even death."[47] I note a parallel between συνάξουσ' in *Homeric Hymn to Demeter* 267 and συνάγῃ in line 2 of Archilochus F 3 West. The verb συνάγω 'to bring together, assemble,' is derived from the same root *ag-* as *agôn*;[48] in Archilochus F 3 West and *Homeric Hymn to Demeter* 267 this verb may express the ideology of cooperation-in-confrontation characterizing the ritual fighting. Strabo (10.1.12) uses the word *agôn* in his description of the stele in Amarynthium: ἀλλὰ συνέθεντο ἐφ' οἷς συστήσονται τὸν ἀγῶνα "but they came to an agreement as to the conditions under which they were to conduct the *agôn*."[49] Strabo contrasts such an *agôn* with a *polemos* in which the participants act willfully (κατὰ αὐθάδειαν); the *agôn*, in Strabo's formulation, has a markedly cooperative flavor, resulting from two verbs with the prefix συν- employed close together: συνέθεντο 'they agreed' and συστήσονται 'they will conduct.'

However, Brelich's suggestion of recurrent ritualized fighting in the Lelantine War has been challenged by an argument that both Herodotus and Thucydides, our earliest sources for

---

[46] Richardson 1974, 246; Pache 2004, 76–77; Nagy 1990a, 121n26.
[47] Richardson 1974, 248.
[48] Nagy 1990a, 136, 386; Chantraine 1968, 17.
[49] It has been shown that Strabo uses *agôn* for fighting conducted according to set rules. Dayton 2006, 31n76; Parker 1997, 117–118; Ellsworth 1971, 56–94; Brelich 1961, 16.

the conflict, appear to refer to a single war.⁵⁰ I propose a modification of Brelich's hypothesis that can account simultaneously for the wording of Archilochus' poem, suggesting a recurrent event,⁵¹ and for Thucydides' and Herodotus' single war. I submit that in the Archaic period the Chalcidians and the Eretrians periodically took part in a ritual battle, which re-enacted the mythical Lelantine War fought by the Curetes/Abantes.

The mentality of reenactment, in which the battle participants *become* the Curetes/Abantes, harmonizes with Archilochus' wording, casting the long-gone Abantes as masters of the present-time battle. The treaty reported by Strabo can be interpreted as a formalization of the rules of the ritual battle. The dissonance between Strabo's description of the Eretrians and Chalcidians as living "in accord with one another" (ὡμολόγουν ἀλλήλαις, 10.1.12) and Archilochus' chilling prophecy of a coming battle can be explained by differences in the standpoints of these sources. Strabo's account preserves, I believe, a historically accurate picture of a relatively peaceful co-existence of Chalcis and Eretria, and a stipulation concerning the conduct of a ritual. Conversely, Archilochus expresses the ideological underpinnings of the ritual battle as an experience of reliving the past in all its gory intensity.

---

⁵⁰ Andrewes 1962, 193; Wheeler 1987, 160.

⁵¹ The impression of a long duration and recurrent nature of the fighting for the Lelantine plain is also produced by Strabo's description of the Curetes as συνεχῶς δὲ περὶ τοῦ Ληλάντου πεδίου πολεμοῦντας (10.3.6), as well as by the multiplicity of battles in Plutarch's ἐν ταῖς περὶ Ληλάντου μάχαις (*Banquet of the Seven Sages* 10 = *Moralia* 153f).

How can my reconstruction of the war as consisting of a mythological core, periodically reenacted by the two cities, explain Thucydides' and Herodotus' references to a single war? The construal of the war as a series of reenactments of the same myth grants unity to the recurrent fighting: all battles are perceived to be ripples of the same original combat, and every new battle is ritually identified with the primeval fighting of the Curetes/Abantes.

However, the ritual reenactment also affects the mythical core. In my reconstruction, the myth of the Curetes, fighting for the Lelantine Plain, actually does not include hostilities between Eretria and Chalcis. The enemies (οἱ πολέμιοι) with which the Curetes are fighting for the Plain are left curiously unspecified (Archemachus ap. Strabo 10.3.6). This vagueness can be accounted for in multiple ways, for example, by proposing that the myth about the Curetes stems from the historical city of Chalcis, and therefore Eretria does not play a role in it. However, I prefer a different explanation. As I have already observed, the alternative name of the mythical Chalcis, Euboea, suggests that the myth had a pan-Euboean status. The location of this mythical city in the Lelantine Plain, between Eretria and Chalcis, as well as its destruction by an earthquake, point in the same direction: Chalcis-Euboea is something that is geographically shared by the historical Chalcis and Eretria, and also is distanced from both of them by the ancient destruction. Therefore, it is appealing to perceive the myth of the fighting Curetes as common to Eretria and Chalcis. In such a scenario, the avoidance of the statement that the Curetes fought specifically in the war between Eretria and Chalcis may derive from a requisite that the figures of the Curetes remain available as the subjects of reenactment both for the Eretrians and the Chalcidians. However, through their repeated reenactments of the mythical war fought by the Curetes, the historical Chalcis and Eretria become integrated as actors into the mythical core of the war: the result is Thucydides' picture of τὸν πάλαι ποτὲ γενόμενον πόλεμον Χαλκιδέων καὶ Ἐρετριῶν (Thucydides 1.15.3). We can visualize such an incorporation of the ritual into the myth through a metaphor of successive ritual layers around the mythical core: from the standpoint of the later layers, the earlier ones can merge with the core. This understanding of the interconnection between myth and ritual in a series of reenactments arises from Gregory Nagy's analysis of the concept of *mîmêsis*. I quote Nagy's formulation: "In that the newest instance of reenacting has as its model, cumulatively, all the older instances of performing the myth as well as the "original" instance of the myth, **mîmêsis** is a current imitation of earlier reenactments."[52]

Some support for my construal of the Lelantine War comes from an examination of other instances in which ποτε and words from the root πάλαι- appear closely together in Thucydides. πάλαι- and ποτε co-occur in a description of a great Ionian festival that happened

---

[52] Nagy 1990a, 43.

in earlier times on Delos, as Thucydides narrates, quoting the *Homeric Hymn to Apollo*.⁵³ They are also found together in a speech of the Argive commander at the start of the battle of Mantinea, urging the Argive army to regain Argos' ancient supremacy and their rightful share of the Peloponnesus.⁵⁴ The third instance is even more interesting: it comes from Thucydides' statement that the Boeotians destroyed the fort of Panactum under the pretext that it was on a territory, disputed between them and the Athenians, which the two parties in ancient times swore to leave uninhabited as a common grazing land.⁵⁵ The last instance of the conjunction between πάλαι- and ποτε in Thucydides that I could find occurs in the description of Alcibiades' annoyance with the fact that the Spartans did not respect his family's ancient

---

⁵³ ἦν δέ ποτε καὶ τὸ πάλαι μεγάλη ξύνοδος ἐς τὴν Δῆλον τῶν Ἰώνων τε καὶ περικτιόνων νησιωτῶν· "Once upon a time, indeed, there was a great assemblage of the Ionians and the neighboring islanders at Delos..." Thucydides 3.104.3.

⁵⁴ Ἀργείοις δὲ ὑπὲρ τῆς τε παλαιᾶς ἡγεμονίας καὶ τῆς ἐν Πελοποννήσῳ ποτὲ ἰσομοιρίας μὴ διὰ παντὸς στερισκομένους ἀνέχεσθαι, καὶ ἄνδρας ἅμα ἐχθροὺς καὶ ἀστυγείτονας ὑπὲρ πολλῶν ἀδικημάτων ἀμύνασθαι· "The Argives [were reminded] that they would contend for their ancient supremacy, to regain their once equal share of the Peloponnesus of which they had been so long deprived, and to punish an enemy and a neighbor for a thousand wrongs..." Thucydides 5.69.1. For the discussion of the connection between this speech and the traditional rivalry between Argos and Sparta over the territory of Cynuria/Thyreatis, signaled by the description of the Spartans as ἀστυγείτονας, see Chapter 6, Section 4.

⁵⁵ ...ἐπὶ προφάσει ὡς ἦσάν ποτε Ἀθηναίοις καὶ Βοιωτοῖς ἐκ διαφορᾶς περὶ αὐτοῦ ὅρκοι παλαιοὶ μηδετέρους οἰκεῖν τὸ χωρίον, ἀλλὰ κοινῇ νέμειν... "...upon the plea that oaths had been anciently exchanged between their people and the Athenians, after a dispute on the subject, to the effect that neither should inhabit the place, but that they should graze it in common..." Thucydides 5.42.1. See the discussion of this passage in Chapter 6, Section 5.

proxenia with Sparta, which had been renounced by Alcibiades' grandfather but cultivated after that lapse by Alcibiades.[56]

These four passages describe remarkably similar situations. All of them, naturally, refer to the past; more interestingly, all of them refer to phenomena in the past that have passed out of existence before the narrative's present time: the ancient Boeotian-Athenian oaths are not honored, and neither is the *proxenia* of Alcibiades' family with Sparta; Argos has lost its equal share of the Peloponnesus, and the grand festival on Delos, featuring contests, has been abolished (Thucydides 3.104.6). Even more fascinatingly, all of these derelict phenomena are resurrected, or are intended to be resurrected, in the narrative's present: the Athenians renew the great Delian festival (Thucydides 3.104.1); Argos strives to regain its share of the Peloponnesus; Alcibiades works on reviving the *proxenia*; and the Boeotians destroy Panactum under the pretext of activating the old oaths. Finally, a theme prominent in these passages is the ancient ritual regulation of relationships between city-states, whether through *proxenia*,

---

[56] ...καὶ κατὰ τὴν παλαιὰν προξενίαν ποτὲ οὖσαν οὐ τιμήσαντες, ἣν τοῦ πάππου ἀπειπόντος αὐτὸς τοὺς ἐκ τῆς νήσου αὐτῶν αἰχμαλώτους θεραπεύων διενοεῖτο ἀνανεώσασθαι. "[Alcibiades was offended] also for [the Spartans] not having shown him the respect due to the ancient connection of his family with them as their *proxenii* which, renounced by his grandfather, he had himself recently attempted to renew by his attention to their prisoners taken in the island." Thucydides 5.43.2.

establishment of a common territory, or an interstate festival.[57] Thucydides' use of πάλαι ποτὲ in application to the Lelantine War indicates that in his perception the war is classed along with semi-obsolete archaic rituals, which, even though suspended long ago, can be reactivated. This ritual quality of the war, and the possibility of its revival, implicit in Thucydides' description, matches our reconstruction.

4. Allies and pillars

Thucydides states that the Greek world was divided in two camps on the occasion of the war between Eretria and Chalcis. As we have seen from the analysis of Thucydides' rhetoric, Thucydides and his audience must have felt that the alliances of the Lelantine War, although Panhellenic in scope, were radically different from the Peloponnesian War's coalitions. Plutarch's story about the assistance rendered by the Thessalian Cleomachus to the Chalcidians provides an instructive case study, helping us to get a better grasp of the character of allied help in the Lelantine War.

---

[57] The Argive aspirations to regain their equal share of the Peloponnesus in a battle seems to be an only example of the four in which a myth, and not a ritual, is invoked; however, see my Chapter 6, Section 4, in which I argue that the oscillation between myth and ritual is crucial for the Argive perception of the battle of Mantinea.

In Plutarch's *Dialogue on Love* (*Moralia* 760e-761a), one of the dialogue's participants narrates that Cleomachus of Pharsalus was summoned by the Chalcidians to lead a cavalry attack in a battle against the Eretrians. Cleomachus came and, filled with ardor by an embrace of his beloved, routed the Eretrian cavalry, bringing victory to Chalcis. However, he himself fell in battle. The Chalcidians buried Cleomachus in their agora, and marked his tomb with a great pillar. They also changed from their previously disapproving view of pederasty, and started to "love and honor" it (ἠγάπησαν καὶ ἐτίμησαν, *Moralia* 761a5).

Cleomachus' story provides a good example of a phenomenon that I have described in my reconstruction of the Lelantine War's nature as a layer of ritual reenactment of the myth being "pressed into" the mythical core. Cleomachus' heroic burial in the *agora*, his public commemoration (evident in the narrator's comment that the Chalcidians kept pointing out Cleomachus' tomb in their *agora* in the present time of the narrative),[58] and, most of all, the aetiology of pederasty, attached to the story, show that we are dealing with a myth.[59] However, as I am going to demonstrate, the battle in which Cleomachus dies, exhibits qualities of a ritual battle. Thus, the story portrays a mythologization of the military help rendered in a ritual battle.

---

[58] *Moralia* 761a2-3. Jeffery 1976, 65; Bakhuizen 1985, 25; Walker 2004, 170.
[59] Brelich 1961, 18. Cf. Lambert 1982, 219.

It is worth quoting a relatively long passage from Plutarch (*Moralia* 760e4–761a1) because of the fascinating information it provides about the motives leading to Cleomachus' invitation by the Chalcidians and about the battle itself:

> Κλεόμαχον δὲ τὸν Φαρσάλιον ἴστε δήπουθεν ἐξ ἧς αἰτίας ἐτελεύτησεν ἀγωνιζόμενος.' 'οὐχ ἡμεῖς γοῦν' οἱ περὶ Πεμπτίδην ἔφασαν, 'ἀλλ' ἡδέως ἂν πυθοίμεθα.' 'καὶ γὰρ ἄξιον' ἔφη ὁ πατήρ· 'ἧκεν ἐπίκουρος Χαλκιδεῦσι τοῦ † Θεσσαλικοῦ πολέμου πρὸς Ἐρετριεῖς ἀκμάζοντος· καὶ τὸ μὲν πεζὸν ἐδόκει τοῖς Χαλκιδεῦσιν ἐρρῶσθαι, τοὺς δ' ἱππέας μέγ' ἔργον ἦν ὤσασθαι τῶν πολεμίων παρεκάλουν δὴ τὸν Κλεόμαχον ἄνδρα λαμπρὸν ὄντα τὴν ψυχὴν οἱ σύμμαχοι πρῶτον ἐμβάλλειν εἰς τοὺς ἱππέας. ὁ δ' ἠρώτησε παρόντα τὸν ἐρώμενον, εἰ μέλλοι θεᾶσθαι τὸν ἀγῶνα· φήσαντος δὲ τοῦ νεανίσκου καὶ φιλοφρόνως αὐτὸν ἀσπασαμένου καὶ τὸ κράνος ἐπιθέντος, ἐπιγαυρωθεὶς ὁ Κλεόμαχος καὶ τοὺς ἀρίστους τῶν Θεσσαλῶν συναγαγὼν περὶ αὑτὸν ἐξήλασε λαμπρῶς καὶ προσέπεσε τοῖς πολεμίοις, ὥστε συνταράξαι καὶ τρέψασθαι τὸ ἱππικόν· ἐκ δὲ τούτου καὶ τῶν ὁπλιτῶν φυγόντων, ἐνίκησαν κατὰ κράτος οἱ Χαλκιδεῖς.

"You know, of course, the story of Cleomachus of Pharsalia and the reason for which he ended his life fighting in a martial contest." "No, we don't," said Pemptides and his party. "But we should be glad to hear it told." "It's worth hearing," said my father. "Cleomachus came to help the Chalcidians when the [Lelantine] War against the Eretrians was at its height. The Chalcidian infantry was thought to have considerable strength, but they found it difficult to resist the enemy cavalry. Accordingly his allies requested Cleomachus, a man of splendid courage, to be the first to charge the horse. His beloved was there and Cleomachus asked him if he was going to watch the contest. The youth said that he was, embraced Cleomachus tenderly, and put on his helmet for him. Filled with ardor, Cleomachus assembled the bravest of the Thessalians about himself, made a fine charge, and fell upon the enemy with such vigor that their cavalry was thrown into confusion and was thoroughly routed. When subsequently their hoplites also fled, the Chalcidians had a decisive victory.

Cleomachus' equestrian participation is unmistakably aristocratic. The emphasis on Cleomachus' courage, and the role of the leader in a cavalry attack, assigned to him, also point to a conspicuously individual quality of his assistance.⁶⁰ Cleomachus is invited as a star player, intended to boost the team after an assessment of the strengths and weaknesses of the sides has been made. The fighting is characterized as an *agôn* (760f2). In the introduction to the story the narrator also says that Cleomachus "ended his life fighting in a martial contest" (ἐτελεύτησεν ἀγωνιζόμενος, 760e5). Both τελευτάω 'to reach fulfillment' and ἀγωνίζομαι 'to participate in a contest'⁶¹ have strong ritual associations, enhanced by the conjunction of the two verbs.⁶² Perhaps the most striking quality of the fighting is its theatrical quality: Cleomachus asks his *erômenos* whether he is going 'to watch the *agôn*' (θεᾶσθαι τὸν ἀγῶνα, 760f1-2). Cleomachus' subsequent brilliant assault and, by extension, his death, are motivated by the fact that he is being looked at by his beloved.

Cleomachus' death has a curious flavor of an unanticipated event: "However, it befell Cleomachus to be killed in the battle" (τὸν μέντοι Κλεόμαχον ἀποθανεῖν συνέτυχε, 761a1-2). It seems to me that the honors, accorded to Cleomachus after his death, paradoxically, underscore the ritual character of the battle: the exceptional terms of commemoration suggest that death in battle for the Plain was perceived as an extremely uncommon occurrence.

---

⁶⁰ Tausend (1987, 510-11) emphasizes the private character of Cleomachus' assistance.
⁶¹ On *telos* 'fulfillment' or 'ritual of initiation' see Nagy 1996, 53; 1990a, 245-246n129; on the ritual aspect of *agôn* see Nagy 1990a, 137.
⁶² I also note the presence of *sunagô* (συναγαγὼν, *Moralia* 760f5), in parallel to Archilochus F 3 West and the *Homeric Hymn to Demeter* 267.

Cleomachus' love-inspired martial fervor transcends the boundaries of the ritual and overflows into myth.

Cleomachus is commemorated by a burial in the agora of Chalcis: "The Chalcidians point out his tomb in the *agora* with the great pillar standing on it to this day" (τάφον δ' αὐτοῦ δεικνύουσιν ἐν ἀγορᾷ Χαλκιδεῖς, ἐφ' οὗ μέχρι νῦν ὁ μέγας ἐφέστηκε κίων, *Moralia* 761a2-4). The burial in the *agora* is an indication of a cult hero status, reserved for the founders and other central figures of the city's past.[63] Cleomachus' cult hero status in Chalcis receives additional support from a parallelism between Cleomachus' death and the end of Athenian Tellus, whose story Solon tells to Croesus (Herodotus 1.30):

> τελευτὴ τοῦ βίου λαμπροτάτη ἐπεγένετο· γενομένης γὰρ Ἀθηναίοισι μάχης πρὸς τοὺς ἀστυγείτονας ἐν Ἐλευσῖνι βοηθήσας καὶ τροπὴν ποιήσας τῶν πολεμίων ἀπέθανε κάλλιστα, καί μιν Ἀθηναῖοι δημοσίῃ τε ἔθαψαν αὐτοῦ τῇ περ ἔπεσε καὶ ἐτίμησαν μεγάλως.
>
> ...his death was most distinguished: when the Athenians were fighting their neighbors in Eleusis, he came to help, routed the enemy, and died most beautifully. The Athenians buried him at public expense on the spot where he fell and greatly honored him.[64]

Details shared between the stories of Tellus and Cleomachus include a motif of military assistance,[65] a feat of routing the enemy, a death in a battle between the neighboring cities and

---

[63] Martin 1951, 197–201; Morris 1987, 193; Hartog 1988, 135 with examples; Kearns 1992, 72; McGlew 1993, 15; Malkin 1994, 127–130, and others.

[64] Trans. by Lynn Sawlivich (revised by Gregory Nagy), modified. On *timê* as 'honor of cult' see Nagy 1990b, 132n51.

an exceptionally honorable burial. Tellus' death is characterized as λαμπροτάτη 'most distinguished'; likewise, Cleomachus attacks λαμπρῶς 'vigorously' (Moralia 760f5). Solon calls Tellus the most fortunate (ὀλβιώτατον) of men. This expression, as Nagy has argued, portrays Tellus as a cult hero, blissful in the afterlife.[66]

Plutarch connects Cleomachus' death with the acceptance of pederasty by the Chalcidians. The traditionality of the connection between the Lelantine War and the endorsement of pederasty is demonstrated by the multiforms of Cleomachus' story, reported by Plutarch. After concluding the story of Cleomenes, Plutarch lists the following variant accounts (Moralia 761a-b):

> καὶ τὸ παιδεραστεῖν πρότερον ἐν ψόγῳ τιθέμενοι τότε μᾶλλον ἑτέρων ἠγάπησαν καὶ ἐτίμησαν. Ἀριστοτέλης δὲ τὸν μὲν Κλεόμαχον ἄλλως ἀποθανεῖν φησι, κρατήσαντα τῶν Ἐρετριέων τῇ μάχῃ· τὸν δ' ὑπὸ τοῦ ἐρωμένου φιληθέντα τῶν ἀπὸ Θρᾴκης Χαλκιδέων γενέσθαι, πεμφθέντα τοῖς ἐν Εὐβοίᾳ Χαλκιδεῦσιν ἐπίκουρον· ὅθεν ᾄδεσθαι παρὰ τοῖς Χαλκιδεῦσιν
> 'ὦ παῖδες, οἳ χαρίτων τε καὶ πατέρων λάχετ' ἐσθλῶν,
> μὴ φθονεῖθ' ὥρας ἀγαθοῖσιν ὁμιλίαν·
> σὺν γὰρ ἀνδρείᾳ καὶ ὁ λυσιμελὴς Ἔρως
> ἐνὶ Χαλκιδέων θάλλει πόλεσιν.'
> Ἄντων ἦν ὄνομα τῷ ἐραστῇ τῷ δ' ἐρωμένῳ Φίλιστος, ὡς ἐν τοῖς Αἰτίοις Διονύσιος ὁ ποιητὴς ἱστόρησε.

---

[65] Herodotus' βοηθήσας (1.30).
[66] Concerning the meaning of *olbios* is the interaction between Croesus and Solon, Nagy argues that "Croesus understands the word only in the non-sacral sense of 'fortunate' while Solon understands it also in the deeper sacral sense of 'blessed,' referring to the blissful state of afterlife enjoyed by local cult heroes like Tellos of Athens..." Nagy 2012, 58-59; a longer discussion of the meanings of *olbios* is in Nagy 1990a, 243-247.

> Formerly they [the Chalcidians] had frowned on pederasty, but now they loved and honored it more than others did. Now Aristotle says that the circumstances of Cleomachus' death in victorious battle with Eretrians were different and that the lover embraced by his friend was one of the Chalcidians from Thrace sent as an ally to the Chalcidians of Euboea. And this, he says, is the reason for the Chalcidian popular song:
>> You boys that have a fair share of the Charites and noble parents,
>> Do not refuse to good men the company of your bloom.
>> For even limb-relaxing Love thrives
>> together with manliness in cities of Chalcis.[67]
>
> Anton was the name of the lover and Philistus was his beloved, as the poet Dionysius relates in his *Origins*.

It is helpful to enumerate all the variants, mentioned in this passage. We learn, that:

1. Aristotle thought that a different story was attached to Cleomachus' death in a battle with the Eretrians.

2. Aristotle also knew a different version in which an *eromenos* from Thracian Chalcis embraced his lover before a battle with the Eretrians. This story was probably also an *aition* of the Chalcidian pederasty.

3. According to a version reported by Dionysius in a poem *Origins*, the names of the lover and the beloved were Anton and Philistus. It is not clear whether this version coincides with Aristotle's story; however, given the name of Dionysius' poem, this version was presumably also giving an aetiology of the Chalcidian pederasty.

4. Aristotle also reported a Chalcidian song, connecting aristocracy, pederasty and manliness.

---

[67] My translation.

The existence of different versions, treated by different authors and belonging to different genres, shows that the stories about foreign allies in the Lelantine War were a well-established subject, and that these stories were traditionally associated with the motif of the Chalcidian acceptance of pederasty.[68] Further, the interconnected topics of the Lelantine War, bravery and pederastic love seem to be strikingly suitable for aristocratic sympotic poetry; the song, cited by Plutarch, appears to be a part of such a tradition. We will return to the connection between the Lelantine War and sympotic poetry when considering Theognis' poems.

Can we date the story of Cleomachus? Bakhuizen observes concerning the pillar on Cleomachus' tomb that grave markers of this form are attested only from the sixth century BC.[69] The story of Cleomachus fits well into the context of the sixth century, I believe.[70] Ritual battles for the Lelantine Plain continued in the sixth century (see below); narrative-wise, Herodotus' story of Tellus provides an early parallel for Cleomachus' tale.

---

[68] An associated subject of the Theban traditional connection between the pederastic love and the battle performance (reaching its zenith in the tradition of the Sacred Band) is invoked by Plutarch immediately after the story of Cleomachus (*The Dialogue on Love* 17 = *Moralia* 761b6-14).
[69] Bakhuizen 1985, 25.
[70] Strictly speaking, Bakhuizen's observation establishes only a *terminus post quem* the detail of the pillar was incorporated into the possibly pre-existing narrative of Cleomachus' help (if Cleomachus had a hero cult in Chalcis, a pillar also could conceivably have been erected in the sixth century at the existing site of the cult).

At the conclusion of this section, I would like to discuss three epitaphs marking tombs of *xenoi* in Eretria: Spartan Pleistias (*IG* XII 9, 286), Aeginetan Mnesitheus (*IG* XII 9, 285) and Athenian Chaerion (*IG* XII 9, 296). All three epitaphs date from the sixth century and have a distinctly aristocratic character; those of Pleistias and Mnesitheus also exhibit prominent similarities with Archaic poetry, painting the departed in heroic colors.[71] Further, the shape of Pleistias' grave marker is a pillar, offering a parallel to Cleomachus' tomb. These three inscriptions provide an attestation of the presence of aristocratic *xenoi* in Eretria in the sixth century BC, and present examples of rhetorical techniques forging an association between the deceased members of the elite and the heroes of the past. As such, they constitute a useful historical background for the mythical story of Cleomachus.

However, I also would like to consider a bolder suggestion concerning at least two of these tombs. As we will see, for several reasons it is difficult to find suitable historical contexts for the deaths of Pleistias and Chaerion. I venture that conceivably these individuals were

---

[71] Mnesitheus' stele, with its metrical elegaic inscription, dates from the sixth century BC. Friedländer 1948, 131 (adding that it "may be too early a date"). The reasons for Mnesitheus' burial in Eretria are uncertain. Walker 2004, 229. I quote Friedländer's (1948, 131) analysis of the epigram: "The Homeric words τύμβωι ἐπ' ἀκροτάτωι (*Iliad* 2.793, *Odyssey* 12.15) make this tomb akin to the tombs of the heroes. ἀκάματον, an epic word in unepic use, and the Homeric flourish at the end of v. 6 (~ Iliad 16.499 [ἤματα πάντα διαμπερές]) promise undying renown." Thus, Mnesitheus' tomb is styled as a tomb of an epic hero. The repetition of the name of Mnesitheus' mother, Timarete, in verses 4 and 7 perhaps emphasizes the theme of honoring (giving *timê* to) her dead son for his military valor (*aretê*). Friedländer (1948, 131) also notes the provincial pronunciation of τύμωι for τύμβωι in verse 5 (compare Pleistias' tomb).

Eretian allies, who fell in ritual battles for the Lelantine Plain. My first example concerns Spartan Pleistias (*IG* XII 9, 286):

> Πλειστίας.
> Σπάρτα μὲν πατρίς ἐστιν, ἐν εὐρυχόροισι Ἀθάναις
> ἐθράφθε, θανάτου δὲ ἐνθάδε μοῖρ' ἔχιχε.

> Pleistias.
> Sparta is his country; he was bred in broad-wayed Athens,
> and the lot of death befell him here.

Pleistias' grave marker, as I have already mentioned, is a pillar, set in a base; it is dated to ca. 550–475 BC.[72] Friedländer compliments the "reticent excellence of the poem" and notes "epical color" of εὐρυχόροισι.[73] The phrase θανάτου ... μοῖρ' ἔχιχε also has closely related counterparts in Archaic poetry.[74] Friedländer further suggests that "the Doric vocalization of Σπάρτα and Ἀθάναις in Ionic Euboea is meant to reveal the unalterable Doricism of the man whose 'country Sparta is.' "[75]

Pleistias thus is emphatically Spartan. However, a law, reported as Lycurgan by Plutarch (*Lycurgus* 27,2), allowed only those Spartans who fell in battle to be commemorated by

---

[72] See Walker 2004, 234n107 for the literature on the stele and a review of suggestions about the stele's date.
[73] Compare *Iliad* 23.299, *Odyssey* 15.1.
[74] Friedländer (1948, 82) cites μοῖρα κίχεν θανάτου of Callinus F 1.15, μοῖρα κίχοι θανάτου of Tyrtaeus F 7.2, Mimnermus F 6.2, Solon F 20.4; I adduce μοῖρα κίχῃ θανάτου of Theognis 340, as well as the Homeric θάνατος καὶ μοῖρα κιχάνει (*Iliad* 17.478; 17.672; 22.436).
[75] Friedländer 1948, 82.

grave markers inscribed with their names. If the law was an Archaic reality, we need to find a sixth-century battle on Euboea for Pleistias to die in; no convincing answer has been suggested so far.[76] Perhaps Pleistias' pillar was earned similarly to that of Cleomachus.

Athenian Chaerion provides another example. The inscription on his Eretrian tomb (*IG* XII 9, 296) is dated ca. 525 by Jeffery:[77]

Χαιρίον
Ἀθηναῖος
εὐπατρίδων
ἐνθάδε κεῖτα[ι][78]

Chaerion
Athenian
from Eupatrids
lies here

The location of Chaerion's tomb in Eretria has been explained as a result of his political exile during the time of the Peisistratidae; εὐπατρίδων has been called a "political manifesto."[79]

However, Aristotle (*Athenian Constitution* 15.2) reports that the regime of Eretrian *hippeis*

---

[76] See Walker 2004, 227–8 for previous literature, discussion of this Lycurgan law and his own interpretation of the inscription; also see an abstract of a talk given at CAMWS 2004 by Marie-Claire Beaulieu, "*IG* XII 9, 286: The Pleistias Epigram." On the commemoration of Spartans who fell in battle, see Hodkinson 2000, 249–259; Low 2006.
[77] Jeffery 1976, 68.
[78] Quoted from Walker 2004, 220.
[79] Davies 1971, 11; similarly, Walker 2004, 221.

supported Peisistratus;[80] this makes Eretria an unlikely haven for the Peisistratidae's enemy. There are also other difficulties: we know that Chaerion set up an altar on the Acropolis around 550 BC;[81] his tomb in Eretria dates from ca. 525, while ca. 520 BC Chaerion's son Alcimachus erected a statue of Chaerion on the Acropolis, describing himself as ἐσθλō πατρὸς hũς.[82] It has been speculated that Alcimachus was "perhaps recalled by the tyrant;"[83] however, it is also added that Alcimachus' erection of the statue of Chaerion, and his self-identification as ἐσθλō πατρὸς hũς "nevertheless made clear his own family sympathies and the limits of the compromise he had accepted."[84]

This elaborate reconstruction of the exiled Chaerion and his uncompromising son is created solely in order to explain the location of Chaerion's tomb; otherwise, nothing in the historical record supports it. A hypothesis of Chaerion's death in a ritual battle between Eretria and Chalcis provides an explanation of the Eretrian tomb, and suits Chaerion's aristocratic profile[85] as well as the wording of the epitaph, proclaiming him to be an aristocrat and a *xenos*.

---

[80] Jeffery 1976, 68.
[81] Davies 1971, 13, Walker 2004, 233n72, citing Raubitschek 1949, 364n330.
[82] Davies 1971, 13, Walker 2004, 221.
[83] Walker 2004, 221.
[84] Davies 1971, 13.
[85] Chaerion was a *tamias* of Athena when he made his dedication around 550 BC; therefore, he must have been a *pentekosiomedimnos*. Davies 1971, 13; Walker 2004, 221.

If I am right in proposing that Chaerion and Pleistias fell in ritual battles for the Lelantine Plain, their memorials offer intriguing comparisons and contrasts to the story of Cleomachus. Cleomachus' death in ritual battle is fully mythologized, complete with the hero cult and the aetiology of pederasty. Chaerion and Pleistias, on the other hand, remain historical individuals, although some heroizing traits, such as the wording of Pleistias' epitaph, and the erection of Chaerion's statue on the Acropolis, are present in their commemoration.

5. Warriors with bangs

One of the multiple functions that the ritual battle for the Lelantine Plain could have in the societies of Eretria and Chalcis is that of a coming-of-age ritual.[86] The coming-of-age associations of the myth of the Lelantine War that I have reconstructed have to do with the Curetes' and the Abantes' special haircuts. Brelich noted a recurrent appearance of the motif of a haircut (or a change of hairstyle) in the descriptions of wars that he classifies as ritual ones; he singled out this motif as being particularly suggestive of a rite of passage.[87]

---

[86] Cf. Brelich 1961, 81–84. Richardson interprets the expression παῖδες Ἐλευσινίων in *Homeric Hymn to Demeter* 266 as "the young men (or boys) of Eleusis," and cites as a parallel a Spartan mock battle described by Pausanias (3.14.8), fought by the ephebes. Richardson 1974, 248.
[87] Brelich 1961, 80–81.

Let us start by looking again at Strabo's description of the Curetes fighting for the Lelantine Plain (Strabo 10.3.6):

> Ἀρχέμαχος δ' ὁ Εὐβοεύς φησι τοὺς Κουρῆτας ἐν Χαλκίδι συνοικῆσαι, συνεχῶς δὲ περὶ τοῦ Ληλάντου πεδίου πολεμοῦντας, ἐπειδὴ οἱ πολέμιοι τῆς κόμης ἐδράττοντο τῆς ἔμπροσθεν καὶ κατέσπων αὐτούς, ὄπισθεν κομῶντας γενέσθαι, τὰ δ' ἔμπροσθεν κείρεσθαι· διὸ καὶ Κουρῆτας ἀπὸ τῆς κουρᾶς κληθῆναι·

> Archemachus the Euboean says that the Curetes settled at Chalcis, but since they were continually at war for the Lelantine Plain and the enemy would catch them by the front hair and drag them down, they let their hair grow long behind but cut short the part in front, and because of this they were called "Curetes," from the cut of their hair.

Plutarch (*Theseus* 5) narrates the same story about cutting of the front hair, but the actors are the Abantes instead of the Curetes:

> Ἔθους δ' ὄντος ἔτι τότε τοὺς μεταβαίνοντας ἐκ παίδων ἐλθόντας εἰς Δελφοὺς ἀπάρχεσθαι τῷ θεῷ τῆς κόμης, ἦλθε μὲν εἰς Δελφοὺς ὁ Θησεύς (καὶ τόπον ἀπ' αὐτοῦ τὴν Θησείαν ἔτι νῦν ὀνομάζεσθαι λέγουσιν), ἐκείρατο δὲ τῆς κεφαλῆς τὰ πρόσθεν μόνον, ὥσπερ Ὅμηρος ἔφη τοὺς Ἄβαντας· καὶ τοῦτο τῆς κουρᾶς τὸ γένος Θησηὶς ὠνομάσθη δι' ἐκεῖνον. οἱ δ' Ἄβαντες ἐκείραντο πρῶτοι τὸν τρόπον τοῦτον, οὐχ ὑπ' Ἀράβων διδαχθέντες, ὡς ἔνιοι νομίζουσιν, οὐδὲ Μυσοὺς ζηλώσαντες, ἀλλ' ὄντες πολεμικοὶ καὶ ἀγχέμαχοι καὶ μάλιστα δὴ πάντων εἰς χεῖρας ὠθεῖσθαι τοῖς ἐναντίοις μεμαθηκότες, ὡς μαρτυρεῖ καὶ Ἀρχίλοχος ἐν τούτοις·
> > Οὔ τοι πόλλ' ἐπὶ τόξα τανύσσεται οὐδὲ θαμειαὶ
> > σφενδόναι, εὖτ' ἂν δὴ μῶλον Ἄρης συνάγῃ
> > ἐν πεδίῳ, ξιφέων δὲ πολύστονον ἔσσεται ἔργον·
> > ταύτης γὰρ κεῖνοι δαίμονές εἰσι μάχης
> > δεσπόται Εὐβοίας δουρικλυτοί.
>
> ὅπως οὖν μὴ παρέχοιεν ἐκ τῶν τριχῶν ἀντίληψιν τοῖς πολεμίοις, ἀπεκείραντο.

> Since it was still a custom at that time for youths who were coming of age to go to Delphi and sacrifice some of their hair to the god, Theseus went to Delphi for this purpose, and they say there is a place there which still to this day is called the Theseia from him. But he sheared only the fore part of his head, just as Homer said Abantes did,

and this kind of tonsure was called Theseïs after him. Now the Abantes were the first to cut their hair in this manner, not under instruction from the Arabians, as some suppose, nor yet in emulation of the Mysians, but because they were war-like men and close fighters, who had learned beyond all other men to force their way into close quarters with their enemies. Archilochus is witness to this in the following words:
> Not many bows will be stretched, neither slings
> plentiful, when Ares joins the throng
> in the plain. It will be the grievous work of the swords.
> For of this kind of battle those ones are masters,
> the lords of Euboea famed for their spears.

Therefore, in order that they might not give their enemies a hold by their hair, they cut it off.

As I have already noted, this commonality of hairstyle and fighting techniques, in addition to associations with bronze, make it appealing to posit an equivalence between the Abantes and the Curetes on Euboea.[88] In Plutarch's narrative, a haircut in the style of the Abantes is connected, through the figure of Theseus, to the coming of age and dedication of hair in a sanctuary.[89] The association between Euboea, Theseus and the Abantic hairstyle may be an old tradition: Theseus sports precisely this hairstyle in the late Archaic sculpture from the pediment of the Temple of Apollo Daphnephoros in Eretria.[90]

---

[88] On the fluidity of distinctions between such categories as Curetes or Corybantes see Strabo 10.3.7, and Blakely 2006, 13-31. Nonnus 13.153-166 is a striking case of fusion and recombination of the Euboean traditions related to the Corybantes, the Curetes and the Abantes. Cf. Chuvin 1991, 42-47.
[89] On the connections between Theseus and the theme of initiation, see Versnel 1993, 56-58.
[90] See Walker 2004, 29, 59n18 for the literature on the Abantic-Curetic hairstyle.

Another interesting observation has been made by Mastrocinque: the danger of being dragged by the front hair implies fighting without helmets, in a sharp contrast with the usual fighting mode.[91] The lack of physical head protection, making the participants more vulnerable, suggests that there were strong social restraints on violence in the battle for the Plain.

The connection between fighting and pederasty, stressed in Plutarch's story of Cleomachus, also fits the context of the coming of age. Pederasty repeatedly features in ancient Greek rites of passage.[92]

Thus, we can conjecture that for the Chalcidian and Eretrian young men, a participation in a ritual battle for the Lelantine Plain, in which they reenacted the Curetes-Abantes, constituted a coming of age ritual for admission into full adulthood.[93] The identification with the Curetes-Abantes was expressed through fighting at close quarters with thrusting-spears and swords (and perhaps also an omission of helmets),[94] as well as though

---

[91] Mastrocinque 1980, 461. Mastrocinque draws a parallel between this example of bareheaded fighting and the accounts of warriors fighting naked (armed with a lance and a shield) in the war between Chios and Erythrae, which has been also identified by Brelich as having a ritual character. Mastrocinque 1980, 462n10 with reference to Brelich 1961, 41.
[92] See the discussion in Ferrari 2002, 127–161.
[93] Compare Tedeschi 1975, 163.
[94] Interestingly, Cleomachus' *eromenos* puts a helmet on him (Plutarch *Moralia* 760f). There could have been differently equipped battle participants. There are several indications that foreign allies in the ritual battle were older men. Plutarch's Cleomachus is an *erastes*, not an

cutting front locks prior to the battle. The omission of the long-range missiles in favor of the close fighting can be thought of in terms of progression from light armor to hoplite equipment.

As we have seen, the myth about the bronze-armed Curetes, fighting for the Lelantine Plain, emphasized the utter destructiveness of their confrontation, resulting in the annihilation of the mythical Chalcis-Euboea by an earthquake. However, in the realm of ritual, the Curetes' warlike character is symbiotic with, not antagonistic to, the conditions of peace and prosperity. The Cretan Palaikastro Hymn is a striking example of such associations of the Curetes.[95] The Curetes' kourotrophic qualities would be essential for the protection of the pre-adult males of Eretria and Chalcis, who went through the dangerous experience of reliving the primordial brutality of fighting for the Plain.[96]

---

eromenos. Athenian Chaerion was old enough to have a son. Similarly, Herodotus' Tellus (1.30), who is said to "assist" the Athenians in battle, saw his children and grandchildren. The presence of helmets on the adult participants would allow them to be easily distinguished in fighting. The helmets offered extra protection, but also may have subjected their wearers to fiercer attacks. Naturally, for the older *xenoi* the battle would not have the function of a coming of age.

[95] Compare Apollonius Rhodius' description (1.1103-1153) of the Argonauts' dance in full armor, clashing their swords and shields, which brings about a divinely sanctioned rush of beauty and fertility, evocative of the Golden Age. On the Palaikastro Hymn and the Curetes, see Blakely 2006, 123-136 with further references.

[96] Compare an Orphic characterization of the Curetes as δαίμονες ἀθάνατοι, τροφέες καὶ αὐτ' ὀλετῆρες "immortal divine beings, both nurturers and destroyers" (*Orphic hymn* 38, 14). Walker 2004, 29, 59n20. On the Curetes and rites of passage see, among others, Muellner 1998, 8, 15-17;

Can this hypothetical reconstruction be connected to the cultic realia of archaic Eretria and Chalcis? Angelo Brelich pointed out several links between the festival of Artemisia at the temple of Artemis at Amarynthus (also called Amarynthia or Amarysia) and the war for the Lelantine Plain.[97] Unfortunately, most of the evidence that we have about the Artemisia is Hellenistic or later, which makes it unreliable for reconstructing the situation in the Archaic period. The festival of Artemisia is associated with various phenomena evocative of a rite of passage; however, at this stage, we cannot say whether these elements continue the older practice of ritual battles or are new developments. Moreover, the location of the temple of Artemis at Amarynthus, about ten kilometers east of Eretria,[98] makes it a somewhat counter-intuitive candidate for playing a primary role in ritual battles for the Lelantine Plain.[99] On the other hand, I note with interest that both Eretria and Chalcis had a month *Hippion* (corresponding to June/July).[100] *Hippion* is an extremely rare month name, attested elsewhere only in Olynthus; Knoefler comments about its association with the aristocratic *Hippeis* and

---

Burkert 1985, 261–262; Jeanmaire 1939, 427–450. Interestingly, Vernant ([1965] 2006, 46) notes that the Bronze Men's entire life cycle consists of the age of *hêbê*.

[97] Brelich 1961, 18–21, 81–82.

[98] Knoepfler 1988.

[99] On the hypothetical temple of Apollo in the Lelantine Plain, indicated by *Homeric Hymn to Apollo* 220–221, see Bruneau 1976.

[100] Knoepfler 1989, 44–46.

Hippobotai of Eretria and Chalcis,[101] who, as we will see, were the primary participants in ritual battles. Perhaps in the Archaic period the ritual battle took place during this summer month.

Below I briefly review the evidence connecting Artemis' temple at Amarynthus and the traditions of the Lelantine War, as well as the links between the festival of Artemisia and rites of coming of age.

The Lelantine War and the temple of Artemis at Amarynthus are connected by two references in Strabo. We have already discussed the first one, describing the prohibition of long-range missiles, inscribed on a stele in the Amarynthium (Strabo 10.1.12). The second reference is similar: Strabo describes another inscription on a stele in the same temple (10.1.10):

> τὴν δὲ δύναμιν τὴν Ἐρετριέων ἣν ἔσχον ποτὲ μαρτυρεῖ ἡ στήλη, ἥν ἀνέθεσάν ποτε ἐν τῷ ἱερῷ τῆς Ἀμαρυνθίας Ἀρτέμιδος· γέγραπται δ' ἐν αὐτῇ τρισχιλίοις μὲν ὁπλίταις ἑξακοσίοις δ' ἱππεῦσιν ἑξήκοντα δ' ἅρμασι ποιεῖν τὴν πομπήν·

> As for the power the Eretrians once had, this is evidenced by the pillar, which they once set up in the temple of Artemis Amarynthia. It was inscribed thereon that they made their festal procession with three thousand heavy-armed soldiers, six hundred horsemen, and sixty chariots.

The procession is frequently considered a part of the Artemisia.[102] The stele is also sometimes connected to the Lelantine War.[103] It is uncertain from Strabo's report whether the

---

[101] Knoepfler 1989, 57.
[102] Ringwood 1929, 386; Brelich 1961, 18–19; Knoepfler 1988, 387; Walker 2004, 34, 122.

two inscriptions were on the same stele, or on different ones, but the military theme unites the two inscriptions.[104] The presence of the sixty chariots makes it clear that the procession evoked the era of heroic fighting,[105] as did the prohibition of missiles.[106] However, the numbers of hoplites and horsemen seem to me to be too great for the Archaic period.[107] More research is necessary on the subject, but perhaps there was a revival of the ritual battle in the Hellenistic period.

The Artemisia was a pan-Euboean festival,[108] possibly also having a federal character.[109] It was grandly celebrated[110] at the end of the month of Anthesterion.[111] The festival continued

---

[103] Burn 1929, 35; Parker 1997, 109–110.

[104] Wheeler (1987, 164) rejects the possibility that the two inscriptions belonged to the same stele, since "a treaty and the description of a religious procession are two very different kinds of documents." Wheeler 1987, 164. However, both the prohibition of missiles and the procession may be regulations for an organization of a festival.

[105] On the chariots in the procession, see Donlan 1970, 138; Walker 2004, 35, 122; Lorimer 1947, 118; Snodgrass 1967, 71; Parker 1997, 32. The established point of view is that the chariots were long obsolete in the Archaic period (references in Van Wees 2004, 291n17; van Wees questions this assumption in pp. 158-60).

[106] See note 41 above on the suggested dates of the two stelae.

[107] Knoepfler (1985, 257; 1988, 387) believes that the stele is archaic.

[108] Ringwood 1929, 386n5, Brelich 1961, 18, Knoepfler 1972; 1988, 391; Sapouna-Sakellaraki 1992, 237; Walker 2004, 33-34. Livy 35.38 refers to the participation of the city of Carystus in the festival.

[109] Knoepfler 1988, 391 with a reference to Picard 1979, 218-220.

[110] Pausanias 1.31.5. Ringwood 1929, 386.

[111] Knoepfler 1988 provides a good overview of the festival.

for several days, and included contests of *mousikê*[112] and athletic competitions.[113] Interestingly, one inscription concerning the festival mentions *xenoi hoi metechontes ton koinon*. It has been argued that this expression refers to the *xenoi* taking part in the athletic competitions.[114] The focus of the festival, and apparently one of the most prestigious and publically attended events of the Eretrian year,[115] was the pyrrhic competition.[116] After Eretria instituted an *ephebeia*, ca. 320 BC, the ephebes were also incorporated in the festival.[117]

There is an illuminating Hellenistic inscription (*ca.* 315-305 BC)[118] in which a group of Eretrian young men is called *pyrrhikistai* in the framework of a contract concerning some public works: apparently, in Eretria *pyrrhikistai* was a term defining males at the later stage of the *ephebeia*, which suggests the centrality of the performance of the pyrrhic in the progression of the coming of age.[119]

---

[112] *IG* XII ix 189. On this inscription see Ringwood 1929, 387, Nagy 2002, 39–53; Rotstein 2012.
[113] Scholia for Pindar *Olympian* 13.159b.
[114] *IG* XII 9, 234, *ca.* 100 BC. Ringwood 1929, 387; Gauthier 1982, 230-231, Knoepfler 1988, 388n27; Chankowski 1993, 24–25; Walker 2004, 61n63.
[115] The pyrrhic *agôn* at the Artemisia was the venue of announcement of honorary decrees. *IG* XII 9, 236, 237, *ca.* 100 BC. Knoepfler 1988, 386; Brelich 1961, 19; Ringwood 1929, 387n1.
[116] Ringwood 1929, 387, Brelich 1961, 19, 76, Sapouna-Sakellaraki 1992, 237, Walker 2004, 34–35 and 61, nn65,68; Chankowski 1993, 27. On the pyrrhic, see Ceccarelli 1998.
[117] Chankowski 1993.
[118] Chankowski 1993, 44.
[119] *IG* XII 9, 191. Brelich 1961, 19; Walker 2004, 35. On age-classes in Chalcis, see Knoepfler 1979, 174–176.

An epigram from the *Greek Anthology* (6.156) by Theodoridas from the third century BC[120] speaks about a dedication of hair in the temple of Artemis at Amarynthus by a young aristocrat Charisthenes.[121] In a striking metaphor, the epigram describes the boy shining like "a foal who has shed his fuzzy dawn" (πωλικὸν ὡς ἵππος χνοῦν ἀποσεισάμενος). It is possible that the reference to the dedication of hair should be connected with the Artemisia, on the model of the Athenian Κουρεῶτις.[122]

It has been proposed that "the Amarynthia are celebrations in honor of Artemis the warrior."[123] In connection with the possible role of Artemis' cult in the ritual battles for the Plain, it is interesting to contemplate Pierre Ellinger's conclusion about Artemis' persistent association with wars of total annihilation, in which the survival of an entire community is at stake.[124] The link between Artemis and savage fighting portrays the goddess as a fitting

---

[120] Leitao 2003, 121.

[121] An epitaph from Chalcis, dating from the second century AD (*IG* 12 Supp. 196.1179, lines 9–12), combines the themes of the long-haired Abantes and the coming of age: "And long locks of hair hang down the back of my head (*opithen komoôsai*). For coming of age (*hebe*) did not cut them, but death struck first." Trans. by Leitao 2003, 123; see his discussion there.

[122] Walker 2004, 35. According to Hesychius s.v. Κουρεῶτις is "a day of the month Pyanepsion on which they sacrifice to Artemis the hair shorn from the heads of boys." Walker 2004, 36. On Athenian Κουρεῶτις see Lambert 1993, 162-64, who suggests a link between Koureotis' haircutting and entry into the phratry. See Lambert 1993, 163n118 for references to haircutting as a rite of passage.

[123] Bornmann 1968, 90, quoted in Walker 2004, 35, 62 n.72.

[124] Ellinger 1993, 335-338.

overseer of the disastrous strife of the Curetes over the Plain.[125] Interestingly, we also have an attestation of the opposite characterization of Artemis Amarynthia as a mediator between warring sides. Knoepfler argues that Artemis' appellation *Metaxu* in the famous inscription concerning the organization of the musical contests at the Amarynthia (*IG* XII 9, 189) is related to Artemis' role as a divine go-between, consolidating the conflicting parties after the Eretrian *stasis* of 341 BC.[126] Perhaps Artemis functioned as a mediator also in the conflict between Eretria and Chalcis.[127]

6. Riders on the earth

So far, I have been visualizing the mode of combat in the ritual battle as the close fighting of hoplites. However, Plutarch's depiction of Cleomachus' participation puts emphasis on the role of cavalry attack. Plutarch's narrative may be influenced by the later development

---

[125] The aetiological story of the origin of cult of Artemis at Amarynthus is also connected to war: the statue of Artemis was set in Amarynthus by Agamemnon, who sacrificed to Artemis a hornless ram, according to the scholia to Aristophanes' *Birds* 873, citing Callimachus F 200b Pfeiffer. Callimachus recounts that Artemis at Amarynthus accepted tailless and one-eyed victims. Similarly, Aelian notes that the Eretrians sacrificed maimed animals to Artemis at Amarynthus (Ἐρετριεῖς δὲ τῇ ἐν Ἀμαρύνθῳ Ἀρτέμιδι κολοβὰ θύουσιν, *On the Nature of Animals* 12.34). Brelich 1961, 20; Walker 2004, 60n53. The sacrifice of maimed animals may be construed as a cultic reference to a quasi-Bronze-Generation *hubris*.
[126] Knoepfler 1997, 376–377.
[127] For Artemis as *kourotrophos* see references in Walker 2004, 60n41.

of the cavalry, but it is probable that horses did play a significant role in the ritual battle.[128] An important attestation is provided by Aristotle (*Politics* 1289b):

> καὶ τῶν γνωρίμων εἰσὶ διαφοραὶ καὶ κατὰ τὸν πλοῦτον καὶ τὰ μεγέθη τῆς οὐσίας, οἷον ἱπποτροφίας (τοῦτο γὰρ οὐ ῥᾴδιον μὴ πλουτοῦντας ποιεῖν· διόπερ ἐπὶ τῶν ἀρχαίων χρόνων ὅσαις πόλεσιν ἐν τοῖς ἵπποις ἡ δύναμις ἦν, ὀλιγαρχίαι παρὰ τούτοις ἦσαν· ἐχρῶντο δὲ πρὸς τοὺς πολέμους ἵπποις πρὸς τοὺς ἀστυγείτονας οἷον Ἐρετριεῖς καὶ Χαλκιδεῖς καὶ Μάγνητες οἱ ἐπὶ Μαιάνδρῳ καὶ τῶν ἄλλων πολλοὶ περὶ τὴν Ἀσίαν)·

> And the upper classes have distinctions also corresponding to their wealth and the amounts of their property (for example in a keeping of horses--for it is not easy to rear horses without being rich, and this is why in ancient times there were oligarchies in all the states whose strength lay in their cavalry, and they used to use horses for their wars against their neighbors, as for instance did the Eretrians and Chalcidians and the people of Magnesia on the Maeander and many of the other Asiatic peoples).[129]

On the basis of this passage, I suggest that the primary participants in the ritual battles were the elites of Eretria and Chalcis, the *Hippeis* and the *Hippobotai*.[130] I am also going to present my reconstruction of the territorial organization of the ritual battle. We know that a significant part of the Lelantine Plain belonged in the Archaic period to the *Hippobotai*. The information comes from Herodotus, who reports that after the Athenian defeat of Chalcis (in 506 BC) the Athenians settled four thousands cleruchs on the land of the Chalcidian *Hippobotai* (Herodotus

---

[128] See Greenhalgh 1973, 90-3, 147-8.
[129] Trans. by H. Rackham.
[130] The ancient references to the Eretrian *Hippeis* are Aristotle *Politics* 1306a; *Athenian Constitution* 15.2; to Chalcidian *Hippobotai*: Herodotus 5.77.2-3; Aristotle F 603 Rose, ap. Strabo 10.1.8. On the interest of the Eretrian elites in the heroic past, as reflected in the Archaic heroizing burials, see Bérard 1970, Crielaard 1998.

5.77.2–3). This account is supplemented by Aelian, who relates that after their victory the Athenians set up a sanctuary to Athena "in the place called Lelanton" (ἐν τῷ Ληλάντῳ ὀνομαζομένῳ τόπῳ, Aelian *Varia Historia* 6.1.3). Probably, most of the Lelantine Plain was in fact owned by the *Hippobotai* and the *Hippeis*. However, I would like to suggest that the battles περὶ Ληλάντου (πεδίου)[131] throughout the Archaic period probably only focused on a circumscribed part of the modern Lelantine Plain. I submit that this fertile but uncultivated territory was considered sacred, and actually belonged to a sanctuary, jointly patronized by the *Hippobotai* and *Hippeis*. Outside of the ritual battle, it functioned as a horse pasture. For examples of important pastures on sanctuaries' lands, I refer to the work of Timothy Howe; a particularly interesting parallel is constituted by the sacred pastures of Delphic Apollo.[132]

The sacred territory would change hands according to the outcomes of periodic ritual battles. The control over this territory metonymically signified the control of the whole Plain. The ritual fighting over the Λήλαντον, and the territory's sacred status, were the grounds on which the *Hippeis* and the *Hippobotai* justified their control over the Plain and their preeminence in their cities.[133]

---

[131] Plutarch *Moralia* 153f, Strabo 10.1.12, Strabo 10.3.6.
[132] Howe 2003; cf. Howe 2008, Chapter 4.
[133] Walker in fact sketches a scenario similar to what I am proposing, but he believes that "the cosy pattern of war games among aristocratic *oikoi*" came to an end *ca.* 825 BC. Walker 2004, 156–157.

This territory was probably believed to occupy the place of the destroyed mythical city of Euboea. The name of this sacred territory must have been Λήλαντον (Strabo 10.1.9);[134] this hypothesis derives from Aelian's notice, which I have already mentioned, that the Athenians established Athena's temple ἐν τῷ Ληλάντῳ ὀνομαζομένῳ τόπῳ (Aelian *Varia Historia* 6.1.3). On my reading, the Athenians substituted the sanctuary belonging to the *Hippeis* and *Hippobotai* by the precinct of their own goddess.

A sacred uncultivated land where horses roam can be a vision of the Golden Age with its spontaneous beauty. A poem by Sappho (F 2), describing a paradisiacal sacred precinct in a sequence of exquisite details, mentions λείμων ἱππόβοτος, a meadow where horses graze. But the uncultivated land where battles take place is equally evocative of the Age of Bronze with its absence of bread (Hesiod *Works and Days* 146).

My interpretation, positing peaceful and cooperative relations between the *Hippeis* and the *Hippobotai*, is corroborated by an attestation of political compatibility between the interests of the *Hippobotai* and the *Hippeis*. The attestation comes from Herodotus' description of events of 490 BC on Euboea (6.100). The Eretrians learn that they are about to be attacked by the Persians, and ask for Athenian help. The Athenians offer the help of their four thousand

---

[134] Λήλαντον may be cognate with ἐλάω/ἐλαύνω 'to ride, to drive;' this toponym (from *leh$_2$-nt-) can mean 'driving/riding place.' I am grateful to Alexander Nikolaev for his help in this question.

cleruchs, occupying the land of the *Hippobotai*. However, a group of Eretrians plans to betray the city to the enemy, "in hope of winning advantages from the Persians" (ἴδια κέρδεα προσδεκόμενοι παρὰ τοῦ Πέρσεω).

> μαθὼν δὲ τούτων ἑκάτερα ὡς εἶχε Αἰσχίνης ὁ Νόθωνος, ἐὼν τῶν Ἐρετριέων τὰ πρῶτα, φράζει τοῖσι ἥκουσι Ἀθηναίων πάντα τὰ παρεόντα σφι πρήγματα, προσεδέετό τε ἀπαλλάσσεσθαι σφέας ἐς τὴν σφετέρην, ἵνα μὴ προσαπόλωνται. οἱ δὲ Ἀθηναῖοι ταῦτα Αἰσχίνῃ συμβουλεύσαντι πείθονται.

> When Aeschines son of Nothon, a leading man in Eretria, learned of both designs, he told the Athenians who had come how matters stood, and asked them to depart to their own country so they would not perish like the rest. The Athenians followed Aeschines' advice.

The Persians arrive and, after a seven days siege, two notable (δόκιμοι) Eretrian citizens, Euphorbus son of Alcimachus and Philagrus son of Cineas, betrayed the city to the Persians (Herodotus 6.101).

It has been suggested by Keith Walker that Aeschines in fact played a part in the same plot as Euphorbus and Philagrus. The three men, according to Walker, were members of the oligarchic faction.[135] (By 490 BC, Eretria was a democracy.)[136] Aeschines' disclosure of the

---

[135] Walker 2004, 280, 286–287n65.
[136] Knoepfler 1998, 105; cf. Walker 2004, 236–262. On Herodotus 5.99, describing the Eretrian aid to Miletus in 498 BC as a repayment of the earlier Milesian military assistance against Chalcis, see the conclusion of this dissertation. The aristocratic ideology of foreign assistance in fighting for the Lelantine Plain, traditionally promoted by the Eretrian *Hippeis* (and the Chalcidian *Hippobotai*), may have been hijacked in this case by a democratic (or perhaps a rival aristocratic) faction. We will encounter a parallel phenomenon in Argos in Chapter 6.

impending betrayal to the Athenians was motivated not by his compassion toward the cleruchs, but rather by the desire to be rid of their presence. The departure of the cleruchs presumably reversed the land of the *Hippobotai* to its previous owners. (In 446 BC, the Athenians needed to expel them once again).[137] Thus, we witness the members of the oligarchic faction in Eretria, whom I think we can identify as the *Hippeis*, attempting to ascend to power and at the same time helping the *Hippobotai* to recover their land.

7. Theognis' stanza

Let us now examine a reference to fighting in the Lelantine Plain in the poetry of Theognis (891-894):

> Οἴ μοι ἀναλκίης· ἀπὸ μὲν Κήρινθος ὄλωλεν,
> Ληλάντου δ' ἀγαθὸν κείρεται οἰνόπεδον·
> οἱ δ' ἀγαθοὶ φεύγουσι, πόλιν δὲ κακοὶ διέπουσιν.
> ὡς δὴ Κυψελιδῶν Ζεὺς ὀλέσειε γένος.

> Alas for cowardice. Cerinthus is ruined,
> The good Lelantine vine plain is being shorn.
> The good ones flee, the bad ones manage the city.
> May Zeus destroy the race of the Cypselids!

---

[137] Plutarch *Pericles* 23.2.

Theognis 891-94 is sometimes connected with the Lelantine War in the modern historical literature, but usually it is considered to be too late for the war.[138] As I have already pointed out, the Panhellenic nature of Theognis' poetry and the Panhellenic tradition of the Lelantine War fit together. Thus, the tradition of the war is probably relevant in some way for the understanding of the poem; however, in what way exactly it remains for us to discover. The poem, in fact, constitutes an oddity in the Theognidean corpus. The poetry of Theognis tends to present situations in generalized, not geographically and historically specific, terms.[139] Thomas Figueira notes a "general absence in Theognis of direct historical allusions," and adds: "One exception is the mention of an otherwise unknown sack of Cerinthus and fighting on the Lelantine plain."[140]

I propose to approach the question of the relevance of the Lelantine War to Theognis 891-94 through a thematic analysis of the poem. The scarcity of historical realia in Theognis implies that the fighting in the Plain and the Cypselids may have some thematic significance.

---

[138] The relevance of Theognis 891-94 for the war is rejected by Burn 1929, 34; Bradeen 1947, 228-230; Parker 1997, 82-88. See also Boardman 1957, 27n160; Wheeler 1987, 160n17; Will 1955, 391-404; Figueira 1985a, 123-4. Figueira 1985b, 288-91 cautiously admits the relevance of these lines.
[139] Nagy 1985, 42; Figueira 1985a, 123; Okin 1985. Similarly to these scholars, I view the corpus of Theognis' poetry as a reflection of a cohesive poetic tradition. Differently, West 1974, 40-64.
[140] Figueira 1985a, 123. Another exception cited by Figueira is Theognis' mention of the Persian invasion, belonging to the latest phase of the poetry.

By tracing patterns, themes, and motifs comprising the poem we may start to comprehend what the Lelantine War means in Theognis.

Importantly, Theognis 784 declares that he has been to Euboea (as well as to Sparta and the land of Sicily):

ἦλθον δ' Εὐβοίης ἀμπελόεν πεδίον

I went to the vine-rich plain of Euboea

This statement, which has been interpreted in a narrowly biographical manner,[141] can be read more thematically. The poetic voice names Sicily, Sparta, and Euboea as audiences of his poetry (as is also evident in the assertion "they made me *philos*," μ' ἐφίλευν, 786). Moreover, I think that the mention of these locales amounts to an acknowledgement that some traditions native to Sicily or Sparta or Euboea constitute themes of Theognis' poetry: ἀμπελόεν πεδίον 'vine-rich plain' parallels οἰνόπεδον 'vine plain' in Theognis 892 too closely not to perceive it as a reference to the Lelantine Plain.[142]

The first step in our analysis is to establish the boundaries of the poetic text to be closely analyzed. I have referred to Theognis 891-894 as a poem; however, it has been suggested that these lines are a part of a larger unit. Keith Walker asserts that Theognis 885-94

---

[141] Bradeen 1947, 229; Walker 2004, 213.
[142] Harrison 1902, 288; Walker 2004, 214-215.

constitutes a unified whole.[143] Walker does not support his suggestion by detailed investigation of the poem; however, his proposal dovetails with the work of Christopher Faraone on the stanzaic structure of early elegiac poetry. Faraone observes a recurrence of five-couplet stanzas in the elegy.[144] I am going to argue below that Theognis 885–94 constitutes precisely such a five-couplet stanza, unified by common motifs and themes. Let me quote this possible poem:

> Εἰρήνη καὶ πλοῦτος ἔχοι πόλιν, ὄφρα μετ' ἄλλων
>   κωμάζοιμι· κακοῦ δ' οὐκ ἔραμαι πολέμου.
> Μηδὲ λίην κήρυκος ἀν' οὖς ἔχε μακρὰ βοῶντος·
>   οὐ γὰρ πατρώιας γῆς πέρι μαρνάμεθα.
> ἀλλ' αἰσχρὸν παρεόντα καὶ ὠκυπόδων ἐπιβάντα
>   ἵππων μὴ πόλεμον δακρυόεντ' ἐσιδεῖν.
> Οἴ μοι ἀναλκίης· ἀπὸ μὲν Κήρινθος ὄλωλεν,
>   Ληλάντου δ' ἀγαθὸν κείρεται οἰνόπεδον·
> οἱ δ' ἀγαθοὶ φεύγουσι, πόλιν δὲ κακοὶ διέπουσιν.
>   ὡς δὴ Κυψελιδῶν Ζεὺς ὀλέσειε γένος.

> May Peace and Wealth attend the city, so that with others
> I may enjoy a revel. I do not lust after evil war.
> And don't exceedingly give ear to the loud cry of the herald,
> for we are not fighting for the land of our fathers.
> But it would be shameful, being present, not to mount swift-footed
> horses and look the tear-causing war in the face.
> Alas for cowardice. Cerinthus is ruined,
> The good Lelantine vine plain is being shorn.
> The good ones flee, the bad ones manage the city.
> May Zeus destroy the race of the Cypselids!

---

[143] Walker 2004, 213; also, already Harrison 1902, 289.
[144] Faraone 2008, 16 and *passim*.

Ewen Bowie has noted that line 885-86, 887-88 and 889-90 "express contrasting attitudes to involvement in war." Lines 885-86 "praise peace;" lines 887-88 "expand this idea;" lines 889-90 seems to constitute a reply.[145] Bowie suggests a sympotic context of performance. He further discusses the meaning of the statement "we are not fighting for the land of our fathers," noting that it depicts the performer and his audience as either mercenaries,[146] soldiers fighting for their *polis* away from their home territory, or "members of an allied force sent by one *polis* to help another."[147]

The mention of an allied force in the context of the Lelantine War sounds singularly relevant. Let us now consider the separate couplets in detail. The first couplet contains a wish for peace (Theognis 885-6):

> Εἰρήνη καὶ πλοῦτος ἔχοι πόλιν, ὄφρα μετ' ἄλλων
> κωμάζοιμι· κακοῦ δ' οὐκ ἔραμαι πολέμου.

> May Peace and Wealth attend the city, so that with others
> I may enjoy a revel. I do not lust after evil war.

---

[145] Bowie 1990, 228-229, with reference to Vetta 1980, xxix-xxx; also Harrison 1902, 289.
[146] West 1974, 160.
[147] Bowie 1990, 228.

Daniel Levine shows that these lines have much in common with Hesiod's depiction of the Golden Generation and the City of *Dikê*, prosperous and untroubled by the war (*Works and Days* 228-29):[148]

> εἰρήνη δ' ἀνὰ γῆν κουροτρόφος, οὐδέ ποτ' αὐτοῖς
> ἀργαλέον πόλεμον τεκμαίρεται εὐρύοπα Ζεύς·

> Peace, the nurturer of the young men, ranges about the land, and never do they have wretched war manifested for them by Zeus who sees far and wide.

The desire for a *kômos* recalls the lifestyle of the Golden Generations, who "took pleasure in banquets" (τέρπovτ' ἐν θαλίῃσι, *Works and Days* 115). Levine observes that "a well-ordered polis allows its citizens to approximate a Golden Age experience."[149]

The next couplet (Theognis 887-8) introduces the situation of fighting away from home. The wish of the Golden-Age-like peace is transformed into a less exalted reluctance to fight:

> Μηδὲ λίην κήρυκος ἀν' οὖς ἔχε μακρὰ βοῶντος·
> οὐ γὰρ πατρώιας γῆς πέρι μαρνάμεθα.

> And don't exceedingly give ear to the loud cry of the herald,
> for we are not fighting for the land of our fathers.

---

[148] Levine 1985, 190, 192.

[149] Levine 1985, 190. Levine calls the city of *dikê* a "multiform" of the Golden Age. Levine 1985, 190, §25n1. On a parallel in Theognis between the morally shocking behavior of the Megarian elite and the *hubris* of the men of the Silver Generation, see Nagy 1985, 58.

Then there is a sharp change, marked by ἀλλ' in line 889: the poetic voice declares that it would be shameful not to participate in the war (Theognis 889-90):

> ἀλλ' αἰσχρὸν παρεόντα καὶ ὠκυπόδων ἐπιβάντα
> ἵππων μὴ πόλεμον δακρυόεντ' ἐσιδεῖν.

> But it would be shameful, being present, not to mount swift-footed
> horses and look the tear-causing war in the face.

The oppositions between war and peace, the reluctance to participate in the fighting and the intention of participation are complemented by a shared feature: in both couplets the speaker is located in a foreign city, which is engaged in war. We have already observed this concerning the lines 887-8; however, it is also appealing to read the participle παρεόντα 'being present at' in line 889 as an indication that the speaker, in fact, is not usually present at the site of the fighting. That is to say, he is a *xenos*, somebody's guest in the city at war.[150]

The tone changes even more dramatically in lines 891–94:

> Οἴ μοι ἀναλκίης· ἀπὸ μὲν Κήρινθος ὄλωλεν,
>   Ληλάντου δ' ἀγαθὸν κείρεται οἰνόπεδον·
> οἱ δ' ἀγαθοὶ φεύγουσι, πόλιν δὲ κακοὶ διέπουσιν.
>   ὡς δὴ Κυψελιδῶν Ζεὺς ὀλέσειε γένος.

> Alas for cowardice. Cerinthus is ruined,
> The good Lelantine vine plain is being shorn.
> The good ones flee, the bad ones manage the city.
> May Zeus destroy the race of the Cypselids!

---

[150] Walker 2004, 213.

The diction in these lines recalls Hesiod's warning about the divine retribution for *hubris*: a whole city suffering because of a bad man (κακοῦ ἀνδρὸς, *Works and Days* 240), and Zeus destroying (ἀπώλεσεν, compare ἀπὸ ... ὄλωλεν in Theognis 891) the city's army or its walls (246).

Theognis can employ *kakos* and *agathos* in the moral sense, not only in reference to social classes,[151] and *kakotês* 'debasement' was shown to be associated with *hubris* in Theognis.[152] The repetition of ἀγαθὸν and ἀγαθοὶ in lines 892 and 892 provides an implicit link, very Hesiodic in spirit, between agriculture and moral goodness. The good Lelantine Plain, with its rich soil,[153] is a perfect place for the good eris of peaceful cultivation (*Works and Days* 21-24). This makes the bad eris in the Plain especially upsetting: a war in a vineyard is particularly painful and monstrous. The destruction is rendered all the more sorrowful through subtle references to an alternative scenario of peaceful prosperity, now impossible. The Hesiodic City of *Dikê* is characterized, in addition to the fertility of its soil and the absence of war, by an exceptional wooliness of its sheep (*Works and Days* 234) and by the presence of honey-bees in oaks (*Works and Days* 233). In the poem of Theognis, perversely, it is a good vineyard, not the sheep, which is shorn. The honey theme is present as well: κήρινθος, as we learn from

---

[151] See Nagy 1985, 44n71 on the interplay of the socio-economic and ethical meanings in the use of *kakos* and *agathos* by Theognis.
[152] See Nagy 1985, 51–53.
[153] Theophrastus, *Historia plantarum* 8.8.5.

Aristotle, means 'bee-bread,' a food of bees that "has a fig-like sweetness" (γλυκύτητα συκώδη ἔχον, Aristotle *Historia animalium* 623b).[154] The repetition of ἀπὸ ... ὄλωλεν and ὀλέσειε in lines 891 and 894 emphasizes the theme of destruction.

The annihilation of the Golden Age in lines 891–894 answers the motif of the Golden Age in lines 885–6; the cohesion is enhanced by the repetition of κακοῦ and κακοὶ in lines 886 and 893, and πόλιν in 885 and 893. Theognis' poem implicitly portrays the devastation of the Lelantine plain and the destruction of Cerinthus as intrusion of *hubris* into the City of *Dikê*. This representation parallels Strabo's description of the collapse of the Golden Age at Pithecussae, as well as Hesiodic associations between Amphidamas of Chalcis and the Bronze Generation. Theognis' reference to the fighting in the Lelantine Plain appears thematically to match other descriptions of the Lelantine War.

8. Earwax and the end of the Lelantine War

But what about Κυψελιδῶν ... γένος in line 894? This expression is usually translated as "the race of the Cypselids." Various conjectures have been made about the otherwise

---

[154] See also Hesychius s.v. κήρινθος. On the associations of Latin *cerinthus* with honey, wax, and bees, and its poetic significance, see Roessel 1990. Interestingly, Probus reports in his commentary on *Georgics* 4.63 that *cerinthon* is a yellow flower, abundant on Euboea. Roessel 1990, 245n8.

unattested involvement of Corinth in the Lelantine War.[155] In fact, the Cypselids do not appear in the manuscripts — they are an emendation, suggested by Hermann. The manuscripts give κυψελίζων (A) and κυψελλίζον (o), "unmetrical and meaningless,"[156] as Figueira describes it. While these variants are indeed unmetrical, they may be not entirely meaningless. A short linguistic excursion is necessary in order to clarify these forms. Through an examination of dirty ears and denominative verbs we may possibly eliminate a whole line of Corinthian tyrants from the poem.

The word κυψέλη, according to LSJ, can signify any hollow vessel, like box or chest; a bee-hive; a hollow of the ear; and, finally, ear-wax, hence the expression in *Comica Adespota* F 620:

κυψέλην δ' ἔχεις
ἄπλατον ἐν τοῖς ὠσίν.

you have boundless amount of earwax in your ears...

Compare also Lucianus' *Lexiphanes* (line 6):

σὺ δὲ κυψελόβυστα ἔοικας ἔχειν τὰ ὦτα

you seem to have ears stopped by the ear-wax...

---

[155] See Bradeen 1947, 229 (who eventually rejects the relevance of the "questionable passage" of Theognis to the Lelantine war, and proposes a different interpretation); Figueira 1985b, 288-291; Walker 2004, 216-219.
[156] Figueira 1985b, 288n13.

The related word κυψελίς means just 'wax in the ears.' The form κυψελίζον (combining the manuscripts' κυψελίζων and κυψελλίζον) can be construed as a neutral participle, characterizing γένος, of the unattested denominative verb *κυψελίζω, derived from κυψελίς. *κυψελίζω should mean something like 'to fill ears with ear-wax.' A metaphorical meaning could be 'to make unable to hear, unresponsive, insensible.' Remarkably, Dondorff, writing about Theognis 891–94, and following an earlier interpretation of Karl Müller, connected κυψελίζον with κυψελίς, and suggested that κυψελίζον ... γένος should signify "obturatum et surdum populum."[157]

My conjecture is that this verse curses somebody for failing to lend military help in the time of war. Deafness can be closely connected with *hubris*, as is illustrated by Plato's description of the bad horse in the soul's chariot (*Phaedrus* 253e):

ὕβρεως καὶ ἀλαζονείας ἑταῖρος, περὶ ὦτα λάσιος, κωφός

...he is the friend of insolence and pride, is shaggy-eared and deaf...[158]

Homeric associations of the adjective κωφός bring us full circle to Theognis' lament about ἀναλκῖης (*Iliad* 11. 390):

κωφὸν γὰρ βέλος ἀνδρὸς ἀνάλκιδος οὐτιδανοῖο

---

[157] Dondorff quoted the Suda for the meaning of κυψελίς, s.v. κυψέλη ... διαφέρει δὲ πρὸς τὴν κυψελίδα, ἥτις ἐστὶν ὁ ἐν τοῖς ὠσὶ ῥύπος. Dondorff 1855, 16–17, cited by Bradeen 1947, 228n22.
[158] Trans. by Harold North Fowler.

...for blunt is the dart of one who is a weakling and a nobody...[159]

Thus, κυψελίζον ... γένος could be cursed for willfully making themselves, or perhaps other people, deaf when their participation is vital.[160]

We have considered how κυψελίζον can function semantically. Another minor emendation can fix the metrical difficulty of the long –ιζ- of κυψελίζον in a short metrical slot. I submit that *κυψελιδόω should mean the same thing as *κυψελίζω, producing the metrically suitable participle κυψελιδοῦν. The development κυψελίς: κυψελιδόω is completely regular, and is paralleled by such examples as κηλίς, 'stain': κηλιδόω 'to defile;' κρηπίς, 'half-boot': κρηπιδόω 'to furnish with boots;' κεραμίς, 'roof-tile': κεραμιδόω 'to make a roof out of shields for protection;' φολίς, 'scale': φολιδόομαι 'to be covered with scales,' etc. In some cases we actually have two denominative verbs, one ending in -ιδόω/-ιδόομαι, and one in -ίζω: στολιδόομαι 'to dress oneself in something,' and στολίζω 'to dress, adorn,' from στολίς, 'garment.'[161]

---

[159] Trans. by A. T. Murray, revised by William F. Wyatt.
[160] The prayer about the destruction of κυψελίζον ... γένος finds a parallel in another Theognis' couplet (Theognis 851-52): Ζεὺς ἄνδρ' ἐξολέσειεν Ὀλύμπιος, ὃς τὸν ἑταῖρον | μαλθακὰ κωτίλλων ἐξαπατᾶν ἐθέλει· "Olympian Zeus destroy the man that is willing to deceive his comrade with the babbling of soft words." Trans. by John Maxwell Edmonds.
[161] In the manuscript tradition, the substitution of κυψελίζω for κυψελιδόω would be straightforward when ζ started to be pronounced as |z| and the syllable was not perceived as long anymore.

I suggest that ὡς δὴ κυψελιδοῦν Ζεὺς ὀλέσειε γένος means "would that Zeus destroy the sort of people who fill their ears with earwax!" This image finds a counterpart in another verse of Theognis' stanza. Remarkably, the only other mention of ears in the corpus of Theognis appears in line 887:

Μηδὲ λίην κήρυκος ἀν' οὖς ἔχε μακρὰ βοῶντος·

And don't exceedingly give ear to the loud cry of the herald...

These verses are precise opposites: one advises not to pay heed to the war summons while in a foreign city, the other curses those who do not respond to the pleas for help. Both verses feature the same image of "turning a deaf ear." The opposition is so specific and accurate that the unity of lines 885-94 as one stanza seems all but certain.[162] We can perceive the stanza as a set of variations on the subject of the participation of foreign allies in the strife for the Lelantine Plain. I quote the passage again, incorporating my new reading (Theognis 885-894):

> Εἰρήνη καὶ πλοῦτος ἔχοι πόλιν, ὄφρα μετ' ἄλλων
> κωμάζοιμι· κακοῦ δ' οὐκ ἔραμαι πολέμου.
> Μηδὲ λίην κήρυκος ἀν' οὖς ἔχε μακρὰ βοῶντος·
> οὐ γὰρ πατρωίας γῆς πέρι μαρνάμεθα.
> ἀλλ' αἰσχρὸν παρεόντα καὶ ὠκυπόδων ἐπιβάντα
> ἵππων μὴ πόλεμον δακρυόεντ' ἐσιδεῖν.
> Οἴ μοι ἀναλκίης· ἀπὸ μὲν Κήρινθος ὄλωλεν,
> Ληλάντου δ' ἀγαθὸν κείρεται οἰνόπεδον·
> οἱ δ' ἀγαθοὶ φεύγουσι, πόλιν δὲ κακοὶ διέπουσιν.

---

[162] On thematic ring compositions as a unifying device in elegiac stanzas, see Faraone 2008, 23-31, with examples from Theognis.

> ὡς δὴ κυψελιδοῦν Ζεὺς ὀλέσειε γένος.
>
> – May Peace and Wealth attend the city, so that with others
> I may enjoy a revel. I do not lust after evil war.
> – And don't exceedingly give ear to the loud cry of the herald,
> for we are not fighting for the land of our fathers.
> – But it would be shameful, being present, not to mount swift-footed
> horses and look the tear-causing war in the face.
> – Alas for cowardice. Cerinthus is ruined,
> The good Lelantine vine plain is being shorn.
> The good ones flee, the bad ones manage the city.
> May Zeus destroy the sort of people who fill their ears with earwax!

The first couplet (885–6) establishes a sympotic context, and prays for a blessing of peace and prosperity to the city. The second couplet (887–8) dramatizes a lighthearted voice of a *xenos* in Chalcis or Eretria, who is "filling with earwax" his audience's ears, advising them (other *xenoi*) not to participate in the war for the Lelantine Plain too eagerly. The third couplet (889–90) forcefully rejects this suggestion; this *xenos* is ready to participate in the fighting. We can remark how the image of mounting the horses is perfectly in tune with out reconstruction of the ritual battle between the *Hippobotai* and the *Hippeis*.[163] Finally, the last quatrain (891–94) provides an even more dramatic shift of mood and point of view: it is a voice of a native Euboean,[164] lamenting the devastation of the Lelantine Plain and cursing those who failed to help out. The vision of the heartbreaking destruction serves as accusatory evidence against

---

[163] Cf. Walker 2004, 214, 232n44.

[164] As Figueira (1985b, 288) observes, the poem leaves unspecified in whose hands the Lelantine plain was at the moment of its destruction.

those whose lack of participation allowed the disaster to happen. Bakker demonstrates that the particle δή conveys an effect of "shared seeing:" the speaker has seen something, and "assumes that the hearer is capable of witnessing the same evidence." The seeing, shared between the speaker and the audience, is a matter of cooperation, as Bakker observes: "the speaker assumes that the listeners are willing to see the evidence produced."[165] Thus, ὡς δὴ κυψελιδοῦν Ζεὺς ὀλέσειε γένος has a sense of "You have seen it [the destruction]. Now, may Zeus destroy those who have let it happen." The disaster in the Lelantine Plain establishes a commonality of vision among the Panhellenic audience of Theognis' poetry.

The stanza starts from a blessing and ends in a curse;[166] the dramatic shifts of voice that it exhibits[167] constitute a virtuoso demonstration of a gamut of possibilities in the poetic treatment of the aristocratic participation in the strife for the Lelantine Plain.[168]

We have analyzed the stanza's rhetoric; now let us shift the point of view and turn to its historical context. It has been observed by numerous scholars that the fleeing ἀγαθοὶ and the

---

[165] Bakker 1997, 75–76.
[166] On ring-compositions of prayers in elegiac stanzas, see Faraone 2008, 27, with Theognis 341-50 as an example.
[167] On the dramatic changes of mood as characteristic for elegiac stanzas, see Faraone 2008, 20–21 and *passim*.
[168] On the poetics of variation, with a discussion of Theognis 215-218 as an expression of ideology of variability, see Nagy 1996, 103; 1990a, 424–425.

κακοὶ who rule the city in line 893 unmistakably suggest the situation of a *stasis*.[169] So, unlike lines 889-90, with their reference to the equestrian contest, lines 891–894 do not speak about the ritual battle. We are amid the destruction in the Lelantine Plain, a democratic revolution seems to be going on, but who is fighting whom? A superbly suitable occasion is the Athenian conquest of the Lelantine Plain in the aftermath of their victory over the Chalcidians in 506 BC.[170] Herodotus reports that the Athenians left 4,000 cleruchs on the land of the Chalcidian *hippobotai* (Herodotus 5.77.2). However, as we have seen, not only the Chalcidian *hippobotai* but also the Eretrian *hippeis* did not want the Athenians to be there. The Athenian take-over of the Plain must have been perceived as a disaster both by the Eretrian and the Chalcidian elites. The destruction of Cerinthus fits the same occasion: Knoepfler and Bakhuizen note that Cerinthus could belong to the territory of Chalcis in (parts of) the Archaic period;[171] the Athenian conquest probably significantly reduced this territory.[172]

But who are κυψελιδοῦν ... γένος, blamed by the poem? Having banished the Cypselids from the primary text of the poem, perhaps now we can cautiously readmit them on the associative level. The idiosyncratic character of the participle κυψελιδοῦν, as well as the

---

[169] Tedeschi 1975, 164; Forrest 1982, 251; Fox 2000, 38; Walker 2004, 213, 217.
[170] A suggestion that Theognis 891-94 refers to the Athenians attack of 506 BC is expressed by Highbarger 1937, 98n38 with further references.
[171] Knoepfler 1997, 406n10; Bakhuizen 1985, 127, 141nn.
[172] From 446 onward Cerinthus clearly belonged to the Athenian colony of Histiaea. Bakhuizen 1985, 127, 141nn39–42 with further references.

verse's similarity to the poetic curse of the Cypselids (ἐξώλης εἴη Κυψελιδῶν γενεά, "May the race of the Cypselids be utterly destroyed!")[173] suggest that the participle was chosen (or constructed) to recall the Cypselids. We are looking then for the historic referent of κυψελιδοῦν ... γένος that fulfills the following requirements: it must be an entity whose lack of participation on the side of Chalcis affected the outcome of the events in 506 BC and it must have some Corinthian connection. The answer is that this entity is the Corinthians themselves.[174] In 506 BC, according to Herodotus, the Spartan army led by Cleomenes and Demaratus, accompanied by armies from allied Peloponnesian cities, including Corinth, invaded Eleusis, about to attack Athens. Simultaneously, Athens was attacked by the Boetians and the Chalcidians (the latter invading and plundering some Attic territories). At this crucial moment of the impending joint attack on Athens, the Corinthians changed their mind (Herodotus 5.75.1, 3):

---

[173] Agaclytus F 1; *Greek Anthology*, appendix, epigram 4; Timaeus, *Lexicon Platonicum*, Photius, *Suda*, s.v. Κυψελιδῶν ἀνάθημα.

[174] Compare the remarkable series of questions, posited by Harrison (1902, 294) in the discussion of Theognis 891-894: "There may be some who would understand Κυψελιδέων of the Corinthians and yet refer the lines to the events of 506. But why should the Corinthians be cursed for the fall of Chalcis? It is true that the Corinthians were the cause of the breaking up of the army of Cleomenes, whereby Athens became free to avenge herself on Boeotia and Chalcis: but why should the poet's resentment be directed against them rather than against the Athenians themselves? And why should he call the Corinthians Κυψελίδαι, when Corinth was in the hands of the party which had expelled the Cypselids?" I hope that my reconstruction satisfyingly answers these questions.

μελλόντων δὲ συνάψειν τὰ στρατόπεδα ἐς μάχην, Κορίνθιοι μὲν πρῶτοι σφίσι αὐτοῖσι δόντες λόγον ὡς οὐ ποιέοιεν δίκαια μετεβάλλοντό τε καὶ ἀπαλλάσσοντο, μετὰ δὲ Δημάρητος ὁ Ἀρίστωνος, ἐὼν καὶ οὗτος βασιλεὺς Σπαρτιητέων καὶ συνεξαγαγών τε τὴν στρατιὴν ἐκ Λακεδαίμονος καὶ οὐκ ἐὼν διάφορος ἐν τῷ πρόσθε χρόνῳ Κλεομένεϊ. [...] τότε δὴ ἐν τῇ Ἐλευσῖνι ὁρῶντες οἱ λοιποὶ τῶν συμμάχων τούς τε βασιλέας τῶν Λακεδαιμονίων οὐκ ὁμολογέοντας καὶ Κορινθίους ἐκλιπόντας τὴν τάξιν, οἴχοντο καὶ αὐτοὶ ἀπαλλασσόμενοι.

When the armies were about to join battle, the Corinthians, coming to the conclusion that they were acting wrongly, changed their minds and departed. Later Demaratus son of Ariston, the other king of Sparta, did likewise, despite the fact that he had come with Cleomenes from Lacedaemon in joint command of the army and had not till now been at variance with him. [...] So now at Eleusis, when the rest of the allies saw that the Lacedaemonian kings were not of one mind and that the Corinthians had left their host, they too went off.

Thus, in Herodotus' presentation, the decision of the Corinthians not to participate in the attack on Athens resulted in the dissipation of the whole expedition. The Corinthians have "filled with earwax" the ears of Chalcis' allies in the struggle against the Athenians. According to Herodotus (5.77.1), the ability of the Athenians to attack Chalcis was a direct result of the dispersal of the Peloponnesian expedition:

διαλυθέντος ὦν τοῦ στόλου τούτου ἀκλεῶς, ἐνθαῦτα Ἀθηναῖοι τίνυσθαι βουλόμενοι πρῶτα στρατηίην ποιεῦνται ἐπὶ Χαλκιδέας.

When this force then had been ingloriously scattered, the Athenians first marched against the Chalcidians to punish them.

They defeated the Boeotians, who rushed to help the Chalcidians out and, crossing on the same day to Euboea, vanquished the Chalcidians in battle (Herodotus 5.77.2). The Lelantine War for the Plain thus was over, and the Athenians were the victors.[175]

Having established the historical context of Theognis 891-894, we can better comprehend the artistry and the ideology of the whole five-couplet stanza. The stanza twists together centuries of ritual fighting and a singular historical act of Athenian geopolitical aggression. The two kinds of fighting are connected: the participation in the ritual battle, whether on the side of Eretria or Chalcis, knits the aristocratic *xenoi* into a Panhellenic community. The deeper theme of lines 891-894 is the break-up (and break-down) of this Panhellenic community, manifested in its failure to assist the aristocratic Chalcis in the clash with the early Athenian democracy. Theognis' poem laments this disintegration and, at the same time, by presenting the devastation of the Lelantine Plain in all its horror, urges the Panhellenic aristocratic community to be more cohesive. The historical incident becomes an enduring moral lesson.

Theognis' poem reworks the themes traditionally associated with the Lelantine War for different purposes. As we have seen, the mythical fighting over the Lelantine Plain is traditionally associated with *hubris*. In Theognis' stanza the *hubris* belongs to the Athenian

---

[175] Cf. Walker 2004, 260-261; Tausend 1987, 508.

cleruchs, shearing the Lelantine Plain of its vineyards.[176] The poem's vision of the beautiful prosperity that is being destroyed by the Athenians implicitly depicts the "good" Lelantine Plain, owned by the "good" people, as belonging to the City of *Dikê*. In other words, the situation before 506 BC, featuring the traditional ritual battles between the *Hippobotai* and *Hippeis*, becomes assimilated into the Age of Gold.

---

[176] The verb κείρεται in line 892 may be making an allusion to the Curetic haircuts of the participants in the ritual battle.

PART II: The Confrontation between Argos and Sparta over the Thyreatis

Chapter 3

Three Hundred Men from Each Side

> ...for today it is necessary to go to Pitana
> by the course of the Eurotas in good time...
> Pindar, *Olympian* 6.28[1]

1. The Argive proposal

The starting point of this chapter is a consideration of the seemingly eccentric terms of a peace treaty, regulating the issue of the territory of Cynuria, put forward by the Argives to the Spartans. It is the year 420 BC. An unstable peace between Sparta and Athens is teetering. In addition, a thirty-year truce between Sparta and Argos has expired, and the Spartans are anxious to renew it in order to avoid fighting with both Argos and Athens. The Argives, on the other hand, worriedly imagine that they are about to confront a coalition between the

---

[1] πρὸς Πιτάναν δὲ παρ' Εὐρώ-
τα πόρον δεῖ σάμερον ἐλθεῖν ἐν ὥρᾳ·

Spartans, Athenians, Boeotians and Tegeans.[2] They curb their aspirations to head an alliance of city-states independent of Sparta, and send envoys to Sparta with the goal of obtaining peace on the best possible terms. Thucydides describes the negotiations:

> καὶ οἱ πρέσβεις ἀφικόμενοι αὐτῶν λόγους ἐποιοῦντο πρὸς τοὺς Λακεδαιμονίους ἐφ' ᾧ ἂν σφίσιν αἱ σπονδαὶ γίγνοιντο. καὶ τὸ μὲν πρῶτον οἱ Ἀργεῖοι ἠξίουν δίκης ἐπιτροπὴν σφίσι γενέσθαι ἢ ἐς πόλιν τινὰ ἢ ἰδιώτην περὶ τῆς Κυνουρίας γῆς, ἧς αἰεὶ πέρι διαφέρονται μεθορίας οὔσης (ἔχει δὲ ἐν αὐτῇ Θυρέαν καὶ Ἀνθήνην πόλιν, νέμονται δ' αὐτὴν Λακεδαιμόνιοι)· ἔπειτα δ' οὐκ ἐώντων Λακεδαιμονίων μεμνῆσθαι περὶ αὐτῆς, ἀλλ', εἰ βούλονται σπένδεσθαι, ἑτοῖμοι εἶναι, οἱ Ἀργεῖοι πρέσβεις τάδε ὅμως ἐπηγάγοντο τοὺς Λακεδαιμονίους ξυγχωρῆσαι, ἐν μὲν τῷ παρόντι σπονδὰς ποιήσασθαι ἔτη πεντήκοντα, ἐξεῖναι δ' ὁποτεροισοῦν προκαλεσαμένοις, μήτε νόσου οὔσης μήτε πολέμου Λακεδαίμονι καὶ Ἄργει, διαμάχεσθαι περὶ τῆς γῆς ταύτης, ὥσπερ καὶ πρότερόν ποτε ὅτε αὐτοὶ ἑκάτεροι ἠξίωσαν νικᾶν, διώκειν δὲ μὴ ἐξεῖναι περαιτέρω τῶν πρὸς Ἄργος καὶ Λακεδαίμονα ὅρων. τοῖς δὲ Λακεδαιμονίοις τὸ μὲν πρῶτον ἐδόκει μωρία εἶναι ταῦτα, ἔπειτα (ἐπεθύμουν γὰρ τὸ Ἄργος πάντως φίλιον ἔχειν) ξυνεχώρησαν ἐφ' οἷς ἠξίουν καὶ ξυνεγράψαντο. ἐκέλευον δ' οἱ Λακεδαιμόνιοι, πρὶν τέλος τι αὐτῶν ἔχειν, ἐς τὸ Ἄργος πρῶτον ἐπαναχωρήσαντας αὐτοὺς δεῖξαι τῷ πλήθει, καὶ ἢν ἀρέσκοντα ᾖ, ἥκειν ἐς τὰ Ὑακίνθια τοὺς ὅρκους ποιησομένους.

What the Argives first demanded was that they might be allowed to refer to the arbitration of some state or private person the question of the Cynurian land, a borderland about which they have always been disputing, which contains the cities of Thyrea and Anthene, and which is occupied by the Spartans. The Spartans at first said that they could not allow this point to be discussed, but were ready to conclude upon the old terms. Eventually, however, the Argive ambassadors succeeded in obtaining from them this concession: -- For the present there was to be a truce for fifty years, but it should be competent for either party, there being neither plague nor war in Sparta or Argos, to give a formal challenge and decide the question of this territory by battle, as on a former occasion, when both sides claimed the victory; pursuit not being allowed beyond the frontier of Argos or Sparta. The Spartans at first thought this mere folly; but at last, anxious at any cost to have the friendship of Argos, they agreed to the terms

---

[2] Thucydides 5.36.1, 5.40.3.

demanded, and committed them to writing. However, before any of this should become binding, the ambassadors were to return to Argos and communicate with their people, and in the event of their approval, to come at the feast of the Hyacinthia and take the oaths.[3]

At this point the relations between Sparta and Athens become even more strained, owing to Alcibiades' intrigues. Alcibiades then orchestrates a treaty between Athens and Argos, persuading the Argives to abandon their agreement with the Spartans. In the following summer (419 BC) Argos enters into a war with the Spartan ally Epidaurus; the following year, the Spartans defeat the Argives in the battle of Mantinea.[4] The Peloponnesian war rolls on, and we are left to ponder the significance of the fleeting and idiosyncratic vision of peace that featured a battle for the disputed territory.

What advantage did the Argives seek by proposing to replay the battle for Cynuria? In the modern scholarship, the Argive suggestion is interpreted as an indulgence in nostalgic archaizing at the cost of realistic engagement with the political situation.[5] However, dismissing the Argive move as an outmoded oddity runs a serious risk of overlooking any pragmatic objectives that the Argives might have had. An attempt to understand the motivation that drove the Argives to propose the rerun of the battle has to begin from the question about the

---

[3] Thucydides 5.41.2-3. Trans. R. Crawley, modified.
[4] Thucydides 5.43-47, 5.53, 5.66-74.
[5] Hanson 2005, 344n37; Hornblower ([1983] 2011, 89) describes the Argive proposal as a "comic moment."

nature of the conflict for Cynuria. Why was Cynuria so central in the negotiations between Sparta and Argos?

It is unlikely that the importance of Cynuria derived from its economic or strategic worth.[6] Cynuria is an isolated mountainous area.[7] The mountain range of Parnon and the ridges of Mt Partheneion separate it, respectively, from both Sparta and Argos. Cynuria's economic value must have been insignificant:[8] it is not rich in natural resources, and poorly suited for agriculture — there are only two plains in it (one of them near the city of Thyrea, on the coast of the Argolic Gulf). Furthermore, the conflict between the Spartans and the Argives, referred to by Thucydides and Lucian, is regularly described in other sources as a conflict over the Thyreatis, the plain near Thyrea:[9] thus, the confrontation apparently focused on only a fraction of Cynuria.

A striking feature of Thucydides' concise presentation of the confrontation over Cynuria/Thyreatis is that the description of the course of the conflict supersedes the account of its causes. We learn a great deal about the conflict's temporal complexity. In the present moment of Thucydides' narrative, Cynuria is inhabited by the Spartans. However, Thucydides

---

[6] See below the discussion of Cynuria's value as a "buffer zone" (Kelly 1970a, 980) between Argos and Sparta.
[7] On the isolation of Cynuria, see Kelly 1970a, 979-980.
[8] Brelich 1961, 22; Kelly 1970a, 980; cf. Robertson 1992, 191.
[9] The ancient authors use the designations Thyrea, Thyreae and the Thyreatis to describe the area. I employ "the Thyreatis" throughout my discussion.

also portrays the Argives and the Spartans as *always* disputing over Cynuria, which is called a "borderland"[10] despite having been under Sparta's control from the middle of the sixth century BC.[11] A further temporal reference is introduced: a certain past occasion on which both Sparta and Argos considered themselves victors. This past occasion is put forward as a blueprint for a future battle for Cynuria.

The mentions of an earlier battle and of the conflict's perpetual nature indicate that the traditional history of the conflict played an important role in the conflict's present. Interestingly, the Argive proposal seeks to remove the issue of Cynuria from history into the safe space of ritual. The condition that in the battle for Cynuria the pursuit cannot proceed beyond the frontiers of Argos and Sparta disconnects the question of possession of Cynuria from the possibility of a wider territorial conquest. Moreover, the fight for this territory becomes the manifestation of concord between Argos and Sparta.

It follows from the prominence of history and ritual in the Argive proposal that the key to understanding the importance of Cynuria/Thyreatis in the Argive-Spartan relationship should be sought not in economic and strategic factors but in the ideology of the conflict over this territory. By the "ideology of the conflict" I mean a conceptual framework, including the

---

[10] γῆς...μεθορίας. Thucydides 5.41.2; also 2.27.2. Figueira (1993, 528–529) points out the peculiarity of Thucydides' definition of the Thyreatis/Cynuria as a borderland.
[11] On the dating of the Spartan annexation of Cynuria, see below.

past course of the conflict as conceived by each side, that informed the perception of the conflict's meaning. In this chapter, I will attempt to elucidate the particular visions of the past that the Argives and the Spartans might have operated with at the moment of the treaty. I will come back to the question concerning the synchronic practical gains the Argives were hoping to achieve by the treaty in Chapter 6. After reconstructing the ideology of the conflict, we will be in a better position to identify the ways in which this ideology was utilized and manipulated by the Argive proposal to ritualize the confrontation over Cynuria.

2. Was there a war?

Our most important source concerning the conflict over Cynuria/Thyreatis is Herodotus' description of the so-called battle of Champions (1.82). This battle is commonly identified with the "former occasion, when both sides claimed the victory," mentioned by Thucydides.[12] Herodotus dates the battle by the time of Croesus' appeal to the Spartans for help against the Persians (in 546 BC, by our reckoning). The Spartans, Herodotus tells us, had just seized the territory of Thyreatis from the Argives, who were ready to fight for the return of their land. The warring sides agreed that in lieu of a full-scale battle, only three hundred

---

[12] Thucydides 5.41.2. Hornblower 2008, 97 with further references.

men from each side should fight. The rest of the two armies departed to avoid involvement in the battle. In the course of fighting, only three men were left alive, two Argives and a Spartan. The Argives returned to Argos, believing that they had won, but the Spartan stripped the enemy corpses of armor and returned to his post in the Spartan camp. The next day, when both armies came back to learn the outcome, a disagreement broke out over who should be considered the victor; the argument turned into a fight, and after both sides had suffered many casualties, the Spartans defeated the Argives. This confrontation, Herodotus says, led to changes in both the Spartan and the Argive customs concerning their hairstyles: the Argives resolved to cut their hair short until they had won the Thyreatis back, while the Spartans started to grow their hair long.

Herodotus' tale about the battle of Champions is not the only surviving story about a military clash focused on Cynuria/Thyreatis. Thucydides' assertion that the Argives and the Spartans "always dispute" over Cynuria is matched by Pausanias' account, portraying Cynuria as a primordial conflict zone. Pausanias dates the first Spartan military involvement in Cynuria by the reign of Echestratus, the son of the eponymous Agis, and even prior to the reign of Prytanis, the son of the eponymous Eurypon.[13] He also refers to a struggle for the Thyreatis

---

[13] Pausanias 3.2.2, 3.7.2.

between the Spartans and Argives in the reign of Theopompus.¹⁴ Furthermore, Plutarch mentions a speech of Polydorus (the Agiad king contemporary with Theopompus, according to the inherited tradition), made on the occasion of the Spartan victory over the Argives, "after the battle of the three hundred."¹⁵ Plutarch's wording is interesting: he says that in the battle of the three hundred the Argives were "again" (πάλιν) defeated by the Spartans, suggesting a previous Spartan victory over the Argives in a battle of three hundred.¹⁶

The sources portray the dispute over Cynuria as remaining unresolved for a long time after the episode during the Peloponnesian War described by Thucydides: Pausanias mentions an arbitration of the disputed territory between Sparta and Argos by Philip and then again, by the Roman senator Gallus.¹⁷

A major advance in the understanding of the ideological underpinnings of the conflict over the Thyreatis was made by Angelo Brelich in his classic study *Guerre, agoni e culti nella Grecia arcaica*. Brelich called attention to the long duration of the conflict, the reports of its inception in legendary antiquity, and the incommensurability between the value of the

---

¹⁴ Pausanias 3.7.5. In addition, Pausanias transmits a tradition of the Spartan defeat by the Argives at Hysiae (Pausanias 2.24.7), which is often connected to the conflict over Cynuria in the modern literature (Wade-Gery 1949, 80; Brelich 1961, 23n29 gives other references); however, see Kelly 1970b.
¹⁵ Plutarch *Sayings of the Spartans* 231e.
¹⁶ Brelich 1961, 25.
¹⁷ Pausanias 7.11.1–2.

disputed territory and the scale of the conflict.[18] He also emphasized the repeated appearance of regulations, mitigating the magnitude of the fighting.[19] Brelich observed that the dispute over the Thyreatis shared these features with the war between Eretria and Chalcis for the Lelantine Plain. He noticed a resemblance between the aetiology of the Spartan and Argive hairstyles given by Herodotus, and a tradition associating the Curetic hairstyle with the Lelantine War,[20] and suggested that the references to hair-cutting tied these border conflicts to ritual initiations of young men into adulthood.[21]

Brelich also pointed out some religious connotations of the conflict over the Thyreatis. The conflict was linked with one of the most important Spartan festivals, the Gymnopaediae. The festival featured choruses of *paides* in honor of the Spartans who fell at Thyrea; the choral leaders wore wreaths called *thyreatikoi*, commemorating the victory at Thyrea.[22] The ritual celebration of the battle for the Thyreatis during the Gymnopaediae occurred in the

---

[18] Brelich 1961, 22, 29, 29–30n38.

[19] *Ibid.*, 29. The examples include the restriction of the number of the participants to three hundred on each side (Herodotus 1.82.3); the Argive proposal that the pursuit in a future battle for Cynuria should not go beyond the borders of Argos and Sparta (Thucydides 5.41.2); Polydorus' insistence in that the aim of the battle was solely the possession of the disputed territory and not the conquest of the enemy's city (Plutarch *Sayings of the Spartans* 231e).

[20] Brelich 1961, 30.

[21] *Ibid.*, 80-81.

[22] *Ibid.*, 30–31. Sosibius ap. Athenaeus 15.678b-c, *Anecdota Bekker* 1, 32, *Suda* s.v. Γυμνοπαίδια.

framework of the cult of Apollo Pythaeus,[23] a divine figure important in Laconia, and at the same time strongly associated with Argos.[24] Brelich remarked that Apollo Pythaeus was connected to the confrontation between Argos and Sparta,[25] and also apparently once united the two city-states in some sort of federal cult.[26] Brelich concluded that the dispute over the Thyreatis (as well as the Lelantine war) originated as a ritual combat for the border territory, during which the participants transitioned from the status of ephebes to adulthood. Over time, these ritual combats were transformed into real wars, leaving only an "aura" of cultic and ritual associations.[27]

However, Brelich himself admitted that such an explanation left some problems unresolved. The relation between the ritual limitation of violence and apparent cases of severe bloodshed is perplexing. For example, in Herodotus' narrative, the regulation limiting the number of the combatants to three hundreds on each side is combined with the annihilation of all but three participants.[28]

---

[23] Pausanias 3.11.9; Brelich 1961, 31.
[24] Brelich 1961, 32, 34. Ancient sources (Telesilla ap. Pausanias 2.35.2) claim that the epithet Pythaeus is originally Argive. We will discuss the traditions connected with Apollo Pythaeus below in more detail.
[25] According to a tradition reported by Pausanias, the cult of Apollo Pythaeus in Asine figured in an ancient episode of the Spartan-Argive hostilities. Pausanias 2.36.4. Brelich 1961, 32.
[26] Thucydides 5.53.1, Diodorus Siculus 12.78.1. Brelich 1961, 33–34.
[27] Brelich 1961, 83–84.
[28] *Ibid.*, 79.

A further and major problem is that Brelich's "ritual aura" does not explain the nature of fighting over the Thyreatis once the ritual combats, according to Brelich's model, were transformed into real confrontations. Brelich perceived the cultic and ritual details, cropping up in our sources in connection to the dispute over the Thyreatis, as synchronically inconsequential, stripped of their "original" initiatory context in the distant past.[29] However, the perpetuation of a ritual at a given moment in time tends to endow it with a range of current functions and significances.[30] Therefore, a proper reconstruction of a ritual must consider its successive modifications in form, content and function over a span of time: the rituals connected to the confrontation over the Thyreatis need to be embedded in their historical contexts. Finally, Brelich's analysis presents an additional methodological problem in that Brelich uses the sources in an undifferentiated fashion, without distinguishing between earlier and later ones.

Indeed, Thomas Kelly, who carefully examined the ancient sources on the history of the strife between Sparta and Argos in a chronological manner, came to the following unsettling conclusion: "the later the writer the more he professes to know about the early warfare

---

[29] Thus, for example, Brelich mentions the Argive proposal to the Spartans of replaying the battle for Thyreatis (Brelich 1961, 17), but he does not offer any remarks on the import of this suggestion in 420 BC.
[30] Kowalzig 2007a, 34.

between the two states."³¹ Kelly asserts that the centuries-long struggle between Argos and Sparta, stemming from the earliest times, was invented in the fourth century BC and then elaborated on by the later historians.³²

The gist of Kelly's argument is as follows. The earliest mention of the conflict between Argos and Sparta is Herodotus' description of the battle of Champions; the passage of Thucydides about the Argive suggestion to replay the battle is the next oldest reference.³³ Both sources portray the conflict as focused solely on the issue of the territory of Cynuria/Thyreatis.³⁴ On this subject Kelly observes that the only accessible road from Sparta to Cynuria passed through the territory of Tegea; the alternative mountainous route was very difficult.³⁵ Kelly infers that a precondition for Sparta's being strategically interested in the occupation of Cynuria (as a buffer zone protecting the Spartans from a potential Argive attack and making a Spartan attack on the Argive plain possible) was Spartan dominance over Tegea.³⁶ Sparta achieved hegemony over Tegea sometime in the middle of the sixth century,³⁷

---

³¹ Kelly 1970a, 1000.
³² *Ibid.*
³³ For a discussion of Tyrtaeus F 23a West, P. Oxy. 3316, not yet discovered at the time of Kelly's article, but now sometimes cited as an Archaic evidence of the war between Sparta and Argos (Cartledge [1979] 2002, 109; Jameson 1994, 70n17; Figueira 1993, 31n59), see below.
³⁴ Kelly 1970a, 974, 979-80.
³⁵ A detailed discussion of the road network in the Thyreatis/Cynuria is in Tausend 2006, 126-136.
³⁶ Kelly 1970a, 980-81.

which therefore must provide a *terminus post quem* for the Spartan military interest in Cynuria. This date fits well with the date of the battle of Champions derived from Herodotus (546 BC); after that point there is an unambiguous record of continual hostilities between Sparta and Argos.[38]

Kelly argues that the ancient writers coming after Herodotus and Thucydides were influenced by the post-mid-sixth-century hostile relations between Sparta and Argos and assumed that the two states were antagonistic throughout their history.[39] The first mention of a specific conflict between Sparta and Argos predating the battle of Champions is found in Ephorus, whom Kelly credits with the introduction of the idea of strife between Argos and Sparta as the defining theme of the early Peloponnesian history.[40] For Pausanias the traditional enmity between the two states was a given. Pausanias makes numerous references to it, providing, for example, a list of six early Spartan kings who engaged in confrontations with the Argives. Kelly remarks that the kings on the list belong to such a remote past that their

---

[37] Kelly 1970a, 975n16 with further references; Cartledge [1979] 2002, 118–120; Thommen 1996, 56, 58–60.
[38] Kelly 1970a, 984.
[39] *Ibid.*
[40] *Ibid.*, 985.

historicity is highly unlikely; for him, the list is an example of a later baroque embellishment on the theme of primordial Argive-Spartan strife.[41]

Kelly's analysis seems to undercut several points of Brelich's argument, such as the early inception of the conflict for the Thyreatis and the long duration of the conflict. However, at this point a crucial distinction must be made between the historical reality of the centuries-long confrontation over Cynuria/Thyreatis and the historical reality of the *tradition* describing such confrontation. I consider Kelly's argument about the mid-sixth century inception of Sparta's military involvement in Cynuria to be persuasive; however, his claim that the tradition of the ancient conflict between Argos and Sparta was invented in the fourth century is less convincing. While it is plausible that the specific details concerning the early confrontation are a later elaboration, already Thucydides states that the two states were "always disputing" over Cynuria.[42] Plato and Xenophon also share a belief in a tradition of the primordial conflict between Sparta and Argos.[43] Further, our earliest source, Herodotus' account, contains elements such as the equal numbers of the battle participants on each side, or the aetiology of haircuts, highly evocative of ritual. Thus, Herodotus does not provide us with a dry military report of the battle of Champions in 546 BC as an inception of Argive-

---

[41] Kelly 1970a, 994–95.
[42] αἰεὶ ... διαφέρονται, Thucydides 5.41.2. Thucydides' wording elicits Kelly's objection, not backed up by any evidence, that αἰεί "cannot be taken in temporal sense." Kelly 1970a, 974n10.
[43] Plato *Laws* 3.686b, Xenophon *Hell.* 3.5.11. Kelly 1970a, 985nn53,54.

Spartan conflict: rather, his description suggests that he is familiar with the tradition of the conflict, endowed with ritual overtones. Let us attempt to reconstruct the various stages of the development of this tradition. The starting point for this reconstruction should obviously be a closer examination of our earliest source, Herodotus.

3. To flee or not to flee

In the next section I will attempt to distinguish separate strands joined together by Herodotus in his account of the battle of Champions. However, before such an analysis, it is important to identify large-scale narrative "adhesive forces" that hold different elements of the episode together. That is to say, we need to understand the place of the battle of Champions in the overall trajectory of Herodotus' narrative.

The tale of the battle of Champions has a clear parallel in the *Histories* in the narrative of Thermopylae. Both battles involve a participation of three hundred Spartans, all but one of whom die.[44] Thus, a reasonable starting point is to assume that the description of the confrontation over the Thyreatis introduces and develops some of the themes that are later

---

[44] Tomlinson 1972, 88–89; Dillery 1996.

sounded in the focal story of Thermopylae. But what exactly does the account of the battle for the Thyreatis contribute to the tale of Thermopylae?

Herodotus portrays the Spartans gaining their distinctive long-haired appearance as an aftermath of the battle for the Thyreatis (1.82.8). The motif of hair resurfaces in the narrative of Thermopylae, when a scout, sent by Xerxes to spy on the enemy before the battle, reports that the Spartans are engaged in combing their locks (7.208.3). Xerxes is astonished, upon which Demaratus explains to him that for the Spartans "it is their tradition that they groom their hair whenever they are about to put their lives in danger" (ἐπεὰν μέλλωσι κινδυνεύειν τῇ ψυχῇ, τότε τὰς κεφαλὰς κοσμέονται, Herodotus 7.209.3).[45] Nicole Loraux notes that in this scene the Spartans may be "preparing to be beautiful corpses:"[46] they are getting ready for the Spartan beautiful death, in which the ethical qualities of bravery and unflinching self-control are fused with the aesthetic vision of corporeal beauty.[47]

The association of long hair with the theme of beautiful death brings out the more somber overtones in the commemoration of the battle for the Thyreatis. The custom of growing long hair turns out to be not only a joyful sign of triumph, but also an expression of readiness, if need be, to die beautifully, in emulation of the three hundred at Thyrea. By

---

[45] Tomlinson 1972, 88; Dillery 1996, 219.
[46] Loraux 1995, 74; David 1992, 16.
[47] Loraux 1995, 65–66, and 275n25.

narrating the story of the battle for the Thyreatis, Herodotus introduces the theme of the Spartan beautiful death at the very inception of the events leading to the Greco-Persian wars, prefiguring the climactic return of this theme at Thermopylae.

The fates of the survivors of the battles of Thyrea and Thermopylae, Othryades and Aristodemus, seem to be thematically connected as well. At the very end of the description of the confrontation over the Thyreatis, Herodotus reports that Othryades committed suicide, ashamed to be the only one left of his three hundred comrades (1.82.8). Many scholars noted that Othryades' act is driven by exceedingly harsh standards of honor, verging on the illogical:[48] it is precisely the *survival* of Othryades that serves as a foundation for the Spartan claim to victory, yet Othryades is ashamed to remain alive. The same harshness of judgment characterizes the story of Aristodemus, the sole survivor of Thermopylae, prevented from participating in the fighting by a severe eye disease (7.229.1). Aristodemus was consequently dishonored at Sparta as a 'trembler,' and then fell at Plataea after proving himself one of the bravest fighters (7.231, 9.71.2). Jean Ducat shows that the fate of Aristodemus was the subject of an ancient debate, in which Herodotus was passionately on the side of Aristodemus'

---

[48] On the anomalous nature of Othryades' suicide see Dillery 1996, 227; Loraux 1995, 73 and 280n112; Arieti 1995, 96; Robertson 1992, 201; Tomlinson 1972, 89; Macan 1908, 341.

defenders.⁴⁹ Herodotus considers Aristodemus "by far the best" fighter at Plataea (9.71.2), in sharp disagreement with the Spartan official judgment, which, as Herodotus reports, refrained from bestowing on Aristodemus any posthumous honors (9.71.4). Thus, in the stories of both battles, the theme of the beautiful death is darkened by an accompanying motif of the fanatical Spartan severity.

The battle of Plataea, in which Aristodemus showed his worth, turns out to be also connected thematically with the battle of Champions. After ten days during which the Greeks and the Persians are just camped opposite each other at Plataea, Mardonius decides to attack. The Greeks are forewarned about Mardonius' plan, and the Spartans change places with the Athenians, so that the Athenians, who have the experience of fighting the Persians at Marathon, will be stationed opposite the Persians also at Plataea. Mardonius notes the maneuver and also shifts his positions, so that the Spartans again face the Persians. The Spartans move back to the Greek right wing, and Mardonius accordingly changes his positions (Herodotus 9.46-47). After this series of actions, Mardonius sends a jeering message to the Spartans (9.48.1-2):

---

⁴⁹ Ducat 2006b, 34-38. The connection between the tales of ignominy, experienced by Spartan lone survivors of Thyrea and Thermopylae, is enhanced by Herodotus' brief mention of Pantites, an alternative 'sole survivor' of Thermopylae, who hanged himself from the dishonor to which he was subjected upon his return to Sparta (Herodotus 7.232).

"ὦ Λακεδαιμόνιοι, ὑμεῖς δὴ λέγεσθε εἶναι ἄνδρες ἄριστοι ὑπὸ τῶν τῇδε ἀνθρώπων, ἐκπαγλεομένων ὡς οὔτε φεύγετε ἐκ πολέμου οὔτε τάξιν ἐκλείπετε, μένοντές τε ἢ ἀπόλλυτε τοὺς ἐναντίους ἢ αὐτοὶ ἀπόλλυσθε. τῶν δ' ἄρ' ἦν οὐδὲν ἀληθές· πρὶν γὰρ ἢ συμμῖξαι ἡμέας ἐς χειρῶν τε νόμον ἀπικέσθαι, καὶ δὴ φεύγοντας καὶ στάσιν ἐκλείποντας ὑμέας εἴδομεν..."

"Men of Lacedaemon, you are said by the people of these parts to be very brave men. It is their boast of you that you neither flee from the field nor leave your post, but remain there and either slay your enemies or are yourselves killed. It would seem, however, that there is no truth in all this, for before we could attack and fight hand to hand, we saw you even now fleeing and leaving your station..."

Mardonius ends his message by challenging the Spartans to fight with the Persians in an equal fight (9.48.4):

τί δὴ οὐ πρὸ μὲν τῶν Ἑλλήνων ὑμεῖς, ἐπείτε δεδόξωσθε εἶναι ἄριστοι, πρὸ δὲ τῶν βαρβάρων ἡμεῖς **ἴσοι πρὸς ἴσους ἀριθμὸν** ἐμαχεσάμεθα;

What is there to prevent us from fighting with equal numbers on both sides, you for the Greeks (since you have the reputation of being their best), and we for the barbarians?

Mardonius' message has prominent points of intersection with the battle of the Champions. The challenge to fight with equal numbers on both sides is one obvious connection; the statement that the Spartans either slay their enemy or are themselves slain is another one. Mardonius' sneer that he previously thought that the Spartans neither flee nor leave their posts (οὔτε **φεύγετε** ἐκ πολέμου οὔτε **τάξιν** ἐκλείπετε, 9.48.1) also has an exact parallel in the battle of the Champions: after the two Argive survivors run to the Argive camp, Othryades strips the Argive corpses and then remains at his assigned post (ἐν τῇ τάξι, Herodotus 1.82.5).

Othryades' behavior is the basis of the Spartan claim of victory, since they assert that the two Argives fled (πεφευγότας, 1.82.6), while their man remained at his post.

Thus, essentially Mardonius challenges the Spartans to have another battle of Champions, with the Persians instead of the Argives. The Spartan answer to this proposition is silence (Herodotus 9.49.1).

Mardonius' offer has an antecedent in the *Histories*. It is Mardonius' famous description of the peculiar Greek style of warfare (Herodotus 7.9b.1):

> καίτοι γε ἐώθασι Ἕλληνες, ὡς πυνθάνομαι, ἀβουλότατα πολέμους ἵστασθαι ὑπό τε ἀγνωμοσύνης καὶ σκαιότητος. ἐπεὰν γὰρ ἀλλήλοισι πόλεμον προείπωσι, ἐξευρόντες τὸ κάλλιστον χωρίον καὶ λειότατον, ἐς τοῦτο κατιόντες μάχονται, ὥστε σὺν κακῷ μεγάλῳ οἱ νικῶντες ἀπαλλάσσονται· περὶ δὲ τῶν ἐσσουμένων οὐδὲ λέγω ἀρχήν· ἐξώλεες γὰρ δὴ γίνονται·

> Besides, from all I hear, the Greeks usually wage war in an extremely stupid fashion, because they are ignorant and incompetent. When they declare war on one another they seek out the best, most level piece of land, and that is where they go to fight. The upshot is that the victors leave the battlefield with massive losses, not to mention the losers, who are completely wiped out.[50]

This passage, also evocative of the battle of the Champions, has been described by Peter Krentz as a foundation of the "agonal model of Greek warfare." Krentz notes: "As Mardonius learned, however, he was mostly wrong."[51] Krentz uses this observation as a jumping board for a

---

[50] Trans. Krentz 2007, 147.

[51] Krentz 2007, 147. Cf. Dayton 2006, 52–53.

historical review of Greek warfare; what interests me now is rather to understand how, and why, Mardonius was wrong in the framework of Herodotus' narrative.

A useful concept to employ is a "war of total annihilation," formulated by Pierre Ellinger.[52] The war of total annihilation is an opposition of agonal warfare; it is a life-and-death situation threatening the existence of the whole community, not just a group of warriors. I think it is fair to say that from Herodotus' point of view, the victory of the Persians similarly threatens the very foundation of Greek identity. Accordingly, when Mardonius suggests that the Spartans and the Persians should fight in the Greek manner, obeying the agonal ethos, he misconstrues the situation: in the case of the Persian wars the rules of *agôn* do not apply.

Herodotus' presentation of the subsequent events at Plataea revolves around the theme of fleeing or staying at one's post. Immediately after Mardonius' challenge, Mardonius, pleased by his "vain victory" (ψυχρῇ νίκῃ, 9.49.1), sends his mounted archers to destroy a spring from which the whole Greek army takes water (9.41.2).[53] The Greeks, deprived of water, decide to relocate. However, Spartan Amompharetus refuses to move (9.53.2):

> ἐνθαῦτα οἱ μὲν ἄλλοι ἄρτιοι ἦσαν τῶν ταξιάρχων πείθεσθαι Παυσανίῃ, Ἀμομφάρετος δὲ ὁ Πολιάδεω λοχηγέων τοῦ Πιτανητέων λόχου οὐκ ἔφη τοὺς ξείνους **φεύξεσθαι** οὐδὲ ἑκὼν εἶναι αἰσχυνέειν τὴν Σπάρτην,

---

[52] Ellinger 1993.
[53] The destruction of the water source interestingly recalls the Delphic Amphyctyony's prohibition to deprive any of its member states of water in time of war or peace (Aeschines *On the Embassy* 115): Mardonius' act demonstrates that the war does not follow the agonal rules.

> Thereupon, all the rest of the captains being ready to obey Pausanias, Amompharetus son of Poliades, the leader of the Pitanate battalion, refused to <u>flee</u> from the barbarians or (save by compulsion) bring shame on Sparta; ...

The Spartan commanders Pausanias and Euryanax attempt to convince Amompharetus to move; they are infuriated at his disobedience but even more worried that the Pitanate battalion will perish (ἀπόληται, 9.53.3) if the rest of the Spartan troops move on. The argument continues and becomes a quarrel, during which Amompharetus puts a huge rock before Pausanias' feet (9.55.2),

> ταύτῃ τῇ ψήφῳ ψηφίζεσθαι ἔφη **μὴ φεύγειν** τοὺς ξείνους, λέγων τοὺς βαρβάρους,
>
> crying that it was the pebble with which he voted <u>against fleeing</u> from the strangers (meaning thereby the barbarians).

In the logic of Herodotus' narrative, Amompharetus misconstrues the situation, believing that the agonal ethos applies to the situation of fighting with the Persians. For this, Pausanias calls Amompharetus an insane madman (9.55.2).

The quarrel continues for the whole night; at dawn, the rest of the Spartan forces finally move, but stop after half a mile (9.57.2):

> ἀνέμενε δὲ τοῦδε εἵνεκα, ἵνα ἢν μὴ ἀπολείπῃ τὸν χῶρον **ἐν τῷ ἐτετάχατο** ὁ Ἀμομφάρετός τε καὶ ὁ λόχος, ἀλλ' αὐτοῦ μένωσι, βοηθέοι ὀπίσω παρ' ἐκείνους.
>
> The reason for their waiting was that, if Amompharetus and his battalion should not leave <u>the place where it was posted</u> but remain there, they would then be able to assist him.

When Amompharetus realizes that his battalion is abandoned, he finally moves and slowly goes toward the main body of Spartan troops. At the moment when he joins them, the Persian cavalry attacks the Spartans (9.57.3). Mardonius watches the Spartans relocating and jeers at them again, repeating that he used to hear that the Spartans do not flee in battle (οὐ φεύγειν ἐκ μάχης), but that he just saw them leaving their battle positions (ἐκ τῆς τάξιος), and running away (διαδράντας). He concludes that the Spartans showed themselves to be nobodies among other Greek nobodies (ὅτι οὐδένες ἄρα ἐόντες ἐν οὐδαμοῖσι ἐοῦσι Ἕλλησι ἐναπεδεικνύατο, 9.58.2).

Thus, the underlying theme of Herodotus' description of the battle of Plataea is a discussion whether it is appropriate to fight the Persians in the style of the battle of Champions, that is, on equal terms and without leaving one's position. Importantly, Herodotus comments that the main factor in the Greek victory at Plataea was that they were armed differently from the Persians: Herodotus' striking formulation is that the Persians "fought, as it were, naked against men fully armed" (πρὸς γὰρ ὁπλίτας ἐόντες γυμνῆτες ἀγῶνα ἐποιεῦντο, 9.63.2).

Herodotus' portrayals of the battles of Thermopylae and Plataea develop themes introduced in the battle of Champions; they do it in opposing and complementary fashions. At Thermopylae, the Spartan emulation of the three hundred Champions against vastly predominant Persian forces is shown as heroic.[54] At Plataea, Amompharetus' attempt to follow the Champions' example is represented as dangerous and senseless. So, while the survival of the Greeks is contingent on the Spartan self-sacrifice at Thermopyale, for victory at Plataea they need to abandon the too-rigid position.[55]

4. What Herodotus has joined together

In Herodotus' presentation of the battle of Champions, the equal number of battle participants on both sides and the extreme lethality of the confrontation are welded together thematically in the picture of fighting as fair as it is devastating. We have seen how this combination functions in Herodotus' narrative. However, if we now apply the criterion of verisimilitude to the passage, it will become obvious that the outcome of the battle of

---

[54] Clarke 2002 detects some darker overtones in Herodotus' description of the fighting at Thermopylae (akin to Amompharetus' "madness").
[55] It is tempting to interpret Herodotus' two variant stories about the best of the Athenians, Sophanes, at Plataea as an expression of the "rigid" and "flexible" points of view: according to the first version, Sophanes had an iron anchor attached to him, which he would throw at his battle position to ensure that he stay there (Herodotus 9.74.1); according to the second version, an anchor was a blazon on Sophanes' shield, "which he constantly whirled round and never held still" (αἰεὶ περιθεούσης καὶ οὐδαμὰ ἀτρεμιζούσης, 9.74.2).

Champions — the death of all but three participants — is extraordinary.[56] A hoplite battle in which all of the participants are killed off is easier accommodated in the world of myth than in the world of military history. A more careful look at the episode also reveals disturbing anachronisms and aberrations. First, it has been observed long ago that Herodotus' description of Argive supremacy in the Peloponnese at the time of the Spartan attack[57] brings to mind the legendary past of Agamemnon's rule over the islands rather than the realia of the sixth century BC.[58] Moreover, Herodotus contradicts himself: a little earlier he noted that at the conclusion of a military alliance with Croesus, "the Spartans had conquered the greater part of the Peloponnese" (ἤδη δέ σφι καὶ ἡ πολλὴ τῆς Πελοποννήσου ἦν κατεστραμμένη, 1.68.6). Furthermore, 546 BC seems late for the Spartan adoption of long hair: representations of long-haired Spartan youths are attested much earlier.[59]

---

[56] The rate of mortality in a hoplite battle has been assessed as three to ten percent for the winning side, and ten to twenty percent for the defeated one. Krentz 1985, 18; Hanson 1999, 302–307.

[57] Ἦν δὲ καὶ ἡ μέχρι Μαλέων ἡ πρὸς ἑσπέρην Ἀργείων, ἥ τε ἐν τῇ ἠπείρῳ χώρῃ καὶ ἡ Κυθηρίη νῆσος καὶ αἱ λοιπαὶ τῶν νήσων. "At this time the land as far as Malis in the west belonged to the Argives, both the mainland and the islands, including Cythera and the rest." Herodotus 1.82.2. All translations from Herodotus are by A. L. Purvis.

[58] Beloch 1912, 204n1; Kelly 1970a, 977–78; Tomlinson 1972, 88; tentatively, Asheri, Lloyd, and Corcella 2007, 139. Cf. Herodotus 1.1.2.

[59] Tomlinson 1972, 89; Lipka 2002, 194. For Plutarch, this custom possessed the antiquity of Lycurgus' ordinance. Plutarch *Lysander* 1.2-3. David 1992, 14. Plutarch's statement that the long hair is Lycurgus' regulation explicitly contests the tradition that the Spartans grew their hair long after the battle over the Thyreatis, reported by Herodotus.

The historical inconsistencies in Herodotus' account of the battle of Champions, which is commonly interpreted as a straightforward chronological account of the past,[60] compel us to examine the battle's dating. As we have seen, the modern date of the battle of Champions (546 BC) matches Kelly's reconstruction that the Spartans became interested in the annexation of Cynuria after they had gained control of Tegea. While we lack a literary source, contemporary or earlier than Herodotus, that would corroborate Herodotus' dating of the Spartan conquest, an archaeologically attested explosive appearance of Spartan settlements in Cynuria in the middle of the sixth century fits the date provided by Herodotus.[61] Thus, it is likely that Herodotus' account of the Spartan annexation of Cynuria in the middle of the sixth century has some foundation in reality.

However, one should observe that the connection between the battle of Champions and Croesus' appeal for help against the Persians, on which the precise dating of the battle is founded, is extremely flimsy. The story of the battle appears in a vignette that turns out to have no causal relation with the Spartan assistance to Croesus:[62] the Spartans decide to help Croesus *despite* their conflict with the Argives (Herodotus 1.83), but then the news of Croesus' capture arrives as they are ready to sail out, so they cancel the expedition. This lack of causal

---

[60] As recently as Kennell 2010, 52.
[61] Kennell 2010, 52. Cartledge ([1979] 2002, 123) also accepts this date for the Spartan annexation of Thyreatis.
[62] Dillery 1996, 221.

relation elicits a suspicion that Herodotus attached the description of the battle of Champions to Croesus' appeal on some other grounds than his rigorous knowledge of the historical link between the two events. Indeed, the presentation of the battle episode at the point of Croesus' appeal is a characteristic Herodotean device of introducing details about events outside the main narrative through a reference to an embassy or exploratory mission.[63] An example of another such excursus, attached to Croesus' story, is a review of the early Athenian and Spartan histories (1.56–69), introduced on the occasion of Croesus' search for Greek allies. The thematic importance of the battle of Champions in the *Histories* suggests that Herodotus could use Croesus' appeal for help as a "peg" on which to hang the story of the battle.

It is reasonable to infer that Herodotus' account of the fighting over the Thyreatis links up a legendary tradition of the lethal battle to Croesus' time. Suggestions along these lines have been made in the past by Richard Tomlinson and Noel Robertson.[64] Yet both these scholars, in different ways, underestimate the potential significance of such a legend. Tomlinson focuses on the historical reality of the interactions between Argos and Sparta in the sixth century BC. Thus, while he notices the "romanticizing" in Herodotus' account and poses a question concerning its causes, he leaves the question unanswered.[65] Robertson asserts that

---

[63] Cf. Dillery 1996, 220 on this digression as explainable by the "structure of archaic narrative."
[64] Tomlinson 1972, 89; Robertson 1992, 184; Kõiv 2003, 131.
[65] Tomlinson 1972, 89.

the story of the battle of Champions was "invented" as aetiology of a certain festival.[66] However, such a privileging of the ritual at the expense of the affiliated myth disregards the interactions between the ritual and the myth, which are arguably central in the generation of messages.[67] My argument will attempt to examine the historical implications of the mythical tradition about the battle for the Thyreatis considered jointly with its allied rituals.

Ritual connotations, as we have already observed, are conspicuous in the description of the battle of Champions. The aetiology of the Spartan and Argive hairstyles suggests an association with rites of passage.[68] Specifically, in Sparta, according to Jean Ducat's reconstruction, men were allowed to grow long hair after leaving the age grade of *hêbôntes*.[69] A subtler point, also indicative of a ritual, is a paradoxical pattern of cooperation between Sparta and Argos, emerging from Herodotus' phrasing. Herodotus reports that the Spartan custom of wearing long hair was established as an opposite of the Argive adoption of short hair.[70] The

---

[66] Robertson 1992, 207.
[67] The definition of myth with which I operate is "a given society's codification of its own traditional values in narrative and dramatic form." Nagy 1990a, 436. Similarly, Lincoln 1999, 147. On the relation between myth and ritual, see the discussion in Kowalzig 2007a, 22-23.
[68] Brelich 1961, 80-81; Robertson 1992, 206; Dillon 1999, 72n50.
[69] Ducat 2006a, 109-111, based on Xenophon *Constitution of Sparta* 11.3. Cf. Pettersson 1992, 85. *Hêbôntes* were men between 20 and 30 years old, the oldest age group that did not have full citizen status (despite its prominence in military service). Ducat 2006a, 104-112; Lupi 2000, 31-46.
[70] Λακεδαιμόνιοι δὲ τὰ ἐναντία τούτων ἔθεντο νόμον· "The Spartans established a contrary regulation." Herodotus 1.82.8.

Argives and the Spartans appear to define themselves through their antagonism; their hair-related customs are contrasting and complementary, operating in one system of signification.

Thus, even a relatively rapid examination of the passage uncovers interlocking elements of history (the Spartan annexation of the Thyreatis), myth (the lethal battle of Champions) and ritual (the hair customs). The joining together of such elements, often stemming from different sources, is at the heart of Herodotus' historical method.[71] Sometimes Herodotus identifies his sources; at other times different narrative strands are amalgamated. Moreover, in many cases it is possible to pinpoint the modifications that Herodotus made in traditional accounts included in his *History*.[72] The following discussion will attempt to determine the outlines of the constituent traditions that Herodotus merged in his description of the dispute over the Thyreatis, and to identify, to the extent possible, the adjustments that he introduced.

---

[71] Bakker 2002, 15, 18–19, 29; cf. Dewald 2002, 283, 286–287; Griffiths 2006, 140.
[72] Burkert 1965; Griffiths 1989; Calame 2003, 86–108; Giangiulio 2001; Giangiulio 2005; Griffiths 2006, 140–141.

5. Beautiful death in the Thyreatis

We have explored the thematic functioning of the motifs recurring in Herodotus' depictions of the fighting at Thyrea and Thermopylae. But what is the nature of these repetitions? How do we explain the striking similarities (the three hundred Spartans, the sole survivor, the reference to hair) between Herodotus' descriptions of the two battles? John Dillery contemplates potential answers to this question.[73] All the possibilities that he considers involve Herodotus, consciously or unconsciously, patterning the accounts of Thyrea and Thermopylae after one another.[74] Dillery concludes that the similarities are not the result of an intentional shaping of the events by Herodotus, but are an outcome of a formulaic thinking on Herodotus' part, unconsciously molding comparable events, such as battles, into analogous shapes.[75] This conclusion, while absolving Herodotus from the accusations of falsifying the historical record,[76] presents a rather unflattering picture of his mental functioning: it is difficult to imagine that Herodotus could have remained unaware of the striking similarities that his mind was allegedly imposing on the descriptions of the two battles. However, I propose an alternative explanation of the aforementioned resemblances: the tradition of the

---

[73] Dillery 1996.
[74] Ibid., 234.
[75] Ibid., 248–249.
[76] Ibid., 236–237.

fighting over the Thyreatis could have molded the tradition of Thermopylae independently and prior to Herodotus.[77] I have suggested in the previous section that the story of the lethal battle of Champions is a myth: as such, it could have influenced both the actual events at Thermopylae and the stories about that battle.[78]

I have proposed that Herodotus combined the mythical tale of a deadly battle for the Thyreatis and some ritual elements (whose nature I will discuss in the next section) with the historically veracious narrative of a large-scale confrontation between Sparta and Argos that resulted in the Spartan appropriation of Cynuria. Furthermore, I have observed that in Herodotus' account, the story of the battle for Thyrea is associated with the Spartan ideology of beautiful death.

The idea that Herodotus combined the myth of a lethal battle and the account of a historical confrontation receives some support from the existence of alternative versions of the fighting for Thyreatis. First, while the references to fighting for the Thyreatis in the time of the Spartan kings Theopompus and Polydorus[79] are likely to be later elaborations of ancient scholars, they demonstrate the perception of the fighting as belonging to legendary antiquity,

---

[77] The tradition of Thermopylae, most likely, retrospectively changed the tradition of Thyrea as well.
[78] See Section 10.
[79] Pausanias 3.7.5, Plutarch *Sayings of the Spartans* 231e.

thus corroborating its mythical character. Further, a version reported by Plutarch presents the battle of six hundred Champions as unaccompanied by further military conflict:

Ἀργείων καὶ Λακεδαιμονίων ὑπὲρ Θυρεάτιδος χώρας πολεμούντων οἱ Ἀμφικτύονες ἔκριναν πολεμῆσαι ἑκατέρ<ων τριακοσί>ους καὶ τῶν νικησάντων εἶναι τὴν χώραν. Λακεδαιμόνιοι μὲν οὖν Ὀθρυάδην ἐποίησαν στρατηγὸν Ἀργεῖοι δὲ Θέρσανδρον. πολεμούντων δὲ δύο ἐκ τῶν Ἀργείων περιελείφθησαν, Ἀγήνωρ καὶ Χρόμιος, οἵτινες εἰς τὴν πόλιν ἤγγειλαν τὴν νίκην. ἠρεμίας δ' ὑπαρχούσης ὁ Ὀθρυάδης ἐπιζήσας καὶ ἡμικλάστοις δόρασιν ἐπερειδόμενος τὰς τῶν νεκρῶν ἁπάντων ἀσπίδας περιείλετο· καὶ τρόπαιον στήσας ἐκ τοῦ ἰδίου αἵματος ἐπέγραψε 'Διὶ τροπαιούχῳ.' καὶ τῶν δήμων στάσιν ἐχόντων οἱ Ἀμφικτύονες αὐτόπται γενόμενοι Λακεδαιμονίους προκρίνουσι· καθάπερ Χρύσερμος ἐν τρίτῳ Πελοποννησιακῶν.

When Argives and Spartans were contending for the Thyreatis, the Amphictyonic Assembly decreed that three hundred of each should fight, and the country should belong to the victors. The Spartans accordingly made Othryades their general and the Argives made Thersander theirs. In the battle two of the Argives survived, Agenor and Chromius, who brought to their city the report of their victory. But when the battlefield was deserted, Othryades revived and, supporting himself on spear-shafts broken in two, despoiled and stripped the corpses of their shields; and when he had erected a trophy, he wrote with his own blood upon it: 'To Zeus, Guardian of Trophies.' And when the two peoples still disputed over the victory,[80] the Amphictyonic Assembly, after a personal inspection of the battlefield, decided in favor of the Spartans. Thus Chrysermus in the third book of his *Peloponnesian History*.[81]

We shall return to the peculiar detail of the Amphictyonic Assembly arbitrating between the Spartans and the Argives. Let us now examine another point of difference between the versions of Herodotus and Plutarch/Chrysermus: the fate and function of the last Spartan to remain alive, Othryades. In Plutarch, Othryades' story lacks the bipartite

---

[80] Compare Thucydides 5.41.2: "when both sides claimed the victory."
[81] Plutarch *Greek and Roman Parallel Stories* 306a-b. Trans. F. C. Babbitt.

development, reported by Herodotus: first the survival, afterwards the suicide. Rather, all lights are trained on the single scene of Othryades' glorious death, unattended by any shame.

The same story is found in several other sources, including an epigram attributed to Simonides (*Greek Anthology* 7.431):[82]

> Οἵδε τριηκόσιοι, Σπάρτα πατρί, τοῖς συναρίθμοις
> Ἰναχίδαις Θυρέαν ἀμφὶ μαχεσσάμενοι,
> αὐχένας οὐ στρέψαντες, ὅπᾳ ποδὸς ἴχνια πρᾶτον
> ἁρμόσαμεν, ταύτᾳ καὶ λίπομεν βιοτάν.
> ἄρσενι δ' Ὀθρυάδαο φόνῳ κεκαλυμμένον ὅπλον
> καρύσσει· "Θυρέα, Ζεῦ, Λακεδαιμονίων."
> αἰ δέ τις Ἀργείων ἔφυγεν μόρον, ἦς ἀπ' Ἀδράστου·
> Σπάρτᾳ δ' οὐ τὸ θανεῖν, ἀλλὰ φυγεῖν θάνατος.

> We, the three hundred, O Spartan fatherland,
> fighting for Thyrea with as many Argives,
> never turning our necks, died there
> where we first planted our feet.
> The shield, covered with the brave blood of Othryades
> proclaims "Thyrea, O Zeus, is of the Lacedaemonians."
> But if any Argive escaped death he was of the race of Adrastus.
> For a Spartan to fly, not to die, is death.[83]

The descriptions of the death of Othryades (and the two hundred ninety nine Spartans) by Plutarch and the epigrams express the Spartan ideology of beautiful death even more

---

[82] On the tentative attribution of *Greek Anthology* 7.431 to Simonides see Bravi 2006, 89–90, with bibliography. Other sources are *Greek Anthology* 7.430; 7.741; Theseus ap. Stobaeus *Florilegium* 3.7.68 (= *FGH* 453 F 2), on which see Corcella 1996, 263, with n15 for further literature. Only one epigram (*Greek Anthology* 7.526) speaks of Othryades' suicide (following the erection of the trophy).

[83] Trans. W. R. Paton.

vigorously than does Herodotus' account. The three hundred Champions apparently enjoyed a heroic status at Sparta.[84] Plutarch describes Othryades as "particularly admired and honored"[85] (μάλιστα θαυμαζόμενον καὶ τιμώμενον, *De Herodoti malignitate* 858d) by the Spartans; this wording might be significant in light of the frequently attested meaning of *timê* as 'honor of cult.'[86]

The evidence provided by Plutarch and the epigrams strongly suggests that at some point the tale of the fighting over the Thyreatis, starring the heroic death of Othryades, was endorsed at Sparta. (I will argue in Chapter 5 that this version dates from the end of the fifth century BC.)[87]

I suspect that Herodotus' division of Othryades' story into the two episodes of survival and suicide has to do with Herodotus' joining of the mythical battle and the historical confrontation. In the process of joining, the figure of Othryades, pivotal at least in some versions of the myth, became marginalized. It is noteworthy that Plutarch (in a passage that I have just cited) vehemently disagreed with the Herodotean version of Othryades' death:

---

[84] See Currie 2005, 99n59 with further references.
[85] Trans. L. Pearson.
[86] On *timê* as 'honor of cult' see Nagy 1990b, 132n51.
[87] I am going to argue in Chapter 5 that the image of Othryades' writing in his blood a dedication announcing that Thyreatis belongs to Sparta (*Greek Anthology* 7.431) is meant to fix the Spartan victory and possession of the land once and for all; thus, the story of Othryades writing on his shield is likely to date to the period after the Spartan annexation of Thyreatis.

"Notice how roughly he has handled Othryades, whom they [the Spartans] particularly admired and honored"[88] (τὸν ἐν αὐτοῖς μάλιστα θαυμαζόμενον καὶ τιμώμενον ὅρα πῶς διαλελύμανται, τὸν Ὀθρυάδαν, *On the Malice of Herodotus* 858d).

I am inclined to believe that Herodotus' presentation of the version in which Othryades commits suicide is influenced by Herodotus' sympathy toward Aristodemus, the survivor of Thermopylae; it also relates to the Herodotean theme, whose presentation in the *Histories* we have traced above, of the excessive Spartan adherence to the ideal of unflinching fighting resulting in death.

Interestingly, we also have traces of an Argive variant of the mythical battle for the Thyreatis. Pausanias reports that the Argives considered themselves victors in a contest (*agôn*) for the Thyreatis with the Spartans, and dedicated a bronze horse at Delphi in honor of the victory (Pausanias 10.9.12). In another passage, he describes seeing in the theater in Argos "a representation of a man killing another, namely the Argive Perilaus, the son of Alcenor, killing the Spartan Othryades"[89] (ἀνὴρ φονεύων ἐστὶν ἄνδρα, Ὀθρυάδαν τὸν Σπαρτιάτην Περίλαος Ἀργεῖος ὁ Ἀλκήνορος, Pausanias 2.20.7). Thus, it appears that at some point the Argives

---

[88] Trans. L. Pearson.
[89] Trans. W. H. S. Jones. In Herodotus, Alcenor is the name of one of the two Argive survivors; Plutarch gives the name of Agenor instead.

presented the death of Othryades as their own victory.[90] The placement of the sculptural group, representing the killing of Othryades, in the theater highlights the public importance of the episode.

This survey of extra-Herodotean traditions connected to the battle of Champions shows that the tales of the battle of Champions, unattended by any mention of a large-scale conflict, enjoyed preeminence both at Sparta and Argos. Furthermore, the two *poleis* promoted alternative competing versions of the mythical confrontation.

6. The ritual battle

The Spartan annexation of Cynuria probably dates to the middle of the sixth century BC, as we have discussed. Can we date the mythical tale of the conflict over the Thyreatis? While living and changing myths are notoriously difficult to date, the detail of the strangely cooperative attitude of the Argives and the Spartans, expressed in the equal number of battle participants on each side, is unlikely to have been first conceived after the Spartan takeover of

---

[90] Asheri, Lloyd, and Corcella 2007, 140.

Cynuria: it probably derives from an earlier period, when Sparta and Argos, as Kelly argues, were not yet enemies.[91]

We arrive at a paradox: the myth of the confrontation between Argos and Sparta, focused on the issue of the Thyreatis, appears to predate any real clash of interests between Argos and Sparta in that area.[92] What was the significance of the *myth* of the confrontation before there was any real confrontation? And how do we account for the traces of cooperation and ritual, noticeable in Herodotus' description of the conflict over the Thyreatis?

As a solution, I propose to adopt a modified form of Brelich's hypothesis that the Argives and the Spartans used to engage in ritual combats for the border territory of Thyreatis. In contrast to Brelich, I do not consign the ritual confrontations to the prehistoric past, but rather suggest that they took place in the Archaic period until Sparta disrupted the tradition by the annexation of Cynuria.[93] The outcome of each battle determined to which city-state the

---

[91] Kelly 1970a, 1001.

[92] For a typological parallel I refer to Jonathan Hall's conclusion concerning the development of perioecic dependency in Sparta: "... while the *fact* of perioikic incorporation argues strongly for the anteriority of the polycentric model, it was achieved at an ideological level by appealing to a largely imagined monocentric model based in part on the memory (however refracted) of Mycenaean Lakedaimon." Hall 2000, 87.

[93] Brelich very cautiously considered a possibility that battles with limited number of participants, analogous to the battle of Champions, were fought in Thyreatis "in tutte le epoche." Brelich 1961, 29–30n38. See also Kõiv 2003, 132. Interestingly, Tyrtaeus' 23a West (P. Oxy. 3316) presents a description in a future tense of a battle between Spartans, Argives and (partly reconstructed) Arcadians. The future tense resembles that of Archilochus F 3 West and

border territory of Thyreatis would belong until the next encounter. I suggest that these ritual battles commemorated and reenacted (in an attenuated form) the mythical deadly battle of the six hundred Champions.

The idea of ritual reenactments of the battle for the Thyreatis helps to explain why Herodotus merged the myth of the battle with the story of the Spartan conquest of Cynuria, which happened only about a hundred years before Herodotus' time.[94] While Herodotus probably was not aware of the past practice of the ritual battles, the reenactments that occurred until the middle of the sixth century could have "modernized" the myth, creating an impression that it took place not in the legendary past, but in a relatively recent historical time.

Herodotus' mention of the Spartan adoption of the long hair in his account of the confrontation over the Thyreatis indicates that this hairstyle may have been linked to participation in the ritual battle. In the Classical period in Sparta the right to wear long hair

---

Homeric Hymn to Demeter 265–67, both of which, as I have argued in Chapter 2, refer to ritual battles. Tyrtaeus' fragment includes a hapax γυμνομάχοι (23a.14 W), indicating a participation of light-armed warriors. The (probable) appearance of the Arcadians implies that the occasion is not a battle for the Thyreatis; perhaps there was also a tradition of triangular ritual confrontations, involving the Spartans, Argives and Arcadians. For the involvement of the Arcadians in the Spartan-Argive relationship, see a difficult fragment of Diodorus (7.13.2), discussed by Kelly 1976, 135–136.

[94] Tomlinson remarks that the "folk-tale versions of events," reported by Herodotus, such as the story of Cypselus, typically "belong to remoter times that the mid-sixth century." Tomlinson 1972, 89.

coincided with the attainment of full citizenship.[95] If we assume that the same custom existed in the Archaic period, we are led to infer that the (hypothetical) ritual battle functioned as a rite of coming of age for its participants, marking their transition into a full adulthood.

We also have an indication confirming that the disputed territory of Thyreatis at some point functioned as an Argive-Spartan federal space of ritual.[96] The attestation comes from an unlikely place, a pronouncement characterized by the ancient paraemiographers as a byword for unintelligibility: Ἄκρον λάβε, καὶ μέσον ἕξεις· ἐπὶ τῶν δυσφράστων καὶ δυσνοήτων "Take the *akron*, and you will have the *meson*: about mysterious and incomprehensible things" (Zenobius I 57). Apparently, this was part of an oracle that the Aeginetans received from Delphi in 431 BC, when they were expelled from Aegina by the Athenians, and given the Thyreatis by the Spartans to settle.[97] The Aeginetans interpreted the oracle by founding a new settlement in the middle (*kata meson*) of a certain promontory (*akrôtêrion*) in the Thyreatis (Zenobius I 57). However, if the right interpretation of the oracle was going to ensure the prosperity of the Aeginetans, they evidently misconstrued it: in 424 BC the city of Thyrea was captured, burnt and pillaged by the Athenians, and the Aeginetans who were not slain in

---

[95] Ducat 2006a, 109-111, on the basis of Xenophon *Constitution of Sparta* 11.3.
[96] I pointed out at the beginning of this exploration the peculiarity of Thucydides' wording, defining the territory of Cynuria — by Thucydides' time long under the Spartan control— as a borderland (γῆ μεθορία) between Argos and Sparta (Thucydides 2.27.2, 5.41.2). Figueira 1993, 528-529.
[97] Zenobius 1,57, *CPG* 1.22-23; Apostolius 1,97, *CPG* 2.264; Thucydides 2.27; Figueira 1993, 535-38.

action were taken to Athens and condemned to death (Thucydides 4.56.2-4.57).[98] While further study is necessary to retrieve the meaning of *akron*, intended by the oracle, I believe that we can make an educated guess about the meaning of *meson*, promised by the oracle to the Aeginetans.[99] I propose that it referred to the territory of Thyreatis as a sacred communal space once shared by Argos and Sparta. We have an attestation of *meson* in the sense of a sacred space shared by a confederation of cities: in the middle of the island of Lesbos there was a locality named *Messon*, which Gregory Nagy describes as "a single communal place reserved for the festivals of this island federation."[100] If I am right in interpreting *meson* as the territory of Thyreatis, this definition harked back to the practices long abolished by 431 BC. The use of the obsolete terminology is suitable for the oracular riddle, which was unfortunately incomprehensible to the Aeginetans. However, it seems appropriate that in the Archaic period

---

[98] Figueira (1993, 536 and n37) notes that the tragic fate of the Aeginetans makes it likely that the fuller version of the tale portrayed them as having misinterpreted the oracle.
[99] Figueira (1993, 535) tentatively suggests "political moderation;" however, a more definite interpretation seems to be needed. Figueira (*ibid.*, 535n35) also cites a suggestion of Pritchett (via a personal communication) that *meson* can be interpreted topographically as the Astros plain (that is, the ancient Thyreatis), adjoining a central promontory as "a vast amphitheater."
[100] Nagy 2007, 24. The double *ss* of Messon is a feature of the Aeolic dialect of Lesbos. On Messon as a shared ritual space for the Lesbian cities, see Cole 2004, 77-79, with further references; Robert 1960b, 300-315.

the Thyreatis, ritually fought over by Argos and Sparta, could be considered a *meson*, the common territory, uniting the two cities.[101]

Earlier we have noted an arresting detail in Plutarch's account of the battle of Champions: the battle was managed by the body called the Amphictyonic Assembly (οἱ Ἀμφικτύονες).[102] Plutarch (on the authority of Chrysermus) credits the Amphictyonic Assembly both with setting up the battle of the six hundred as a solution of the Argive-Spartan dispute over the Thyreatis, and with the authoritative ruling of the Spartan victory. While many elements of Plutarch's account, such as the story of the death of Othryades, clearly stem from the *myth* of the battle for Thyrea, it is tempting to interpret the reference to the Amphictyonic Assembly as a memory of the supervision of the Argive-Spartan ritual battles by an alliance of city-states. We will return to the discussion of the identity of the Ἀμφικτύονες later in the chapter.

---

[101] On the semantic field of the name 'Thyrea,' including the concepts of doors, frontiers and foreignness, see Sauzeau 2005, 169.
[102] Plutarch *Greek and Roman Parallel Stories* 306a–b.

7. Fighting at the Gymnopaediae

I have proposed that in the archaic period the Argives and the Spartans fought in ritual battles for the territory of Thyreatis. What follows is an attempt to reconstruct further details concerning the setting and organization of such battles.

We have already mentioned Brelich's observation of the connection between the tale of the battle for the Thyreatis and an important Spartan festival, the Gymnopaediae,[103] which involved choruses in honor of the Spartans fallen at Thyrea, as well as wreaths, called *thyreatikoi*, worn by choral leaders in memory of the Spartan victory at Thyrea.[104] Currently, the *communis opinio* is that commemoration of the battle for the Thyreatis is a later addition to the festival. A detail, reported by Athenaeus on the authority of Sosibius, of choruses at the Gymnopaediae performing songs of Alcman and Thaletas,[105] creates an impression of festival

---

[103] Brelich 1961, 30–31. The Gymnopaediae was one of the principal Spartan festivals, as attested by Pausanias 3.11.9. Its importance is also apparent in earlier periods: Ducat 2006a, 266; Nagy 1990a, 348n56. The festival was attended by strangers at least from the Classical period on: Xenophon *Memorabilia* 1.2.61, Plutarch *Agesilaus* 29.1, Plutarch *Cimon* 10.6. My presentation is based on the recent discussion of the Gymnopaediae by Ducat 2006a, 265–274; see also Bölte 1929; Jeanmaire 1939, 531–540; Brelich 1969, 139, 171–173, 187–191; Pettersson 1992, 42–56; Robertson 1992, 147–165; Richer 2005.
[104] Sosibius ap. Athenaeus 15.678b-c, *Anecdota* Bekker 1, 32, *Suda* s.v. Γυμνοπαίδια.
[105] Athen. 15.678c. Trans. Ducat 2006a, 269.

practices that predate 546 BC (the accepted date of the battle at Thyrea).[106] However, as I have argued, the myth of the battle of the six hundred Champions should be detached from the date of 546 BC; once this is done, nothing prevents us from assuming that the myth of the battle at the Thyreatis was a primary component of the Gymnopaediae. I propose that this myth, with its underlying ideology of beautiful death, was the *aition*[107] of the Gymnopaediae. At present, no convincing hypothesis exists concerning the aetiology of the Gymnopaediae. Previously, the accepted position was Wade-Gery's suggestion that the festival was instituted by the Spartans in 668 BC (the traditional date of the Gymnopaediae, deriving from Eusebius) as a morale-boosting measure following their defeat by the Argives at Hysiae in 669 BC.[108] However, this idea has been criticized by Kelly, who contends that Pausanias 2.4.7 is the only mention of the battle of Hysiae; moreover, the battle's date (669 BC) is a result of a modern emendation.[109] The battle of Thyrea provides a much likelier candidate for an *aition*. Further, I suggest, as a working hypothesis, that the Archaic predecessor of the Gymnopaediae (which I will call the

---

[106] Wade-Gery 1949, 80; Ducat 2006a, 271; cf. Kõiv 2003, 130–131.
[107] I adopt Nagy's definition of an *aition*: "a myth that *traditionally* motivates an institution, such as a ritual." Nagy [1979] 1999, 279§2n2. Nagy stresses that the aetiological tradition is not derivative, but parallel to the ritual.
[108] Wade-Gery 1949, 80–81.
[109] Kelly 1970b, 32, 34.

"proto-Gymnopaediae") constituted for the Spartans the framework in which the ritual battles with the Argives took place.[110]

The conjectured role of the ritual battle as a coming-of-age rite matches the "initiatory themes"[111] perceptible in the accounts of the Gymnopaediae from the Classical period onwards. It seems that the age-group of ephebes played a particularly prominent part at the Gymnopaediae.[112] The festival's name suggests that the participating *paides* (whom we probably can identify as the ephebes[113]) were naked — an impression confirmed by ancient texts.[114] The nakedness strengthens the resemblance to an initiation ritual.[115] The Spartan Megillus in Plato's *Laws* describes the Gymnopaediae as "a fearful act of endurance practiced in our own community, where people have to fight against fierce and stifling heat" (ἔτι δὲ κἀν ταῖς γυμνοπαιδίαις δειναὶ καρτερήσεις παρ' ἡμῖν γίγνονται τῇ τοῦ πνίγους ῥώμῃ διαμαχομένων,

---

[110] On the Argive festival associated with the ritual battles, see below.
[111] Ducat 2006a, 274; cf. Pettersson 1992, 55.
[112] Pausanias 3.11.9. See Kennell 1995, 68–69 (who thinks it is a late feature).
[113] Ducat (2006a, 268) remarks that the *paides*, frequently mentioned in the ancient sources as the participants of the Gymnopaediae, must have been *paidiskoi*, adolescents in their late teens. (He comments, however, that -παιδία probably is not derived from παῖς 'child,' but is rather related to παίζειν 'to play, to dance.' Ducat 2006a, 266.)
[114] Athen. 14.678c, citing Sosibius; Hesychius s. v. Γυμνοπαίδια. Ducat 2006a, 272–273; Ferrari 2002, 120. While it seems very likely that γυμνός in various descriptions of the festival denotes literal nakedness, the prominence of *paides* and ephebes in the sources on the Gymnopaediae suggests that the other sense of γυμνός, 'light-armed,' can be equally relevant. On the possibility of the light-armed pre-adults' participation in the ritual battle, see below.
[115] Ducat 2006a, 274.

Plato *Laws* 1.633c).[116] This portrayal of the festival as an ordeal is particularly reminiscent of an initiation rite. Interestingly, a little earlier the same speaker mentions "collective bare-hand combats" (ἔν τε ταῖς πρὸς ἀλλήλους ταῖς χερσὶ μάχαις, Plato *Laws* 1.633b).[117] The scholion on the passage interprets this phrase as related to the Gymnopaediae, reporting that "the *paides*, practicing in the sun, hit each other until victory" (γυμνάζοντες γὰρ τοὺς παῖδας ἐν ἡλίῳ τύπτειν ἀλλήλους ἐποίουν μέχρι νίκης, schol. Plato *Laws* 1.633b s.v. ταῖς χερσί):[118] thus, the Gymnopaediae possibly included ritual bare-hand combats.

One more indication of the connection between the Gymnopaediae and the rituals of coming of age can be derived from a peculiar Spartan law, whose introduction Plutarch ascribes to Lycurgus. Plutarch relates that the Spartans who failed to marry at the proper age were excluded from watching the Gymnopaediae; in wintertime, they were made to march naked around the agora, singing a self-imprecating song.[119] Gloria Ferrari discerns the logic behind this seemingly eccentric chastisement: the bachelors are compelled to participate in a

---

[116] Trans. Ducat 2006a, 273, modified. I am particularly interested in Plato's use of the military language in the figure of "battling with the heat." While such representation of the festival as an endurance test is unique in our sources (Ducat 2006a, 273–274), it must be taken seriously as an early evidence.
[117] Trans. Ducat 2006a, 2009.
[118] Pettersson 1992, 42.
[119] Plutarch *Lyc.* 15.1.

disgraceful parody of the Gymnopaediae, happening in the same location[120] but in the winter instead of the summer. Thus, the men who failed to actualize their manliness via the normative practice of marriage were forced to undergo repeatedly "a perversion of the ritual through which they had attained manhood."[121]

We note that the adult bachelors and the ephebes — two categories of males linked with the coming-of-age rituals at the Gymnopaediae — belong to very different age groups. There is more evidence indicating that distinct groups of different ages participated in the festival. Athenaeus reports on the authority of Sosibius that at the Gymnopaediae choruses of *paides* and *andres* were staged in commemoration of the victory at Thyrea (Athen. 15.678b). It is usually assumed that there is a lacuna in the text, which contained a mention of another chorus, presumably, of old men.[122] It is further reconstructed that these three choruses performed the Spartan song-and-dance of *trichoria*, in which old men, men in their prime, and

---

[120] The agora as the setting of the Gymnopaediae is attested in Pausanias 3.11.9, Hesychius s. v. Γυμνοπαίδια.

[121] Ferrari 2002, 120.

[122] This assumption is based on the asymmetry of Athenaeus' sentence as it stands now: "The choruses are as follows: in front, the chorus of *paides*, and on the left the chorus of *andres*" (χοροὶ δ' εἰσὶν τὸ μὲν πρόσω παίδων τὸ δ' ἐξ ἀρίστου ἀνδρῶν, Athen. 15.678b, trans. Ducat 2006a, 269). It is reasonable to expect that a chorus in front and a chorus on the left would be accompanied by a third chorus on the right. *Ibid*.

boys ritually praised their past, current or future excellence.¹²³ In addition to the performance of the *trichoria*, the Gymnopaediae apparently included competitions between choruses, again organized by age-groups: Xenophon mentions a men's chorus engaged in a competition (τοῦ ἀνδρικοῦ χοροῦ, *Hell.* 6.4.16), and Ducat suggests that other choral competitions were in the groups of *paides* and *hêbôntes*.¹²⁴ Thus, in historical times the festival involved the entire Spartan society, with the special prominence of the *paides*-ephebes.¹²⁵ On the other hand, we have hypothesized that the ritual battle served as a rite of passage into full adulthood. Thus, the age group participating in the battle must have been the *hêbôntes*. We will return to the discussion of a more "adult" profile of the ritual battle in comparison with the historical Gymnopaediae.

A question arises concerning the location of the proto-Gymnopaediae. If this festival featured the ritual battle, then at least a part of the festival must have taken place at the battle site in the territory of Thyreatis. The historical Gymnopaediae, in contrast, was celebrated

---

[123] Plutarch *Lyc.* 21.3; *Institutions of the Spartans* 238a-b; *On Praising Oneself Inoffensively* 544e; scholia for Plato *Laws* 1.633a, s.v. συσσίτια; Pollux 4.107; Sosibius F 8 ap. Zenobius 1.82. Ducat 2006a, 268–270, *contra* Kennell 1995, 68–69.

[124] Ducat 2006a, 272.

[125] Linked rites of coming of age are expected in a society comprehensively structured by age-classes, where "the initiation of one group precipitates the promotion of all." Davidson 2006, 35.

solely in Sparta. How do we explain this difference between the conjectural proto-form of the festival and its attested form?

We know of a Spartan festival that was connected to the battle for the Thyreatis and celebrated in that territory: it is the Parparonia.[126] Georgius Choeroboscus mentions Parparus as a site of a battle between the Argives and the Spartans in the Thyreatis;[127] Hesychius speaks of *agôn* and *choroi* established at that site.[128] The festival of Parparonia, attested in the famous Damonon inscription (5 c. BC), included athletic competitions.[129] The situation in which both the Gymnopaediae and the Parparonia were connected to the myth of the confrontation over the Thyreatis is explicable if the proto-Gymnopaediae, previously celebrated both in Sparta and in the Thyreatis, was restructured following the elimination of the ritual battle in the sixth century. In the absence of the ritual battle, the part of the Gymnopaediae taking place in Sparta would have probably gained prominence.[130] Subsequently, the celebration in the

---

[126] Wade-Gery 1949, 79n7; Brelich 1961, 31n42; Billot 1989–1990, 87-88; Robertson 1992, 179–207; de Polignac 1995, 55n54; Kõiv 2003, 127-8.

[127] Choeroboscus *Commentary on Theodosius* 297, 4–6. Phaklaris 1990, 110–111, 183–185.

[128] Hesychius s.v. Πάρπαρος. I note with great interest Phaklaris' suggestion that the Parparonia was celebrated in honor of Apollo Pythaeus. Phaklaris 1987, 116. Differently, Billot 1989–1990, 87-79; cf. Shaw 1999, 292–93.

[129] *IG* V 1, 213 lines 44-9, 62-4.

[130] The idea of a transfer of some of the rites performed in Thyreatis to the Gymnopaediae in Sparta might help to explain a peculiar wording in Athenaeus, perhaps revealing a "seam" between different sets of the festival practices. Athenaeus, on the authority of Sosibius, gives information about the Thyreatic wreaths, worn "in commemoration of the victory at Thyrea,

Thyreatis could have become detached from the festival of the Gymnopaediae, turning into a separate festival.

Interestingly, we have an ancient reference, connecting the establishment of the Gymnopaediae with foundations of an Argive and an Arcadian festival (Pseudo-Plutarch, *On Music* 1134b–c):

> Ἡ μὲν οὖν πρώτη κατάστασις τῶν περὶ τὴν μουσικὴν ἐν τῇ Σπάρτῃ, Τερπάνδρου καταστήσαντος, γεγένηται· τῆς δὲ δευτέρας Θαλήτας τε ὁ Γορτύνιος καὶ Ξενόδαμος ὁ Κυθήριος καὶ Ξενόκριτος ὁ Λοκρὸς καὶ Πολύμνηστος ὁ Κολοφώνιος καὶ Σακάδας ὁ Ἀργεῖος μάλιστα αἰτίαν ἔχουσιν ἡγεμόνες γενέσθαι· τούτων γὰρ εἰσηγησαμένων τὰ περὶ τὰς Γυμνοπαιδίας τὰς ἐν Λακεδαίμονι λέγεται κατασταθῆναι, <καὶ> τὰ περὶ τὰς Ἀποδείξεις τὰς ἐν Ἀρκαδίᾳ, τῶν τε ἐν Ἄργει τὰ Ἐνδυμάτια καλούμενα.

> Now music was first organized at Sparta, under the direction of Terpander; for its second organization Thaletas of Gortyn, Xenodamus of Cythera, Xenocritus of Locri, Polymnestus of Colophon, and Sacadas of Argos are said to have been chiefly responsible, since it was at their suggestion that the festival of the Gymnopaediae at Lacedaemon was instituted and so too the Apodeixeis in Arcadia and the so-called Endymatia {festival of Apparelling} at Argos.[131]

There are several noteworthy features in the passage. The linkage of the poets from different parts of Greece to the inception of the Gymnopaediae depicts the festival as

---

by the leaders of the choruses which are staged during the festival which also involves the Gymnopaidiai" (ὑπόμνημα τῆς ἐν Θυρέᾳ γενομένης νίκης τοὺς προστάτας τῶν ἀγομένων χορῶν ἐν τῇ ἑορτῇ ταύτῃ, ὅτε καὶ τὰς Γυμνοπαιδιὰς ἐπιτελοῦσιν, Athen. 15.678b, trans. Ducat 2006a, 269). It seems that this wording distinguishes between the part of the festival commemorating the victory at Thyrea, and the Gymnopaediae proper. Cf. Ducat 2006a, 270–271.

[131] Trans. B. Einarson and P. H. de Lacy.

characterized by a strong pan-Hellenic trend. It is particularly remarkable to find an *Argive* poet, Sacadas, connected to the foundation of this festival. *On Music* presents Sacadas as a quintessential pan-Hellenic figure: in addition to crediting Sacadas with a series of victories at the inception of the Pythian games, the treatise also attributes to him the composition of a chorus that combined three systems of tuning — the Dorian, the Phrygian, and the Lydian.[132] Another figure connected to the foundation of the Gymnopaediae, Polymnestus of Colophon, is similarly pan-Hellenic, described by Pindar as "the voice common to all."[133]

The story of the institution of three Peloponnesian festivals upon the advice of the same "committee" suggests a possibility of a historical connection between the festivals. Moreover, Gregory Nagy observes a semantic link between the names of the Spartan Gymnopaediae and the Argive Endymatia: they contain "opposite notions of ritual undressing and dressing."[134] Such opposition strikingly recalls Herodotus' report of the Spartan decision to wear long hair in contrast to the short hair of the Argives.[135] Pseudo-Plutarch's account seems to contain traces of the same cooperation-in-opposition as does Herodotus' aetiology of the

---

[132] Ps.-Plutarch, *On Music* 1134a. Compare Nagy 1990a, 89–91. Pausanias (2.22.8) also ascribes to Sacadas the distinction of inventing the Pythian *nomos*.
[133] Strabo 14.1.28.
[134] Nagy 1990a, 344; also Ducat 2006a, 187–188.
[135] Herodotus 1.82.7.

hairstyles. It is plausible that the Endymatia was the festival associated with the ritual battle on the Argive side.[136]

8. Border games

The hypothesis that there was an Archaic Spartan tradition of ritual battles, serving as rites of passage, finds a typological parallel in later attestations of Spartan group combats, bearing initiatory overtones.[137] One such ritual combat is the Platanistas, a competition

---

[136] Leitao (1995, 143) suggests that the Endymatia was "the occasion on which young men in Argos assumed warrior garb for the first time." Similarly, Calame [1977] 2001, 204; Robertson 1992, 207, who connects the festival to the tradition of the battle for Thyreatis; Ceccarelli 1998, 119. A passage from Polybius about Arcadian customs might be portraying the festival: καὶ μὴν ἐμβατήρια μετ' αὐλοῦ καὶ τάξεως ἀσκοῦντες, ἔτι δ' ὀρχήσεις ἐκπονοῦντες μετὰ κοινῆς ἐπιστροφῆς καὶ δαπάνης κατ' ἐνιαυτὸν ἐν τοῖς θεάτροις ἐπιδείκνυνται τοῖς αὐτῶν πολίταις οἱ νέοι. "Their young men again practice a military step to the music of the pipe and in regular order of battle, producing elaborate dances, which they display to their fellow-citizens every year in the theatres, at the public charge and expense." Polyb. 4.20.12, trans. E. S. Shuckburgh. Ceccarelli 1998, 222. Numerous attempts were made to identify the Endymatia with other Argive festivals: with the Hybristica, whose origins Plutarch connects with the battle of Sepeia (Plutarch *Virtues of Women* 245e-f; *Encyclopaedia Britannica*, s.v. "Telesilla," 11th ed., 1911, vol. 26, 573); with the Heraea (Scheid and Svenbro 1996, 31, 77); with an unspecified festival of Hera's appareling (Webster 1970, 67); with a festival of Athena's bathing (Wilamowitz 1924, 14, called a "pure conjecture" by McKay 1962, 82). However, since the Endymatia is a hapax, all of the above identifications are entirely speculative, derived from the etymology of the festival's name. My interpretation, building on the parallelism between the Endymatia and the Gymnopaediae, has the advantage of being grounded in the text of Plutarch.

[137] Hodkinson (1997, 49) comments about the "unusual prominence" of team games in Sparta.

between two bands of ephebes for the control of a plane-tree grove, encircled by a water channel. The victory belonged to the team who succeeded in pushing all the members of the opposing team into the water. The competition was preceded by sacrifices to Enyalius and Achilles, and followed by choral performances.[138]

The Spartan practice of the ball games is even more relevant for our purposes. The games took place in the theater, and featured a competition between two teams, called *sphaireis*. Most interestingly, Nigel Kennell shows that, at least in the Roman period, the game was "a type of graduation ceremony, marking the transition from ephebe to adult."[139] It was organized as a tournament, in which pairs of ephebic teams (*sphaireis*), representing five *ôbai*, the ancient constituent villages of Sparta, competed against each other:[140] this detail is particularly valuable, since it attests to the existence of ritual fighting between geographically distinct Spartan communities. While we do not have much direct evidence about the details of the Spartan ball game, it is very likely that it was the same as the ball game known under the names of *episkuros* or *sphairomakhia*.[141] The *episkuros* was played by two teams, who contended over the control of the playing field. The field was divided in the center by a boundary line

---

[138] Our main source is Pausanias (3.14.8-10); also Lucian *Anacharsis* 38. See the discussion in Ducat 2006a, 208; Kennell 1995, 55-59. The evidence, admittedly, is late: there are no references to the Platanistas before the first century BC.
[139] Kennell 1995, 40. See also *ibid.*, 59-64. See also Muellner 1998, 6.
[140] Kennell 1995, 40.
[141] *Ibid.*, 61; Crowther (1997, 6) is more cautious.

(*skuros*), on which the ball was placed at the beginning of the game; the teams' home base lines were also marked. During the game, one team hurled the ball toward their opponents, who strove to catch it and to hurl it back; as the ball was passed back and forth, the teams attempted to push their opponents over their home base, gaining the field. The alternative name of the game, *ephebike*, suggests its strong connection with the ephebes.[142] In a recent article David Elmer demonstrates the centrality of the notions of boundaries and territorial possession in *episkyros*, as well as the deep affinity between the details of the game and the imagery traditionally associated with conflicts over boundary territories.[143] Elmer proposes that the game can be interpreted as "a symbolization of a boundary dispute."[144] He also convincingly argues that *episkuros* is an implicit referent of an Iliadic simile — a suggestion that reinforces the possibility that the game was already present during the Classical period and possibly earlier.[145]

If the Spartan ball game was indeed identical to *episkuros*, this Spartan tradition presents a striking analogy to the conjectured ritual battle. While *episkuros* displays a higher

---

[142] The main source on *episkuros* is Pollux 9.103-107. See Crowther 1997; Elmer 2008.
[143] Elmer 2008.
[144] *Ibid.*, 420.
[145] *Ibid.* For the plausible iconographical attestation of *episkuros* in the six century, see Crowther 1997, 5 (with bibliography), and Elmer 2008, 414-415n6.

degree of stylization and abstraction, both the game and the ritual battle are characterized by a nexus of a boundary dispute and a rite of passage.[146]

Finally, we have an attestation of a ritual battle between communities of the Argive Plain. According to Pausanias (2.25.7), a fight between Proitus and Acrisius was commemorated by a building in a form of a pyramid, decorated by shields; this structure was believed to be a common tomb of those who fell in battle on both sides:

> ἐρχομένοις δὲ ἐξ Ἄργους ἐς τὴν Ἐπιδαυρίαν ἐστὶν οἰκοδόμημα ἐν δεξιᾷ πυραμίδι μάλιστα εἰκασμένον, ἔχει δὲ ἀσπίδας σχῆμα Ἀργολικὰς ἐπειργασμένας. ἐνταῦθα Προίτῳ περὶ τῆς ἀρχῆς πρὸς Ἀκρίσιον μάχη γίνεται, καὶ τέλος μὲν ἴσον τῷ ἀγῶνι συμβῆναί φασι καὶ ἀπ' αὐτοῦ διαλλαγὰς ὕστερον, ὡς οὐδέτεροι βεβαίως κρατεῖν ἐδύναντο· συμβάλλειν δὲ σφᾶς λέγουσιν ἀσπίσι πρῶτον τότε καὶ αὐτοὺς καὶ τὸ στράτευμα ὡπλισμένους. τοῖς δὲ πεσοῦσιν ἀφ' ἑκατέρων— πολῖται γὰρ καὶ συγγενεῖς ἦσαν—ἐποιήθη ταύτῃ μνῆμα ἐν κοινῷ.

> On the way from Argos to Epidauria there is on the right a building made very like a pyramid, and on it in relief are wrought shields of the Argive shape. Here took place a fight for the throne between Proetus and Acrisius; the contest, they say, ended in a draw, and a reconciliation resulted afterwards, as neither could gain a decisive victory. The story is that they and their hosts were armed with shields, which were first used in this battle. For those that fell on either side was built here a common tomb, as they were fellow citizens and kinsmen.

---

[146] The scholion on the speech of Spartan Megillus in Plato's *Laws*, discussed above, in fact mentions ball-playing as a part of the Gymnopaediae: ἐνίοτε δὲ καὶ σφαῖραν ἢ ἄλλο τι ἐρρίπτουν, ὥστε τὸν πρῶτον ἁρπάσαντα νικᾶν "sometimes they hurl a ball or some other thing, so that the first one to snatch it wins." Schol. Plato *Laws* 1.633b s.v. ταῖς χερσί. Pettersson 1992, 43, 46–47.

The aetiology of the invention of shields, the draw in the battle, as well as the common tomb, resemble the fighting for the Thyreatis. We further learn from Hesychius that the battle was commemorated by an Argive festival Daulis: Δαῦλις· ἑορτὴ ἐν Ἄργει, μίμημα τῆς Προίτου πρὸς Ἀκρίσιον "Daulis. A festival in Argos, an imitation of the battle between Proitus and Acrisius." Thus, it is likely that at some point the Tirynthians and the Argives participated in a ritual battle, reenacting the mythical confrontation between the fighting forces led by Proitus and Acrisius.[147]

9. Apollo Pythaeus

A consideration of the figure of Apollo Pythaeus, the deity presiding over the Gymnopaediae, further illuminates the paradoxical antagonistic concord between Argos and Sparta. We have briefly reviewed Brelich's findings about the worship of this deity in both Argos and Sparta,[148] the association between Apollo Pythaeus and the tradition of Argive-

---

[147] Kõiv 2003, 335-336n228; Dowden 1989, 218n6; Nilsson 1906, 416.
[148] Kowalzig (2007, 145-146) gives a concise summary of the literary and epigraphic attestation of the cult of Apollo Pythaeus in the Argolid and around the Argolic Gulf, including Cynuria, where two sixth-century inscriptions to Apollo Pythaeus were found in Tyras and Kosmas. The sanctuaries of Apollo in these two locales produced numerous dedications of weapons (both full-sized and miniature) and a bronze sixth-century statuette of a hoplite. Phaklaris 1990, 176,

Spartan confrontation, and Brelich's suggestion concerning the existence of a federal cult of Apollo Pythaeus, which apparently counted both Argos and Sparta as members.[149] However, how do these separate pieces of evidence coalesce into a historically nuanced understanding of the Argive-Spartan relations in the Archaic period, and how do they clarify the nature of the dispute over the Thyreatis?

Barbara Kowalzig makes a major step forward in answering these questions. Kowalzig notices the frequent association between the cult of Apollo Pythaeus and inter-*polis* boundaries.[150] She proposes that the Archaic cult of Apollo Pythaeus at Asine[151] had the function of mediating between communities of the Argolid in their long-standing territorial disputes. Importantly, Kowalzig argues that the cult operated not by resolving the conflicts but by embracing the competing versions of the disputing sides and commemorating their irreducible variance through recurrent rituals.[152]

179–182; de Polignac 1995, 54. On the cult of Apollo Pythaeus see also Billot 1989–1990; Kõiv 2003, 304–308; and Kowalzig 2007a, 132–154 (discussed below).

[149] Brelich 1961, 33–34, on the basis of Diodorus Siculus 12.78.1 and Thucydides 5.53.1.

[150] Kowalzig 2007a, 147–148; similarly, de Polignac 1995, 54n52; Jameson 1994, 63–64n11.

[151] The cult of Apollo Pythaeus at Asine is attested by Pausanias 2.36.4 and Bacchylides *Paean* (F 4); Barrett 1954.

[152] Kowalzig 2007a, 132–154, esp. 147–149, 153–154.

Kowalzig also notes the prominence of Apollo Pythaeus in the conflict over the Thyreatis,[153] but she considers the deity to be an embodiment of the *real* hostility between the two states.[154] However, Kowalzig's reconstruction of the character of archaic Apollo Pythaeus as a mediator between communities at variance perfectly fits the idea that this deity oversaw the *ritual* battles between Argos and Sparta in the framework of the Gymnopaediae, uniting the two *poleis* in their confrontation.

The situation that I tentatively reconstruct is that in the Archaic period the sanctuary of Apollo Pythaeus in Asine was the center of an association of cities, including Argos, Epidauros and Sparta, concerned with a regulation of contested border spaces. Such a suggestion about Argos and Epidaurus has been well developed in the scholarship;[155] what I am adding is an observation that the contest over the Thyreatis is homologous to other border disputes associated with the worship of Apollo Pythaeus.

The story of the destruction of Asine is important in my reconstruction. The story is narrated by Pausanias (2.36.4-5), according to whom Asine was destroyed by the Argives as a

---

[153] Kowalzig 2007a, 155-157.
[154] "Apollo Pythaieus stood for what separated Argives and Spartans, imbued with connotations of the Spartano-Argive conflict." *Ibid.*, 156.
[155] Kowalzig 2007a, 132-149; Kõiv 2003, 304-310; Jameson 1994, 63-64n11; Kelly 1976, 172-3n53 for earlier literature. See also Forrest 2000, 284. Kowalzig (2007, 149-153) connects the worship of Apollo Pythaeus with the Archaic Calaurian amphictyony; however, my impression is that the tradition of the Calaurian amphictyony is not directly connected to the cult of Apollo Pythaeus.

retaliation for the participation of the Asinaeans in the Spartan invasion into the Argive territory, led by the early Spartan king Nicander (conventionally dated to the eighth century BC). Pausanias reports that when the Argives destroyed the wall of Asine, the Asinaeans abandoned their city and sailed away with their families. The Argives leveled Asine to the ground but left the sanctuary of Apollo Pythaeus standing (Pausanias 2.36.5):

> Ἀργεῖοι δὲ ἐς ἔδαφος καταβαλόντες τὴν Ἀσίνην καὶ τὴν γῆν προσορισάμενοι τῇ σφετέρᾳ Πυθαέως τε Ἀπόλλωνος ὑπελίποντο <τὸ> ἱερὸν—καὶ νῦν ἔτι δῆλόν ἐστι—καὶ τὸν Λυσίστρατον πρὸς αὐτῷ θάπτουσιν.
>
> the Argives, while levelling Asine to the ground and annexing its territory to their own, left the sanctuary of Apollo Pythaeus, which is still visible, and by it they buried Lysistratus.

There is archaeological evidence of violent destruction in Asine in the last third of the eighth century.[156] On the basis of the correspondence between Pausanias' account and the archaeological data, Pausanias' narrative has been frequently accepted as historically accurate. However, the historicity of the account is extremely questionable. It has been shown by Thomas Kelly that the destruction of Asine in the eighth century was unlikely to take place in the framework of Argive-Spartan hostilities.[157] Further, Jonathan Hall has demonstrated that the perception of the destruction of Asine as an early example of the Argive expansionistic

---

[156] See details in Hall 1995, 581 with further references.
[157] Kelly 1967. Similarly, Billot 1989–1990, 38.

tendencies[158] cannot be substantiated historically.[159] Moreover, it is now clear that the eighth-century destruction was not complete; the site of Asine shows indications of continuous occupation after the destruction.[160]

The historical problems with Pausanias' account do not mean that it should be completely discarded as evidence. The destruction of Asine can be interpreted as a charter myth of the association of cities around the cult of Apollo Pythaeus in Asine.[161] Such a suggestion is paralleled by the myth of the destruction of Crisa by the Delphic Amphictyony in the First Sacred War.[162] Thus, I propose that an earlier version of the myth featured a joint destruction of Asine by Argos, Epidauros and Sparta.[163] As in the case of Crisa, such destruction could be motivated by ascribing a conspicuously transgressive behavior to the Asinaeans.

---

[158] Kelly 1967.
[159] Hall 1995, 582–583; cf. Ratinaud 2004.
[160] Wells 2002; Luraghi 2008, 40; Ratinaud 2004; Hall 1995, 581; Jameson 1994, 63n11.
[161] Compare Ellinger 1993, 312–322.
[162] For the analysis of the tradition of the First Sacred War, see Hall 2002, 145–154; Howe 2003.
[163] The suggestion that the destruction of Asine was a joint venture of Argos and Epidaurus has been made by Jameson. Thucydides 5.53 reports that (in 419 BC) the Argives accused the Epidaurians of neglecting to send their sacrifices ὑπὲρ βοταμίων to the temple of Apollo Pythaeus, whose main overseers (κυριώτατοι) were the Argives. The temple in question is believed to be Apollo's temple in Asine (Barrett 1954). I quote Jameson's analysis: "Participation by Epidauros in a festival under Argive leadership points to a regional center [...]. We suggest that Epidauros participates and contributes to the sacrifice in payment for its share of the rewards in the destruction of Asine, namely, the land of Iria and, perhaps, Kandia. Iria belonged to Epidauros in the Classical period but is much more likely to have been Asinaian when the community existed. There is a late cent.-V dedication to Apollo *Puthês* from

This (conjectural) mythical reason for the destruction of Asine may dovetail with the historical reason of the attack on the city in the eighth century. Jonathan Hall observes that the settlement plan and mortuary practices attested in Asine are unparalleled in the Argive Plain, signaling "an identity self-consciously distinct from other neighbouring sites."[164] Hall further speculates that perhaps "the settlers were, in fact, pirates whose continued harassment of shipping in the Argolic Gulf was responsible for provoking the Argive attack."[165] In connection with this suggestion, Hall quotes a fragment of Pherecydes, describing the Dryopians (who, according to the ancient tradition, inhabited Asine)[166] as ληστρικὸν δὲ τὸ ἔθνος 'a piratical people.'[167] At this point we crossover to mythical parallels: exactly the same

---

the Iria plain (SEG XXIV 274). Thucydides speaks of the sacrifices as being "on behalf of the *botamia*" (*huper botamiôn*). [...] What is expected here is some easily understandable word or phrase indicating why the Epidaurians send sacrifices. *Botanai*, "pastures," has been proposed. A suggestion found in some of the later manuscripts, but not discussed in recent years, is *parapotamia* (or *parapotamioi*), i.e., "the land [or, "the people"] besides the river," which Bursian (1872: 61, 77) takes to refer to the Bedheni valley and the Iria plain, traversed by the Bedheni river." Jameson 1994, 63-64n11. We will return to the question of Thucydides' ὑπὲρ βοταμίων in Chapter 6; I will argue that a comparison with another passage in Thucydides (5.42) strengthens the interpretation of this term as referring to common grazing territory.
[164] Hall 1997, 137.
[165] Hall 1995, 582.
[166] The destruction of Asine is connected in Pausanias' account with the traditions of the Messenian Asine, inhabited by the Dryopians. On the traditions concerning the Dryopians, see Kowalzig 2007a, 132-54; Luraghi 2008, 40-43; Strid 1999; Hall 1997, 74-7; Billot 1989-1990, 44-50.
[167] Scholia for Apollonius Rhodius 1212-19 = Pherecydes *FGrHist* 3.19. Hall 1995, 582.

reason, *lêisteia* 'robbery/piracy' is given by Pausanias (3.2.2) as a reason for the ancient removal of all the Cynurians of military age by the Spartans:

> ἐπὶ δὲ Ἐχεστράτου τοῦ Ἄγιδος βασιλεύοντες ἐν Σπάρτῃ Κυνουρέας τοὺς ἐν τῇ ἡλικίᾳ Λακεδαιμόνιοι ποιοῦσιν ἀναστάτους, αἰτίαν ἐπενεγκόντες ὡς τὴν Ἀργολίδα συγγενῶν σφισιν ὄντων Ἀργείων **λῃσταί** τε ἐκ τῆς Κυνουριακῆς κακουργοῖεν καὶ αὐτοὶ καταδρομὰς ἐκ τοῦ φανεροῦ ποιοῖντο ἐς τὴν γῆν.

> When Echestratus, son of Agis, was king at Sparta, the Lacedaemonians removed all the Cynurians of military age, alleging as a reason that freebooters from the Cynurian territory were harrying Argolis, the Argives being their kinsmen, and that the Cynurians themselves openly made forays into the land.

The peculiar concern exhibited by the Spartans for the Argives in this passage may be a trace of the earlier stage of the myth in which the establishment of the Thyreatis as a sacred border territory between Argos and Sparta was predicated on the removal of the criminal locals.[168]

The folk etymology of Asine as a "harmless" city, attested in Bacchylides' paean (F 4.47), finds parallels in myths about such "pre-cultural" people as ancient Lemnians and Pelasgians:

> Philochoros says that the Pelasgians were called Sinties because they raped the Athenian girls, for *sinesthai* means to harm. According to Eratosthenes, the Sinties/Pelasgians were *goetes* who invented *deleteria pharmaka*; Hellanikos said that the Lemnians were called Sinties because they first invented weapons for war, and Porphyrios that they were called Sinties because they first invented weapons for war, which harm people.[169]

---

[168] Pausanias adds that the Cynurians were Argives, and their founder was Cynurus, son of Perseus (3.2.2); the mention of Perseus indicates that this addition in all probability derives from an Argive tradition, post-dating the Argive adoption of Perseus in 460s BC. See Hall 1997, 95–99, and Chapters 4 and 5 below.

[169] Sourvinou-Inwood 2003, 136. Philochorus *FGrHist* 328 F 101; Eratosthenes *FGrHist* 241 F 41; Hellanicus *FGrHist* 4 F 71; scholia BT for *Iliad* 1.594.

The destruction of Asine by a coalition of cities makes it "harmless," and serves as a foundation of the orderly resolution of border conflicts between the league's members. This conjecture is corroborated by Plutarch's fascinating reference to the Ἀμφικτύονες, organizing a battle between Argos and Sparta over the Thyreatis.[170]

The association of cities around Apollo Pythaeus in Asine must have experienced major changes after the cessation of the ritual battles for the Thyreatis in the middle of the sixth century. Barbara Kowalzig notes the "varied geographic origin" of the votive deposits in Apollo's temple in Asine in the seventh and sixth centuries; however, on the basis of the archaeological evidence she suggests "a rebuilding of the temple under Argive auspices" around 500 BC.[171] We will repeatedly return in the following chapters to the role of Apollo Pythaeus in the relations between Argos, Sparta and Epidaurus, and to the Argive efforts to "appropriate" Apollo Pythaeus.

---

[170] Plutarch *Greek and Roman Parallel Stories* 306a-b, referring to "Chrysermus in the third book of his *Peloponnesian History*."
[171] Kowalzig 2007a, 144.

10. The transformation of the *hippeis*

I have suggested that the ritual battle happened in Sparta in the framework of the Archaic precursor of the Gymnopaediae (and perhaps in the framework of the precursor of the Endymatia in Argos), and served as a coming of age rite for its participants. But who were these participants? Whose rite of passage was it? A consideration of the Spartan institution of *hippeis*, which has not been taken into account until now, can help us answer this question.

The Spartan *hippeis* were an elite corps of hoplites (their equestrian appellation notwithstanding), who numbered three hundred. In the Classical period, the *hippeis* fought in close proximity to the king and had the task of protecting him. They also served as the Spartan "emergency force" in cases of internal or external danger.[172] The *hippeis* were chosen competitively from the body of *hêbôntes*,[173] the Spartiates between 20 and 30 years old, who constituted the oldest age group not yet having full citizen rights.[174]

The relevance of the *hippeis* to the present discussion stems from their character as picked troops and from their number, coinciding with the number of the Spartan warriors at Thyrea. In a recent article, Thomas Figueira suggests that the three hundred Spartans who

---

[172] Figueira 2006, 58-60. Similarly, Detienne 1968, 135.
[173] Xenophon *Constitution of Sparta* 4.3-4. Figueira 2006, 62-67.
[174] On the *hêbôntes* see Ducat 2006a, 104-112.

fought in the battle of Champions must have been *hippeis*: "It would be incongruous for the Spartans to choose another elite group of the same size, inasmuch as the *hippeis* probably already existed."[175] In light of the previous discussion, we can modify Figuiera's suggestion: the battle, in which all the Spartan participants die heroically, can be construed as a foundation myth of the *hippeis*, setting a benchmark for their fighting conduct.

Here, however, a question arises. I have hypothesized previously that the battle of Champions is a foundation myth for the Gymnopaediae; now the battle seems to fit also as a foundation myth for the institution of *hippeis*. Are the Gymnopaediae and the *hippeis* related to each other, and if yes, what is the nature of their connection?

My first observation is that the mythical battle of Champions is linked to the *hippeis* and to the Gymnopaediae by very different details. The *hippeis* and the battle of Champions are not connected explicitly, but share the prominent detail of three hundred Spartan warriors. Conversely, the number of three hundred does not play any role in the Gymnopaediae as far as we can see; however, we have the explicit ancient attestation that the festival featured "Thyreatic wreaths" and hymns honoring the fallen at Thyrea. It is appealing to bring these different pieces of evidence together, and to suggest that in the Archaic period the three hundred *hippeis* were the Spartan participants in the ritual fighting reenacting the mythical

---

[175] Figueira 2006, 60.

battle of Champions. I will label these hypothetical Archaic *hippeis*, who took part in the ritual battle, as "proto-*hippeis*."

The idea that the "proto-*hippeis*" fought in the ritual battle, which, as I hypothesized, was a coming-of-age ritual, implies that the status of "proto-*hippeis*" was an age grade.[176] Thus, I reconstruct the ritual battle as an initiation into the category of "proto-*hippeis*," which marked full adulthood. On the other hand, the historical institution of *hippeis* was certainly not an age grade. While the *hippeis* were chosen from the age grade of *hêbôntes*, only some of the *hêbôntes* were promoted to the status of *hippeis*. Age-grade transition, on the contrary, involves all members of a particular age-class.[177]

However, while the historical *hippeis* did not constitute an age grade, they apparently were sometimes perceived as such. Aristophanes of Byzantium in his treatise on the terms describing age categories, charts the following progression of the ages: *meirakion, meirax,*

---

[176] My use of the term "age grade" is based on the discussion by Bernardi 1985, 2-4. A grade "corresponds to a social position, that is, a status with special prerogatives acquired by a class as a right, which, in any case, is only a temporary right;" "after a definite period a class is expected to abandon the grade and leave it for the following class." *Ibid.*, 3.

[177] This statement does not imply that all members of an age-class always actively participate in the rites of coming of age: some rituals can be undergone by a selected group on behalf of the whole age-class. Bernardi 1985, 4-5 calls such rites of passage "promotional rites," and remarks that "promotional rites, [...] even though they may be carried out by official representatives of the class, alter the status of all class members." However, my point is that in an age-class society *all* members of an age-class, by default, make a transition to the next level in the age structure. On the egalitarian distribution of power in age-class societies see Bernardi 1985, 24-37; and Davidson 2006, 35-36 in application to Greece.

neaniskos, neanias. Concerning the latter he says: "The Spartans called these *hippeis*, and those who manage them *hippagretai*."[178] This "flavor" of an age grade displayed by the historical *hippeis* might be an echo of the prehistory of this institution.

Who were the Archaic "proto-*hippeis*"? The idea of the age grade provides an answer. The *hippeis* can be an age grade only in the society where "everybody who counts" is a *hippeus*. That is to say, the ritual battle could serve as a coming-of-age rite only at the stage when Sparta had an oligarchic regime of aristocratic *hippeis*.

Let us now attempt to sketch the trajectory of the development and obliteration of the ritual battles between Argos and Sparta alongside with the changes in the character of the *hippeis*. The first stage strikingly resembles the reconstruction of the fighting over the Lelantine Plain between the Eretrian *Hippeis* and the Chalcidian *Hippobotae*. The Spartan *hippeis* must have been a body of aristocratic horsemen,[179] and the ritual battle constituted a rite of passage for the young aristocrats reaching adulthood. I believe that both on Euboea and in the battles for the Thyreatis, the fighting in the ritual battle at this aristocratic stage was not restricted only to the young men who were reaching adulthood on the given year. Rather, all younger *hippeis* would probably take part in the battle. This suggestion is based on numerical

---

[178] Aristophanes of Byzanium *Nomina aetatum* (fragmenta) 275.8-9. Figueira 2006, 64.
[179] Figueira 2006, 68; Nafissi 1991, 89-90; 153-162; Detienne 1968, 136-37.

reasoning: in any given year, there were too few aristocratic young men coming of age to constitute an acceptable fighting force on their own.

Next, in the period of the Spartan "sixth-century revolution,"[180] the aristocratic *hippeis* were transformed from the elite age grade into an elite corps.[181] I quote Thomas Figueira's description of this process:

> Instead of the previous corps, based on birth and wealth, a new elite body was created whose membership was determined by public recognition of ἀρετή in its Spartan connotations. The empanelment of the new *hippeis* embodied a particularly Spartan

---

[180] Finley 1981, 25–26; Whitby 2002, 23; Cartledge [1979] 2002, 134; Nafissi 2009, 124.

[181] On the major reorganization of the Spartan army in the sixth century see Singor 2002; 2009, 600. A transformation of an age grade into a military unit finds the following typological parallel. The Spartan military system had been long compared with that of the Zulu. Ferguson 1918; Jeffery 1976, 130; Cartledge 1987, 206. In fact, the analogy pertains to a specific historical period: the early nineteenth century emergence of the Zulu state under the leadership of Shaka, who introduced a number of innovations into the traditional tribal practices of the Nguni people (of whom the Zulus constituted a clan). Murray [1978] 1993, 178. Shaka's reform that is particularly relevant for our purposes is the one that Bernardi describes as a transformation of "the age class system of the ancient Nguni into a regimental model." Bernardi 1985, 163; also 41, 112–119. The former age-classes were converted into regiments; the point at which a new regiment was formed was decided by the king. The rite of the regiment formation concluded with a formal distribution of arms (spears and shields) to the warriors on king's behalf. The transition to the regimental model was accompanied by an increased atmosphere of competitiveness, an introduction of strict discipline, and, on a more general level, a profound militarization of the age-class structure, and a centralization of power in the hands of the king. *Ibid.*, 116–119. The regimental model, as Bernardi observes, is a unique phenomenon, emerging in distinctive historical circumstances (*ibid.*, 119). This historical specificity makes the Zulu case a particularly valuable parallel to the proposed development of the *hippeis*.

mode of meritocracy, one in which confirmation of agonistic 'excellence' radiated down from older exemplars.[182]

Perhaps the creation of the corps of *hippeis* was in fact related to the ritual battle. The elite military unit, competitive admission into which was open to all *hêbôntes*, provided a more democratic access for participation in the previously exclusively aristocratic tradition of ritual battles. I believe that the detail of the six hundred mythical Champions stems from this stage of the ritual confrontation: the increased Spartan pool of potential participants in the battle would require explicit limits imposed on their numbers.[183] The ritual battle at this point ceased to be a coming-of-age rite for the Spartans, since the *hippeis* were not an age grade any more; instead, it played the role of an initiation into the elite corps. The festival that I have called the proto-Gymnopaediae, which constituted the framework for the aristocratic ritual battle, was probably reorganized at this stage, receiving a form closer to the historically attested Gymnopaediae. The focus of the festival shifted to the younger age grade of the *paides*, more democratically inclusive, because it preceded the split into *hippeis* and non-*hippeis*.

---

[182] Figueira 2006, 68. Cf. Detienne 1968, 138. Figueira (2006, 69) further suggests that the democratic reform also converted the *hippeis* from horsemen into hoplites. However, as we have seen on the example of the fighting over the Lelantine Plain, the close combat is very aristocratic, and the Archaic aristocratic Spartan *hippeis* probably already fought for the Thyreatis in a hoplite phalanx.

[183] The earlier aristocratic version of the myth of fighting for the Thyreatis probably did not specify the numbers of the participants.

The strategy of choosing the best soldiers among all *hêbôntes*,[184] rather than manning the field at Thyrea indiscriminately with the younger aristocrats, must have resulted in a much stronger fighting force with higher chances of victory. This development probably made the fighting over the Thyreatis more aggressive. These changes in all likelihood gradually eroded the perception of the Thyreatis as the sacred common territory, bringing Argos and Sparta together. At some point around the middle of the sixth century, Sparta adopted more aggressive expansionist politics in the Peloponnese, and annexed the whole region of Cynuria, including the Thyreatis.[185] The ritual hostilities became real.

The democratic transformation of the *hippeis* from the hereditary aristocracy into an elite force was attended by ideological developments. As Figueira notes, the new *hippeis* became a paradigmatic embodiment of Spartan virtues. The ideology of the beautiful death, expressed in the myth of the Battle of Champions, was applicable first and foremost to them. Nicole Loraux observes that the *hippeis*' code of behavior on the battlefield was stricter than that of usual hoplites, obliging them, for example, to die with a king.[186]

---

[184] On the highly competitive nature of the membership in the *hippeis*, see Figueira 2006, 64-66.
[185] See Singor 2009, 599-601.
[186] Loraux 1995, 73 and 280n113 with reference to Isocrates *On the Peace* 143. An indirect but nevertheless important piece of evidence concerning the ideology of the *hippeis* comes from Herodotus' narrative of Thermopylae. The three hundred Spartans at Thermopylae apparently were not *hippeis*: according to Figueira's reconstruction of the situation, Leonidas was denied the corps of *hippeis* by the ephors, but managed to recruit "an equivalent force from former

However, despite the reform, the *hippeis* remained a primarily aristocratic organization. Moreover, as I hope to show, the aristocratic associations were part of the ideological underpinnings of the *hippeis*.

We learn that an alternative appellation of the *hippeis* was simply *ko(u)roi*, 'youths.'[187] The designation *koroi* appears on an Archaic relief from Sparta with a dedicatory inscription: "[The] *koroi* [dedicate this image of] Theocles son of Nam[——]"([τοὶ] κόροι Θιοκλê Ναμ[— — — — ἀνέθηκαν — — —], *IG* V, 1 457).[188] The relief has been dated by Alan Wace to ca. 556-520 BC.[189]

---

hippeis who had children." Figueira 2006, 62, on Herodotus 7.205.2. However, Figueira (*ibid.*, 61, 62) suggests that in the "spirit of institutional metonymy," the death of the three hundred at Thermopylae was associated with the corps of *hippeis*, augmenting its glory. I have suggested earlier that the myth of Thyrea influenced the shaping of the narrative of Thermopylae. Now I note Nicole Loraux' observation that the last stand of the Spartans at Thermopylae, as described by Herodotus (7.223-225), seems to belong to the mythic past in all its pre-civilized savagery. Loraux 1995, 71-73. Going far beyond the ritual imitation, the literal reenactment of the death of the three hundred Champions by the heroes of Thermopylae crosses over into the territory of myth; in the words of Loraux (*ibid.*, 72), it is "as if the Spartans' deaths reached back beyond hoplitic tradition to reenact the mad exploits of mythical warriors." One more episode of the death of 300 warriors is attested by Herodotus, in a brief mention of the fate of Arimnestus, who fell with his three hundred men in a battle against "all of the Messenians" (9.64.2, referring to the helot revolt of 465 BC). Figueira understands the episode as involving the corps of *hippeis*. Figueira 2006, 60; Loraux 1995, 72. It looks as if the *hippeis* kept fatally reenacting the deaths of the Champions, or, at least, that stories of such lethal reenactments of the myth by the three hundred *hippeis* were generated again and again.

[187] Figueira 2006, 67; Kennell 1995, 139. The information comes from 'Archytas' (ap. Stobaeus *Florilegium* 4.1.138 = 34.16-27 Thesleff) who names *hippagretai* (the supervisors of *hippeis*) and *ko(u)roi* as democratic components of the Spartan constitution.

[188] Jeffery [1961] 1990, 200 no. 29, with further literature.

It represents a standing young man, holding a spear in his left hand, and offering a round object with his right hand to a serpent. The relief provides evidence of the communal worship of the heroized Theocles.[190] Judging from his short hair and the absence of a beard, Theocles died before reaching adulthood.[191] Kennell notes the lack of hoplite equipment and remarks that "within the bounds of propriety, he [Theocles] is attired as one of the Dioscuri." Kennell concludes that "the *koroi* were, to all appearances, the mortal counterparts of the *Dioskoroi*."[192]

The designation of the *hippeis* as *koroi*, as well as Theocles' resemblance of the Dioscuri, provide a noteworthy parallel to the centrality of the Curetes in the myth of fighting for the Lelantine Plain.[193] The heroization of Theocles recalls Plutarch's Cleomachus and the Eretrian grave markers that I have discussed in Chapter 2. Conceivably, Theocles, a *hêbôn*, could die during an initiation into the corps of *hippeis* in one of the last battles for the Thyreatis;

---

[189] Wace 1937, 219; Kennell 1995, 139; *SEG* 46 399. Jeffery ([1961] 1990, 193) dates the relief to ca. 510–500 BC.
[190] Kennell 1995, 139–141; Hodkinson 2000, 244; Jeffery [1961] 1990, 193.
[191] Kennell 1995, 140.
[192] *Ibid.*, 141.
[193] Kennell also notes the abundance of the representations of horses and horsemen in the sanctuary of Artemis Orthia, and suggests "the involvement of young horsemen in Orthia's cult." He further connects the "Laconian rider motif" (iconographically linked with Artemis Orthia) with the *hippeis*, enjoying Artemis' protection. Kennell 1995, 142, with further references. This link between the *hippeis* and Artemis recalls the possible role of the cult of Artemis Amarynthia in the ritual battles for the Lelantine Plain.

Theocles' comrades in initiation, who successfully became *hippeis*, commemorated his death by establishing a hero cult.

Whether we accept this interpretation of Theocles' death or not, the relief is also interesting in another respect. The relief was found in modern Magoula, the ancient Spartan village of Pitana.[194] The association between the *hippeis* and Pitana brings us back to the obstinate Amompharetus, the leader of the Pitanate battalion (τοῦ Πιτανητέων λόχου, Herodotus 9.53.2).

The existence of the Pitanate battalion was famously denied by Thucydides (1.20.3). Herodotus' designation almost certainly was technically faulty, since the attested Spartan *lochoi* have different names; Herodotus seems to have used the term *lochos* in a broader sense of a body of troops.[195] The term "Pitanate *lochos*" is not limited to Herodotus' usage; Herodian (4.8.3) reports that Caracalla "summoned picked young men from Sparta and formed a unit which he called his Laconian and Pitanate battalion" (ἀπό τε Σπάρτης μεταπεμψάμενος νεανίας Λακωνικὸν καὶ Πιτανάτην ἐκάλει λόχον). Douglas H. Kelly has suggested on the basis of

---

[194] Hodkinson 2000, 244; Jeffery [1961] 1990, 193.
[195] Lupi 2006, 191; Cartledge [1979] 2002, 218-219; cf. Hornblower 1991, 57-58. On Thucydides' interest in precise technical appellations, see Hunt 2006, 385.

Thucydides' text that the Pitanate *lochos* should be identified with the corps of *hippeis*.[196]

Recently Marcello Lupi has convincingly developed this interpretation, showing on the basis of a broad spectrum of evidence that the Pitanate *lochos* must have consisted of young men in their twenties.[197]

The identification of Amompharetus as a commander of the corps of *hippeis*,[198] and a *hippeus* himself,[199] perfectly suits the thematic links between the battle of Plataea and the battle of Champions, which we have detected earlier. Amompharetus leads the corps that is

---

[196] Kelly (1981, 32) notes that Thucydides objects to a belief that there is the Pitanate *lochos* "to the Spartan kings;" the association between the kings and the *lochos* identifies the Pitanates as *hippeis*.

[197] Lupi 2006, 190-195. The suggestion that the Pitanate *lochos* consisted of young men has been made already by Chrimes 1949, 318.

[198] Lupi (2006, 198) suggests that Amomphareus' force is only a part of the *hippeis* corps.

[199] Herodotus (9.85.2) reports that after the battle the Spartans buried Amompharetus and other preeminent warriors in a separate tomb; the text of Herodotus says that this tomb was reserved for the priests (ἱρέας), but this word is commonly emended to ἰρένας (*eirenes*). (Differently, Hodkinson 2000, 258 with references). Lupi (2006, 190-193) defends this emendation, interpreting *eirên* as a young man in his twenties. (Lupi's argument that the Pitanate *lochos* consisted of young men does not hinge on the acceptance of this emendation). Lupi's interpretation of *eirên* makes it synonymous with *hêbôn*. It is disputed whether the term *eirenes* identifies young men only in their twenty-first year, or a broader category of 20-30 years old; Lupi embraces the latter position. For references to both opinions, see Lupi 2006, 209n21. The identification of Amompharetus as a young man, to which Kelly (1981, 34-36) objects because of the excessive insubordination that it seems to imply, actually makes the dynamics of the quarrel between Amompharetus and Pausanias psychologically convincing: Pausanias responds to Amompharetus' obstinacy with a parent-like mixture of exasperation and anxiety for his safety.

supposed to embody the three hundred Spartans who sacrificed their lives fighting for the Thyreatis. Amompharetus is eager to reenact their fate.

What is the connection between the *hippeis* and Pitana? Pausanias (3.14.2) reports that the royal tombs of the Agiad house were in Pitana. Pindar (*Olympian* 6.28) and Herodotus (3.55) attest to the aristocratic character of some of Pitana's inhabitants. The elite associations of Pitana matches the elite history of the *hippeis*; as Stephen Hodkinson observes, "[a]lthough success in the Spartiate upbringing was in principle based upon merit, it is likely that boys from privileged families fared better in the selection procedures by which the future military leaders were chosen."[200] Thus, it is likely that the corps of *hippeis* was largely comprised of aristocratic Spartans. However, the significance of Pitana is broader than its elite overtones. Marcello Lupi shows that Pitana "was the main village and the political and cultic centre of the city."[201] Pitana was located in the west and north-west of the city and included the Spartan acropolis.[202] In Euripides' *Trojan Women* (1112), Pitana seems to be used as a synonym of Sparta: the chorus prays that Menelaus should never see the city of Pitana and the temple of Athena of the Brazen House on the acropolis. The connection between Menelaus and Pitana is further attested by Hesychius, s.v. Πιτανάτης στρατός· ὁ τῶν Ἑλλήνων, ἤτοι ἀπὸ μέρους, ἢ διὰ τὸν

---

[200] Hodkinson 2000, 259.
[201] Lupi 2006, 204.
[202] Shipley 2003, 131, reviewing the results of Kourinou 2000.

Μενέλαον, ὃς ἦν Πιτανάτης, οὗ χάριν ἐστράτευσαν. ἔστι δὲ ἡ Πιτάνη φυλή "The Pitanate host. The host of the Greeks, either [called so] on account of its part, or because of Menelaus, who was Pitanate, and for whose sake they waged war. There is also Pitana *phule*." Thus, Pitana had an enormous metonymic force: the name of the village could designate all of Greece and evoke times as distant as the Trojan War. Hesychius' gloss represents Pitana not only as the heart of Sparta, but as the heart of Greece. The *hippeis*' bond to Pitana, expressed by the dedication of Theocles' relief, emphasizes their status of paradigmatic Spartan warriors.

The three hundred Spartans who fought over the Thyreatis defined what it is to be a Spartan. In death they were imagined to come back not just to Sparta, but to their world's center, Pitana:

> τὰν Πιτάναν Θρασύβουλος ἐπ' ἀσπίδος ἤλυθεν ἄπνους
> ἑπτὰ πρὸς Ἀργείων τραύματα δεξάμενος,
> δεικνὺς ἀντία πάντα· τὸν αἱματόεντα δ' ὁ πρέσβυς
> παῖδ' ἐπὶ πυρκαϊὴν Τύννιχος εἶπε τιθείς·
> "Δειλοὶ κλαιέσθωσαν· ἐγὼ δὲ σέ, τέκνον, ἄδακρυς
> θάψω, τὸν καὶ ἐμὸν καὶ Λακεδαιμόνιον."

> Thrasybulus came to Pitana on his shield, lifeless,
> having received seven wounds from the Argives,
> showing them all in the front. Placing his blood-covered
> child on the funeral pyre, old Tynnichus said:
> Let the cowards weep. But I without tears
> will bury you, son, both mine and Sparta's.[203]

---

[203] Dioscorides, *Greek Anthology* 7.229 = Plutarch, *Sayings of the Spartans* 235a.

Chapter 4

City of Women: Democratic Argos and the Battle of Sepeia

> And I almost forgot to mention the spirit of freedom and equal
> rights in the relation of men to women and women to men.
> Plato, Republic 8.563b[1]

1. Harnessing the energy of the myth

In the previous chapter I have argued that in the Archaic period the aristocratic young men of Argos and Sparta participated in ritual battles for the territory of the Thyreatis. We will return to the subject of ritual battles in Chapter 6, which explores the political subtext of the Argive proposal to the Spartans to replay the ancient battle for the Thyreatis/Cynuria in the framework of a peace treaty (420 BC, Thucydides 5.41.2–3). However, we will reach that point only after Chapters 4 and 5, dealing with different issues. How do these chapters function in the framework of my argument?

First, these chapters attempt to bridge the gap between the Archaic ritual battles and the Argive proposal of 420 BC. It is clear from Thucydides' testimony that the idea of ritual battles did not disappear with the cessation of the actual ritual confrontations in the sixth

---

[1] ἐν γυναιξὶ δὲ πρὸς ἄνδρας καὶ ἀνδράσι πρὸς γυναῖκας ὅση ἡ ἰσονομία καὶ ἐλευθερία γίγνεται, ὀλίγου ἐπελαθόμεθ' εἰπεῖν.

century. The ritual seems to have been "dormant" for more than a hundred years before its brief political resurrection. However, the revivification of the ritual after such a period of inactivity implies that there was a group of people in Argos who kept the memory of the ritual alive. As will become apparent from my analysis, this group can be identified with the Argive fifth-century aristocrats, forming the oligarchic faction in the city. In the course of my exploration I attempt to detect traditions concerning Argive-Spartan relations that can be attributed to this socio-political group.

However, searching for appearances of the "keepers" of ritual battles in the historical record is far from being the central concern of the next two chapters. I am primarily interested in investigating the ideological role of the Argive-Spartan confrontation in the fifth-century Argos. The previous chapter has suggested that the theme of the confrontation between Sparta and Argos was ideologically highly charged in the Archaic period, lying in the foundation of the myth-ritual complex of battles over the Thyreatis. After the Spartan annexation of Cynuria and the inception of the real Argive-Spartan hostilities, the tradition of the confrontation between Argos and Sparta must have remained thematically highly potent. In other words, even though the ritual battles between Argos and Sparta ceased, the myth of the confrontation between Argos and Sparta remained, and presumably was reinforced by the real violence of the Spartan annexation of Cynuria and the battle of Sepeia. The appreciation of the mythical potential of the Argive-Spartan antagonism leads us to expect that the topic of confrontation with Sparta could have been harnessed for various ideological purposes at the focal points of Argive fifth-century history. Indeed, in the next two chapters I demonstrate that the battle of Sepeia acquired a mythical status in fifth-century Argos, becoming contested ideological grounds for Argive self-definition. The battle of Sepeia and the figure of Apollo Pythaeus, the deity that formerly watched over the ritual battles between Argos and Sparta, become implicated in the foundational narratives of the establishment of the Argive democracy and the consolidation of the Argive Plain under the control of Argos.

2. Cleomenes' ruses

Herodotus' account of the battle of Sepeia (6.77–80) indicates from the outset that the fighting between the Spartans and the Argives is not going to follow the agonistic model: the Argives are not afraid of "fair fighting," but are worried that the Spartans might use a trick (*dolos*, 6.77.1). The trick indeed follows, and it is hard to imagine a stratagem that would enact more vicariously the breakdown of the agonistic mode of combat. The Argives decide that the best way to protect themselves from the trickery is to follow commands of the enemy's herald: therefore, they repeat all the actions of the Spartans. This is a moment of a perfect symmetry between the sides, recalling the symmetry of the three hundreds against the three hundreds of the Battle of Champions. Then the symmetry is treacherously broken: "When Cleomenes saw that the Argives did whatever was signaled by his herald, he commanded that when the herald cried the signal for breakfast, they should then put on their armor and attack the Argives" (6.78.1).[2] The ruse succeeds and many Argives are killed at breakfast, which they take "in obedience to the herald's signal" (ἐκ τοῦ κηρύγματος, 6.78.2).[3] Thus, the Argives are made vulnerable by their reliance on symmetry and their trust in the overt meaning of communications.[4]

Cleomenes' next move also involves perverted communication. The surviving Argives flee to take refuge in a sacred grove of Argos. Cleomenes sends a herald, who calls out names of individual Argives, announcing to them that they are ransomed; when they emerge one by one from the sacred grove, they are killed. Importantly, Herodotus places this atrocity against the backdrop of normal pan-Peloponnesian practices: "Among the Peloponnesians there is a fixed ransom of two minae to be paid for every prisoner" (6.79.1).

---

[2] Cleomenes evidently finds a way to communicate his treacherous message to his army bypassing his herald. Thus, the breakdown of the traditional mode of agonistic fighting is also dramatized as going beyond the conventional means of transmitting military information. Cf. Thucydides 5.66.
[3] Compare Peisistratus' attack on the Athenians during the afternoon meal/rest in Herodotus 1.63.
[4] This trust in the heralds can be contrasted with the "herald-less" war (πόλεμον ἀκήρυκτον), waged by the Aeginetans against the Athenians (Herodotus 5.81.2).

Cleomenes' rampage culminates in a burning down of the sacred grove of Argos, together with the Argive soldiers taking refuge there; then Cleomenes disregards local sacred rules, disobeying a priest who prohibits him to sacrifice at the Heraion, since he is a stranger; Cleomenes orders the priest be whipped (6.81).

Herodotus' description of the battle of Sepeia portrays the events as a massacre unbounded by any social, moral and religious constraints. An important theme is the breakdown of trustworthy communications as embodied in the figure of the herald.[5] The impression of outrage is intensified by the strong appeal to the agonistic norms of fighting, present in the text: the notions of symmetry and honesty, and the limitation of violence in the form of established ransom.[6]

The Sepeia campaign as depicted by Herodotus is not only an instance of an unusually vicious aggression: it is a representation of a world that is profoundly in disarray. Such a reading of the episode stems from the consideration of the Delphic oracle, given to the Argives, which opens Herodotus' description of the fighting (Herodotus 6.77.2):

ἀλλ' ὅταν ἡ θήλεια τὸν ἄρσενα νικήσασα

---

[5] Fittingly, Cleomenes ultimately is himself caught in a divine double entendre, when he realizes that the capture of Argos, promised by Apollo, turns out to refer to his capture of the grove of Argos (Herodotus 6.80).

[6] Connor (1988, 19n74) describes Herodotus' account of Cleomenes at Sepeia as "an almost paradigmatic inversion of the warrior code."

ἐξελάσῃ καὶ κῦδος ἐν Ἀργείοισιν ἄρηται,
πολλὰς Ἀργείων ἀμφιδρυφέας τότε θήσει.
ὥς ποτέ τις ἐρέει καὶ ἐπεσσομένων ἀνθρώπων
δεινὸς ὄφις τριέλικτος ἀπώλετο δουρὶ δαμασθείς.

When the female defeats the male
and drives him away, winning glory in Argos,
she will make many Argive women tear their cheeks.
As someday one of men to come will say:
the dread thrice-coiled serpent died tamed by the spear.

The image of the female defeating the male, and the mixing of glory and grief portray the world in a topsy-turvy state. The theme of topsy-turvy conditions reappears in Herodotus' statement that after the battle of Sepeia slaves took control of the Argive affairs[7] (I will return to this subject at length). Arguably, the non-agonistic, deceptive mode of fighting employed by Cleomenes is a feature of the same disordered world. This inference is borne out by the text: the Argives' fear of the Spartan trick arises precisely from their knowledge of the oracle (despite the fact that no trick is explicitly mentioned by the oracle).[8] So, the motif of underhanded violence and the topsy-turvy state of the world are interrelated in Herodotus' description.

---

[7] Vidal-Naquet 1986, 210; Miller 1999, 243.
[8] ἐνθαῦτα δὴ οἱ Ἀργεῖοι τὴν μὲν ἐκ τοῦ φανεροῦ μάχην οὐκ ἐφοβέοντο, ἀλλὰ μὴ <u>δόλῳ</u> αἱρεθέωσι: <u>καὶ γὰρ</u> δή σφι ἐς τοῦτο τὸ πρῆγμα εἶχε τὸ χρηστήριον τὸ ἐπίκοινα ἔχρησε ἡ Πυθίη τούτοισί τε καὶ Μιλησίοισι, λέγον ὧδε. "There the Argives had no fear of fair fighting, but rather of being captured by a trick. This was the affair referred to by that oracle which the Pythian priestess gave to the Argives and Milesians in common, which ran thus: ..." Herodotus 6.77.1–2.

An anecdote transmitted by Plutarch attributes a different trick to Cleomenes at Sepeia: Cleomenes makes a truce of seven days with the Argives, but attacks them on the third night, while they are asleep. His justification is that the truce included only days and not nights. While historically the two stories rule each other out, on the level of narrative they function as variations on the same theme of unfair fighting.[9] Cleomenes' stratagem of including only days in the truce is in fact a stock story, reappearing in a number of contexts.[10] Strabo (quoting Ephorus), Zenobius, and Polyaenus ascribe the stratagem to the Thracians; the stratagem was the source of the proverbial expression "Thracian pretext." The attribution of the stratagem to the Thracians places it in a realm of archetypically savage behaviors.[11]

Cleomenes' night attack resembles Pierre Ellinger's concept of "war of total annihilation." A narrative belonging to this type presents a conflict in opposition to a normative hoplite battle. Wars of total annihilation are unequal, extreme, transgressive, full of ruses;[12] the fighting frequently happens at night. Summarizing Ellinger's work, Vernant describes wars of total annihilation as situations "where the prize is no longer the victory of

---

[9] On the broader theme of the Spartan duplicity, see Bradford 1994.
[10] Ephorus ap. Strabo 9.2.4; Zenobius 4.37; Cicero, *De Officiis* I 10, 33; Polyaenus 7.43; 6.53. Hendricks 1980, 346.
[11] Another variation, in Polyaenus 6.53, makes the Athenian Hagnon the truce-breaker in his dealing with barbarians on the river Strymon. We see, again, that the trick of counting the days and not night belongs to the dealings with barbarians, not to the civilized Greek world.
[12] Ellinger 1993, 336.

one city over another but the survival of an entire human community." He continues: "In such excess and all-or-nothing stakes, war goes beyond the civilized boundaries within which rules of military engagement are maintained and veers abruptly into savagery."[13]

The presentation of the Sepeia campaign as an uncivilized, topsy-turvy affair occurs also in other accounts of the battle. I have already mentioned Herodotus' report that slaves ruled in Argos after the battle. Pausanias and Plutarch narrate that the battle saw the participation of women (and slaves as well, according to Pausanias). The involvement of women in war is a typical feature of the wars of total annihilation: as Ellinger describes it, in such situations the boundaries, normally dividing the world of warriors from the female world, collapse.[14]

It is important to emphasize that depicting the Sepeia campaign as a war of total annihilation is a *way of presenting* the conflict.[15] We have traces of an alternative presentation of the battle that portrays Cleomenes as respecting certain boundaries in his assault. The strongest evidence is Herodotus' report that when Cleomenes returned to Sparta, he was blamed for not making an attempt to capture Argos: this tradition, running, as we will see, directly counter to the traditions transmitted by Pausanias and Plutarch, does not espouse the

---

[13] Vernant 1991, 246.
[14] Ellinger 1993, 336.
[15] For folk motifs in Herodotus' description of the disaster at Sepeia, see Griffiths 1989, 57.

representation of the battle as threatening Argos' survival. In a different entry of the *Sayings of the Spartans* Cleomenes is even credited with a riposte that seems more appropriate for the practice of ritual battles than for lethal warfare (*Moralia* 224b):

> Εἰπόντος δέ τινος «Διὰ τί πολεμοῦντας ὑμῖν Ἀργείους πολλάκις κρατήσαντες οὐκ ἀνῃρήκατε;» «Οὐδ' ἂν ἀνέλοιμεν» ἔφη, «ὡς ἂν γυμναστὰς τοῖς νέοισιν ἔχωμεν.»
>
> When someone said, "Why have you not killed off the people of Argos who wage war against you so often?" he said, "Oh, we would not kill them off, for we want to have some trainers for our young men."

The issue of the different presentations of the Sepeia campaign opens a question of the causes and purposes of any particular account. A related problem is, what are the sources from which the stories that we possess originate? I will attempt to tackle these questions in the following sections.

3. Women and slaves disentangled: varieties of inversion

Two other main accounts of the Sepeia campaign, by Plutarch (*Virtues of Women* 245c-e) and Pausanias (2.20.8-10), introduce a narrative element that is absent in Herodotus. These authors report that after the battle of Sepeia Cleomenes brought his army to attack Argos, which was completely stripped of the males of military age. At that point an Argive poetess, Telesilla, led the resistance. Pausanias recounts that Telesilla positioned very young and old men, as well as slaves, on the walls of Argos. Pausanias and Plutarch both tell that the women then valiantly fought the Spartans, who eventually turned back, unable to capture the city.

Plutarch's version contains some especially remarkable details. On the authority of the Argive historian Socrates, Plutarch reports that the women not only repulsed Cleomenes' army, but also drove out the army of Demaratus that somehow managed to get inside Argos. Plutarch describes the Argive commemoration of the women's valor, and adds that on the anniversary of the battle, the Argives to his day celebrated a festival called Hybristica, characterized by cross-dressing.

The versions of Plutarch and Pausanias have found little favor with modern scholars of Greek history. Many details seem untrustworthy. The report that Cleomenes' army attacked Argos contradicts Herodotus' version of the events, which seems by far the more reliable.[16] The materialization of Demaratus' army in Argos looks even less credible. Further, the story of Telesilla and the brave Argive women appears to many scholars to be just a later attempt to

---

[16] Herodotus (6.82) specifically reports that Cleomenes was brought to trial in Sparta for not attacking Argos, the information that seems to be based on the Spartan sources.

explain the oracle about the female defeating the male, quoted by Herodotus.[17] The aetiological connection between the battle and the Hybristica is also commonly viewed with suspicion.[18]

While the usefulness of Pausanias' and Plutarch's accounts for a historical reconstruction of the events surrounding the Sepeia campaign may be limited, these stories have historical value of their own as reflections of Greek perceptions of the past. This value can be particularly great if we succeed in establishing when, and why, these stories were created. One way to approach this task is to study the ideologies of these narratives, investigating the respective particular versions of the past that they promote.

The tales of the Argive disaster at Sepeia are frequently studied by scholars that are interested in patterns of mythical thinking. An analysis by Vidal-Naquet has greatly influenced the scholarship on the subject;[19] thus, reviewing Vidal-Naquet's argument and the place of the Argive narratives in it is a good way to start the investigation of the narratives' ideology.

Vidal-Naquet investigated the question of a potentially parallel perception of women and slaves, two classes of people excluded from power in a Greek polis. Vidal-Naquet performed his analysis on the material of myth-historical accounts and utopias inverting the

---

[17] Herodotus' omission of any reference to Telesilla is often interpreted as a strong indication that the story was not yet current when Herodotus was gathering information; see discussion below.
[18] I discuss the issue below in more details.
[19] Vidal-Naquet 1986, 205–223.

normative order of the polis; he searched for traditions "linking the exercise of power by women and by slaves."[20] He found four examples of such a pairing, including the Argive cluster of narratives. Vidal-Naquet observed that there was a distinction between Athens and the societies that he dubbed "archaic" (such as Sparta or Locri): in Athens, tales of the rule of women were never linked with the rule of slaves. Vidal-Naquet inferred that the civic status of women was problematized in democratic Athens, but that slaves were irrevocably excluded from the civic system; conversely, in the "archaic societies" the statuses of slaves and women were perceived as analogous.[21]

A comprehensive reevaluation of Vidal-Naquet's argument would distract from my present investigation; however, I wish to reexamine the points that specifically relate to Argos. Vidal-Naquet noted that in Herodotus' narrative the rule of women (the oracle's victory of the female) and the rule of slaves were not connected, while the later versions linked the slaves and the women. However, the difference between Herodotus and the later sources did not concern Vidal-Naquet, whose aim was "not to reconstruct the 'facts' but to understand the logic of the myths."[22] Indeed, owing to Vidal-Naquet's research we clearly perceive the parallelism in the inversion tales about the rule of women and slaves in Argos. But were all

---

[20] Vidal-Naquet 1986, 209.
[21] *Ibid.*, 217–18.
[22] *Ibid.*, 210.

inversions created equal? That is to say, what is the importance of the paradigmatic substitution of woman vs. slave in a topsy-turvy situation?[23] Vidal-Naquet's consideration of the Athenian example already indicates that there can be a significant difference between narratives that feature both women and slaves, and those that mention only one category. I propose to descend from the bird's-eye view, adopted by Vidal-Naquet, and to examine separate versions in their uniqueness. I would like to clarify the ideologies endorsed by different versions; as I have said earlier, I hope that such a clarification, in turn, will be helpful in dating the stories.

To begin, I would like to appraise the evidence for the connection between women and slaves in the Argive stories. Among our sources, Herodotus, as we have just discussed, mentions women in the oracle only, and does not draw any connection between this reference and slaves. Plutarch's narrative stars women as the fighting force; at the only point that Plutarch mentions slaves and women in the same breath, he does so to refute Herodotus. "To repair the scarcity of men they did not unite the women with slaves, as Herodotus records," he protests.[24] (In fact, in our inherited text, Herodotus never makes such an assertion.) Pausanias is the only source that portrays women alongside slaves: Telesilla stations slaves, and males of

---

[23] Sourvinou-Inwood (1974, 193–4n9) notes potentially different functions of stories concerning the rule of women and rule of slaves after the battle of Sepeia.
[24] *Moralia* 245f.

non-military age, on the walls of Argos and then the women engage in a combat (Pausanias 2.20.9). However, in Pausanias' version the role of the slaves, manning the walls of Argos alongside the old and young Argives, is that of a supporting cast; the focus of attention is squarely on the women.[25]

Thus, the slaves and the women tend to appear separately in the accounts of Sepeia and post-Sepeia. Moreover, there is some conflict between the traditions precisely on the point of the relation between the women and the slaves, with Plutarch contesting the details of what he perceived to be Herodotus' account. Since I would like to figure out the difference in the function of the women and the slaves in the inversion tales, I will pay particularly close attention to the versions where they appear on their own: I will now analyze Plutarch's version of the story of Telesilla, and, in Chapter 5, I will examine Herodotus' passage concerning the rule of the slaves.

---

[25] Pausanias' version is an amalgam of several sources, including Herodotus' narrative (Pausanias repeats the story of the burning of the grove of Argos), so it is possible that the appearance of the slaves in Pausanias' version is influenced by the rule of the slaves in Herodotus. Piérart 2003, 280 observes that Pausanias "has Herodotus in mind" throughout his account.

4. Liberating the Pamphyliacum

Plutarch provides a detailed description of the defense of Argos by women (*Virtues of Women* 245c–e):

Οὐδενὸς δ' ἧττον ἔνδοξόν ἐστι τῶν κοινῇ διαπεπραγμένων γυναιξὶν ἔργων ὁ πρὸς Κλεομένη περὶ Ἄργους ἀγών, ὃν ἠγωνίσαντο Τελεσίλλης τῆς ποιητρίας προτρεψαμένης. ταύτην δέ φασιν οἰκίας οὖσαν ἐνδόξου τῷ δὲ σώματι νοσηματικὴν εἰς θεοῦ πέμψαι περὶ ὑγιείας· καὶ χρησθὲν αὐτῇ Μούσας θεραπεύειν, πειθομένην τῷ θεῷ καὶ ἐπιθεμένην ᾠδῇ καὶ ἁρμονίᾳ τοῦ τε πάθους ἀπαλλαγῆναι ταχὺ καὶ θαυμάζεσθαι διὰ ποιητικὴν ὑπὸ τῶν γυναικῶν. ἐπεὶ δὲ Κλεομένης ὁ βασιλεὺς τῶν Σπαρτιατῶν πολλοὺς ἀποκτείνας (οὐ μήν, ὡς ἔνιοι μυθολογοῦσιν, ἑπτὰ καὶ ἑβδομήκοντα καὶ ἑπτακοσίους πρὸς ἑπτακισχιλίοις) ἐβάδιζε πρὸς τὴν πόλιν, ὁρμὴ καὶ τόλμα δαιμόνιος παρέστη ταῖς ἀκμαζούσαις τῶν γυναικῶν ἀμύνεσθαι τοὺς πολεμίους ὑπὲρ τῆς πατρίδος. ἡγουμένης δὲ τῆς Τελεσίλλης ὅπλα λαμβάνουσαι καὶ παρ' ἔπαλξιν ἱστάμεναι κύκλῳ τὰ τείχη περιέστεψαν, ὥστε θαυμάζειν τοὺς πολεμίους. τὸν μὲν οὖν Κλεομένη πολλῶν πεσόντων ἀπεκρούσαντο· τὸν δ' ἕτερον βασιλέα Δημάρατον, ὡς Σωκράτης φησίν ἐντὸς γενόμενον καὶ κατασχόντα τὸ Παμφυλιακὸν ἐξέωσαν. οὕτω δὲ τῆς πόλεως περιγενομένης, ...

Of all the deeds performed by women for the community none is more famous than the struggle against Cleomenes for Argos, which the women carried out at the instigation of Telesilla the poetess. She, as they say, was the daughter of a famous house but sickly in body, and so she sent to the god to ask about health; and when an oracle was given her to cultivate the Muses, she followed the god's advice, and by devoting herself to poetry and music she was quickly relieved of her trouble, and was greatly admired by the women for her poetic art. But when Cleomenes king of the Spartans, having slain many Argives (but not by any means seven thousand, seven hundred and seventy-seven, as some fabulous narratives have it) proceeded against the city, an impulsive daring, divinely inspired, came to the younger women to try, for their country's sake, to hold off the enemy. Under the lead of Telesilla they took up arms, and, taking their stand by the battlements, manned the walls all round, so that the enemy were amazed. The result was that Cleomenes they repulsed with great loss, and the other king,

Demaratus, who managed to get inside, as Socrates says, and gained possession of the Pamphyliacum, they drove out. In this way the city was saved.

Plutarch is familiar with numerous accounts of the events surrounding the battle of Sepeia. He disagrees with some authors (such as Herodotus, or an unnamed source that asserted that the number of the Argives killed at Sepeia was seven thousand seven hundred and seventy-seven); he reserves his judgment regarding other rival versions, such as those concerning the day of the month when the battle occurred, and reports them side by side. Most importantly for my investigation, Plutarch reveals his source for the eccentric detail about the army of Demaratus getting inside the Argive walls and taking possession of Pamphyliacum, only to be driven out by the Argive women: on this point Plutarch invokes the authority of the Argive historian Socrates (*Moralia* 245e). While there is no scholarly consensus about whether the story of Telesilla's leadership was also reported by Socrates, or was inherited by Plutarch from a different source,[26] the story of Telesilla and the story about the Argive women seizing the Pamphyliacum are strongly connected thematically and are likely to belong to the Argive version(s) of the events at Sepeia.[27]

Plutarch's narrative about the women liberating the Pamphyliacum has a high

---

[26] See Stadter 1965, 52–53, n73 with further references; Kiechle (1960, 181) thinks the whole Telesilla story is from Socrates.

[27] On the Argive sources of the stories of Telesilla and the female defense of Argos, see Stadter 1965, 45–53, 136–137.

concentration of mythologizing patterns.[28] The joint appearance of Cleomenes and Demaratus creates a dramatic effect, producing the impression that the Argive women face the attack of the whole of Spartan manpower. Another element exhibiting mythological overtones is the story of Telesilla. Telesilla's accomplishments in war are represented as corresponding to her accomplishments in the art of poetry. I note the parallel between the two occurrences of the verb θαυμάζω 'marvel at,' describing, in the first case, the reception of Telesilla's poetry by the Argive women, and in the second, the amazement of the enemy at the sight of the women encircling the city. Moreover, Telesilla's defense of Argos is portrayed as deriving from her role as a chorus leader.[29] The women's resistance is described in terms reminiscent of a choral dance: they stand by the battlements in a circle, "enwreathing" the walls.[30] Thus, the female defense of Argos is depicted in terms evocative of a sacred ritual activity.

Plutarch presents the assault of Cleomenes and Demaratus on Argos as a war of total annihilation. Plutarch's narrative portrays the community on the brink of disappearance, with

---

[28] It seems apt to quote here a remark of Nicole Loraux (1995, 234–5) that "introducing armed women into a narrative essentially amounts to freeing the text from all concerns with reality."
[29] On Telesilla's defense of Argos as similar to a choral performance, see Kowalzig 2004, 50, Goff 2004, 241. The only surviving fragment ascribed to Telesilla is a choral piece; thus, perhaps the persona of Telesilla was traditionally choral. On the role of Telesilla and her poetry in coming-of-age rituals, see Dowden 1989, 103; Ingalls 2000, 14–16.
[30] On the circularity of the lyric chorus, see Calame [1977] 2001, 34–35, especially p. 35: "It is appropriate here to recall that Hesychius himself defined the chorus as a circle or a crown" (Hesychius s.v. χορός).

the men already dead and the women about to succumb to the unified assault of both Spartan kings. Then comes the salvation by the women. Importantly, the women's defense constitutes not just a rescue, but also a victory over the Spartans, since Cleomenes retreats with heavy losses.

The female triumph that saves the city of Argos at the same time marks the end of the old community: Argos, whose males are extinct, and whose females acts like males, is a new city. It is relevant to mention here that among Vidal-Naquet's four examples of the joint rules of the women and slaves, two are foundation tales, of Ephizephyrian Locri and Tarentum.[31] I suggest that we should similarly read the story of the women's defense as a foundation tale of a new phase for Argive society.

Can we establish at which phase of Argive history the story of the women's defense, in the form that Plutarch narrates it, could have been used as a foundation tale? Plutarch's account provides a clue about the character of this phase: Plutarch reports that after the battle the Argives united their women "with the best of the *perioikoi*, whom they made Argive citizens."[32] Many scholars have seen this statement, describing a broadening of the franchise, as an expression of a transition to a more democratic constitution. While I do not subscribe to

---

[31] Sourvinou-Inwood 1974, 193–4.
[32] I assume here that the word *perioikoi* has a standard meaning of 'dwellers around;' I defend this interpretation of the *perioikoi* in Chapter 5.

the historical interpretation inferring that Argos transitioned to a more democratic stage after Sepeia, I do think that the detail about the enfranchisement of the *perioikoi* is a manifestation of the democratic ideology. Thus, *if* it can be shown that the part about the *perioikoi* and the story of the women's defense are intrinsically connected, and were not merely brought together by Plutarch, we can conclude that the story of the women's defense functioned as a foundation tale of the Argive democracy.

I will presently examine the connection between the story of the women's defense and the reference to the *perioikoi*. However, first I would like to establish what period of Argive history the democratic detail about the enfranchisement of the *perioikoi* fits best. The enfranchisement constitutes a synoecism, in the most literal of the senses: the best of the *perioikoi* are made to cohabit (συνῴκισαν) with the Argive women. While our knowledge of Argive history is imperfect, the period of 460–450 BC appears to provide a remarkably suitable setting for the tale featuring the reference to the synoecism and *perioikoi*. By that time, as has been convincingly demonstrated by Jonathan Hall, Argos finally acquired control over the previously independent neighboring communities of the Argive Plain. The inscriptional evidence reflects a major restructuring of the Argive citizen body sometime before the middle of the fifth century; it has been suggested that this restructuring indicates a democratic reform, connected with Argive acquisition of the new territories and a subsequent integration of new citizens from the dependent communities.[33] Thus, I conjecture that Plutarch's account of the enfranchisement of the *perioikoi*, as well as the story of the women's defense of Argos, stem from the historical milieu of 460–450 BC. These tales express the ideology of democratic Argos, retrojecting the establishment of democracy all the way back to the times of Sepeia.

As a crucial next step in my argument, I need to show that the story of the women's defense, as reported by Plutarch, is thematically connected and contemporaneous with the detail about the *perioikoi*.[34] I believe that indeed there is a clue in the story that substantiates this suggestion: it is the point about the liberation of the Pamphyliacum.

In Plutarch's version, the liberation of the Pamphyliacum by the women is presented as a climactic moment of the salvation of Argos. The mention of the liberation is followed by the statement: "in this way the city survived." I propose that the importance of the Pamphyliacum derives from the visualization, inherent in that designation, of the totality of the citizen body as composed of different *phylai*.

We have strong reason to think that the concept of *phylai* had a particular significance in Argos in the middle of the fifth century. The restructuring of the citizen body that I have

---

[33] Hall 1995, 590; Hornblower 2002, 80; Piérart 1997, 332.
[34] I do not exclude the possibility that the story of the female defense of Argos could have circulated in some form in Argos prior to the transition to democracy. My claim is that Plutarch's account includes some details allowing to connect the composition of that particular version of the tale with the establishment of the democratic regime in 460s BC.

just mentioned apparently involved a (re)division of each tribe into twelve phratries. It is also likely that there was some redistribution of people across the tribes. In addition, by the mid-fifth century the emergence of the fourth Argive tribe, the Hyrnathioi, must have been relatively recent history. We do not know exactly when this tribe was added to the three traditional Dorian *phylai*, but our best guess is that the addition of this tribe is also connected to the Argive territorial conquests and the resulting enfranchisement of new citizens (I address the issue in more detail below).[35] Thus, if we accept the mid-fifth century dating of the story of the women's defense, the detail about the liberation of the Pamphyliacum, previously overlooked, can be seen as meaningful, thematically connected to the subjects of enfranchisement and synoecism.

The appellation Pamphyliacum also can denote, of course, an entity belonging to the tribe of the Pamphyloi. It has been regularly assumed that the word refers to a quarter, or perhaps a sanctuary, of the Pamphyloi.[36] This interpretation (with which I agree, favoring the meaning 'sanctuary') does not exclude my previous point about the word's reference to all *phylai*, since the name of the tribe functions as a *pars pro toto*, metonymically denoting the

---

[35] The model that seems reasonable to me is that of a two-stage process, involving first an addition of the Hyrnathioi to the tribal system, followed by the reorganization of the four tribes into the forty-eight phratries sometime in 460–450 BC.

[36] Pamphyliacum as a city quarter: Stadter 1965, 45n46; Jones 1987, 115n20; as a sanctuary: Jones 1987, 115. The Pamphyliacum also could have been a sanctuary of all *phylai*.

whole community.[37]

Importantly, it has been argued that the Pamphyloi occupied the lowest rank in a traditional hierarchy of the Doric tribes.[38] Even more interestingly, it has been even suggested on the basis of the inscriptional evidence that the Argive Pamphyloi were at some point promoted in the tribal hierarchy. Their place vis-à-vis two other Doric tribes remained the same, but they began to outrank the tribe of the Hyrnathioi that had been preceding the Pamphyloi in the earlier inscriptions. While a suggestion that the context for this promotion was the democratic reforms of the 460-450 BC is conjecture,[39] it fits very well with my interpretation of the reference to the liberation of the Pamphyliacum. In my reading, the story of the women's defense of Argos singles out the tribe of the Pamphyloi — the notional "common people" of Argos — as the chief beneficiaries of the female victory.

The idea that the account of the Sepeia campaign starring the women's victory has a distinct democratic background recalls Vidal-Naquet's observation that in democratic Athens, the inversion tales featured only women, not slaves. The Argive women seem equally democratic and equally prone to inversions. The next sections continue the investigation of the theme of female supremacy as related to Argive democracy. In particular, I am going to

---

[37] Nagy 1990b, 281, with a comparison to the identical phenomenon in the case of the Hindu vaiśya.
[38] Jones 1980, Nagy 1990b, 279-282.
[39] Jones 1980, 206; Nagy 1990b, 280.

explore the significance of two elements that Plutarch's account connects to the battle of Sepeia: a strange Argive custom according to which a married woman should wear a beard, and the cross-dressing festival of Hybristica.

5. The bearded bride

I will start by quoting the rest of Plutarch's passage (*The Virtues of Women* 245e-f):

> οὕτω δὲ τῆς πόλεως περιγενομένης, τὰς μὲν πεσούσας ἐν τῇ μάχῃ τῶν γυναικῶν ἐπὶ τῆς ὁδοῦ τῆς Ἀργείας ἔθαψαν, ταῖς δὲ σωθείσαις ὑπόμνημα τῆς ἀριστείας ἔδοσαν ἱδρύσασθαι τὸν Ἐνυάλιον. τὴν δὲ μάχην οἱ μὲν ἑβδόμῃ λέγουσιν ἱσταμένου μηνός, οἱ δὲ νουμηνίᾳ γενέσθαι τοῦ νῦν μὲν τετάρτου, πάλαι δ' Ἑρμαίου παρ' Ἀργείοις, καθ' ἣν μέχρι νῦν τὰ Ὑβριστικὰ τελοῦσι, γυναῖκας μὲν ἀνδρείοις χιτῶσι καὶ χλαμύσιν, ἄνδρας δὲ πέπλοις γυναικῶν καὶ καλύπτραις ἀμφιεννύντες. ἐπανορθούμενοι δὲ τὴν ὀλιγανδρίαν οὐχ, ὡς Ἡρόδοτος ἱστορεῖ, τοῖς δούλοις, ἀλλὰ τῶν περιοίκων ποιησάμενοι πολίτας τοὺς ἀρίστους, συνῴκισαν τὰς γυναῖκας· ἐδόκουν δὲ καὶ τούτους ἀτιμάζειν καὶ περιορᾶν ἐν τῷ συγκαθεύδειν ὡς χείρονας. ὅθεν ἔθεντο νόμον τὸν κελεύοντα πώγωνα δεῖν ἐχούσας συναναπαύεσθαι τοῖς ἀνδράσι τὰς γεγαμημένας.

> Thus the city was saved. The women who fell in the battle they buried close by the Argive Road, and to the survivors they granted the privilege of erecting a statue of Ares as a memorial of their surpassing valour. Some say that the battle took place on the seventh day of the month which is now known as the Fourth Month, but anciently was called Hermaeus among the Argives; others say that it was on the first day of that month, on the anniversary of which they celebrate even to this day the 'Festival of Impudence,' at which they clothe the women in men's shirts and cloaks, and the men in women's robes and veils. To repair the scarcity of men they did not unite the women with slaves, as Herodotus records, but with the best of their neighbouring subjects, whom they made Argive citizens. It was reputed that the women showed disrespect and an intentional indifference to those husbands in their married relations from a feeling

that they were underlings. Wherefore the Argives established a law commanding married women to wear beards while sleeping with their husbands.[40]

Many scholarly accounts conflate the two items recounted by Plutarch, the description of the festival of Hybristica, and the law compelling the Argive women to wear beards. We repeatedly hear of a Hybristica where women wore beards, or of a Hybristica that featured group marriages (with beard-endowed brides), etc.[41] Such interpretations are not impossible, but they should not be arrived at implicitly. Plutarch describes the festival and the law separately, and it is important to analyze them separately, each in its own right. I will first examine the tale about the law obliging the women to wear beards.

A prevalent current assumption is that Plutarch's story about the Argives establishing a law according to which a married woman should sleep with her husband while wearing a beard is a result of Plutarch's erroneous connection between the story of Sepeia and a traditional Argive marriage rite, involving the transvestism of the bride.[42] This assertion rests on a broader claim that female transvestism was a widespread custom in Greece. It is this assumption that I would like to examine first.

The remarkable fact is that despite the claims that female transvestism during marriage rites was a common phenomenon, the *only* two cases that are cited in the literature

---

[40] Trans. Frank Cole Babbitt, 1931, modified.
[41] Stadter 1965, 50n67 with references to older literature.
[42] Clark 2012, 118; Ament 1993, 18.

are Plutarch's description of a marriage ceremony of Spartan women, during which the bride's hair was cut and she was dressed in a male cloak,[43] and our Argive story.[44] We should observe that the Argive story does not explicitly talk about transvestism during the marriage ceremony: rather, Plutarch reports a law prescribing a certain behavior of the married women. Two cases, out of which one is not explicitly characterized as a marriage custom, cannot support an assertion that female transvestism was a regular feature of marriage ceremonies.

Male transvestism during marriage rites, on the other hand, is much more robustly attested. So, what we seem to face is an instance of an asymmetry in marriage rites between the genders. Such asymmetry, of course, is not very surprising if we think of the drastic gender inequality in the Greek society. The meaning of marriage was different for men and for women; thus, male and female transvestism potentially could have operated in very different frames of reference. David Leitao, an expert in matters related to the phenomenon of transvestism in ancient Greece, observes this divergence in the functions of male and female marriage transvestism: "When the bridegroom donned the clothing of the opposite sex, it was to dramatize before the community his final transition from the world of women to the world of men. Brides, however, did not undergo a comparable transformation of gender at puberty,

---

[43] Plutarch *Lycurgus* 15.3. For a discussion of that passage, see Lupi 2000, 71-5.
[44] For example, Clark 2012, 188; Gagné 2006, 8; Miller 1999, 243 and n79; Leitao 1995, 162; Serwint 1993, 421.

and therefore a different interpretation must be sought."⁴⁵ As a solution, Leitao has proposed that female transvestism had a very different function, a psychological one, aiming "to ease the anxiety of the individual bridegroom," unaccustomed to heterosexual relationships.⁴⁶ The effectiveness of the bride's false beard in alleviating the anxieties of the individual Argive bridegrooms remains uncertain; in addition, Leitao's explanation does not sufficiently account for such a prominent characteristic of female marriage transvestism as its extreme rarity.

The peculiarity of the (hypothetical) image of a bride wearing a beard is thrown into a sharper relief by Gloria Ferrari's fundamental discussion of the significance of the asymmetrical nature of male and female rites of passage in ancient Greece. Ferrari emphasizes, concerning the social status of a woman, that "the formalities of female rites of passage and the conception of marriage insistently suggest that an adult is what she must never become."⁴⁷

---

⁴⁵ Leitao 1995, 162–63.

⁴⁶ *Ibid.*, 163.

⁴⁷ Ferrari 2002, 8. Ferrari observes an underdeveloped character of female rituals of coming of age, in comparison to male ones, and emphasizes their "poverty" and "incoherence" (p. 176). The existing female rites of passage typically appear as paler reflections of the corresponding male rites, featuring important asymmetries (a phenomenon attested in age-class societies, Ferrari 2002, 176–77 and 299n77, with a reference to Chapter 11 of Bernardi 1985). For example, Ferrari points out concerning the Spartan wedding transvestism of a bride, seemingly analogous to the male attainment of the adult status through a pederastic relationship, that the bride's transition from *parthenos* to *gune* is brought about by a man, not a woman (p. 165); further, she observes, like Leitao, that female transvestism does not change the gender of the bride (p. 176). According to Ferrari (p. 177), this imperfect patterning of the female rites on the male ones expresses the "notion that scholars express with the oxymoron

In this context, how can we make sense of a married woman (as in Plutarch) or a bride (according to the modern reinterpretations) flaunting a full beard, indicating, in the case of a male, an adult status?

Given the stress on the sub-adult status of women in the framework of marriage, a bride's wearing of a beard, that is, her temporary assumption of the identity of an adult male, would have constituted a striking conceptual oddity in a routine marriage ritual.[48] Therefore, I suggest that we should abandon the conjecture that Plutarch mistakenly linked a traditional marriage ritual to the story of the battle of Sepeia. Instead, let us consider Plutarch's text as it stands.

As soon as we come back to Plutarch's original presentation, the idiosyncratic detail about the married women wearing beards finds a correspondingly exceptional context: the extraordinary moment in the past when the Argive females had a higher status than the perioecic males. The transmission of citizenship by uterine descent, formalized by the marriage of the citizen women to the *perioikoi*, is an anomaly; the beards worn by the married woman give this anomaly a dramatic expression.

'women of citizen status,'" namely, the dependence of women on men for having a share in the polis, which the women can achieve only "as daughters, wives and mothers of citizens."
[48] "[I]nversion does not make sense in rituals involving persons whose identities are changing: to represent a ritual actor who is in the process of becoming "X" as "anti-X" is to obscure the very process of change which such transformative rituals aim to bring about." Leitao 1999, 256.

The logic of the Argive law, as reported by Plutarch, both articulates the superiority of the women over their perioecic husbands by means of giving them beards, and at the same time presents this superiority as something temporary, unnatural, un-female. The aim of the law is to cut the women down to size, so that they would not disrespect their husbands, and the false beards do it through presenting the female supremacy as grotesque. A woman with a beard is laughable, as the following dialogue from Aristophanes' *Assemblywomen* shows. After the Athenian women have tied on their false beards, in order to disguise themselves as men, one woman complains to Praxagora (*Assemblywomen* 124–128):

Γυνὴ
δεῦρ' ὦ γλυκυτάτη Πραξαγόρα, σκέψαι τάλαν
ὡς καὶ καταγέλαστον τὸ πρᾶγμα φαίνεται.
Πραξάγορα
πῶς καταγέλαστον;
Γυνὴ
ὥσπερ εἴ τις σηπίαις
πώγωνα περιδήσειεν ἐσταθευμέναις.

Woman: Look, my dear, and see how really ludicrous the thing looks.
Praxagora: In what way ludicrous?
Woman: It's as if someone tied a beard on to lightly browned cuttlefishes![49]

The story about the law obliging women to wear beards features the same motif of the Argive women behaving in a manly manner as does the story of the female defense of Argos; however, the two narratives present opposite, tragic and comic, viewpoints on such a behavior. The

---

[49] Trans. Alan H. Sommerstein, modified.

story of the female defense of Argos portrays the manly conduct of the women positively, as a heroic feat in an extreme situation. The law concerning the women's beards portrays the female manliness as detrimental, and attempts to regulate it, bringing it under control through ridicule.

What can we say about the nature of the law regarding the women's beards, reported by Plutarch? I consider the information that Plutarch transmits to be based on a genuine Argive tradition; however, was it a real law that was endorsed once upon a time? Since, as I have argued in the previous section, the tradition about the enfranchisement of the *perioikoi* after the battle of Sepeia is likely to have been coined around the time of the establishment of the Argive democracy in the 460s, the story about the contemptuous Argive women and the law ordering them to wear beards in all probability should belong to the same historical period. Thus, the law is a mythical invention. I submit that, along with the story of the female defense of Argos, the story about the wives of *perioikoi* sporting beards served as an *aition* for the cross-dressing festival of Hybristica.[50] As I have noted, the two tales are complementary, expressing opposite attitudes toward the motif of the female manliness. Taken together, these two myths motivate both the celebration of the topsy-turvy situation of gender reversal, and the transition back to normalcy.

---

[50] Similarly, McInerney 2003, 336-337.

6. Women in arms: the glory, the farce and the permanent changes

I have proposed that the heroic tale of the female defense of Argos and the comic tale of the beard-wearing wives of the *perioikoi* constitute the foundation myths of the establishment of democracy in Argos. The references to the Pamphyliacum and to the *perioikoi* connect the heroic and comic myths to the central issues of the synoecism and the restructuring of the *phulai* that were taking place during the democratic reforms in the 460s BC. I am going to adduce more evidence for the use of the battle of Sepeia as a foundation myth of the Argive democracy in Chapter 5.

The festival of Hybristica, on the other hand, does not exhibit any clearly democratic details. Despite that, the festival *is* strongly linked to the democratic myths of the female defense of Argos and of the beard-wearing women through the theme of gender inversion. The theme of gender inversion, in fact, helps to explain the name of the festival. A gnome of Democritus of Abdera states that "to be ruled by a woman is the ultimate *hybris* for a man" (ὑπὸ γυναικὸς ἄρχεσθαι ὕβρις εἴη ἂν ἀνδρὶ ἐσχάτη).[51] Thus, *Hybristica* appears to be an apposite term for a festival memorializing the bizarre situation of women in charge.

---

[51] Democritus ap. Stobaeus IV 23, 39.

The question that I would like to examine now is, why does the motif of gender inversion, and of armed women in particular, play a central part in the myth-ritual complex celebrating the establishment of democracy? I have suggested above that the story of the extinction of the male population of Argos dramatizes a break with the past; perhaps the women's presence, conversely, establishes a sense of continuity. However, in what ways, if any, does the fact that the women are armed relate to the function of the tale as a foundation myth?

The motif of the women in arms can be viewed in the context of a broader ancient discourse on primitive life. The subject of the Greek imagination of the primitive life, an existence in a pre-civilized state at chronologically and/or geographically distant points, is extraordinary rich and varied.[52] A recurrent feature that is relevant to the present discussion is the equality between the genders: most pertinently, we encounter both men and women training for war.[53] Women in arms also appear in another mode of envisioning the ancient past, that of the Heroic age: the Amazons are an obvious pan-Hellenic example, but the Argive Danaids also can be represented as hunting and riding chariots.[54]

---

[52] Ferrari 2003, 44–51; Topper 2009; Kearns 2012; Versnel 1993, 286–8 and *passim*; Vidal-Naquet 1986, 285–301.
[53] Ferrari 2002, 170, citing Plato *Critias* 110b5–c2.
[54] Dowden 1989, 153, 155; the *Danais*; Melanippides ap. Athenaeus 14.651f.

The women in arms thus resemble the primitive life or the age of heroes. One can envision the usefulness of such an anciently flavored motif being linked to the battle of Sepeia. The linkage imbues the recent past with the traits of the long-ago, so that it becomes more suitable for being featured in a foundation myth. However, the primitive and heroic pasts are not the only realms in which women in arms are encountered. There are several stories in which women in arms act in times more recent than the age of the heroes (from the point of view of the Greeks); these stories, and their associated rituals, closely parallel to the Argive myth-ritual complex in question, shed further light on the functioning of the motif of the armed women. Let me present these narratives, along with the most important studies done on them.

1. Pausanias (8.47–48) narrates apropos an image of Ares that was situated in the agora of Tegea and called *Gynaecothoenas* ('He who entertains women') a story of an invasion of Tegea by the Spartan king Charillus. The Tegean women armed themselves and joined the battle out of an ambush from under a hill. The women put the Spartans to flight, and took many of them prisoners. Marpessa, surnamed Choera, was the woman who particularly distinguished herself by her fighting; Pausanias saw her shield displayed in the Tegean temple of Athena Alea (Pausanias 8.47.2). After the battle Charillus, who had been also captured by the women and then released without a ransom, swore that the Spartans would never attack Tegea again; later

he broke that oath. Since then the women of Tegea sacrifice to Ares in commemoration of their victory, and the men receive no share of the sacrificial victim (Pausanias 8.48.4–5). A fragment of the historian Deinias of Argos contains an apparent variant of this story, reporting that Spartan prisoners, kept in bonds, were working the plain by the river Lachas in the reign of Tegean Perimede, popularly called Choera (FGrH 306 F4).

2. Lactantius (*Divine Institutes* 1.20, 29–32) recounts a tale of the Messenians slipping away from under a Spartan siege and attacking Sparta, only to be put to flight by the Spartan women, who armed for that purpose. The Spartans realized that they have been deceived and came in pursuit of the Messenians. Instead, they encountered the armed Spartan women, who had come out of the city. The women thought that the approaching armed men were the Messenians, and stripped naked. The aroused Spartan men, still armed, copulated with the women at random. A temple of armed Aphrodite was founded to commemorate this event.

3. Polyaenus (4.1) reports that when the Talauntians made a campaign against the Macedonians, Argaeus (an early Macedonian king) ordered the Macedonian *parthenoi* to arm themselves and to attack the enemy from behind a mountain. The *parthenoi* attacked, some equipped with thyrsoi and ivy crowns. The Talauntians fled, and the victorious Argaeus established a temple to Dionysus Pseudanor. From that point the *parthenoi*, who previously had been called Clodones, received an appellation Mimallones, since they imitated men.

An influential analysis by Fritz Graf examines the topos of women in arms in these narratives, along with the tale of Telesilla's defense of Argos. Graf points out that the stories operate as *aitia* explaining odd cultic or ritual phenomena,[55] such as the statue of an armed Aphrodite in Sparta, or the worship of Ares by the Tegean women. Importantly, Graf seems to suggest that the ritual and cultic constituents are primary, serving as a source for the creation of mythical stories: "the story of women fighting to save the polis is a narrative device pointing to a representation of cult or a ritual with unusual features, those of inverted normality."[56]

Graf's perception of the myths as merely derivatives of the rituals of inversion conflicts with the diversity of sights and rituals associated with the stories of women in arms. At least by the times of Plutarch and Pausanias, the myths of armed women were woven into polis life, both geographically, through monuments, and temporally, through rituals. The two better attested cases of Tegea and Argos provide the following lists. In Tegea, there are the statue of Ares in the agora of Tegea and the sacrifice to Ares done by the women; there is also the shield of Marpessa in the temple of Athena Alea. In Argos, we have our familiar festival of Hybristica, the tombs of the women who fell in the battle, the statue of Ares erected by the women, and the statue of armed Telesilla in the temple of Aphrodite. The quantity of the commemorative

---

[55] Graf 1984, 249.
[56] *Ibid.*, 252–253.

phenomena suggests that the tales of the armed women occupied an important place in the cities' past.

The trend of regarding the myth about the armed women as secondary to their ritual counterparts is even more prominent in the work of Bremmer and Hatzopoulos. These scholars see the myths as echoes of the (unattested) female rites of passage during which the women were armed.[57] I believe that the reasoning that I have employed in my critique of the interpretations of the story about the beard-wearing women as a marriage rite is also applicable in this case. Bremmer and Hatzopoulos base their interpretations on a postulation of an essential symmetry between the male and female rites of passage; thus, they perceive a woman's temporary assumption of a male identity through arming as a stage in the transition to a new social status.[58] However, as I have pointed out above, in ancient Greece the male and female rites of passage are characterized by sharp asymmetry; thus, the connotations of the female assumption of the male identity may be very different from the male assumption of the female one. Moreover, by interpreting the myths about the women in arms as vestiges of

---

[57] Bremmer 1999; Hatzopoulos 1994, 73–85.
[58] Conveniently, Bremmer (1999, 192) articulates this line of reasoning: "...[W]e cannot fail to note that the order boy-"female"-male which characterized early Greek male initiation must once have had a counterpart in the order girl-"male"-woman, as exemplified by the legend of the Macedonian Mimallones [...]. The legends about girls/women in arms thus reflect real practices, which, however, must have disappeared in the course of the Archaic period."

vanished rituals of female fighting, Bremmer passes over a possibility that these myths may be valid synchronically, that is, that they may express a coherent message in their attested form.

What messages do the myths of armed women and their associated rituals communicate? Let me start from analyzing the structure of these myths. A remarkable characteristic of the tales of women in arms that has thus far escaped scholarly discussion is a comic strand that is intertwined with the heroic one in these narratives. I have already discussed the combination of the heroic and the comic in the myths about the female defense of Argos and the ensuing Argive decree compelling the women to wear beards. The myth about the female defense of Tegea from the Spartans offers a nice parallel. The nickname of the preeminent Tegean female fighter, Marpessa, is Choera: this detail is apparently thematically central, given that it recurs in an otherwise disparate version given by Deinias.[59] 'Choera' means 'pig,' but the name also unmistakably suggests the female genitalia.[60] The brave Choera's nickname acquires particular interest in conjunction with the name of the Spartan king, Charilaus (or Charillus). This name, which can be translated, among other possibilities, as 'whose people have mirth,' occurs in a fragment by Archilochus. Gregory Nagy has argued that Charilaus, whom Archilochus' poem addresses with a promise to bring him the pleasure of

---

[59] Noted, with surprise, by Leahy 1958, 151.
[60] Sauzeau 1999, 155n79; Henderson 1991, 132; Loraux 1995, 326n37; Graf 1984, 248n25. Cf. Versnel 1993, 256-7.

laughter, is a stock character whose name expresses the communal reaction to the iambic poetry of Archilochus.[61] If we return to the Spartan king who bore this cheerful name, we will find that the tradition about him also has distinct comic overtones. We learn that Charilaus was characterized by timorousness and excessive gentleness (even toward scoundrels).[62] Such traits, the opposite of the normative virtues of a Spartan king, in conjunction with Charilaus' name, open a possibility that the figure of Charilaus originated in the realm of the comic, and only later was streamlined into the fabric of early Spartan history by the Hellenistic historians.[63] The story of Charilaus' defeat and capture by Choera and other Tegean women belongs, I suggest, to such a comic tradition.

The story about the Spartan women defeating the Messenians, transmitted by Lactantius, also has a manifest comic twist. When the Spartan women see approaching men, whom they believe to be the Messenians, they strip naked: this reaction, presumably prompted by the women's fear, runs counter to their previous heroic defense and gives the tale a bawdy slant.

The tale of the Macedonian Mimallones does not preserve conspicuously comic overtones, but the Dionysiac setting makes the existence of such overtones quite plausible.

---

[61] Nagy [1979] 1999, 91–92.
[62] See Plutarch, *Lycurgus* 5.5 on Charilaus running to an altar in fear of Lycurgus' thirty men.
[63] On the Spartan king-lists, see Kelly 1970a, 995–996.

The motif of women in arms, presented ambiguously both as a victorious achievement and a travesty, constitutes a recurrent pattern, as these examples show. The combination of the heroic and the comic shows the ambivalent perception of armed women in the Greek cultural imagination. The ambivalence has been beautifully described by Barbara Goff, who uses the concept of a "latent citizenship" to express women's status in the polis. The latent citizenship is a pattern of women's regular exclusion from participation in the affairs of the city, along with their intermittent inclusion under highly marked circumstances, such as a performance of a ritual or an extreme peril. Goff comments apropos the Hybristica and the female festival of Ares in Tegea (where men were excluded from partaking of the sacrificial meat):

> The women's latent citizenship, emerging in their military actions and in the rituals, can be a problem for the city as well as a deliverance, because if women participate in the city's preservation, men will inevitably begin to lose the signs of their participation and experience instead the feminine contours of exclusion. What is signified by these ritual anomalies is not simply an inversion of roles, but rather the zero-sum structure of Greek gender ideology; according to this uncompromising arithmetic, if women start to behave like men, men will become women.[64]

As I have already suggested in the Argive case, the ridicule is meant to "disarm" the women, to return them to their traditional gender role. The ridicule has a very distinct ribald quality, obvious in the case of Choera and the naked Spartan women; in the slightly more subtle Argive

---

[64] Goff 2007, 56. Similarly, Gherchanoc 2003, 781–782.

case, the statement that the women were looking past their perioecic husbands when they were sleeping with them (ἐν τῷ συγκαθεύδειν) has strong sexual overtones,[65] and the theme is picked up by the law that orders the women to wear beards when they sleep with their husbands (συναναπαύεσθαι τοῖς ἀνδράσι τὰς γεγαμημένας). The lewdness is not just the most effective way to remind the women of their femininity:[66] what is at stake is the continuation of the polis. The women who saved the polis in battle now need to submit to the males in sex, so that a new generation of the citizens could be produced.[67] Thus, the name of Hybristica is likely to refer to two kinds of hubris: the *hubris* of the women's attempt to rule over the men, and the *hubris* of the men's counter-offensive lewdness toward the women.

We have established what the myth-ritual complexes starring the motif of the armed women communicate concerning the role of the women in the polis: they locate the armed women exclusively in the past, and the ridicule allows to transform the armed women into the progenitors of the community, thus bridging between the past and the present.

However, these myth-rituals can be also read from a different angle: we can ask how does the motif of armed women function in the construction of the *polis'* past. I have already

---

[65] LSJ; see Aristophanes *Assemblywomen* 1009, Plato *Laws* 838b.
[66] Compare Livingston 2001, 227 on John Fletcher's *The Woman's Prize:*"...the men, by dwelling on female genitalia, are attempting to use bawdy in order to re-emphasize the female gender of their opponents in the face of the women's 'masculine' conduct." See also Ferrari 2002, 169 on the inherently laughable nature of the female public nudity (Plato *Republic* 5.451e6–452b5).
[67] Similarly, Loraux 1995, 233.

posed this question about Argos; now I formulate it in broader terms on the basis of multiple conflicts involving women in arms. The conflicts in which armed women are said to participate are also attested in variants that do not mention women.[68] What is the special point of the versions that do involve armed women?

I am going to approach the answer not historically — that is, by an attempt to reconstruct the circumstances in which the tales of the armed women made their way into the histories of certain conflicts[69] — but rather, typologically. I will try to describe the mindset behind the association of the armed women with particular moments in the history of different *poleis*.

I propose that the employment of the motif of armed women in a representation of a specific past conflict emphasizes the irreversible impact of that past event. The logic of this inference works as follows. In the here-and-now of the *polis*, women must be confined to their subordinate position; therefore, the women's past victory is absolutely unrepeatable.[70] (This mindset is an exact opposite of the mentality of the recurrent ritual battles that I have been

---

[68] Herodotus 1.66 (the battle of Fetters), and 6.77–80 (the battle of Sepeia).

[69] I am going to explore the historical relation between Herodotus' version of the Battle of the Fetters and the tale of the armed Tegean women defeating the Spartans in a different project.

[70] Compare McInerney's (2003, 332) observation about the abundance of "ktistic stories" in Plutarch's *Virtues of Women*. McInerney comments: "It is as if the crisis of founding a polis authorizes actions which are at odds with normative behavior and permit temporarily a suspension of the usual restrictions on women." McInerney's 2003, 333.

investigating in the previous chapter.) The victory of the armed women exists beyond the possibility of a rerun and thus produces indelible consequences for the polis.

The story of the Tegean women defeating the Spartans has a detail supporting my suggestion that the motif of women in arms expresses the ineradicable imprint of a given past event. Pausanias reports that after Charillus, who had been captured by the women, was released without ransom, he "swore to the Tegeans that the Lacedaemonians would never again attack Tegea, and then broke his oath" (8.48.5). That is to say, the story admits that the Spartans attacked Tegea repeatedly; however, the attacks after the women's victory are *qualitatively different* since they involve the breach of the oath.[71] The feeling of irrevocability, produced by the motif of the women in arms, fits with the abundance of aetiologies associated with the motif: the permanent changes in the order of things, effected by the singular involvement of the armed women, are memorialized through recurrent rituals.[72]

---

[71] The mentality according to which the armed female participation in a conflict creates an impasse is also expressed by Pausanias in the case of the Argive women (2.20.9): ἐνταῦθα οἱ Λακεδαιμόνιοι, φρονήσαντες ὡς καὶ διαφθείρασί σφισι τὰς γυναῖκας ἐπιφθόνως τὸ κατόρθωμα ἕξει καὶ σφαλεῖσι μετὰ ὀνειδῶν γενήσοιτο ἡ συμφορά, ὑπείκουσι ταῖς γυναιξί. "Then the Lacedaemonians, realizing that to destroy the women would be an invidious success while defeat would mean a shameful disaster, gave way before the women."

[72] Another story starring the female participation in a foundational conflict is the narrative of the Romans' fight with the Latins, in which the Romans were assisted by the serving-maids. The victory of the Romans was celebrated in a festival called the Capratine Nones, in which the maidservants fought in mock battles. Plutarch's Romulus 29.4-6; *Camillus* **4**.

My aim in this long comparative detour was to establish that the situation in which women put on arms and defeat the enemy is a stable motif, repeatedly used in the construction of the imaginary past and ritual present of different *poleis*. As a trope, expressing an event's irrevocable outcome, the motif of the armed women's defense of a *polis* seems highly suitable for a foundation legend.

7. The Hybristica and the democratic dissolution

I have noted above that that the myths that provide the aetiology of the Hybristica feature distinct democratic motifs, which the festival of Hybristica itself lacks. The Hybristica, in fact, conforms to the generic contours of a festival of reversal, as is indicated by its swap of the gender roles and the mockery in the festival's name.[73] Interestingly, however, myths and festivals of reversal and dissolution seem to have proliferated in Argos in the 460s, perhaps serving as a means of creating the new community of citizens.[74] This section considers the myth-ritual complex of the manly Argive women and the Hybristica in relation to other contemporary Argive myths and rituals featuring dissolution and gender inversion. I hope that

---

[73] Sauzeau 1999, 159; Sauzeau also mentions the celebration of the festival at the new moon, and its link to Hermes through the month of Hermaeus. See also Halliday 1909–1910.
[74] See below.

such an embedding of the particular myth-ritual in the context of other civic myths and rituals will foster our understanding of the factors that affected its formation and introduction.

An Argive myth that provides a fascinating counterpart to the story of the female defense of Argos is the confrontation between Dionysus and Perseus, in which Perseus and Argive men fought Aegean women, the followers of Dionysus. The myth is attested in a number of versions, according to some of which Perseus killed Dionysus.[75] Pausanias saw in Argos a common tomb of the women slain in the battle by the victorious Perseus (Pausanias 2.22.1), as well as a separate monument to the high-ranking maenad Chorea (Pausanias 2.20.4).

Two instances of women fighting men in Argos are an interesting coincidence; however, what makes the comparison between the Argive women against the Spartans and the Dionysiac women against Perseus really instructive are the arguably democratic overtones of the latter myth. Barbara Kowalzig discerns the presence of the myth in two fragmentary Pindaric dithyrambs (1 and 4), which, she suggests, were Argive commissions. According to Kowalzig, the reenactment of the Dionysiac myths in the communal performance of the dithyrambs was instrumental in shaping a new sense of a community, "characterized not by shared ancestry but by shared mystic experience and the 'criterion' of initiation;" thus, the performances of Pindar's dithyrambs perhaps played a role in the democratic reform of the

---

[75] See Ogden 2008, 28–32 for the list of ancient sources. See also Sourvinou-Inwood 2005, 191–192; Arrigoni 2003; 1999; Piérart 1996a.

Argive society.⁷⁶ Moreover, Kowalzig observes that the dithyrambs helped in establishing Perseus as an Argive hero. As Jonathan Hall has demonstrated, Argos appropriated Perseus only after the destruction of Mycenae.⁷⁷ Pindar's dithyrambs introduce Perseus into Argos in the paradoxical role of an antagonist of the ultimately triumphant god.⁷⁸ In Kowalzig's view,

---

⁷⁶ Kowalzig 2007a, 169.
⁷⁷ Hall 1997, 95-99.
⁷⁸ The paradoxical policy of the Argive appropriation of Perseus in a transgressive role of Dionysus' adversary perhaps finds a counterpart in a tale about the Argive tyrant Perilaus, who, according to Pausanias, destroyed a bronze chamber, in which Danae was kept under guard by Acrisius (2.23.6-7). The story of Perilaus' destruction of the site of Perseus' conception immediately precedes Pausanias' mention of the war between Perseus and Dionysus (2.23.7); the ruined Danae's chamber and Dionysus' precinct were adjacent. Thus, we can hypothesize that the destruction of the chamber was probably motivated as some kind of retaliation for Perseus' offensive behavior toward the god. The next question is, what is the nature of such a story, and what is its date? If we accept Hall's argument that Perseus was appropriated by Argos only after the sack of Mycenae, the story of the chamber's destruction cannot stand as historically true, since the chamber of Danae would be only *set up* in Argos after 468 BC. It is therefore appealing to construe the story of the chamber's destruction as an effort to establish Perseus in Argos. The story of the destroyed chamber, which in reality never existed, elegantly manages both to locate Perseus in the Argive sacred landscape, and to explain the lack of the monument to his conception and birth. The prudent ascription of the chamber's destruction to a morally ambiguous figure of the bygone tyrant avoids the pitfall of taking sides in the god-hero ritual antagonism. Perilaus' destruction of Danae's chamber parallels Cleisthenes of Sicyon's dealings with the hero Adrastus, as reported by Herodotus (5.67). It has been recently convincingly argued by Sara Forsdyke that the tale of Cleisthenes' enmity toward Adrastus is a later folk story, attributing the tyrant with an impious conduct toward the hero (Forsdyke 2012, 98-99). I will return to the use of the figure of Perilaus in the Argive myth in the next chapter. On Perilaus, see Berve 1967, 35; Tomlinson 1972, 189; de Libero 1996, 216-217.

the eventual subordination of Perseus to Dionysus (as expressed by the establishment of Dionysus' cult) allows Perseus' incorporation into the city on more democratic terms.[79]

Dionysus' and Telesilla's women share, it turns out, not only fighting abilities, but also an ability to promote democratic ideology and (cultic or political) unification of the Argive Plain under Argos' control. The belligerent women appear to have been an expedient trope in the period of the establishment of the Argive democracy.

The comparison between these two episodes of female fighting brings us to a broader topic of the Dionysiac affinities of the Hybristica and its aetiological myths.[80] We have seen that one of the parallel instances of the armed women defending their polis, namely, the Macedonian Mimallones, had a Dionysiac context. Dionysiac myths are characterized by dissolution and abound with women fighting under the god's influence, and Dionysiac festivals are exemplary cases of ritual reversals. By pointing out the similarities between the Dionysiac myth-rituals and the Hybristica and its myths I am not trying to suggest that the Hybristica was celebrated in honor of Dionysus. Rather, I propose that the Dionysiac myth-rituals could have served as an inspiration for the establishment of the new myth-ritual complex. Let me explain what I mean by this suggestion.

---

[79] Kowalzig 2007a, 170; Kowalzig 2007b, 227–228, 242–45.
[80] Sauzeau 1999, 160.

The confrontation between Perseus and Dionysus is not the only Dionysiac resistance myth attested in Argos. Another variant tells of the women of Argos being affected by Dionysus, so that they roamed the wilds, feeding on the flesh of their infants (Apollodorus 3.5.2).[81] The appearance of the Argive women in such a gender-inappropriate setting constitutes a nightmarish variation on the theme of masculine Argive women. Importantly, this variant is attested as early as Herodotus (9.34), although Herodotus does not mention the god who induced the women's madness. Nor do the variants end here: other versions name the daughters of king Proitus as Dionysus' victims.[82] Kowalzig notices these mythical multiforms and suggests that their existence indicates shifts in the groups comprising the god's worshippers; such shifts, in their turn, are a sign of social change.[83] We cannot ascribe a date to these transformations, or to an emergence of numerous other versions of the myths of the Proitids/women of Argos; however, the sheer amount of variants shows that the myth was contested, reshaped and replicated over and over. The offended deity can be Hera or Dionysus,[84] and the versions can incorporate various Peloponnesian locales.[85] Temporally, the

---

[81] On these reversal myths, see Burkert 1983, 161–196.
[82] Bacchylides 11, Hesychius s.v. Ἀγράνια.
[83] Kowalzig 2007a, 169n104.
[84] Hera: Bacchylides 11, Hesiod ap. Apollodorus 2.2.2; Dionysus: Acusilaus ap. Apollodorus 2.2.2, Vitruvius 8.3.21; Ovid *Metamorphoses* 15.325.
[85] Herodotus 9. 34, Diodorus Siculus 4.68 (Argos); Bacchylides 11 (Tirynth, Lusae); Apollodorus 2.2.2, Pausanias 2.7.8 (Sicyon); Kowalzig 2007a, 267–319; on the variability of the Peloponnesian

events can be set in the time of king Proitus or his grandson Anaxagoras.[86] It would seem that the myth of the Proitids as maidens should be organically connected with the wrath of Hera, while the Dionysiac madness typically affects married women; however, the cross-pollination between these versions has a long history, since the Proitids' connection to Dionysus apparently figured already in Hesiod.[87] I am enumerating these permutations and amalgamations in order to illustrate the remarkable "pliability" of the myths of the Proitids/Argive women. That is to say, the abundance of variations, resulting from the repeated refashioning of these myths, generated a fertile ground for the production of further variants. It seems likely that the pliable quality of these myths was already present in the middle of the fifth century BC: as I have mentioned, several versions are attested already in Hesiod and Herodotus, and the Proitids' myth was relocated from its Tirynthian setting to Argos by the Archaic period.[88] The ritual counterparts of these myths, festivals of reversal, must have been similarly malleable. Indeed, we know of the Argive festival of Agr(i)ania, which, on comparative grounds, should have been a festival of reversal, dedicated to Dionysus

---

myths about Melampous, see Jost 1992; see Levaniouk 2008, 32-33 on the variant accounts of the Proitids' story as an example of the "two-pronged" variety of the myths, featuring versions involving both unmarried girls and mothers; see also Sauzeau 2005, 119-137.

[86] The events are set during Anaxagoras' reign in Diodorus Siculus 4.68.4-5; Pausanias 2.18.4.
[87] Hesiod F 131 Merkelbach-West ap. Apollodorus 2.2.2.
[88] Hall 1997, 98.

and celebrated by married women;[89] however, Hesychius reports that the festival was celebrated in honor of one of the Proitids.[90] Thus, the Agr(i)ania shows evidence of accretive layers of aetiological myths.

In fifth-century Argos, the festivals of reversal and dissolution, associated with the myths of the Proitids/Argive women, must have had a rich history of being vehicles for new mythical variations. One could formulate a recipe for the inauguration of a new myth *à la argienne*: 1. Adjust the mythical part according to the necessity. 2. Celebrate a dissolution festival (in culinary terms, "shake well"). I suggest that this familiar strategy of the introduction of new mythical material via a festival of reversal is at work also in the adaptation of the Hybristica, a generic reversal festival, to the celebration of a radically new myth, the establishment of the Argive democracy after the battle of Sepeia.

8. The Sepeia oracle: an immodest proposal

I have attempted to show how the Hybristica and its myths fit the traditional patterns of Greek cultural imagination, as well as the local Argive myth-ritual configurations. However,

---

[89] Dowden 1989, 81. Cf. Casadio 1994, 51–122.
[90] Hesychius s.v. Ἀγράνια· ἑορτὴ ἐν Ἄργει ἐπὶ μιᾷ τῶν Προίτου θυγατέρων. Hesychius has a different entry s.v. ἀγριάνια· νεκύσια παρὰ Ἀργείοις: the festival seems to have a tendency of multiplying.

thus far the discussion scarcely mentioned a factor that is widely considered to exert a crucial influence on the emergence of the myth of Telesilla and the Argive women, that is, the oracle about the victory of the female over the male, quoted by Herodotus in his description of the Battle of Sepeia. What place does the oracle have in my reconstruction of the events, which stresses the democratic context of the Hybristica and its myths, and dates their formation by the 460s BC?

Herodotus reports that the oracle was a joint prediction, given in Delphi to the Milesians and the Argives (although he never cites together the parts concerning Miletus and Argos). Here is the Argive part of the pronouncement (Herodotus 6.77.2), which I have already quoted:

> ἀλλ' ὅταν ἡ θήλεια τὸν ἄρσενα νικήσασα
> ἐξελάσῃ καὶ κῦδος ἐν Ἀργείοισιν ἄρηται,
> πολλὰς Ἀργείων ἀμφιδρυφέας τότε θήσει.
> ὥς ποτέ τις ἐρέει καὶ ἐπεσσομένων ἀνθρώπων
> δεινὸς ὄφις τριέλικτος[91] ἀπώλετο δουρὶ δαμασθείς.

When the female defeats the male
and drives him away, winning glory in Argos,
she will make many Argive women tear their cheeks.
As someday one of men to come will say:
the dread thrice-coiled serpent died tamed by the spear.

---

[91] The variant ἀέλικτος, attested in *Greek Anthology* 14.90, will be discussed below.

A widespread current view takes this oracle to be the source from which the myth of the heroic female defense of Argos was derived.[92] The development of this myth is typically considered to postdate Herodotus, since Herodotus does not mention it in his presentation of the events.[93] Another argument in favor of the oracle's chronological primacy is the incomplete correspondence between the story of the heroic Argive women and the oracle, which features a seemingly unrelated image of a snake subdued by a spear.[94] However, the latter observation introduces a more general difficulty: Herodotus' narrative also fails to comment on the image of the snake, and a convincing interpretation of the oracle, connecting the image of the victory of the female and the vanquished snake, has proved to be remarkably elusive.

I postpone the discussion of Herodotus' silence concerning Telesilla and her companions until my detailed analysis of the Herodotean tale about the rule of the slaves in Argos in the next chapter. My aim in this section is to establish a more dialogical connection between the oracle, on the one hand, and the Hybristica and its myths, on the other, than has been acknowledged so far. I accept the possibility that the oracle may have influenced the formation of the myth about the female defense of Argos. However, I believe that the

---

[92] Piérart 2003, 281; Jacoby 1955, 46, Stadter 1965, 48; Bury 1902, 20 and n4 for the earlier literature.
[93] Among others, Suárez de la Torre 2004, 253-55.
[94] Piérart 2003, 282.

connection goes both ways, and that we can discern traces of the Hybristica and its myths in the oracle.⁹⁵ Exploring such a bidirectional connection between the oracle and the festival will allow us, I hope, to arrive to a cohesive interpretation of the oracle.

A recent analysis of the Sepeia oracle by Marcel Piérart argues that the oracle, which is linked by Herodotus and the *Greek Anthology* to a prophesy of the fall of Miletus, stems from the setting of the Ionian revolt (the oracle's reference to the Argives, Piérart maintains, was initially construed as denoting the Greeks in general).⁹⁶ Piérart suggests that the oracle was later embraced by the Argives as alluding to the events of the battle of Sepeia.⁹⁷ For Piérart, the *terminus ante quem* for such an adoption is ca. 450 BC, the date which he ascribes to Herodotus' visit to Argos in search of the information about the Spartan-Argive relationship.⁹⁸ A treatment of the subject by Pierre Sauzeau discusses at length various Argive "readings" of the oracle, resulting in the "rewriting" of Argive history and a creation of the myth of the victorious

---

⁹⁵ The influence of Telesilla's story on the oracle has been suggested already by Macan 1895, 336.
⁹⁶ Piérart 2003, 290–296.
⁹⁷ *Ibid.*, 284. See below for a more detailed discussion of the reasons for Piérart's dating of Herodotus' activity in Argos by 450 BC. One important consequence of the dissolution of the primary link between the Battle of Sepeia and the oracle is that it abolishes the reasons to date the battle by the end of Cleomenes' reign (the dating which contradicts the information provided by Pausanias 3.4.1, who places the battle in the beginning of Cleomenes' career). Piérart 2003, 296.
⁹⁸ *Ibid.*, 284.

Argive women.[99] Yet, despite Piérart's and Sauzeau's acute appreciation of the importance of the Argive phase of the oracle, they treat the text of the oracle as a constant, which could be only reinterpreted, not changed, throughout its history. I would like to revise this perception of the oracle as a fixed entity, by taking into account Lisa Maurizio's important work on the oral character of the Delphic oracles.[100]

Maurizio makes a case that "the primary means of transmission of Delphic oracles was word of mouth, and that the Delphic tradition was an oral one."[101] Thus, the oracles were not only repeatedly reperformed and reinterpreted, but also *recomposed* in the process of the reperformance. Given the prominent Argive phase in the transmission of the Sepeia oracle, we can expect to see in it traces of the Argive recomposition. Moreover, since, as Piérart argues, Herodotus collected the oracle in Argos,[102] the Argive context should be particularly significant. That is to say, the oracle as a whole should be understandable from the Argive perspective, since the oral tradition typically maintains the details that are meaningful for the current audience.[103]

---

[99] Sauzeau 1999.
[100] Maurizio 1997.
[101] *Ibid.*, 313.
[102] Piérart 2003, 284.
[103] Forsdyke 1999, 362; Vansina 1985, 100-114.

The part of the oracle about the victory of the female over the male, of course, does not present any problem in this respect: the myth of Telesilla and the Argive women provides the Argive referent. The crucial element to be explained is the snake, subdued by the spear. As I have already mentioned, this part of the oracle, which Piérart calls "one of the most obscure passages in oracular literature"[104] currently lacks a convincing interpretation. Earlier attempts to construe the image of the snake as the city of Argos are difficult to substantiate, and none of the explanations achieves an organic connection between the triumphant female and the defeated snake.

Let us consider the wording of the oracle. After the passage about the victory of the female and the grief of the Argive women, the image of the snake is introduced by the following line:

ὥς ποτέ τις ἐρέει καὶ ἐπεσσομένων ἀνθρώπων

as someday one of men to come will say...

This verse features a remarkable change in the temporal point of view: while the previous segment of the poem speaks about the future disaster as foreseen from the present time, the image of the snake is introduced *as a past from the standpoint of the future generations*. From the perspective of future people, the battle of Sepeia has happened already, and is now

---

[104] Piérart 2003, 292; similarly, Sauzeau 1999, 134.

contemplated as a past event. In other poetic texts, the future middle forms of the verb ἔπειμι are repeatedly associated with commemoration. In Theocritus' *Idyll* 12, the future people (ἐπεσσομένοις, Theocritus 12.11) become the audience of a song into which two lovers are transformed. In a poem inscribed on a stone herm, quoted by Aeschines, the future Athenians (ἐπεσσομένων, Aeschines 3.184) are imagined as the audience, reading the inscription. Most interestingly, the *Homeric Hymn to Demeter* promises that an unwilting honor will always attach to the baby Demophon (τιμὴ δ' ἄφθιτος αἰὲν ἐπέσσεται, *Homeric Hymn to Demeter* 264), since a goddess was his nurse. What follows is a description of ritual battles that the Eleusinians shall recurrently celebrate in Demophon's honor (*Homeric Hymn to Demeter* 266-268). Thus, ἐπέσσεται introduces the future of hero-cult honors.[105] So, the future middle forms of ἔπειμι signal the transition to a commemorative mode, through monuments, song, or cult. Importantly, what is represented as a future from the poems' interior point of view, is in fact the *present* for the poems' audience: for the Athenians reading the herm, for the listeners of Theocritus' song, for the worshippers of the baby Demophon. On this reasoning, the line

ὥς ποτέ τις ἐρέει καὶ ἐπεσσομένων ἀνθρώπων

as someday one of men to come will say...

---

[105] On *timê* as the 'honor of cult' see Nagy 1990b, 132n51. On ritual fights as Demophon's cult honors see Pache 2004, 75-78.

should refer to the commemoration of the Battle of Sepeia. Given the Argive setting of the poem's performance, we can expect this commemoration to be specifically Argive: that is to say, the image of the snake is likely to refer either to one of the several monuments, memorializing the deeds of the Argive women, or to the festival of Hybristica.

At this point it is relevant to consider an alternate reading of the oracle: the *Greek Anthology* 14.90 and some Herodotean manuscripts attest ὄφις ἀέλικτος 'uncoiled snake' instead of ὄφις τριέλικτος 'thrice-coiled snake.' The word ἀέλικτος is a *hapax* and a *lectio difficilior*, and therefore should command our attention. What does an uncoiled snake remind us of?

I suggest that the festival of Hybristica provides a suitable setting for the following answer: the uncoiled snake refers to a phallus, and the passage describes, in a riddling manner, the loss of masculinity suffered by the male Argives as a result of the female defense of Argos,[106] and seasonally re-experienced by them during the gender reversal of the Hybristica. A snake as a symbolic representation of a penis is widely attested cross-culturally; Greek literature furnishes examples of this symbolism.[107] If a snake suggests a penis, the uncoiled snake evokes the same idea much more strongly. The first and second parts of the oracle

---

[106] It is relevant to quote here again Barbara Goff's formulation: "if women start to behave like men, men will become women." Goff 2007, 56.

[107] See McMahon 1998, 139–141; Henderson 1991, 127. In *Greek Anthology* 11.22, ὄφις refers to a penis; double entendres are suspected in *Assemblywomen* 906–910 and *Lysistrata* 758–759.

correspond to the tragic view of the events during the Spartan attack of Argos, articulated by the myth of Telesilla, and the comic view, expressed by the myth of the women wearing beards and the festival of Hybristica.[108]

The ribald interpretation of the image of the snake that I have offered is supported by the resemblances between the Sepeia oracle and comic oracles, found in Aristophanes. The combination of the solemn Homeric diction with obscenities is part and parcel of Aristophanic oracular jokes. One Aristophanic oracle features a serpent (δράκων, *Knights* 198), and also includes expressions ἀλλ' ὁπόταν...τότε, ἀπόλλυμι and κῦδος (*Knights* 197-200); the oracle's interpretation, given in the play, singles out the serpent's most phallic quality: ὁ δράκων γάρ ἐστι μακρὸν ὅ τ' ἀλλᾶς αὖ μακρόν "for the serpent is long, and the sausage is also long" (207). Another Aristophanic prophesy, bearing a conspicuous similarity to the Sepeia oracle, comes from *Lysistrata* (770-773):

> ἀλλ' ὁπόταν πτήξωσι χελιδόνες εἰς ἕνα χῶρον,
> τοὺς ἔποπας φεύγουσαι, ἀπόσχωνταί τε φαλήτων,
> παῦλα κακῶν ἔσται, τὰ δ' ὑπέρτερα νέρτερα θήσει
> Ζεὺς ὑψιβρεμέτης—
>
> Yes, when the swallows hole up in a single home,
> Fleeing the hoopoes and leaving the phallus alone,
> Then are their problems solved, and high-thundering Zeus

---

[108] The risqué quality of the second part of the Sepeia oracle perhaps has something to do with female *aischrologia*. On women's use of the obscene speech as an extreme form of gender inversion, see Versnel 1993, 244; McClure 1999, 51.

Shall reverse what's up and what's down—

Sauzeau speaks of "des similitudes troublantes" between this prediction and the Sepeia oracle.[109] Indeed, both oracles feature a reversal motif, coupled with the appearance of θήσει in the line-final position. Moreover, my interpretation of the snake as a phallus is paralleled by Aristophanes' reference to χελιδόνες 'swallows,' a slang term for female genitals.[110]

The profusion of oracles in Aristophanes' plays indicates that there must have been a strongly developed sub-genre of comic oracles. The similarities between the Sepeia oracle and the Aristophanic oracles that I have discussed probably stem from shared genre conventions.[111] Perhaps some of the similarities also derive from Aristophanes' direct familiarity with the Hybristica and the associated myths. A joke from the *Assemblywomen* (127-128), which I have already cited, describes the women disguised with false beards in the following manner:

ὥσπερ εἴ τις σηπίαις
πώγωνα περιδήσειεν ἐσταθευμέναις.

It's as if someone tied a beard on to lightly browned cuttlefishes!

Christoph Auffarth has recently argued that the absurd image of the bearded cuttlefishes (σηπίαις) is in fact a punning reference to the tradition of the Argive women wearing beards

---

[109] Sauzeau 1999, 146.
[110] Henderson 1987, 168 with further references; Sommerstein 1990, 197.
[111] Sauzeau 1999, 146.

after the battle of Sepeia.[112] If Auffarth is right, the pun indicates Aristophanes' acquaintance with the Argive myths celebrated by the Hybristica;[113] it also seems to imply that the Athenian audience in the beginning of the fourth century (or at least some part of the audience) was sufficiently familiar with these myths as to catch a fleeting reference.[114]

The fourth-century Athenians might have been fluent in the Argive comic tradition concerning the aftermath of Sepeia, but what about Herodotus? The "hybristic" interpretation that I have proposed clashes spectacularly with the solemn mood of Herodotus' account, in which he quotes the Sepeia oracle. How do I explain this striking dissonance? To preview my conclusions, I shall argue in Chapter 5 that Herodotus' tale about the rule of the slaves in Argos expresses an aristocratic point of view on the events after the battle of Sepeia. I will also make a case that Herodotus gathered his information in Argos after 450 BC, when the aristocratic party was in power, and the democratic tale of Telesilla and the heroic Argive women was temporarily "out of vogue." I submit that in fact we can see a further step in the recomposition

---

[112] Auffarth 2004, 48. The Aristophanic scholiast thought the comparison to be "not to the point" (ἀπρόσλογος, scholia for *Assemblywomen* 126). Ussher 1973, 93. If a pun is involved, the comparison acquires a point. The word order, in which the word σηπίαις comes close to the beginning of the sentence and is immediately followed by πώγωνα, seems to foreground the punning part.

[113] Aristophanes' pun constitutes the earliest attestation of the myth of the female defense of Argos.

[114] Auffarth 2004 argues for a pervasive presence of the Hybristica and the associated Argive tales in the *Assemblywomen* as a meaningful background for the play's action.

of the oracle in Herodotus' version. The case in point is the variant τριέλικτος, which is predominant in the Herodotean manuscripts. The image of the three-coiled snake excludes the phallic reading. It seems very appealing to view ὄφις τριέλικτος as a recomposition of the oracle that bleaches out the democratic overtones. I believe that Herodotus received this version of the oracle with an attendant reinterpretation of the rest of the imagery: the victory of the female over the male was construed as an expression of a generally topsy-turvy state of the world, rather than a reference to the specific myth of the female defense of Argos.

Chapter 5

Cobwebs on Shields: Scenes from the Argive Synoecism

> ...it [the city] consists only of a face and an obverse, like a sheet of paper, with a figure on either side, which can neither be separated nor look at each other.
> Italo Calvino, *Invisible Cities*[1]

1. The demise of the seventh

At this point we are going to part from the heroic Argive women and the festival of Hybristica. The central claim of Chapter 4, that the tales of the female defense of Argos, and of the Argive women wearing beards, are myths introduced by the Argive democratic regime in the 460s, so far rests on two details: the references to the Pamphyliacum and the perioecic husbands. This section adduces further evidence that the Argive defeat at Sepeia was represented as a point of transition to democracy.

A brief but highly significant reference to the Argive political reforms after the Battle of Sepeia comes from Aristotle's *Politics* (1303a6-8).

καὶ ἐν Ἄργει τῶν ἐν τῇ ἑβδόμῃ ἀπολομένων ὑπὸ Κλεομένους τοῦ Λάκωνος ἠναγκάσθησαν παραδέξασθαι τῶν περιοίκων τινάς,

---

[1] ...[la città] consiste solo in un dritto e in un rovescio, come un foglio di carta, con una figura di qua e una di là, che non possono staccarsi né guardarsi.

...and at Argos when those in the seventh had been destroyed by the Spartan Cleomenes the citizens were compelled to admit some of the *perioikoi*, ...[2]

This remarks contains an obscure expression ἐν τῇ ἑβδόμῃ, which is currently translated either as "of the seventh tribe," or "on the seventh day."[3] I believe that a better solution is available.

The key is making a search for ἕβδομος in the *Politics*. The only other occurrence of the word comes from a passage in which Aristotle describes categories of people constituting a polis (*Politics* 1290b.38-39):

καὶ γὰρ αἱ πόλεις οὐκ ἐξ ἑνὸς ἀλλ' ἐκ πολλῶν σύγκεινται μερῶν, ὥσπερ εἴρηται πολλάκις.

For states also are composed not of one but of several parts, as has been said often.

Aristotle then itemizes the categories, such as farmers, merchants, artisans, warriors and other groups; category number seven is the wealthy (1291a.33-4):

ἕβδομον δὲ τὸ ταῖς οὐσίαις λειτουργοῦν, ὃ καλοῦμεν εὐπόρους.

---

[2] Trans. by H. Rackham, modified.
[3] Rackham 1950, 385 translates ἐν τῇ ἑβδόμῃ as "those in the seventh tribe;" similarly, Warrington 1959. Keyt 1999, 87 mentions the interpretation "on the seventh day of the month," suggested by Newman 1902, 303; similarly, Lord 1984, 259, admitting uncertainty. The interpretation of ἐν τῇ ἑβδόμῃ as "on the seventh day" draws on Plutarch's comment that according to some sources, the battle happened on the seventh day of the fourth month (*Virtues of Women* 245e7).

And a seventh class is the one that serves the community by means of its property, the class that we call the rich.

It is highly appealing to conclude on the basis of this search that when Aristotle speaks of those "from the seventh" who died at Sepeia, he is referring to people constituting the seventh category in the polis, that is, the affluent.[4] Such a conclusion is strengthened if we consider the context of the remark about the Argive "seventh." Significantly, Aristotle again is speaking about different parts constituting the polis (without spelling them out). He asserts that revolutions in the constitution of a state happen when a certain part of the population grows out of proportion (1302b.33-34). Sometimes the change also happens accidentally (διὰ τύχας, 1303a3), Aristotle continues, and he gives the following three examples of a transition to a different regime:

> ...οἷον ἐν Τάραντι ἡττηθέντων καὶ ἀπολομένων πολλῶν γνωρίμων ὑπὸ τῶν Ἰαπύγων μικρὸν ὕστερον τῶν Μηδικῶν δημοκρατία ἐγένετο ἐκ πολιτείας, καὶ ἐν Ἄργει τῶν ἐν τῇ ἑβδόμῃ ἀπολομένων ὑπὸ Κλεομένους τοῦ Λάκωνος ἠναγκάσθησαν παραδέξασθαι τῶν περιοίκων τινάς, καὶ ἐν Ἀθήναις ἀτυχούντων πεζῇ οἱ γνώριμοι ἐλάττους ἐγένοντο διὰ τὸ ἐκ καταλόγου στρατεύεσθαι ὑπὸ τὸν Λακωνικὸν πόλεμον.

---

[4] The wealthy people who died at Sepeia must have belonged simultaneously to the fifth category of warriors (Aristotle, *Politics* 1291a6-7). There is no contradiction here, since in the course of his discussion, Aristotle comments that the categories that he is talking about are not mutually exclusive (1291a28-31): καὶ ταῦτ' εἴτε κεχωρισμένως ὑπάρχει τισὶν εἴτε τοῖς αὐτοῖς, οὐθὲν διαφέρει πρὸς τὸν λόγον· καὶ γὰρ ὁπλιτεύειν καὶ γεωργεῖν συμβαίνει τοῖς αὐτοῖς πολλάκις. "And it makes no difference to the argument whether these functions are held by special classes separately or by the same persons; for it often happens for the same men to be both soldiers and farmers."

> ...as for instance at Tarentum, when a great many notables were defeated and killed by the Iapygians a short time after the Persian wars, a constitutional government was changed to a democracy; and at Argos when those in the seventh had been destroyed by the Spartan Cleomenes, the citizens were compelled to admit some of the surrounding people; and at Athens when they suffered disasters by land the notables became fewer because at the time of the war against Sparta the army was drawn from a muster-roll.

The Argive category of "the seventh" is precisely paralleled in the passage by the class of

γνώριμοι 'notables' both in Tarentum and in Athens.[5]

---

[5] Aristotle's remark is a summary of an Argive myth, but there is some evidence suggesting that at the Battle of Sepeia Cleomenes' attack was actually directed toward the elites. The indication comes from the part of Herodotus' narrative dealing with the strife between Athens and Aegina. Unexpectedly, this part of Herodotus' account depicts Cleomenes as friendly to Athens. Herodotus portrays Cleomenes coming to Aegina at the suggestion of the Athenians, in order to punish the Aeginetan medizers (Herodotus 6.49–50). There a group of Aeginetans accuses Cleomenes of having been bribed by the Athenians and contests his authority as Spartan king. Herodotus remarks that these Aeginetans had been instructed in their behavior by a letter of Demaratus. In time, Cleomenes succeeds in removing ten of the wealthiest and most aristocratic Aeginetans to Athens as hostages (6.73). Later in Herodotus' account it transpires that there was a sharp political division on Aegina between Athenian-supported democrats and oligarchs, resulting in a bloody civil strife and the victory of the oligarchs (6.91). I think it is justifiable to conclude from this information that the anti-Athenian Aeginetan group that confronted Cleomenes was oligarchic. (The pattern of hostility between the oligarchic Aeginetans and democratic Athens should be viewed against the background of the previous Archaic entente between Aegina and Pisistratid Athens, on which see Nagy 2011b, 78, with reference to Figueira 1993.) Thus, we get a glimpse of Cleomenes who, at least at some point of his trajectory, has democratic sympathies. Is it too much to suspect that at the battle of Sepeia, Cleomenes' violence was directed against the Argive aristocrats? In the scene of Cleomenes' devastation of the grove of Argos, Herodotus mentions Argive deserters (6.79, 80), who provide Cleomenes with the names of the Argives inside the grove. Thus, it is possible that the attack of Cleomenes was actually advantageous to, if not actively supported by, a (quasi)-democratic faction in Argos. The continuous existence of a political division in Argos soon

All three cases that Aristotle lists feature a decline in the number of affluent citizens. It is clear that these cases are meant to be examples of democratic revolutions,[6] even if Aristotle's thinking is not totally free of difficulties.[7] The combination of democracy and the *perioikoi* unmistakably brings to mind the democratic Argive myth of the *perioikoi* and their

---

after the battle of Sepeia is illustrated by the Herodotean story about the Aeginetans asking the Argives for help against the Athenians (6.92). The Argive state refuses, on the pretext that the Aeginetan ships had been used by Cleomenes to transport his army to the Argolis, and therefore Aegina owed Argos a fine. However, a thousand Argives, led by an athlete Eurybates, come of their own accord, and are subsequently largely killed by the Athenians, according to Herodotus. The extermination of the thousand Argives is in all probability a propagandistic exaggeration: the story has been analyzed by Jonathan Hall as functionally parallel to the story of the disaster at Sepeia, aimed "to explain the weakness of the Argive élite at the beginning of the fifth century." However, the elite nature of the account, underscored by Eurybates' athletic prowess, is noteworthy. The oligarchic Aeginetans that appealed to the Argives for help must have been very hostile to Cleomenes' memory. If so, it is tempting to see the ground on which the Argive state refused its help as a pretext, and the assistance by the thousand Argives as a gesture of support for fellow aristocrats. (So Forrest 1960, 225). Thus, it seems that the democratic faction ascended to power in Argos at some point soon after the Battle of Sepeia. The use of Cleomenes' attack as a pretext shows how quickly the Battle of Sepeia started to be exploited in political maneuvering; perhaps the figure of Cleomenes was invoked by the democratic faction in power precisely in an (unsuccessful) effort to discourage the support of Aegina by the Argive aristocrats. For the suggestion that the post-Sepeia Argive democratic government was on good terms with Sparta, see O'Neil 1981, 344.

[6] Immediately after the quoted passage Aristotle states: "And this happens also in democracies, although to a smaller extent" (1303a11-12). Therefore, before this assertion he has been thinking of oligarchies turning democratic. Adshead 1986, 374.

[7] The Athenian case cannot be properly called a change in constitution. Andrewes 1990, 176. Andrewes (1990, 176n20) also notices the implausibility of Aristotle's suggestion that the system of drafting men from a muster-roll resulted in higher elite casualties. Adshead 1986 demonstrates the heterogeneous nature of the three examples (Tarentum, Argos, Athens) that Aristotle gives.

Argive wives that we have encountered in Plutarch's rendering. However, the important difference between Plutarch's and Aristotle's account is that in Plutarch's version, the democratic context can be only deduced; Aristotle's report explicitly describes a transition to democracy, and provides the new piece of information that the dead at Sepeia were believed to have been elites. It seems certain that Aristotle is recounting a variant of the Argive democratic myth. Significantly, Aristotle's abridged version brings together the annihilation at Sepeia and the enfranchisement of the *perioikoi*, constituents that in Plutarch's detailed depiction are kept apart (as tragic and comic myths, in my description).

2. The curious incident of the missing conquest

We have analyzed the function of the motif of women in the foundation myth of the Argive democracy. But what is the role of the *perioikoi* in the Argive democratic myth? I shall presently attempt to answer this question; however, let me first spell out who these *perioikoi* are, and are not, in my opinion.

I have assumed throughout the discussion that the word *perioikoi* in Plutarch's and Aristotle's accounts of the Argive affairs has a basic sense of 'dwellers around.' Moreover, given the proposed historical background of Plutarch's and Aristotle's tales concerning the *perioikoi* — that is, the conquest of the Argive Plain by Argos, followed by the incorporation of new citizens from the communities of the Plain — the meaning of *perioikoi* as "inhabitants of the surrounding communities controlled by Argos" is surely relevant, even though it is not absolutely explicit. However, this is not a point of view that is currently widely accepted. Let me examine the established interpretation of the meaning of *perioikoi* in the Argive context.

A widespread notion is that, while in Plutarch's account the Argive *perioikoi* are indeed inhabitants of the surrounding dependent communities, in Aristotle's text the word refers to a different group of people, such as slaves or agricultural laborers.[8] It is claimed that Plutarch's version resulted from a misreading of Aristotle, in which Plutarch did not realize that Aristotle had used the word in a special sense.[9]

Scholars are motivated to argue that Plutarch and Aristotle mean different things when they talk about the Argive *perioikoi* on the basis of two lines of reasoning. Firstly, the appearance of the *perioikoi*, in the sense of "citizens of the dependent communities," immediately after the battle of Sepeia is anachronistic, since Argos did not control the Argive Plain at that point.[10] Such an anachronism in Plutarch is felt to be acceptable; in the case of the much earlier and well-informed Aristotle, it is more disturbing. Therefore, it is tempting to get

---

[8] Willetts 1959, 496; Lotze 1959, 8–9; the idea is already in Newman 1902, 304. Seymour 1922, 29 argues against it.
[9] O'Neil 1981, 343; Lotze 1971, 103.
[10] O'Neil 1981, 342–343.

rid of it by claiming that Aristotle used the word in a different sense. Secondly, many scholars feel that Aristotle's enfranchised *perioikoi* should be equated with a group that Herodotus describes as slaves who came to power in Argos after the battle of Sepeia; for such a scenario to be possible, Aristotle's *perioikoi* need to denote a category of Argive residents.

The scenario according to which Plutarch misunderstood Aristotle's remark seems implausible to me, in light of my analysis of Plutarch's version, presented above. Plutarch's account is based on Argive sources and shows Plutarch's remarkable familiarity with the Argive tradition. Further, the argument concerning the anachronistic quality of the *perioikoi* after Sepeia loses its force if we adopt my interpretation of the post-Sepeia enfranchisement of the *perioikoi* as a piece of political mythology. The second argument, suggesting the equivalence between Herodotus' slaves and Aristotle's *perioikoi*, is also dispensable: as I am hoping to show later in this exploration, a more satisfying and coherent understanding of Herodotus' tale is achieved if we do not merge it with Aristotle's remark, keeping the slaves and the *perioikoi* distinct.

Thus, the motives inducing scholars to argue that Aristotle's Argive *perioikoi* are not inhabitants of the dependent communities are by themselves expendable. Now let us consider the actual evidence on the basis of which it is claimed that Aristotle meant 'serfs' when he spoke about the Argive *perioikoi*.

The groundwork for these claims has been supposedly carried out in a paper by R. F. Willetts, to which more recent treatises routinely refer. The main part of Willetts' argument is deductive: he aims to prove that the Argive *perioikoi* in Aristotle are serfs through asserting that in the *Politics* Aristotle uses the word *perioikos* exclusively in this meaning. Since Willett's discussion of the subject is so frequently invoked and is so short, it is worth citing it here in its entirety:

> Normally in the *Politics* Aristotle uses περίοικοι to mean "serfs" and not *perioikoi*. There is one single possible exception where the meaning "*perioikoi*" or "subject population" might be preferred. This normal usage strongly favours the meaning "serfs" in the remaining passage under discussion here. Elsewhere in the *Politics* ἄπορος is contrasted with εὔπορος. This too would be a more justifiable general term for "serfs" rather than for "*perioikoi*."[11]

Willett's supporting point about the contrast between ἄπορος and εὔπορος is based on the equation between the Argive *perioikoi* and τῶν ἀπόρων πλῆθος, "the mass of poor people," whose growth brings about transitions to democracy, according to Aristotle (1303a2–3). However, this identification is unwarranted,[12] since in Aristotle's three examples of Tarentum, Argos and Athens the unifying thread is not the multiplication of the poor but a decrease in the number of the rich. Now, to Willetts' main argument about Aristotle's use of the work

---

[11] Willetts 1959, 496.
[12] As seen already by Forrest 1960, 223n7.

perioikos. Willett's note gives an unadorned list of the occurrences of the word *perioikos* in the *Politics*.[13] Let us take a closer look at Aristotle's usage.

Aristotle's mentions of the *perioikoi* in the *Politics*, with the exception of the Argive case, belong to two clusters. The first one is a cluster of five references to the Cretan *perioikoi*, in Aristotle's comparison between the constitutions of Sparta and Crete.[14] Another cluster is comprised of three references to non-Greek *perioikoi*, who are to till soil and serve as sailors in Aristotle's ideal state.[15] Thus, Aristotle's other references to the *perioikoi* are limited to just two specific groups with markedly inferior status.[16] It is methodologically unsound to extend the connotations of *perioikoi* for these two groups to the third unrelated group, the Argive *perioikoi*.[17]

---

[13] Aristotle, *Politics* 1269b3, 1272a18, 1327b11, 1329a26, 1330a29, Willetts 1959, 496n5. Willetts (ibid., 496n6) also cites the "single possible exception," 1271b30. The list is in fact partial, although the missing entries (1272a1, 1272b18) are similar to the ones that are included.

[14] Aristotle, *Politics* 1269b3, 1272a1, 1271b30, 1272a18, 1272b18.

[15] Aristotle, *Politics* 1327b11, 1329a26, 1330a29. The *perioikoi* are characterized as *barbaroi* in 1329a26 (as emended by Susemihl) and 1330a29. Aristotle makes a reference to the city of Heraclea, famous for its barbarian subjects the Mariandynians, immediately after speaking about the *perioikoi* in 1327b11. Van Wees 2003, 46.

[16] Aristotle compares the Cretan *perioikoi* to the Spartan helots in *Politics* 1269b3, 1272a1, 1272b18.

[17] Similarly, Forrest 1960, 223n7, whose point of view is accepted by Andrewes 1990, 173n8.

Moreover, even the Cretan *perioikoi* are not unambiguously serf-like in Aristotle's presentation.[18] Willetts' "one single possible exception" (1271b30) depicts the *perioikoi* of the Cretan city of Lyctus using the system of laws attributed to Minos. It was pointed out by Jakob Larsen that the mention of laws rules out the possibility that these *perioikoi* were serfs.[19] How the status of the *perioikoi* of Lyctus relates to the status of other Cretan *perioikoi* in Aristotle is a separate question, but for my purposes it is important as a clear attestation that, at least once in the *Politics*, Aristotle in fact uses *perioikoi* in a sense other than 'serfs.' Thus, Willetts' deduction that the Argive *perioikoi* in Aristotle must be serfs is completely unwarranted.

Let us then return to the basic meaning of the word. Graham Shipley's careful analysis of the meanings of *perioikos* emphasizes the importance of the primary meaning 'dweller around.' Following an authoritative earlier discussion by Gschnitzer, Shipley points out that this topographical sense is nearly always dominant (apart from the Spartan contexts).[20] Perhaps, Shipley suggests, the topographical sense alone can provide a satisfactory

---

[18] The real status of the inhabitants of the dependent communities on Crete is a disputed question. A careful analysis by Perlman 1996 is notable; see also Larsen 1936; Willetts 1955, 37-39; Willetts 1967, 12; Andrewes 1990, 173-174; Link 1994, 32; van Wees 2003, 58-61.

[19] Larsen 1936, 12 and n6. Willetts himself admitted the validity of Larsen's argument in Willetts 1955, 37; 1967, 12n50.

[20] Shipley 1997, 196; Gschnitzer 1958, 146-147.

understanding of such occurrences of the word as in Aristotle's reference to the Argive *perioikoi*.[21]

What Shipley seems to visualize is a situation in which the Argives grant citizenship to the members of sovereign communities in the surroundings of Argos. As I have already said, the dependent status of the Argive *perioikoi*, following the Argive conquest of the Plain, was an important reality in the period when the story of the post-Sepeian enfranchisement of the *perioikoi* was coined; the dependency must be taken into account in our interpretation of Plutarch's and Aristotle's references. Yet Shipley's suggestion helps to pinpoint the peculiarity inherent in the Argive myth about the *perioikoi*: the myth completely elides the violent process of the acquisition of the Argive Plain by Argos. The disparity between myth and historical reality provides a glimpse into the processes of construction of the imagined past, and allows us to infer the myth's agenda.

The myth represents the *perioikoi* already in existence right after Sepeia. At first glance, this may appear to be merely an anachronistic retrojection of the mid-fifth century situation; however, the rhetoric is probably subtler. The range of possible meanings of *perioikoi* leaves the status of the Argive *perioikoi* before the enfranchisment conveniently fuzzy. What the employment of the word does produce is not a relocation of the Argive military successes

---

[21] Shipley 1997, 197.

further back in time, but a delicate adjustment of Argos' past status, depicting it as the unchallenged leader of the Plain by the time of Sepeia. Even when *perioikos* is employed in the primary topographical sense of 'dweller around,' the word conveys a worldview in which there is a center and a periphery, and the center is, typically, more important (notable, powerful, violent) than the periphery.[22] Argos, even in the desperate post-Sepeian straits, is given preeminence through the mention of its *perioikoi*.

After this initial sleight of hand, the stage is set for introducing a vision of a peaceful synoecism. As Barbara Kowalzig observes, the narrative ties together synoecism and democratization. The synoecism, an admission of the *perioikoi* into citizenship, becomes an embodiment of democratization. Further, the myth casts the enfranchisement as an unavoidable step that the Argives were compelled (ἠναγκάσθησαν) to make because of the severity of their losses. That is to say, the transition from the pre-Sepeian oligarchy to the synoikized democracy is portrayed as an inevitable outcome of a particular set of circumstances, not as the product of actively pursued and aggressive policies. The only violence that is allowed into the picture is that of the Spartans, not of the Argives. The variant

---

[22] Good examples of such a hierarchy in power, implied by the use of *perioikoi*, are Herodotus 1.166.1 (the Phocaeans who live in Cyrnus plunder all the *perioikoi*) and Herodotus 5.91.2 (the power of Athens grew after the city became democratic, as their *perioikoi*, the Boeotians and the Chalcidians, had learned well). Both instances are defined by Shipley as the 'topographical' use of the word. Shipley 1997, 218, 219.

transmitted by Plutarch adds an overtone of desirability: the information that the Argives chose "the best of the perioikoi" to become their citizens by means of marriage presents the enfranchisement as a privilege.

3. The *Hyrnathioi* and other migrants

Who were the real-life counterparts of the privileged enfranchised *perioikoi* of the myth? We know that by the 460s BC, Argos had annexed the *poleis* of Mycenae, Tiryns, and Midea.[23] We also know that by the mid-fifth century Argos had a fourth tribe of *Hyrnathioi*, in addition to the three Dorian tribes.[24] We do not know when the tribe of the *Hyrnathioi* was added to the system.[25] However, it is appealing to assume that the foundation of the new tribe

---

[23] Hall 1995, 589 and n84; Kritzas 1992, 233 (479-460); Moggi 1974. We do not know when exactly between 479 and 460 BC Tiryns was captured. Dorati 2004, 309n65 with further references.

[24] In earlier scholarship, the *Hyrnathioi* are often assumed to be non-Dorian, a view to which I do not subscribe. O'Neil 1981, 343n93, Tomlinson 1972, 189-190.

[25] Piérart 2000, 298; Charneux 1984, 222; Wörrle 1964, 13. A piece of circumstantial evidence that has been proposed to be relevant for the dating of the institution of the fourth Argive tribe are two sixth-century inscriptions attesting boards of nine and six *damiourgoi* in Argos, which suggests a tripartite tribal division in that period (*SEG* 11.336, 11.314). An inscription dated to 460-450 BC explicitly attests four *hieromnamones*, representing the four tribes (*IG* IV 517). Hammond 1960, 36n1; Roebuck 1975, 489; Kelly 1976, 173n56; Jones 1987, 112, 116-117; Ruzé 1997, 252.

was related to the incorporation of the new citizens from the subjugated communities.[26] Perhaps the *Hyrnathioi* originally were comprised of the populace brought from the cities subdued by Argos.[27] The names of the phratries that make up the *Hyrnathioi* when we first encounter the tribe in the epigraphic record in the 450s partly seem to reflect non-Argive origins of their members, such as the *Naupliadai*; on the other hand, we come across the supremely Argive *Temenidai* in the same list, which, together with an artificial-looking division of the four tribes into twelve phratries each, suggests that there was a reshuffling of the phratries between the tribes before the middle of the fifth century.[28]

Several ancient sources give information about the fates of the inhabitants of the conquered cities.[29] Pausanias says that the inhabitants of destroyed Mycenae went away to Cleonae, Ceryneia and Macedonia (Pausanias 7.25.5-6); Diodorus reports that they were sold into slavery by the Argives (Diodorus 11.65.5). The occupants of Midea apparently moved to Halieis (Strabo 8.6.11, emended). The most interesting case is that of the Tirynthians.

---

[26] Wörrle (1964, 12) tentatively connects the institution of the new tribe with the democratization after the battle of Sepeia. For the earlier literature on the *Hyrnathioi*, see Ruzé 1997, 251n27.

[27] Kritzas 1992, 236n10; see also Lewis 1992, 101n17. A suggestion by van Wees (2003, 40) that the Sicyonian tribe of *Aigialeis* was comprised of the inhabitants of Pellene, Donoussa, Aigeira and other dependent communities provides a parallel for this construal of the first stage of the *Hyrnathioi*.

[28] Kritzas 1992, 236. This democratic reorganization is evoked by the myth of the defense of the Pamphyliacum, discussed above.

[29] See Piérart 1997, 329–331.

Pausanias says that the Argives transplanted the Tirynthians to Argos as *synoikoi*, in order to enlarge the population (2.25.8).[30] Other authors relate that the Tirynthians emigrated to Epidaurus and Halieis (Strabo 8.6.11, Ephorus *FGrHist* 70.56, Herodotus 7.137). Tiryns is also mentioned in Herodotus' narrative about the rule of the slaves in Argos, as a city that was taken by the slaves after they had been expelled from Argos (Herodotus 6.83). I will return to this detail in the next section; however, I would like to note already now that the appearance of Tiryns in the tale of the slaves suggests that the occupation of Tiryns was a particularly important and memorable event.

The conflicting traditions about the fate of the Tirynthians after the destruction of their city (synoecism with Argos vs emigration to Epidaurus or Halieis) indicate that the memory of the event was contested between different groups that were representing the past in different ways. Of course, the different outcomes for different sub-populations were in all probability also a historical reality. Kowalzig suggests that the Tirynthians who were exiled were "some members of the local elites," while the other inhabitants were synoikized into Argos.[31] Kritzas notices that when Plutarch describes the Argives enfranchising the best of the *perioikoi* (τῶν περιοίκων ποιησάμενοι πολίτας τοὺς ἀρίστους), the "best" has to mean "the most

---

[30] There is also a passage in Pausanias (8.27.1), which states that the Argives brought in the populations of Tiryns, Hysiai, Orneai, Mycenae and Midea. The difficulties of the passage and its time frame are discussed by Moggi 1974.
[31] Kowalzig 2007a, 164–165, and n.92.

well-disposed toward Argos," since admitting hostile men into the civic body would be "une vraie bombe" for the Argive state.[32] Thus, a plausible scheme is that after the Argive takeover and the attending democratic coup, the oligarchic-minded aristocrats left for Epidaurus and Halieis, while the supporters of democracy became Argive citizens, strengthening the position of the democrats in Argos.[33]

The pro-democratic Tirynthians presumably were an important constituent of the *Hyrnathioi* when the tribe was first instituted. In this respect, it is interesting to observe the parallel between the twofold fortunes of the inhabitants of Tiryns and the story of Hyrnetho. Like the Tirynthians, who are divided between Argos and Epidaurus,[34] Hyrnetho is torn between the same two cities. Hyrnetho, a daughter of Temenus and wife of Deiphontes, lived with her husband in Epidaurus. It is clear that there existed alternative accounts of Hyrnetho's life and deeds, since Pausanias (2.23.3) explicitly says that he is adopting the Epidaurian

---

[32] Kritzas 1992, 233.

[33] This scenario resembles the model of a "partial synoecism" that was earlier proposed by Forrest (1960, 224): "...there were two political groups in Argos before 494, an aristocratic group in power and a democratic group who favoured or were prepared to accept synoecism; [...] there were similarly two groups in the perioecic towns, a democratic group who favoured synoecism and their opponents who preferred independence; [...] the defeat {at Sepeia} brought the democrats to power in Argos and with them a partial synoecism." O'Neil (1981, 341) points out various difficulties in accepting the existence of such a partial synoecism soon after Sepeia, when Argos did not control the Plain yet.

[34] The relation of the story of emigration of the Tirynthians to Halieis to other tales about the fates of the Tirynthians needs further research.

version, rather than the Argive one.³⁵ According to this version, a rivalry between Deiphontes and the sons of Temenus causes the sons of Temenus to plot a separation between Deiphontes and their sister. After Hyrnetho refuses her brothers' pleas to abandon Deiphontes and return to Argos, her brothers forcibly abduct her from Epidaurus. Deiphontes and the Epidaurians chase them. The pregnant Hyrnetho dies in the close combat between her husband and her brother Phalces from being violently dragged by Phalces. Deiphontes buries Hyrnetho near Epidaurus, and Hyrnetho is honored by the Epidaurians with a hero-cult in the precinct around her tomb, called *Hyrnethion*.³⁶

We do not have the Argive version of the life and death of Hyrnetho. However, we do know that the Argives laid claim to having Hyrnetho's body: this is evident from Pausanias' remark in which he reports seeing the grave of Hyrnetho in Argos. Pausanias only allows the possibility that it is a cenotaph, since he subscribes to the Epidaurian version of events (2.23.3).³⁷ However, despite Pausanias' disparagement, it is clear that the Argives did not think the grave was empty.

---

³⁵ The ancient references to Hyrnetho are Pausanias 2.19.1; 2.23.3; 2.26.2; 2.28.3–7; Apollodorus 2.8.5;
Nicolaus of Damascus *FrGrHist* 90 F 30. On the Epidaurian claim to Hyrnetho see Jameson 1994, 61; on the Argive one, see Kowalzig 2007a, 152.
³⁶ Pausanias 2.28.3–7.
³⁷ Tomlinson 1972, 219; Piérart 2004a, 20.

So far, the question of why the *Hyrnathioi* were called in this manner has not been convincingly resolved.[38] It seems to me appealing to me to draw a link between Hyrnetho's body's final return to Argos from Epidaurus (according to the Argive claim), and the *Hyrnathioi* as the *perioikoi* who came to Argos instead of moving to Epidaurus. In both cases, the alternative Epidaurian version of the event is invoked, only to be ultimately rejected in favor of the Argive version.[39]

The hypothesis that the aristocratic Tirynthians moved to Epidaurus is no more than speculative. However, we do have an attestation of a comparable phenomenon. The case in point is an inscription on a bronze plaque found in the Epidaurian temple of Apollo Maleatas (*SEG* 26.449):

> Κάλλιπος Ηικέτας
> Εὐκλέος Ηυιὸς
> τὸν Ἐπιδαύριον
> παρ' Ἀπόλλονος
> Πυθίο Ἀργεῖος
> ἀρχὸς καὶ Ϝοικιάται

> Along with his household, the Argive leader Callipus, the son of Eucles, was a suppliant of the Epidaurians at the behest of Pythian Apollo.[40]

---

[38] See Valdés Guía 2005, 106-108, discussing the Hyrnetho and the *Hyrnathioi* as an instance of the prominence of women in the Argive democratic myths; Tomlinson 1972, 219 on Hyrnetho marking the non-Dorian identity of the *Hyrnathioi*.

[39] Compare Kowalzig 2007a, 152, characterizing the relationship between Argos and Epidaurus as "a mixture of allegiance and conflict."

[40] Trans. by Naiden 2005, 78.

The inscription is dated to 475–450 BC.⁴¹ Callipus, describing himself by a poetic term ἀρχὸς,⁴² was undoubtedly an aristocrat.⁴³ The plaque indicates that Callipus, along with his household, was accepted by the Epidaurians.⁴⁴ This situation, in which an Argive aristocrat finds refuge in Epidaurus, constitutes a good parallel to the posited migration of the elite anti-democratic Tirynthians to Epidaurus.⁴⁵ I believe that Callipus left Argos at some point in 475–450 BC, when the Argive democrats gained enough power to make the existence of that particular aristocrat untenable.

What makes the inscription particularly interesting for my purposes is Callipus' invocation of Apollo Pythaeus. As I suggested in Chapter 3, in the Archaic period Apollo Pythaeus presided over an alliance of states, including Argos, Sparta and Epidaurus. Callipus' statement about approaching the Epidaurians παρ' Ἀπόλλονος Πυθίο "at the behest of Apollo Pythaeus," that is, with the god's backing,⁴⁶ appears to call upon that alliance between Argos and Epidaurus.⁴⁷ The relations between Epidaurus and the new democratic Argos, from which

---

⁴¹ On *SEG* 26.449 see Lambrinoudakis 1990, Klees 1975, 176–77.
⁴² On the term ἀρχὸς in the inscription, see Lambrinoudakis 1990, 177.
⁴³ Kowalzig 2007a, 165n92. Differently, Lambrinoudakis 1990, 178 and n19.
⁴⁴ Naiden 2005, 78, 80.
⁴⁵ So Kowalzig 2007a, 165n92. See also Piérart 2004a, 27.
⁴⁶ Naiden 2005, 80.
⁴⁷ The peculiar word order of the inscription results in 'the Epidaurians' and 'the Argive' framing 'Apollo Pythaeus' in the middle: thus, Argos and Epidaurus are iconically united

Callipus flees, have changed: Apollo Pythaeus does not unite them any more.[48] However, an individual nobleman like Callipus can still summon the old aristocratic ties consecrated by Apollo, binding him to the elite Epidaurians.

Our exploration of the myths and realities related to the movement of people between Argos and the neighboring cities allows us to piece together a picture of a rapidly changing world, in which internal changes of constitution are intrinsically connected to the shifting patterns of inter-polis rivalries and alliances. The democratic Argive myth about the enfranchisement of the *perioikoi* elides this complexity, barely hinting at the underlying disagreements in its reference to the "best" of the *perioikoi*. We will now shift to the exploration of a more acerbic viewpoint on the post-Sepeian developments, transmitted by the narratives stemming from an aristocratic presentation of the events.

4. Slaves and other villains

Let us consider Herodotus' account of the rule of the slaves in Argos. In current scholarship, the story of the "servile interregnum" is commonly amalgamated with Plutarch's

---

through Apollo.

[48] I explore the role of Apollo Pythaeus in the later relations between Argos and Epidaurus in the next chapter.

and Aristotle's references to the enfranchisement of the *perioikoi*.[49] Very frequently, an equivalence between the 'slaves' and the '*perioikoi*' is posited, and the two appellations are viewed as stemming from different value judgments or tenors of description: Gomme's "those called περίοικοι by their friends and δοῦλοι by their enemies" provides a succinct example, as does Hornblower's characterization of Aristotle's reference to the *perioikoi* as a "watered down" version of Herodotus' "startling statement" about the slaves' take-over.[50] Opinions vary concerning the underlying identity of the actual group alternatively called 'slaves' and '*perioikoi*.' A frequent idea is that these are agricultural laborers, specifically Argive *gymnetes*, tribute-paying peasants.[51] Other scholars prefer to see Herodotus' "slaves" as a derogatory term for *perioikoi* in the sense of 'members of the dependent communities around Argos.'[52] Finally, some researchers do not fuse the different sources together, and perceive the reforms related to the 'slaves' and the '*perioikoi*' as different steps in the process of the Argive democratization.[53]

---

[49] For example, Lambrinoudakis 1990, 178 and n18 and Valdés Guía 2005, 103, both with further references.
[50] Gomme 1957, 257n8; Hornblower [1983] 2011, 85.
[51] Newman 1902, 304; Kirsten 1942, 93; Willetts 1959, 497; Lotze 1971, 102; Tomlinson 1972, 98-99; Moggi 1974, 1260-1263; Zambelli 1974, 451; O'Neil 1981, 343; Vidal-Naquet 1986, 210; Lambrinoudakis 1990, 178; cf. Hall 1997, 71-72.
[52] Macan 1895, 340; Lewis 1992, 101; Hornblower [1983] 2011, 85; Piérart 1997, 327-331; Piérart 2004b, 605;
[53] Seymour 1922; Adshead 1986, 375-377; Kritzas 1992, 233; cf. Ruzé 1997, 254-261.

Even the scholars who analyze separately the accounts concerning the slaves and the *perioikoi* do not devote much attention to the discussion of the nature of these accounts. Rather, they typically "translate" the events described in the sources into modern historical language and then attempt to generate a temporal scheme for these events. And yet, as I hope I have shown in the case of the *perioikoi*, an analysis that first aims to identify the underlying ideology of a given passage can produce new insights into the historical significance of the text. Let us therefore take a closer look at Herodotus' story of the slaves' regime (Herodotus 6.83), paying attention to the distinctive aspects of its portrayal of the events following the battle of Sepeia, and especially to its divergences in structure and tone from the Argive democratic myths:

> Ἄργος δὲ ἀνδρῶν ἐχηρώθη οὕτω ὥστε οἱ δοῦλοι αὐτῶν ἔσχον πάντα τὰ πρήγματα ἄρχοντές τε καὶ διέποντες, ἐς ὃ ἐπήβησαν οἱ τῶν ἀπολομένων παῖδες. Ἔπειτέ σφεας οὗτοι ἀνακτώμενοι ὀπίσω ἐς ἑωυτοὺς τὸ Ἄργος ἐξέβαλον· ἐξωθεόμενοι δὲ οἱ δοῦλοι μάχῃ ἔσχον Τίρυνθα. Τέως μὲν δή σφι ἦν ἄρθμια ἐς ἀλλήλους, ἔπειτε δὲ ἐς τοὺς δούλους ἦλθε ἀνὴρ μάντις Κλέανδρος, γένος ἐὼν Φιγαλεὺς ἀπ' Ἀρκαδίης· οὗτος τοὺς δούλους ἀνέγνωσε ἐπιθέσθαι τοῖσι δεσπότῃσι. Ἐκ τούτου δὲ πόλεμός σφι ἦν ἐπὶ χρόνον συχνόν, ἐς ὃ δὴ μόγις οἱ Ἀργεῖοι ἐπεκράτησαν.

> But Argos was so wholly deprived of men that their slaves took possession of all affairs, ruling and governing until the sons of the slain men grew up. Then they recovered Argos for themselves and cast out the slaves; when they were driven out, the slaves took possession of Tiryns by force. For a while they were at peace with each other; but then there came to the slaves a prophet, Cleander, a man of Phigalea in Arcadia by birth; he persuaded the slaves to attack their masters. From that time there was a long-

lasting war between them, until with difficulty the Argives got the upper hand.

The story follows a circular trajectory. At the story's end, Argos finally returns to the situation disrupted by the disaster at Sepeia: the sons of the slain are in power, the slaves are defeated. This essential lack of change, notwithstanding the numerous perturbations, sharply contrasts with the democratic myth, depicting the foundation of the new city and the admission of the outsiders into the community. Further, in Herodotus' story, the representation of Sepeia's aftermath is purely negative: the battle's bleak consequence is a demeaning government of slaves. The brighter aspects of the story, such as the heroism of Telesilla or the comedy of the bearded wives of the *perioikoi*, are lacking. Finally, the story abounds in violence: in addition to the destruction at Sepeia, there is a forceful expulsion of the slaves from Argos, the slaves' assault on Tiryns, and an ensuing long war between the slaves and the Argives.

The emphasis of the birthright of the sons of the slain and the ultimate return to the pre-Sepeian regime indicate that the story of the slaves derives from an aristocratic view of the events, which rejects the democratic widening of the constitution. Similarly, the unmitigated pessimism with which Sepeia's consequences are portrayed is a sign of refusal to accept the battle's role in the democratic foundation tale of the new society. Thus, the "sons of the slain" is a self-representation of the Argive aristocrats.[54] (As we have seen, the democratic myth similarly depicts those fallen at Sepeia as aristocrats.) However, in the course of the story, the designation "sons of the slain" mutates into "the Argives." In this way, the Argive elites are presented as coextensive with Argos itself. The slaves, conversely, are consistently associated with non-Argive elements in the story. They are extraneous to the Argive bloodlines; they are expelled from Argos to Tiryns; even their attack is motivated by the external influence of Cleander from Phigalia. Thus, the story emphasizes that the slaves are alien to the Argive *polis*.

The 'slaves' probably had multiple referents in the real world. The Argive democrats were certainly among these; the *gymnetes*, most likely, were not.[55] It is not easy to disentangle the story's blend of "political abuse,"[56] mythical thinking portraying a topsy-turvy, disordered world,[57] and echoes of real, complicated events.[58] What is clearer is how the story of the slaves interacts with the democratic myth of the enfranchisement of the *perioikoi*. Both the

---

[54] Forrest 1960, 222–223. On the aristocratic pattern of assimilation of non-elites into the category of "slaves," see Hunt 1998, 136.
[55] In Forrest's apt formulation (1960, 223), "*gymnetes*, even the best of them, are not the stuff of which governments are made."
[56] *Ibid.*
[57] Vidal-Naquet 1986, 209–210; Piérart 2004c, 178.
[58] I am particularly interested in exploring in a different project the significance of the reference to the agitation of the Argive slaves by the prophet Cleander from Phigalea (Herodotus 6.83) for understanding the Argive-Arcadian relations of the period.

aristocratic story of the slaves, which pitches true Argives against servile interlopers, and the democratic account of enfranchisement and synoecism are concerned with the relations between inside and outside, between Argive and non-Argive. These narratives are talking to each other, and they are saying drastically different things. We have observed the profusion of violence in the story of the slaves: this depiction of numerous hostilities pointedly contrasts with the omission of any reference to the brutal conquest of the Argive Plain in the democratic myth. On the other hand, the aristocratic myth, while highlighting the aggression and the complexity of the events transpiring in the Plain, does not include any mention of the synoecism: nothing is said about the fate of Tiryns after the slaves are defeated by the Argives. This is understandable, since the synoecism of the Plain was clearly the main point of pride of the Argive democrats. Thus, the democratic and the aristocratic tales create irreconcilably different representations of the Argive history, by highlighting the elements omitted by their opponents and omitting the elements most important for the alternative account.[59]

In this discussion, I have been treating the democratic and the aristocratic tales as more or less contemporary. The democratic myths, as I have argued, date from the 460s BC. Can we establish a date for the story of the slaves?

---

[59] The incompatibility of the aristocratic and democratic tales perhaps explains why detailed and careful attempts by Forrest 1960 and O'Neil 1981 to work out a chronology that would fit both the story of the slaves and the enfranchisement of the *perioikoi* have not produced credible results.

I believe that a clue for the dating comes from the very end of the slaves' story, usually neglected in historical reconstructions: with difficulty, the Argives win. This description of the events indicates that the aristocrats were in a position of power when Herodotus gathered the tale. It is improbable that such an occurrence took place during the 460s, the acme of democratic developments in Argos. On the other hand, the period after 451 BC is a plausible setting. While in 462/1 BC Argos entered into an alliance with Athens, and in 458 BC a thousand Argives joined the Athenians in fighting the Spartans in the battle of Tanagra, in 451 BC Argos performed what was described by Victor Ehrenberg as a "most remarkable" "political somersault"[60] and concluded a thirty years' peace with Sparta.[61] The shift in Argive foreign policy was in all probability accompanied by changes in the domestic situation, strengthening the oligarchic faction. (We will see more examples of the interrelations between Argive domestic and foreign policies in Chapter 6).[62]

Independently, Marcel Piérart comes to the conclusion that Herodotus' research of Argive history during and after the battle of Sepeia should be dated no earlier than 450 BC. A

---

[60] Ehrenberg [1968] 2010, 179. Ehrenberg suggests that there must have been some connection between the Argive-Spartan peace and a five-years truce concluded between Athens and Sparta the same year.
[61] See the discussion in Hornblower [1983] 2011, 81, 85–87.
[62] Cerri 2004 argues that in Euripides' *Suppliants* Argos is associated with aristocracy/ oligarchy. Cerri suggests that this representation stems from the Athenian resentment of the Argive thirty years peace with Sparta and the power wielded by the Argive aristocracy. Cerri 2004, 197.

chronological indication comes from Herodotus' report of the Argives' justification of their neutrality in the Persian wars. That account claims that when the messengers of the Greeks came to Argos with an appeal to help against the Persians, the Argives requested as a precondition for their participation in the war that a thirty years' peace should be concluded between Argos and Sparta (Herodotus 7.148.4, 7.149.1). Piérart suggests that the idea of the thirty years' peace at the time of the Persian wars was inspired by the Argive-Spartan peace of 451 BC.[63] For my purposes, it is relevant to note here that in Herodotus' account, the passage describing the Argive request for a peace treaty is linked with the story of the slaves' rule via a statement that the Argives needed time for their sons to grow into manhood after Sepeia (7.149.1, 7.148.2).[64] The association probably implies that these narratives stem from the same source, and thus both should be dated after 451 BC.

Piérart also points out that an alternative account of the motives for the Argive neutrality, reported by Herodotus (7.150–151), features an incidental reference to an Athenian embassy to Persia, led by Callias, datable to the middle of the fifth century.[65] Pietro Vannicelli, who has studied that version, unfavorable to Argos, argues that it derives from Athens and

---

[63] Piérart 2003, 284 and n50 with a reference to Bengtson 1975, 46–47n144.
[64] Asking for a thirty years' truce around 480 BC in order to recover from the losses of Sepeia seems to be overestimating the amount of time necessary for the Argive children to grow up. The miscalculation argues against the possibility that the story dates to 480 BC.
[65] Piérart 2003, 284.

tentatively connects it with the cooling off of the Argive-Athenian relationship after the Argive-Spartan peace of 451 BC.[66]

Accepting 451 BC as a *terminus post quem* for Herodotus' accounts of the battle of Sepeia and the slaves' rule reverses the established viewpoint of the chronological precedence of Herodotus' narrative over the story of the female defense of Argos. On this new construal, by the time of Herodotus' interactions with his Argive informants, the stories of Telesilla, of the heroic Argive women, of the bearded wives of the *perioikoi*, as well as the "hybristic" version of the Sepeia oracle, were already out of commission. These narratives were obviously not forgotten: rather, the new oligarchic regime probably actively censored them as manifestations of democratic ideology. Instead, Herodotus was presented with the oligarchic version of events.[67]

---

[66] Vannicelli 2004, 293. This version asserts that Xerxes sent an envoy to the Argives before the war, appealing to a common descent from Perseus (Herodotus 7.150.2). If we accept Hall's argument that Perseus was adopted by Argos only after the Argive conquest of Mycenae (Hall 1997, 98), then Perseus' appearance in the narrative provides another indication for dating it no earlier than the 460s.

[67] On Herodotus' aristocratic informants, see Forrest 1960, 222-223.

5. The shields of Archinus

I submit that we have a good parallel to Herodotus' story of the slaves, displaying a similar anti-democratic stance and comparable rhetoric, and also postdating the 460s. The case in point is the following account by Polyaenus (3.8):

> Ἀρχῖνος Ἀργείων ὅπλα ποιουμένων δημοσίᾳ πᾶσι τοῖς πολίταις ἐπιμελητὴς τῶν ἐργαζομένων ἀποδειχθείς, καινὸν ὅπλον ἑκάστῳ τῶν πολιτῶν διδοὺς τὸ παλαιὸν ἐλάμβανεν ὡς ἀναθήσων τοῖς θεοῖς· καὶ γὰρ οὕτως ἦν τοῖς Ἀργείοις δεδογμένον. ἐπεὶ δὲ τὰ παλαιὰ πάντων ὅπλα μόνος ἤθροισεν, ὁπλίσας <u>ξένους καὶ μετοίκους καὶ ἀτίμους καὶ πένητας</u> τὴν Ἀργείων τυραννίδα κατέσχεν.

> When the Argives were making weapons for all citizens at public expense, Archinus was appointed an overseer of the task. Giving a new shield to each of the citizens, he took the old ones to be dedicated to the gods, as it had been decreed by the Argives. But, when he singly mustered everybody's arms, he armed foreigners, resident aliens, people deprived of civic rights and day-laborers, and achieved the tyranny in Argos.

The story pits the members of the Argive body politic against those who lack Argive citizenship and are armed by Archinus. The realism of a situation in which all citizens are on one side of a political division, while the non-citizens are on the other, is questionable. Accordingly, I suggest that the tale of Archinus' ruse should be not taken at face value, but rather perceived as a fictional representation of a broadening of the franchise. The story transforms the extension of citizenship to new groups of people into an act of arming the outsiders with the hoplite panoply, an emblem of citizen status.[68] Archinus' usurpation of power, on the same reasoning, is a dramatic description of a transition to a democratic regime.[69] Thus, the story is an expression of an oligarchic worldview in the face of political change. We can observe resemblances to the story of the slaves: again, the oligarchic faction represents itself as "the Argives," while the democrats are depicted as lacking legitimacy and being supported only by the alien elements and the poor. The emphasis on the theme of enfranchisement, together with the proposed dating of the story to the fifth or fourth century BC,[70] open up the possibility that the tale of Archinus' ruse refers to the same phase of Argive history as does the Herodotean story of the slaves' rule.

The interpretation of Archinus as a major figure behind the democratic reforms, not a tyrant, finds a parallel in the figure of Euphron of Sicyon, as analyzed by Sian Lewis.

---

[68] On the hoplite armor/status as the key image of the citizenship, see Aristotle, *Politics* 1279a39–b5; Loraux [1981] 2006, especially 349–350; Cartledge 1998, 62–64; Hunt 1998, 219–220.
[69] The mentality of perceiving democracy as tyranny is attested both in Aristotle (*Politics* 1292a17–24; 1312b6, 1312b33–38 and in Plato (*Republic* 564d-e, 572d–573a); Neel 1994, 108; Beiner 2005, 184–186; compare also Herodotus' association between the democratic reforms of Athenian Cleisthenes and the activities of Cleisthenes the tyrant of Sicyon (Herodotus 5.67–69); cf. Henderson 2003; Kallet 2003; Hall 2010.
[70] De Libero 1996, 215. De Libero's dating is based on the tale's representation of the citizenship as a closed category, as well as the similarity of Archinus to the Aristotelian formula of the tyrant supported by the common people (Aristotle *Politics* 1310b12–16). Cf. Piérart 1996b, 175.

Xenophon, our nearly exclusive source for Euphron's short rule (368–366 BC),[71] portrays a ruthless greedy despot. A detail relevant for the comparison with Archinus is Xenophon's claim that Euphron paid his mercenaries in temple treasures (*Hellenica* 7.1.46, 7.3.8):[72] the despoiling of the temples in order to fund Euphron's armed force nicely matches Archinus' arming of his supporters with the armor that was supposed to be dedicated to the gods. And yet, Lewis discerns "an underlying positive tradition [...] contained in Xenophon's account. It is plain, for instance, that Euphron was popular with the Sicyonian *dêmos*: he established a democracy at the outset of events and consistently supported that democracy against the aristocratic faction."[73] Lewis suggests that Xenophon's accusatory remark that Euphron gave freedom and citizenship to the slaves (*Hellenica* 7.3.8) is evidence of his democratic reforms.[74] The exact identity of the slaves is still debated: Whitehead takes them as chattel-slaves,[75] whereas Cartledge and van Wees suggest two different historically attested groups of helot-like Sicyonian serfs as candidates.[76] While it may remain unclear what social category

---

[71] Apart from Xenophon, *Hellenica* 7.1.44-6 and 7.3, the only other mention of Euphron is Diodorus Siculus 15.70.3. Lewis 2004, 65.
[72] *Ibid.*, 70.
[73] *Ibid.*, 71.
[74] *Ibid.*
[75] Whitehead 1980, 177–178.
[76] Cartledge 1980; van Wees 2003, 38. Van Wees and Cartledge analyze further instances of the motif of the enfranchisement of slaves; see also Fisher 1993, 33; Cartledge 2001, 225n85; and my next note. To the list of the stories of enfranchisement of slaves cited by the above scholars we

Xenophon's "slaves" denoted in real life (probably several different groups), the image of slave enfranchisement strikingly recalls the version of the Argive events that Plutarch ascribes to Herodotus: the story that after Sepeia the Argives married their women to slaves.[77] Plutarch rejects the version angrily in favor of the enfranchisement of the best of the *perioikoi* (*Moralia* 245f). So, Plutarch contrasts the positive presentation of the enfranchisement with its negative presentation.[78]

Returning to Euphron: after being assassinated in Thebes, he was buried in Sicyon's agora and honored with a hero cult (Xenophon *Hellenica* 7.3.12). Lewis argues that this honor was bestowed upon Euphron as the founder of the Sicyonian democracy.[79] She infers: "The conflict at Sicyon, despite being presented as that of liberator versus tyrant, was clearly a *stasis* between democrats and aristocrats; the opponents of Euphron are described at various junctures as the *beltistoi*, the *kratistoi* and the *plousiotatoi*, indicating a division along class

---

can add a reference to the enfranchisement of their slaves by the Samians (Aristotle fr. 575 Rose ap. Photius *Lexicon* Σ 498.17, Suda Σ 77).

[77] On the topos of the marriage of citizen women to slaves, see Asheri 1977; Trampedach 1994, 64n24; van Wees (2003, 38, 46).

[78] Herodotus' rule of the slaves constitutes a different topos from the enfranchisement/marriage of the slaves (although the two topoi are obviously connected) and therefore, as I have argued above, it is not just a negative mirror image of the story of the enfranchisement of the *perioikoi*.

[79] Lewis 2004, 72.

lines."⁸⁰ Lewis' conclusion is that "[v]iewed from the right perspective, almost any ruler or regime could be claimed as a tyranny, and the judgement we make on any given regime depends to a large extent on the ideology of the historian who described it."⁸¹

The shift of attention from the figure of the tyrant to the attitude of the narrator, which Lewis advocates, is an important general point, but in the specific case of Archinus, do we have traces of the alternative positive presentation? I submit that we do. It is the only other reference to Archinus that we have, coming from a Pindaric scholion (O.7.152d):

> ἄλλως· ἐν Ἄργει, ἐν τῷ Ἑκατομβαίων ἀγῶνι, χαλκὸς τὸ ἆθλον δίδοται, ὅτι Ἀρχῖνος Ἀργείων γενόμενος βασιλεὺς, ὃς καὶ ἀγῶνα πρῶτος συνεστήσατο, ταχθεὶς ἐπὶ τῆς τῶν ὅπλων κατασκευῆς, ἀπὸ τούτων καὶ τὴν τῶν ὅπλων δόσιν ἐποιήσατο.

> According to another source. In Argos, in the games of Hecatombaea, bronze armor is given as a prize, because Archinus, when he became king in Argos — he was the first who organized the games — having been appointed over the provision of armor, from those means also established the award of the armor.

The point shared by both references to Archinus is his connection to the provision of armor;⁸² however, in Polyaenus this leads to his tyranny, while according to the scholion the result is

---

⁸⁰ Lewis 2004, 71, with note 30 referring to De Ste. Croix 1981, 297. Lewis also points out a parallel for her analysis of Euphron in Bosworth's study of the Ephesian tyrant Hegesias (Polyaenus 6.49). Bosworth construes Hegesias "not as a 'genuine' tyrant, but as one of the leaders of the democratic faction whose pre-eminent position [...] laid him open to accusations of tyranny." Lewis 2004, 72–73 and note 40 referring to Bosworth 1980, 132.
⁸¹ Lewis 2004, 74.
⁸² Piérart 1996b, 175.

just a glorification of the festival. The story is frequently dated to the Archaic period;[83] an alternative early hypothesis is to date it to 266-263 BC, the time of the Chremonidean War.[84] However, as Piérart has shown, the latter dating is historically impossible.[85] If we look at the text of the scholion, the combination of βασιλεὺς 'king' and ταχθεὶς 'having been appointed' suggests that Archinus' kingship belongs to the period when the king was just an eponymous official.[86] Now, it has been proposed by Jonathan Hall that there was a reorganization of the Hekatombaia in the 460s. Hall connects the reorganization with Argos finally gaining control over the Heraion. One of the crucial pieces of evidence that has led Hall to propose the reorganization is the sudden appearance in 470-460 BC of a series of bronze hydriai with inscriptions identifying them as coming from the games of Hera Argeia.[87] The reorganization of the games, which saw the expansion of the bronze prizes, provides a perfect fit for the story

---

[83] Mitsos 1952, 47-48; Berve 1967, 35; Zörner 1971, 148; Kõiv 2003, 219-220.
[84] Droysen 1878, 240; Cook 1914, 446n8; Pritchett 1979, 249-250.
[85] Piérart 1996b, 175 and n18 with further references.
[86] Tentatively suggested by de Libero 1996, 216; on eponymous kingship in Argos, see de Libero 1996, 214n42.
[87] Hall 1995, 612. Similarly, Piérart 1996b, 176. In 460-450 BC, the Heraion also saw the construction of the South Stoa, a project carried out by the Argive democracy, as argued by des Courtils 1992, 244-247. Cf. Hall 1995, 611.

of Archinus as reported by the scholion.[88] Thus, both accounts of Archinus' activities fit very comfortably in the 460s.

---

[88] On the Hecatombaea/Heraea, see Nilsson 1906, 42; Arnold 1937; Zeitlin 1970, 659; Burkert 1983, 162-167; Moretti 1991; Piérart 1996b, 173-176; Nagy 2010, 292-297. I hope to explore the ideology of the Hekatombaia after the Argive democratic reform in a different project; here are a few preliminary remarks. The only explicit attestation of the festival's *aition* is an account by Hyginus (*Fabulae* 170): after Danaus' death, his grandson Abas reports the news to Lynceus, his father. The scene is apparently set in the temple of Hera. Lynceus looks around for a gift for Abas and sees a shield of Danaus, which Danaus carried in his youth and then dedicated to Hera. Lynceus takes the shield down from the temple's wall and gives it to Abas. Then Lynceus establishes sacred games in which a shield is given to the runners. It is appealing to see in the oligarchic tale about Archinus' arming of his supporters a parody of this *aition*: Archinus' appropriation of the old shields that were supposed to be dedicated to the gods caricatures Lynceus' "recycling" of the shield that had been dedicated to Hera. (One can also compare a detail, reported in Pausanias, that Telesilla and the Argive women armed themselves with armor taken from sanctuaries, Pausanias 2.20.9). A possible indication that Hyginus' *aition* was current in the 460s is supplied by the strong democratic associations of Hypermestra (Danaus' daughter, Lynkeus' wife and Abas' mother): Hypermestra is acquitted by vote of the Argive people (Aesch. *Suppl.* 600-624; Pausanias *2. 19. 6; 2.20.7;* 2.21.1; see discussion in Bultrighini 1990, 96-100. On the parallelism between Hypermestra and Telesilla, see Sauzeau 1999, 158. In addition, a tradition casting Hypermestra as a priestess of the Argive Hera is attested (Hellanikus, Jacoby *FGrHist* I 1 544; Burkert 1983, 164 and n11; Sauzeau 2005, 314-15): this detail amounts to an Argive claim on the festival. Another interesting subject is the relation between the story of Cleobis and Biton (Herodotus 1.31) and the Argive aspirations to control the Heraion. On Cleobis and Biton and their connection with the Hekatombaia/Heraia, see Seaford 1988, 123-124; Chiasson 2005; McInerney 2010, 121. Fascinatingly, a multiform of the story of Cleobis and Biton is attested by Pausanias: in the very heart of Argos, in the sanctuary of Apollo Lyceus, near the throne of Danaus, there was a statue of a man with a bull on his shoulders, whom Pausanias, on the authority of the Argive poet Lyceas identified as one Biton, who carried a bull to the sanctuary of Zeus at Nemea when the Argives performed a sacrifice there (Pausanias 2.19.5). The feat of this Biton is likely to be connected to the Argive interest in the sanctuary at Nemea (see Diodorus Siculus 11.65.2). Perhaps staking the Argive claim to the Heraion was one of the primary purposes of the story of Cleobis and Biton when it was

The negative and the positive representations of Archinus' actions — which we can describe as the "oligarchic" and "democratic" versions — exhibit numerous similarities to, respectively, the story of the slaves' rule and the Argive democratic myths, discussed above. The oligarchic narratives promote the ideal of the unchanging franchise, expressed as the sons of the slain claiming their patrimony, or as the renewal of the old armor. The rhetoric of the oligarchs tends to emphasize the aggression of their opponents, their illegitimacy and low status; it also consistently omits any reference to the Argive political or cultural synoecism. The democratic stories, on the other hand, are strikingly nonviolent. In the same way that the tale about the enfranchised *perioikoi* omits any mention of the Argive conquest of the Plain, the democratic depiction of Archinus' innovations elides any reference to internal Argive conflict; instead, it focuses on the glorification of the Hecatombaea, expressing the peaceful control of Argos over the Plain. Further, the enfranchisement of the lower Argive classes is given a distinctly low profile in the democratic discourse. It is reasonable to infer from a comparison of the democratic and the oligarchic versions of Archinus' official capacity that the "provision of armor" supervised by Archinus had to do with the arming of new citizens who could not afford a hoplite panoply. However, this is never spelled out in the democratic version, just as the *perioikoi*, and not the Argive poor, are the only enfranchised group explicitly mentioned in

---

circulating in Argos. The version reported by Herodotus, with its numinous character, probably derives from Delphi, as argued by Regenbogen (1965, 383-389).

the democratic myth. Finally, the statement that Archinus was the first to organize the festival, portraying him as the founder of the games,[89] casts the Argive democratic reform of the festival as its establishment. We can compare to this the primeval quality of the motif of women in arms and the way in which the female defense of Argos is presented as a foundation of a new city. The democracy depicts itself as the beginning of a new era, but the beginning is moved back in time, so that recent events are assimilated into the ancient past.

6. A farewell to arms and the moveable Apollo Pythaeus

In Chapter 3 I proposed a tentative reconstruction of an Archaic association of cities around the cult of Apollo Pythaeus in Asine. I have suggested that the league included Argos, Epidaurus and Sparta, and that its charter myth was the story of their joint destruction of the wayward community of Asine, making it "harmless."

I am now going to present an analysis of Bacchylides' paean (F 4), a song composed for performance in the sanctuary of Apollo Pythaeus in Asine.[90] I hope to demonstrate that the paean reflects the ideology of the Argive democracy of the 460s BC, constituting a striking reworking of several aspects of the reconstructed Archaic myth.

---

[89] Compare Nagy's construal of Archinus as a culture hero. Nagy 2010, 293nn73, 74.
[90] The fundamental reconstruction of the Paean is Barrett 1954.

The first extant scene of the paean is Heracles' arrival in the house of Ceyx, king of Trachis (21-25). A lacuna of uncertain length follows. Next, there is a fragmentary scene (understandable on the basis of an account in Pausanias 4.34.9), in which Apollo commands Heracles to bring the Dryopes, whom Heracles has conquered, from Delphi to Asine (39-43). Heracles performs this act, and, as another of Pausanias' accounts (2.28.2) elucidates, apparently twists olive trees to mark the borders of the Asinaeans, making the Asinaeans "harmless" (Ἀσινεῖς, 47).[91] Next, we learn that the seer Melampous came to Asine from Argos and established a cult of Apollo (50-58):

> μάντι]ς ἐξ Ἄργευς Μελάμ[πους
> ἦλ]θ' Ἀμυθαονίδας
> βω]μόν τε Πυθα<ι>εῖ κτίσε[
> καὶ] τέμενος ζάθεον
> κείν]ας ἀπὸ ῥίζας τόδε χρ[
> ἐξό]χως τίμασ' Ἀπόλλων
> ἄλσο]ς, ἵν' ἀγλαΐαι
> τ' ἀνθ]εῦς[ι] καὶ μολπαὶ λίγ[ειαι·

> ...(the seer) Melampus, son of Amythaon, (came) from Argos and founded an alter for Pythaeus and a holy sanctuary. From that root (came) this (precinct), and Apollo gave it exceptional honor, a place where festivities blossom and clear songs; ...[92]

The next twenty-five lines of the paean (55-80) develop a striking vision of peace, featuring an image of unused arms and armor, left to spiders and rust.

---

[91] Barrett 1954, 426, 430.
[92] Trans. by David A. Campbell.

The first remarkable feature of Bacchylides' paean is that it represents the foundation of the cult of Apollo in Asine as an export from Argos by the seer Melampous, a figure with strong Argive associations.[93] It has been argued by numerous scholars on the basis of both literary and archaeological data, that the cult of Apollo in Asine is older than its Argive counterpart.[94] However, the paean insists on the primacy of the Argive cult. A similar claim is reported by Pausanias (2.24.1), according to whom the Argive temple of Apollo Pythaeus was built by a character named Pythaeus when he came from Dephi. This description portrays the Argive temple as dependent only on Delphi and not on any other temple. Another reference in Pausanias is illuminating: Pausanias remarks concerning the temple of Apollo Pythaeus in Hermione that the Hermionians "learned the name Pythaeus from the Argives, for Telesilla tells us that they were the first Greeks to whose country came Pythaeus, who was a son of Apollo (τὸ μὲν δὴ τοῦ Πυθαέως ὄνομα μεμαθήκασι παρὰ Ἀργείων· τούτοις γὰρ Ἑλλήνων πρώτοις ἀφικέσθαι Τελέσιλλά φησι τὸν Πυθαέα ἐς τὴν χώραν Ἀπόλλωνος παῖδα ὄντα, 2.35.2). In light of what we have established about Telesilla as an emblematic figure of the Argive democracy, the reference to her authority amounts to an acknowledgment that the tradition

---

[93] Kowalzig 2007a, 137.
[94] Barrett 1954, 438-441; Vollgraff 1956, 33; Morgan and Whitelaw 1991, 83; Hall 1995, 581; Kowalzig 2007a, 154-155.

about the primacy of the Argive cult of Apollo Pythaeus is a variant promoted by the Argive democratic regime of the 460s.[95]

The democratic claim that the cult of Apollo Pythaeus originated from Argos should be viewed, I suggest, against the backdrop of the earlier aristocratic league of the Peloponnesian cities, worshipping Pythaeus, with its center in Asine. The Argive democracy in the 460s was not interested in the perpetuation of these old ties. However, during the same period we have traces of the other, inter-polis aristocratic version of Apollo in the appeal of the Argive leader Callipus, who sought refuge in Epidaurus "at the behest of Pythian Apollo."[96] While the Argive democracy was claiming ownership of Apollo Pythaeus, Callipus, fleeing from the new regime, invoked the patronage of the god connecting the Argive and Epidaurian aristocrats.

Another interesting feature of Bacchylides' paean is its treatment of the fate of the Dryopes/Asinaeans. In Chapter 3 I have analyzed Pausanias' tale of the Argive destruction of Asine (2.36.4-5). Bacchylides' paean, on the other hand, apparently recounts that Heracles

---

[95] Barrett 1954, 439 asserts that the "shadowy figure of Pythaieus" is a "late invention."
[96] SEG 26.449, inscribed on a bronze plaque found the temple of Apollo Maleatas, 475–450 BC. Morgan and Whitelaw (1991, 81) note a "relatively high proportion" of Argive dedications at the temple of Apollo Maleatas at Epidaurus from the early seventh century.

brought the Dryopes to Asine from Delphi. Are the two stories compatible?[97] Pausanias thought so, since he reported the two events as consecutive (4.34.9):

> ἀναχθέντες δὲ ἐς Πελοπόννησον χρήσαντος Ἡρακλεῖ τοῦ θεοῦ πρῶτα μὲν τὴν πρὸς Ἑρμιόνι Ἀσίνην ἔσχον, ἐκεῖθεν δὲ ἐκπεσόντες ὑπὸ Ἀργείων οἰκοῦσιν ἐν τῇ Μεσσηνίᾳ, …
>
> When brought to Peloponnese according to the god's instructions to Heracles, they first occupied Asine by Hermion. They were driven from there by the Argives and lived in Messenia.

However, in the logic of Bacchylides' narrative, the move of the Dryopes to Asine cannot be followed by the Argive destruction of the city: Heracles makes the Dryopes 'harmless' (Ἀσινεῖς) and marks out their boundaries for them. The further destruction of Asine is unwarranted.

I have suggested that an earlier version of the story of Asine's destruction served as a charter myth of the Archaic association of cities around Apollo Pythaeus. On this reasoning, the Argive democracy of the 460s did not need the myth of the destruction of Asine. Indeed, I shall show now that Pausanias' belief in the destruction of Asine does not derive from Argive sources.

The destruction of Asine by Argos and the migration of Asine's population to Messenia were narratives embraced as foundations of communal identity by Messenian Asine. Nino

---

[97] Hall (1997, 76, citing Piérart 1985, 278) suggests that Heracles' relocation of the Dryopes served "as an aetiological doublet for the Argive action." Billot (1989–1990, 43–47) argues that the myth of Apollo commanding Heracles to bring the Dryopes to Asine is Argive invention; similarly, Luraghi 2008, 41.

Luraghi discusses the importance of being Dryopian for that city: the ethnic self-definition as Dryopes allowed the inhabitants of Asine not to be Messenian, and from the fifth century onward the political trajectory followed by Asine repeatedly differed from the rest of Messenia.[98] Pausanias returns to the story of the relocation of the Asinaeans to Messenia several times (3.7.4, 4.8.3, 4.14.3, 4.34.9-11); thus, for him, Asine's destruction is an essential historical episode. Pausanias' conviction that Asine was destroyed by Argos made him skeptical when he encountered a different tradition. Here is Pausanias' description of the boundary between Epidaurus and Asine (Pausanias 2.28.2):

> ἐς δὲ τὸ ὄρος ἀνιοῦσι τὸ Κόρυφον, ἔστι καθ' ὁδὸν Στρεπτῆς καλουμένης ἐλαίας φυτόν, αἰτίου τοῦ περιαγαγόντος τῇ χειρὶ Ἡρακλέους ἐς τοῦτο τὸ σχῆμα. εἰ δὲ καὶ Ἀσιναίοις τοῖς ἐν τῇ Ἀργολίδι ἔθηκεν ὅρον τοῦτον, οὐκ ἂν ἔγωγε εἰδείην, ἐπεὶ μηδὲ ἑτέρωθι ἀναστάτου γενομένης χώρας τὸ σαφὲς ἔτι οἷόν τε τῶν ὅρων ἐξευρεῖν. ἐπὶ δὲ τῇ ἄκρᾳ τοῦ ὄρους Κορυφαίας ἐστὶν ἱερὸν Ἀρτέμιδος, οὗ καὶ Τελέσιλλα ἐποιήσατο ἐν ᾄσματι μνήμην.

> As you go up to Mount Coryphum you see by the road an olive tree called Twisted. It was Heracles who gave it this shape by bending it round with his hand, but I cannot say whether he set it to be a boundary mark against the Asinaeans in Argolis, since in no land, which has been depopulated, is it easy to discover the truth about the boundaries. On the top of the mountain there is a sanctuary of Artemis Coryphaea (of the Peak), of which Telesilla made mention in an ode.

The detail of an olive, twisted by Heracles as a marker of the boundary between Epidaurus and Asine, perfectly corresponds to στ]ρέψας ἐλαίας 'having twisted olive-trees' of Bacchylides' paean (line 46). However, Pausanias' tone is extremely hesitant: he evidently mistrusts the

---

[98] Luraghi 2008, 39-43.

tradition that he himself reports. Paola Bernardini notes Pausanias' uncertainty and suggests that Pausanias experienced a cognitive dissonance between the idea of the widely dispersed Dryopian population, living on Euboea, in Cyprus and the Cyclades, and the instance in which the Dryopes of Asine seemed to be contained by "confini troppo precisi e limitativi."[99]

The mention of Telesilla in the context of setting boundaries between Epidauros and Asine again suggests the Argive democratic reworking of the previous aristocratic system of relations between Argos and Epidauros, focused on regulating various border territories.[100] The substitution of the myth of Asine's destruction by the more peaceful myth of Heracles' setting boundaries for the Dryopians in Asine is in line with the Argive democracy's elision of references to its aggressive conquest of the Argive Plain.

The subject of the Argive conquest of the Plain brings us to the paean's magnificent description of peace. Bernardini argues that the paean should be dated to the period after 462 BC, when Argos experienced a period of calm. She proposes that the paean's brilliant vision of peace is linked with the memories of the recent wars that the Argives went through.[101] The background of the previous wars, from the trauma of Sepeia to the Argive wars of conquest, is certainly relevant for the appreciation of the paean's depiction of peace; however, it is

---

[99] Bernardini 2004, 139.
[100] Billot 1989–1990, 44.
[101] Bernardini 2004, 140–141.

tempting to consider the images of peace also in the context of the earlier tradition of ritual battles between Argos and Sparta. Amid the festive sacrifices and songs of the peaceful city, the paean portrays the decay of the unused armor (69–78):

> Ἐν δὲ σιδαροδέτοις πόρπαξιν αἰθᾶν
> ἀραχνᾶν ἱστοὶ πέλονται,
> ἔγχεα τε λογχωτὰ ξίφεα
> τ' ἀμφάκεα δάμναται εὐρώς.
>
> χαλκεᾶν δ' οὐκ ἔστι σαλπίγγων κτύπος,
> οὐδὲ συλᾶται μελίφρων
> ὕπνος ἀπὸ βλεφάρων
> ἀῷος ὃς θάλπει κέαρ.

> On iron-pinned shieldgrips are found the spinnings of red-brown spiders, and sharp-pointed spears and double-edged swords and subdued by rust. [a lacuna of two lines] There is no din of bronze trumpets, and sleep, honey for the mind, still soothing the heart at daybreak, is not pillaged from men's eyelids.

The role of Apollo Pythaeus as the overseer of the ritual battles between Argos and Sparta induces me to infer that these lines not only depict the end of the real hostilities, but also allude to the obsolescence of the aristocratic ritual fighting. The paean's Apollo Pythaeus continues to be the god of young men (lines 67, 80); however, the deity who used to preside over the inter-polis aristocratic ritual battles now is imagined as watching over his native democratic Argos, as the city enjoys the bliss of peace.

7. Writing on the shield

In this and the previous chapter I have explored at length the emergence of new networks of myths and rituals in Argos after the disruption of the ritual battles with Sparta in the middle of the sixth century. I have attempted to show that by the 460s the battle of Sepeia became a new mythical point of reference, a formative event that was claimed to have shaped Argive social and political organization. At the conclusion of this chapter I would like to turn to Sparta and to consider the ways in which the Spartan annexation of the Thyreatis and the subsequent hostilities with Argos were presented in the Spartan accounts of these events.

First, it is relevant to observe a striking difference in the Spartan perception of the battle of Sepeia. Herodotus reports that Cleomenes' enemies accused him of being bribed, and brought him to trial before the ephors on the charge of not taking Argos (Herodotus 6.82). This information in all likelihood derives from Spartan sources. This view of the Sepeia campaign portrays it as a half measure and a disappointment — a far cry from the fateful carnage, resulting in the establishment of a new city, of the Argive democratic myth. In the Spartan historical imagination the battle of Sepeia apparently did not amount to a seminal event.

It is the Spartan annexation of the Thyreatis that finds its way into the myth.

I suggest that we can detect the Spartan ideological claims concerning the irrevocable and rightful possession of the Thyreatis in the tale of the death of Othryades, as presented by Chrysermus (cited in Plutarch), the poems in the *Greek Anthology*, and other sources. Mortally wounded, Othryades makes a trophy and with his own blood inscribes a shield, proclaiming the Spartan ownership of the Thyreatis.[102] Below I shall argue that the act of inscribing the victory in blood is meant to fix the outcome of the battle for all time. Construed in this way, the image presents a stark contrast to the perennially changing outcomes of the ritual battles.

Thus, I suggest that the tale of Othryades' inscription dramatizes the point of transition from the ritual battles to Spartan control of the Thyreatis. This reading is certainly conjectural. We do not have direct means of establishing when the detail of the writing on the shield in blood was incorporated in the narrative of the battle of Champions. However, as I hope to demonstrate, several other stories that derive from Sparta and are probably datable to the first half of the fifth century, feature similar imagery and rhetoric.

The first account, whose relevance to Othryades' story will require some explaining, is a bizarre tale found in Stephanus of Byzantium. In an entry on the town of Anthana (Anthene), Stephanus narrates that it was so called in honor of Anthes, son of Poseidon, whose skin Cleomenes stripped off and inscribed. Meineke suggested that the text must have a lacuna

---

[102] Chrysermus ap. Plutarch *Greek and Roman Parallel Stories* 306a-b; *Greek Anthology* 7.430; 7.431; 7.741; Theseus ap. Stobaeus *Florilegium* 3.7.68 (= FGH 453 F 2).

after "son of Poseidon," containing a reference to an unfortunate citizen of Anthene, flayed by Cleomenes; later scholars put forward various identifications of the missing person.[103] However, Alan Griffiths has made a compelling case for the validity of the inherited text. Griffiths argues that the narrative portrays Cleomenes' desecration of a tomb of the hero Anthes. Here is the text of Stephanus' note:

> Ἀνθάνα, πόλις Λακωνική, μία τῶν ἑκατόν· κέκληται δὲ, ὡς Φιλοστέφανος, παρὰ Ἄνθην τὸν Ποσειδῶνος, ὃν Κλεομένης ὁ Λεωνίδου ἀδελφὸς ἀνελὼν καὶ ἐκδείρας ἔγραψεν ἐν τῷ δέρματι τοὺς χρησμοὺς ὧδε τηρεῖσθαι.

> Anthana, a Laconian polis, one of the hundred. It is called, according to Philostephanus, for Anthes son of Poseidon, whom Cleomenes the brother of Leonidas disinterred, flayed and wrote on his skin, thus the oracles were kept.

The pivotal point is the meaning of the participle ἀνελών, previously translated as 'killed.' Griffiths argues that it should be translated as 'disinterred' and quotes as a parallel Thucydides' use of the same participle in a passage describing Cleomenes' removal of the bones of the Alcmaeonidae from Athens: τῶν τεθνεώτων τὰ ὀστᾶ ἀνελόντες ἐξέβαλον "having taken up the bones of the dead, they cast them out" (Thucydides 1.126.12). Thucydides' passage beautifully does double duty, producing a clear attestation of the meaning 'disinter,' and an example of a tradition claiming that Cleomenes dug up the dead.[104]

---

[103] References in Griffiths 1989, 62–63.
[104] Griffiths 1989, 66.

No matter how intriguing on its own terms, Cleomenes' writing on the skin of a dead hero does not appear particularly similar to Othryades' writing on a shield. However, if we examine further details of Stephanus' narrative, the two tales start to converge. First of all, as Griffiths observes, Anthene lay in the Thyreatis, close to the town of Thyrea (Pausanias 2.38.6).[105] Griffiths also compares Cleomenes' disinterment of Anthes with the stories about finding the bones of Orestes, Tisamenus and Theseus, which were "used *to establish claims to disputed territory*"(Griffiths' italics). Accordingly, Griffiths proposes that Cleomenes' actions had the same aim.[106] At this point, a common pattern starts to emerge: both Cleomenes and Othryades express a claim to the disputed territory of Thyreatis through an act of writing, in which the material or medium is derived from a human body.

In order to understand the significance of this pattern, we need to clarify the rhetoric of Cleomenes' actions. Griffiths believes that what Cleomenes does to Anthes amounts to desecrating the remains of the enemy's eponymous hero.[107] This construal is based on Griffiths' assumption that the Thyreatis "had traditionally been *Argive* land" and therefore "its town will

---

[105] Herodotus (6.76.2) attests to Cleomenes' presence in the Thyreatis: he reports that before the battle of Sepeia, Cleomenes led his army to Thyrea, from where, after a sacrifice, they crossed the Argolic gulf on ships toward Tiryns and Nauplia. Robertson (1992, 193) believes that the Spartans actually seized the Thyreatis for the first time on this occasion.
[106] Griffiths 1989, 67.
[107] *Ibid.*, 66.

have had Argive mythical oikists."¹⁰⁸ However, the Thyreatis was not simply Argive territory but rather a borderland contested by Sparta and Argos; thus, Anthene's eponymous hero should not be defined as Argive. What was the logic of Cleomenes' actions, in this case? Or was he indeed mad?

I propose that despite its apparent striking gruesomeness, Cleomenes' treatment of Anthes does not have to be perceived as abuse. There are traditions claiming that the Spartans preserved skins of Pherecydes and Epimenides, both figures revered at Sparta. An investigation of these traditions will give us new insights into the tale of Cleomenes and Anthes, as well as of Othryades.

The story of Pherecydes' skin is known from a brief mention in Plutarch's *Pelopidas* (21.2):

> Φερεκύδην τε τόν σοφὸν ὑπὸ Λακεδαιμονίων ἀναιρεθέντα¹⁰⁹ καὶ τὴν δορὰν αὐτοῦ κατά τι λόγιον ὑπὸ τῶν βασιλέων φρουρουμένην
>
> ...Pherecydes the wise man, who was put to death by the Lacedaemonians, and whose skin was preserved by their kings, in accordance with some oracle...¹¹⁰

---

[108] Griffiths 1989, 64; the emphasis is his.
[109] I note the recurrence of ἀναιρέω here as in Stephanos' note on Anthes. While in Plutarch's text the word clearly means 'killed,' I wonder whether perhaps in Plutarch's source it was also used in the meaning 'disinterred.'
[110] Trans. by Bernadotte Perrin.

We learn that Pherecydes was highly honored at Sparta from another fleeting reference in Plutarch's *Agis* (10.3).[111] Diogenes Laertius (1.116) also tells of Pherecydes' prophecy to his Messenian host about an imminent Spartan conquest.[112]

The myths concerning Epimenides at Sparta are somewhat better attested. First, Pausanias (3.11.11) mentions Epimenides' tomb at Sparta, in the Old Ephoreia (which served in Pausanias' time as the Prytaneion).[113] Pausanias also reports that Epimenides was considered to be the founder of a circular shrine of Zeus and Aphrodite at Sparta (3.12.11). Diogenes Laertius (1.115) similarly narrates that Epimenides' body was guarded by the Spartans "in accordance with some oracle" (κατά τι λόγιον). Further, an entry by Diogenianus Grammaticus (8.28), explaining a proverbial expression τὸ Ἐπιμενίδειον δέρμα, claims that Epimenides' skin was stored up (κατέκειτο) at Sparta.[114] Most remarkably, we learn about this skin that a long time after Epimenides' death it was found tattooed with letters.[115]

The traditions about the skins of Pherecydes and Epimenides at Sparta connect them with the highest authority (the kings in the case of Pherecydes, the Ephoreia in the case of

---

[111] Munn 2006, 48n128.
[112] Tigerstedt 1965, 62, 366n465.
[113] On the Old Ephoreia as the Spartan Prytaneion in late Hellenistic and Imperial periods, see Spawforth 2002, 127.
[114] On the variants of the Spartan possession of Epimenides' whole body or only his skin, see Lupi 2001, 190.
[115] Suda s.v. Ἐπιμενίδης = *FGrH* 457 T 2, Hesychius s.v. Ἐπιμενίδης.

Epimenides). Another striking common detail is the statement that the Spartans guard Pherecydes' and Epimenides' remains κατά τι λόγιον "in accordance with some oracle" (Plutarch *Pelopidas* 21.2, Diogenes Laertius 1.115).[116] The vagueness of the expression suggests that the oracles in question are a secret tradition. The custody of the highest authority and the secretiveness, surrounding the skins, point to their talismanic value. The function of a hero's body as a talisman protecting the polis is famously attested in the case of Oedipus (Sophocles, *Oedipus at Colonus*, 1524-25, 1533-34). Importantly, the knowledge about the location of Oedipus' corpse is a secret, restricted to the lineage of priests reaching back to Theseus.[117]

The importance of guarding Epimenides' skin seems also to be reflected in the explanation of the proverbial expression τὸ Ἐπιμενίδειον δέρμα, given by several ancient sources: ἐπὶ τῶν ἀποθέτων[118]. Current scholarship on the subject understands ἀποθέτων as denoting secret, hidden, obscure things.[119] Without arguing with this aspect of the translation, I would like to point out that ἀπόθετος can also mean 'stored up' (LSJ), and that the meaning 'hidden, secret' is probably an extension of that core meaning. Diogenianus' use of κατέκειτο, "stored up," in the reference to Epimenides' skin at Sparta, supports this interpretation of

---

[116] Hughes 1991, 237n143.
[117] Sophocles, *Oedipus at Colonus* 1520-32, 1761-3; Nagy 1990b, viii.
[118] Diogenianus 8.28, Suda s.v. Ἐπιμενίδης, Michael Apostolius s.v. Ἐπιμενίδης.
[119] Dodds 1951, 163n43; Griffiths 1989, 69; Robertson 1992, 193; Svenbro 1993, 137; Lupi 2001, 180; Catarzi 2001, 319n8.

ἀπόθετος. Thus, I suggest that the proverbial "skin of Epimenides" signified things that were stored up and away to ensure their absolute safety.[120]

Besides the accounts locating Epimenides' body at Sparta, a rival version situated his tomb in Argos.[121] Pausanias (2.21.3) relates that the Argives showed Epimenides' grave before the temple of Athena Trumpet. The accompanying story was that the Spartans were at war with the Cnossians, and captured Epimenides alive; subsequently they killed him for inauspicious prophesies, at which point the Argives took up the body[122] and buried it in their city.[123] Pausanias explicitly states that the Argive and the Spartan accounts are at variance, since the Spartans denied ever fighting the Cnossians (3.12.11). Pausanias also chooses the

---

[120] The mythical pattern, according to which the safety of a *polis* can be contingent upon the preservation of a human skin, is replicated in a euhemeristic version of the myth of the Golden Fleece, reported by Diodorus Siculus (4.47.5-6). Phrixus' attendant, whose name was Crius (Ram), was sacrificed to the gods in Colchis; his body was flayed and "the skin was nailed to the temple, in accordance with some custom" (προσηλωθῆναι τῷ νεῷ τὸ δέρμα κατά τι νόμιμον, 4.47.5). Later, the king of Colchis Aeëtes received an oracle that he would die when the skin of Crius was carried off; this made the king build a wall around the precinct and guard the skin most vigilantly. This account is certainly late, and interests me as a typological parallel to the stories of Pherecydes and Epimenides (observed in Hughes 1991, 236n143); in addition, it has been argued by Rusten that Diodorus' version of Crius' story was in fact inspired by the tales about Epimenides' and Pherecydes' skins. Rusten 1982, 94 and addendum, 182; Stephens 2003, 40n63.
[121] Compare the rivalry between Argos and Epidaurus over the possession of Hyrnetho's grave.
[122] Interestingly, the verb describing the Argives taking Epimenides' body up after his death is ἀναιρέω again.
[123] On the Argive affinities of Epimenides' poetry, see Breglia Pulci Doria 2001, 305-311. Diogenes Laertius 1.114-115 reports that Epimenides foretold to the Cretans the defeat of the Spartans by the Arcadians, on which see Leahy 1958; Dušanić 1977, 27-28; Mele 2001, 274.

Spartan story as the more credible of the two competing versions (3.11.11).

Thus, in parallel to their contention over the Thyreatis, Argos and Sparta vie for possession of Epimenides' true grave.[124] It is tempting to connect the two subjects, and to wonder whether the possession of Epimenides' grave, his authority and his favorable prophecies were felt to be crucial for the rightful ownership of the Thyreatis. Interestingly, the figure of Pherecydes is also inscribed in a territorial conflict, albeit not the Argive-Spartan one: Diogenes Laertius (1.117-118, 120-121) narrates, on the basis of an earlier account by Hermippus, that there was a war between the Ephesians and the Magnesians. Pherecydes, who wished the Ephesians to win, was the only recipient of a particular oracle concerning their victory. He ensured the Ephesians' success by dying in the territory of Magnesia, and giving instructions to the Ephesians to bury him on the spot of his death, when they conquer that territory. The Ephesians defeated the Magnesians and buried Pherecydes with great honor.[125]

The tales about the roles of Epimenides and Pherecydes in the Argive-Spartan and Ephesian-Magnesian enmities illustrate the productivity of the mythical pattern that features an obscure oracle and the body of a hero as a talisman in an interstate opposition. Similarly, the stories concerning the skins of Pherecydes and Epimenides show the productivity of a related mythical pattern, in which a hero's *skin* has talismanic value: this pattern seems to be a

---

[124] See Levaniouk 2012, 392 (and pp. 395-397 on the Argive-Spartan rivalry in Crete).
[125] Pherecydes' death is discussed in Schibli 1990, 6-10.

local Spartan specialty.[126]

At long last, let us return to Anthes and Cleomenes. The tale of Cleomenes' treatment of Anthes shares several motifs with the accounts concerning Epimenides' body at Sparta: the image of the hero's skin, which is written upon; the setting of the Argive-Spartan conflict; and the hazy reference to an oracle. It is reasonable to conclude that rather than abusing Anthes as the enemy's champion, Cleomenes' actions were intended to ascertain the irrevocable Spartan possession of the hero, and, by extension, the permanent Spartan control of the Thyreatis. Getting rid of the antagonistic component in our perception of Cleomenes' behavior toward Anthes makes more valid Griffiths' comparison between Anthes and heroes like Orestes or Theseus, whose bones were instrumental in making territorial claims.[127]

Cleomenes' writing on Anthes' skin is connected in some way with the oracles:

---

[126] The question whether there was some direct borrowing between the stories of Pherecydes' and Epimenides' skins is not essential for my purposes, since I am interested in this case not in establishing a historical relation between the versions, but merely in demonstrating the replication of the mythical pattern in different stories. Bremmer (1993, 236) explains the similarities between the tales of Pherecydes' and Epimenides' skins as resulting from borrowing; for a discussion of a parallel example of legends shared between Pherecydes and Pythagoras, see Bollansée 1998, 146–152 (who comments that some of the similarities may have resulted from the application of common mythical patterns).

[127] Griffiths acknowledges that Cleomenes' desecration of Anthes' tomb is imperfect as a parallel to the use of the bones of Orestes, Tisamenus and Theseus in assertions of territorial possessions. Griffiths 1989, 67.

Stephanus' note contains a difficult expression τοὺς χρησμοὺς ὧδε τηρεῖσθαι "thus the oracles were kept."[128] Griffiths offers several conjectural explanations but admits that the meaning is ultimately unclear. While many pieces of the puzzle are missing, it seems to me that we can broadly reconstruct how the act of writing on the skin and the oracles fit together. This is where the tale of Othryades' death becomes crucial.

As I have noticed above, both Cleomenes and Othryades assert Sparta's rights over the Thyreatis through an act of writing that uses human skin or blood. We should also remember that Othryades writes on a shield, which has strong traditional associations with an ox-hide. The link between shields and hides is deeper than a simple reference to the construction material: it goes back to the Proto-Indo-European theme of equating one's shield, as well as one's skin, with one's self.[129] Thus, the motif of *writing on the human skin*, expressed in the tale of Cleomenes and Anthes, is split in Othryades' case into the components of *writing* in *human blood* on a shield's *skin*. The two stories seem to be instantiations of the same prototype. Epimenides' skin, covered with letters, provides a possible third example. It appears plausible that this prototype was at some point expressed by an oracle, pronouncing that lasting

---

[128] Griffiths (1989, 77n52) suggests an emendation of τηρεῖσθαι to τελεῖσθαι or πληροῦσθαι.
[129] Nagy 1990b, 264. Nagy quotes three cognates, Indic *tvác-* 'hide,' Greek *sakos* 'shield', and Hittite *tweka-* 'body, self' as a reflection of this theme.

possession of the Thyreatis can be gained only when the victory is inscribed onto a skin,[130] and that the writing needs to be done on, or with, a human body. Accordingly, Cleomenes' writing on Anthes' skin is a fulfillment of this oracle, ensuring the Spartan possession of the Thyreatis.

Regardless of whether or not I am right in positing the existence of such an oracle, and whether or not Epimenides' tattooed skin and Cleomenes' treatment of Anthes are historically related to Othryades' story, the images of writing on the human skin provide a good typological parallel for Othryades' inscribing the shield with blood. Can we date these accounts?

It has been argued by Marcello Lupi that the Argive version of Epimenides' death, according to which he was killed by the Spartans after being captured in a war with the Cnossians, fits well the period of 455–450 BC, when a treaty between Argos, Cnossus and Tylissus was concluded (prior to the thirty years peace between Argos and Sparta). Lupi suggests that the Argive version is constructed in polemic with the Spartan account of Epimenides' life and death, and so its date provides the *terminus ante quem* for the Spartan version.[131]

---

[130] The word δέρμα, used for skins of Anthes and Epimenides, can also refer to the shield's hide (*Iliad* 6.117).
[131] Lupi 2001, 177.

There are also some indirect cues for dating the story of Cleomenes stripping Anthes' skin off. Griffiths suggests that this narrative may lie in the background of the account of Cleomenes' death, given by Herodotus (6.75.3), according to which Cleomenes sliced with a knife his own body into pieces from the shins up. Griffiths perceives a connection between this story of Cleomenes' death and Cleomenes' treatment of Anthes: since Cleomenes has purportedly "flayed a holy corpse, popular tradition provides him with a homologous end."[132] If Griffiths is right and the story of Cleomenes' terrible end is partly informed by the story of his actions toward Anthes, then the narrative about Cleomenes and Anthes should at least predate Herodotus' account.

The story of Cleomenes' writing on Anthes' skin could have been created at some point as propaganda of Cleomenes' endeavors to stake the Spartan ideological claim to the Thyreatis. The story is obviously not veristic: the idea that Cleomenes writes on Anthes' skin is based on a mystical visualization of the body of the hero as intact in death.[133] The act of writing on the hero's skin is especially appropriate for staking a claim for the *border* territory: "bodily inscriptions are all about boundaries, a perennial theme in anthropology — between self and

---

[132] Griffiths 1989, 61, 70.
[133] *Contra* Griffiths 1989, 67, who conceives of an ancient tradition envisaging "the disinterred bones of the legendary Anthes [...] to have scraps of skin still adhering." For the preservation of hero's body after death, see Herodotus 9.120.2 (Protesilaus); Nagy 1990a, 269-273; Philostratus, *On Heroes* 10.2-4, 11.2; Nagy 2001b, xxvii-xxviii nn20, 21.

society, between groups, and between humans and divinity."[134] By writing on Anthes' skin, Cleomenes permanently inscribes the Spartan presence into the Thyreatis. However, as other things done by Cleomenes, this story is "messy:" it can be easily converted from pro-Spartan into anti-Spartan propaganda.[135] I submit that the tale of Othryades' inscription on the shield is a subsequent "cleaner" account expressing the same ideology of fixity. On the basis of comparisons with the parallel stories that I have considered, it should be dated to the first half of the fifth century.[136]

---

[134] Schildkrout 2004, 338.

[135] Cf. Forrest 1980, 86.

[136] The figure of Othryades as a symbol of the irrevocable Spartan possession of the Thyreatis may have provoked an Argive reaction. I have mentioned earlier a sculpture that Pausanias saw in the theater in Argos: "a representation of a man killing another, namely the Argive Perilaus, the son of Alcenor, killing the Spartan Othryades" (ἀνὴρ φονεύων ἐστὶν ἄνδρα, Ὀθρυάδαν τὸν Σπαρτιάτην Περίλαος Ἀργεῖος ὁ Ἀλκήνορος, Pausanias 2.20.7). The rhetorical point of this image lies in focusing the attention of the viewer on the fact of Othryades being killed, and thus suggesting that the victory belongs to Argos. The identity of Othryades' slayer, Perilaus, may hint that this sculpture dates to the 460s BC, the period of the democratic regime. We have discussed in Charter 4 the story of the Argive tyrant Perilaus destroying the bronze chamber of Danae, the site of Perseus' conception (Pausanias 2.23.6–7). I have proposed that the story paradoxically expresses the Argive appropriation of Perseus, and therefore should be dated to the period after the Argive conquest of Mycenae. If Perilaus the tyrant and Perilaus the slayer of Othryades are the same figure, perhaps the sculpture in the theater of Argos also belongs to the period of the Argive democracy, which found Perilaus "good to think with." Shaw (1999, 288) assumes that the tyrant and the killer of Othryades are the same person; Kõiv (2003, 219n18) doubts it. The Argives employed the newly-acquired figure of Perseus in formulating their claims for Cynuria: Pausanias (3.2.2) reports a tradition according to which the Cynurians are Argives by descent, and their founder is Cynurus, son of Perseus.

We have explored how the historical events of the Spartan annexation of the Thyreatis and the battle of Sepeia became mythologized in Argos and Sparta. The list of the Spartan-Argive hostilities in the first half of the fifth century is certainly not exhausted by the battle of Sepeia. The Spartans and the Argives fought several times: at Tegea, at Tanagra, perhaps at Oinoe.[137] However, we know extraordinary little about these battles, just their locations and sometimes the date. The disparity between the opacity of these confrontations and the richness of the traditions associated with the Battle of Sepeia and the Spartan takeover of the Thyreatis is not necessarily explainable by the differences in the scale of fighting or the battles' strategic importance. Rather, it seems to be the difference between the historical events that became absorbed into mythological traditions, and the ones that did not.

---

[137] Herodotus 9.35; Pausanias 1.15.

Chapter 6

As They Did in the Past: The Dispute over the Thyreatis in Argive Politics of 421-417 BC

> *Have the temperament of a complex octopus, who*
> *looks like whatever rock with which he is associated.*[1]
> Theognis 215-216

1. The ritual battle as an oligarchic motion

Let us return to our starting point in Chapter 3, the Argive proposal to the Spartans of replaying the battle for the Thyreatis in the framework of a peace treaty (Thucydides 5.41.2-3).[2] I have argued that ritual battles for the Thyreatis between Argos and Sparta took place in the Archaic period; however, by 420 BC the ritual had been obsolete for more than a hundred

---

[1] πουλύπου ὀργὴν ἴσχε πολυπλόκου, ὃς ποτὶ πέτρῃ
τῇ προσομιλήσῃ, τοῖος ἰδεῖν ἐφάνη.

[2] Thucydides does not speak about the battle for the Thyreatis but rather for Cynuria (5.41.2), which can refer to a larger territory, of which the plain of Thyreatis is a part. Thucydides speaks about the territory of Thyreatis proper in 6.95.1, defining it as the territory on the Argive border, and in 2.27.2, again defining it as γῆ μεθορία τῆς Ἀργείας καὶ Λακωνικῆς. There is a possibility that Thucydides uses 'Cynuria' and 'Thyreatis' synonymously, because when he speaks about Cynuria in 5.41, he mentions only the cities of Thyrea and Anthene, located in the Thyreatis; in 4.56.2 he describes Cynuria as μεθορία δὲ τῆς Ἀργείας καὶ Λακωνικῆς. Since I assume that the Argive proposal intended to revive the Archaic practices, I continue to employ the expression "battles over the Thyreatis" in the discussion below.

years. What were the motives of the Argives for attempting to bring the ritual back to life? The Spartans seem to be surprised by the proposal: they consider it nonsense (μωρία, 5.41.2). Therefore, perhaps the rationale for the proposal should be sought not in the relations with Sparta, but in Argive internal affairs of the years around 420 BC.

We know that between 421 and 417 BC there were strong political tensions in Argos, eventually developing into an open strife between the oligarchic and democratic factions.[3] The democratic-oligarchic opposition needs to be deduced from our sources before 418;[4] however, in that year there was an oligarchic coup in Argos, followed by a democratic countercoup in 417 BC.

Another feature, prominent in Thucydides' account, is the occurrence of abrupt shifts in Argive foreign policy, oscillating between Sparta and Athens. One such shift happened immediately after the Argive proposal to replay the battle for Thyreatis had been presented to the Spartans. While the Argive ambassadors were in Sparta, discussing the terms of the peace treaty, relations between Sparta and Athens deteriorated. Alcibiades, who was both politically

---

[3] Hornblower [1983] 2011, 89-90; Bearzot 2006; Bultrighini 1990, 128-140; Kelly 1974.
[4] A last-minute cancellation of a battle between Sparta and Argos in 418 BC, achieved through personal negotiations between two prominent Argives and the Spartan king Agis, who concluded a truce of four months between Argos and Sparta (Thucydides 5.59.4-601), as well as the unwillingness of "the Argives" to let the Athenian reinforcement that arrived soon after the cancelled battle negotiate with the Argive *dêmos* (Thucydides 5.61.1), are examples of the events that may have been instigated by the Argive oligarchs. Bultrighini 1990, 131-136; Ruzé 2006, 270.

and personally interested in the termination of the Athenian treaty with Sparta and the establishment of an alliance with Argos, privately sent a message to the Argives, informing them about an opportunity to conclude a pact with Athens (5.43). This information induced the Argives to abandon their treaty-in-the-making with Sparta; importantly, the reasoning that Thucydides attributes to the Argives at the point of their switch to the alliance with Athens singles out the Athenian democratic system as an asset (5.44.1):

> οἱ δὲ Ἀργεῖοι […] τῶν μὲν ἐν Λακεδαίμονι πρέσβεων, οἵ σφίσι περὶ τῶν σπονδῶν ἔτυχον ἀπόντες, ἠμέλουν, πρὸς δὲ τοὺς Ἀθηναίους μᾶλλον τὴν γνώμην εἶχον, νομίζοντες πόλιν τε σφίσι φιλίαν ἀπὸ παλαιοῦ καὶ **δημοκρατουμένην ὥσπερ καὶ αὐτοὶ** καὶ δύναμιν μεγάλην ἔχουσαν τὴν κατὰ θάλασσαν ξυμπολεμήσειν σφίσιν, ἢν καθιστῶνται ἐς πόλεμον. ἔπεμπον οὖν εὐθὺς πρέσβεις ὡς τοὺς Ἀθηναίους περὶ τῆς ξυμμαχίας·

> ...the Argives paid no further attention to the embassy which they had just sent to Lacedaemon on the subject of the treaty, and began to incline rather towards the Athenians, reflecting that, in the event of war, they would thus have on their side a city that was not only an ancient ally of Argos, but a sister democracy and very powerful at sea. They accordingly at once sent ambassadors to Athens to treat for an alliance.

Thus, the alliance with Athens was in the interest of the Argive democrats. In the description of the subsequent events Thucydides calls the Argive oligarchic faction simply "the Spartan party" (οἱ ἄνδρες οἱ τοῖς Λακεδαιμονίοις, 5.76.3). As we will see, Thucydides explicitly links foreign policy and internal political division at Argos, presenting the peace with Sparta after the battle of Mantinea as an element of the oligarchs' scheme of taking over Argos (5.76.2).

It seems reasonable to conclude on the basis of the entente between the Argive democrats and Athens, and the Argive oligarchs and Sparta,[5] that the Argive suggestion of replaying the battle for the Thyreatis in the framework of a peace treaty with Sparta was a motion backed by the oligarchic faction.[6] Such a suggestion harmonizes with what we have learned about the earlier ideologies of ritual and real confrontations with Sparta, espoused by different groups in Argos: I have argued in Chapter 3 that the ritual battles for the Thyreatis were an elite tradition, and we have seen in Chapters 4 and 5 that the real confrontation between Argos and Sparta at Sepeia became the core of the foundation myth of the Argive democracy.

2. The versatile Thousand

Who were the Argive oligarchs? I have mentioned Thucydides' "Spartan party." Thucydides also reports that the oligarchic coup in 417 BC was executed by one thousand Argives, assisted by one thousand Spartans (5.81.2). Diodorus Siculus (12.80.2) also says that the coup was performed by group of one thousand Argives:

> περὶ δὲ τοὺς αὐτοὺς χρόνους ἐν τῇ πόλει τῶν Ἀργείων οἱ κατ' ἐκλογὴν κεκριμένοι τῶν πολιτῶν χίλιοι συνεφώνησαν, καὶ τὴν μὲν δημοκρατίαν ἔγνωσαν καταλύειν,

---

[5] Thucydides (3.82.1) asserts that such an alignment between Athens and oligarchs, and Sparta and democrats, was ubiquitous in Greece during the Peloponnesian wars.
[6] Thus Kelly 1974, 93.

ἀριστοκρατίαν δ' ἐξ αὐτῶν καθιστάναι.

And about the same time in the city of the Argives the Thousand who had been selected out of the total muster of citizens came to an agreement among themselves and decided to dissolve the democracy and establish an aristocracy from their own number.

Diodorus gives more information about this group. He speaks about the Argive prosperity, resulting from a long peace, and about the glory of the Argive past, and narrates that "a large number of cities joined together and selected the city of the Argives to hold the position of leader" (πολλαὶ πόλεις συνίσταντο, καὶ προῆγον τὴν τῶν Ἀργείων πόλιν ἐπὶ τὴν ἡγεμονίαν, 12.75.5). In these promising circumstances, the Argives decided in 421 BC to establish an elite military force (12.75.7):

> οἱ δ' Ἀργεῖοι νομίζοντες αὐτοῖς συγχωρηθήσεσθαι τὴν ὅλην ἡγεμονίαν, ἐπέλεξαν τῶν πολιτῶν χιλίους τοὺς νεωτέρους καὶ μάλιστα τοῖς τε σώμασιν ἰσχύοντας καὶ ταῖς οὐσίαις· ἀπολύσαντες δὲ αὐτοὺς καὶ τῆς ἄλλης λειτουργίας καὶ τροφὰς δημοσίας χορηγοῦντες προσέταξαν γυμνάζεσθαι συνεχεῖς μελέτας. οὗτοι μὲν οὖν διὰ τὴν χορηγίαν καὶ τὴν συνεχῆ μελέτην ταχὺ τῶν πολεμικῶν ἔργων ἀθληταὶ κατεστάθησαν.

> The Argives, believing that the entire leadership was to be conceded to them, picked out one thousand of their younger citizens who were at the same time the most vigorous in body and the most wealthy, and freeing them also from every other service to the state and supplying them with sustenance at public expense, they had them undergo continuous training and exercise. These young men, therefore, by reason of the expense incurred for them and their continuous training, quickly formed a body of athletes trained to deeds of war.

Diodorus' narrative does not explicitly identify the Thousand as oligarchic at the point of their establishment; however, the happy coincidence that the chosen young men were *both* "the most vigorous in body and the most wealthy" marks the Thousand as upper-class: the amalgamation of wealth and bodily superiority is central to an elite self-definition (the ideal of *kalokagathia*). I propose that in the case of a ratification of the Argive peace treaty with Sparta, these thousand aristocratic young men would have been the ones to fight with the Spartans in the rerun of the ancient battle for the Thyreatis.[7] It is appealing to conjecture that one of the main practical points of the oligarchic suggestion to revive ritual battles over the Thyreatis was ensuring the existence of the elite (and pro-oligarchic) corps, intended for the participation in ritual battles, during times of peace.

This idea encounters two difficulties. First, some scholars doubt that the one thousand Argives who performed the coup according to Thucydides can be identified with the elite corps described by Diodorus. Thucydides mentions the one thousand picked Argive men, trained at public expense, in the description of the battle of Mantinea (5.67.2, 72-73). However, he does not explicitly connect the two references. This lack of explicit connection convinced Gomme that Thucydides intentionally kept the two thousands apart as different entities.[8] Gomme's point of view has been followed by a number of scholars, most recently, Simon Hornblower. Hornblower believes that Diodorus' version, as well as Pausanias' account (2.20.1-2, to which we shall return), derive from Ephorus, who misread Thucydides, creating a

---

[7] Piérart (2009, 278) makes this suggestion.
[8] Gomme 1970, 105–106.

spurious connection between the two unrelated mentions of a thousand Argives.[9] Further (and this is the second difficulty), Hornblower considers the discrepancy in the stances toward Sparta of the Thousand at Mantinea (anti-Spartan) and the Thousand of the oligarchic coup (pro-Spartan) to be an additional strong reason against identifying the two groups as one.[10]

We are going to explore below the contradictory attitudes toward Sparta, exhibited by the Argive Thousand; however, I believe that neither this inconsistency nor the lack of an overt connection between the two mentions of the Thousand in Thucydides are sufficient grounds to presume that there were two separate entities consisting of a thousand men in Argos between 421 and 417 BC. Hornblower's objection that the Thucydidean references to the Thousand have to be kept apart, since Thucydides does not connect them, is an argument from silence.[11] In addition, the accounts of Argive affairs of 421–417 BC by Diodorus (12.75.5–80.3), Aristotle (*Politics* 1304a25–26), and Pausanias (2.20.1–2) differ significantly from Thucydides' narrative and from each other. They do not seem to be easily reducible to a single preceding source that misconstrued Thucydides; in all probability, they incorporate several different traditions about the Argive history of the period that are independent of Thucydides. As we will see, a part of Diodorus' version stems from a tradition more sympathetic toward the

---

[9] Hornblower 2008, 178; similarly, Gehrke 1985, 28.
[10] Hornblower 2008, 178.
[11] David 1986, 118.

Thousand than Thucydides is,[12] while Pausanias' account is based on a distinctly lowbrow version of the events.[13]

Thus, we may accept that there was only one force of one thousand elite young men in Argos in 421–417 BC, who fought the Spartans at Mantinea in 418 BC and, approximately half a year later, executed an oligarchic coup.[14] This configuration of events, however, requires us to account for the about-face that occurred in the attitude of the Thousand toward Sparta in the few short months between the battle of Mantinea and the coup. There are other apparent inconsistencies in the aggregate portrayal of the Thousand. I have suggested the elite corps of the Thousand as a candidate for fighting in the peace-time battle with the Spartans; yet, Diodorus' account of the creation of the Thousand situates this occasion in the period of Argive dreams of political supremacy, a year before the treaty with Sparta was proposed. Moreover, the Thousand later distinguished themselves fighting at Mantinea. Why, and how, did the Thousand shift between ritual and real confrontations, between conflict and alliance with the Spartans?[15]

Aristotle's succinct analysis of Argive political dynamics in 418 BC provides a cue for

---

[12] David 1986, 116.
[13] *Ibid.*, 122.
[14] Scholars who accepts this view of the events include Andrewes (in Gomme 1970, 106); David 1986; Bultrighini 1990, 128–140; van Wees 2002, 78; Sauzeau 2008, 6–18.
[15] Cf. Bultrighini 1990, 130–131; Sauzeau 2008, 8.

understanding the motives of the Thousand's exceptional political volatility.[16]

Aristotle observes, as an illustration of his thesis that political revolutions happen when some section of the *politeia* grows in power or prestige, that "at Argos the notables having risen in repute in connection with the battle against the Spartans at Mantinea took in hand to put down the people" (καὶ ἐν Ἄργει οἱ γνώριμοι εὐδοκιμήσαντες περὶ τὴν ἐν Μαντινείᾳ μάχην τὴν πρὸς Λακεδαιμονίους ἐπεχείρησαν καταλύειν τὸν δῆμον, *Politics* 1304a25–26).[17]

If indeed the success of the oligarchic coup was predicated on the earlier heroic conduct of the Thousand at Mantinea, then the prompt reorientation from fighting the Spartans to joining forces with them must have been an essential tactical move for the Thousand. But how was such a sharp change of political course feasible in a brief span of time?

Perhaps one of the propagandistic devices that assisted the Thousand in switching fluently between pro-Spartan and anti-Spartan attitudes was the manipulation of the myth-ritual complex of the confrontation over Thyreatis. We can envisage the usefulness of the concept of ritual battle as a stepping stone between war and peace: by substituting the exhortation to battle with an exhortation to ritual battle, a spokesman of the Thousand could

---

[16] David 1986, 115–116.

[17] Diodorus' account presents a similar picture: he notes that the oligarchic coup by the Thousand was facilitated by the Thousand's numerous exponents, who supported them because of the prominence that "their wealth and brave exploits" gave them (ταῖς οὐσίαις καὶ ταῖς ἀνδραγαθίαις, 12.80.3).

employ the charismatic rhetoric of military valor and struggle for the primordially Argive land, even if the underlying message was one of peace, not war. When it became necessary to maneuver in the opposite direction, from endorsing peace with Sparta to backing war, then the proponents of the ritual battle with their belligerent diction presumably would have been able to distance themselves from their earlier conciliatory policy more easily than if they had initially been supporting an openly dovish stance. Probably, such adaptable rhetoric was also employed by the oligarchic faction in the process of persuading the Argive community to establish the corps of the Thousand and to provide public funding for its training in 421 BC.[18]

Thus, hypothetically we can conceive of gains in political flexibility resulting from adroitly emphasizing or obscuring the connection between the myth of the ancient struggle for the Thyreatis and the ritual battle for that territory. The vital question is whether we can detect traces of such manipulations of the relation between myth and ritual in the historical record. The Argive suggestion to replay the battle for Thyreatis is one clear example of the employment of myth in tandem with ritual for political purposes. Below I am going to argue that in the period of 421-417 BC, the tradition of the confrontation between Argos and Sparta

---

[18] Bultrighini (1990, 131) describes the creation of the Thousand as "un'astuta manovra delle correnti oligarchiche" in Argos. For a glimpse of procedures concerning interstate negotiations in Argos in 421 BC, and their possible relevance to the power-struggles between the democrats and oligarchs, see Thucydides 5.27.2-3 (discussed in Robinson 2011, 11-12; Bearzot 2006, 126-128).

and the figure of Apollo Pythaeus was contested territory in the political struggle between the Argive democratic and oligarchic factions.

3. Apollo Pythaeus: a democratic move

Thucydides narrates that after the Argives entered into an alliance with Athens (in 420 BC) they declared war on Epidaurus (in the summer of 419 BC). Thucydides provides a remarkably precise analysis of the motives of this confrontation (5.53.1):[19]

> τοῦ δ' αὐτοῦ θέρους Ἐπιδαυρίοις καὶ Ἀργείοις πόλεμος ἐγένετο, προφάσει μὲν περὶ τοῦ θύματος τοῦ Ἀπόλλωνος τοῦ Πυθαέως, ὃ δέον ἀπαγαγεῖν οὐκ ἀπέπεμπον ὑπὲρ βοταμίων Ἐπιδαύριοι (κυριώτατοι δὲ τοῦ ἱεροῦ ἦσαν Ἀργεῖοι)· ἐδόκει δὲ καὶ ἄνευ τῆς αἰτίας τὴν Ἐπίδαυρον τῷ τε Ἀλκιβιάδῃ καὶ τοῖς Ἀργείοις προσλαβεῖν, ἢν δύνωνται, τῆς τε Κορίνθου ἕνεκα ἡσυχίας καὶ ἐκ τῆς Αἰγίνης βραχυτέραν ἔσεσθαι τὴν βοήθειαν ἢ Σκύλλαιον περιπλεῖν τοῖς Ἀθηναίοις. παρεσκευάζοντο οὖν οἱ Ἀργεῖοι ὡς αὐτοὶ ἐς τὴν Ἐπίδαυρον διὰ τοῦ θύματος τὴν ἔσπραξιν ἐσβαλοῦντες.

> The same summer war broke out between the Epidaurians and Argives. The pretext was that the Epidaurians did not send an offering for their pasture-land to Apollo Pythaeus, as they were bound to do, the Argives having the chief management of the temple; but, apart from this pretext, Alcibiades and the Argives were determined, if possible, to gain possession of Epidaurus, and thus to insure the neutrality of Corinth and give the Athenians a shorter passage for their reinforcement from Aegina than if they had to sail round Scyllaeum. The Argives accordingly prepared to invade Epidaurus by themselves, to exact the offering.

---

[19] See Hornblower 2008, 140–142 with further references.

We have repeatedly referred to this passage earlier (in Chapters 3 and 5): the description of the Argives as κυριώτατοι 'main overseers' of Apollo's temple serves as a central piece of evidence for the reconstruction of the Archaic alliance of states around the temple of Apollo Pythaeus in Asine.[20] Now we encounter the passage in its contemporary context. The striking peculiarity of this context is that the accusation of the Epidaurians for not sending their sacrificial dues, which evokes the distinctly aristocratic Archaic alliance, comes from the Argive democrats, associated with Athens. We have analyzed in Chapter 5 the ideological appropriation of Apollo Pythaeus by the Argive democracy, as attested by Bacchylides' paean and references to Telesilla's poetry. However, one of the democratic transformations that Apollo Pythaeus endured in the 460s was a relocation of the original cult of the god from the sanctuary in Asine to Argos. As I have argued, this reworking of the mythical tradition was connected precisely with the disintegration of the Archaic aristocratic alliance around Apollo in Asine; the democratic Argos of the 460s was not interested in preserving the elite connections with Epidaurus. However, in 420 BC the situation changed: the old alliance provided a perfect pretext for announcing war with the Epidaurians.

Diodorus provides a detail that differs from Thucydides' information in a fascinating way. He reports that the Argives accused the *Spartans* of not delivering the sacrifice to Apollo

---

[20] Barrett 1954; see above for other references.

Pythaeus (12.78.1–2):

> ἐπὶ δὲ τούτων Ἀργεῖοι μὲν ἐγκαλέσαντες τοῖς Λακεδαιμονίοις ὅτι τὰ θύματα οὐκ ἀπέδοσαν τῷ Ἀπόλλωνι τῷ Πυθαεῖ, πόλεμον αὐτοῖς κατήγγειλαν· καθ' ὃν δὴ χρόνον Ἀλκιβιάδης ὁ στρατηγὸς τῶν Ἀθηναίων ἐνέβαλεν εἰς τὴν Ἀργείαν ἔχων δύναμιν. τούτους δὲ οἱ Ἀργεῖοι παραλαβόντες ἐστράτευσαν ἐπὶ Τροιζῆνα, πόλιν σύμμαχον Λακεδαιμονίων, καὶ τὴν μὲν χώραν λεηλατήσαντες, τὰς δὲ ἐπαύλεις ἐμπρήσαντες, ἀπηλλάγησαν εἰς τὴν οἰκείαν.

> In this year the Argives, charging the Lacedaemonians with not paying the sacrifices to Apollo Pythaeus, declared war on them; and it was at this very time that Alcibiades, the Athenian general, entered Argolis with an army. Adding these troops to their forces, the Argives advanced against Troezen, a city which was an ally of the Lacedaemonians, and after plundering its territory and burning its farm-buildings they returned home.

The "Lacedaemonians" of Diodorus' testimony are commonly understood as either an erroneous substitution for Thucydides' Epidaurians, or as not the Spartans themselves, but their allies the Troezenians.[21] However, in my investigation I have already accepted Diodorus' passage at face value. Diodorus' testimony is the basis on which Angelo Brelich has first hypothesized about the existence of an Archaic federal cult of Apollo Pythaeus, including Sparta and Argos.[22] My reconstruction of the Archaic relationship between Sparta and Argos does not depend exclusively on Diodorus' testimony, so methodologically the reasoning is not circular. However, now we need to consider Diodorus' information in the context of Argive-Spartan relations in 420 BC.

---

[21] Recently, Kowalzig 2007a, 145; Barrett 1954, 442n1.
[22] Brelich 1961, 33–34.

It is appealing to connect the appearance of Apollo Pythaeus in the record of Argive-Spartan hostilities with the proposal of the ritual battle, made by the Argives to the Spartans just a year earlier. We may be witnessing a democratic "hijacking" of the oligarchic suggestion of the ritual battle, which transforms it from an offer of peace into a declaration of war. Apollo Pythaeus, who presided over the ritual battle between the Argives and Spartans and united the aristocrats of Sparta, Argos and Epidaurus, now caters to the needs of the Argive democracy.

Yet the struggle for Apollo's possession was not over. We will return to the subject, and discuss the meaning of the difficult expression ὑπὲρ βοταμίων 'over the pasture-land' (?), qualifying the Epidaurians' debts to Apollo in Thucydides 5.53.1, when we investigate the terms of alliance between Argos and Sparta in the beginning of winter of 418/417 BC. However, before that let us consider the confrontation between Argos and Sparta in the summer of 418 BC, at the battle of Mantinea.

4. Heroic and unscathed at Mantinea

The battle of Mantinea was the oligarchs' revanche. They succeeded in utilizing the real battle with the Spartans, in which Argos suffered a defeat, as their springboard for gaining power. A propagandistic presentation of the events of the battle of Mantinea as an extension of the myth of the lethal struggle for the Thyreatis may have played a role in this accomplishment.

Thucydides recounts the words of encouragement addressed to the Argives by their commander before the battle (Thucydides 5.69.1):

> Ἀργείοις δὲ ὑπὲρ τῆς τε παλαιᾶς ἡγεμονίας καὶ τῆς ἐν Πελοποννήσῳ ποτὲ ἰσομοιρίας μὴ διὰ παντὸς στερισκομένους ἀνέχεσθαι, καὶ ἄνδρας ἅμα ἐχθροὺς καὶ ἀστυγείτονας ὑπὲρ πολλῶν ἀδικημάτων ἀμύνασθαι·

> The Argives [were reminded] that they would contend for their ancient supremacy, to regain their once equal share of the Peloponnesus of which they have been so long deprived, and to punish an enemy and a neighbor for a thousand wrongs.

The "equal share of the Peloponnesus" refers to the myth of the division of the Peloponnesus by the Heracleidae into Argos, Sparta and Messenia.[23] The mention of the "ancient supremacy" (παλαιᾶς ἡγεμονίας) takes us even further back into the mythical past. Thucydides speaks about the Argive hopes "to gain the supremacy of the Peloponnesus" (τῆς Πελοποννήσου ἡγήσεσθαι, Thucydides 5.28.2) in 421 BC, when Sparta was commonly perceived as lacking power, and Argos enjoyed sudden political ascendancy.[24] The notion of the "ancient supremacy" therefore describes the Argive position in the Peloponnesus free of Sparta's interference, that is to say, before the arrival of the Dorians. This interpretation is supported

---

[23] Hornblower 2008, 63–64, 183.
[24] Compare Thucydides 5.40.3, where the Argive desire of supremacy is associated with the refusal to renew a treaty with Sparta.

by Diodorus' assertion, at the point of describing the Argive aspirations of 421 BC, that the Greek kings of the greatest importance all came from Argos "until the return of the Heracleidae" (Diodorus Siculus 12.75.6). Herodotus' reference to the Argive control of a large part of the Peloponnesus before the battle of Champions (Herodotus 1.82.2) also fits this picture, if we take into account the telescoping of myth and history that occurs in the passage, and understand the Argive domination as taking place before the mythical battle, not before the Spartan annexation of the Thyreatis in the sixth century. Finally, the description of the Spartans as the *astugeitones* also invokes the traditional theme of confrontation between neighboring cities for border territory, and implicitly refers to the Spartan annexation of Cynuria.[25]

The exhortation before the battle of Mantinea thus presents the Argives as determined to reset the historical clock by means of battle, which is envisaged as an occasion on a par with the mythical events defining Argive-Spartan relations. Mantinea was to be an expanded and corrected version of the battle of Champions, in which Sparta might be decisively vanquished, and the Argive supremacy established once and for all.

However, the Argives were defeated. Moreover, the battle of Mantinea is famous for some very odd military moves, initiated by the Spartan king Agis, which generated suspicions

---

[25] See Introduction, Section 3.

among a number of modern scholars that the course of the battle was informed by an ulterior agreement between Agis and the Argive oligarchs.[26] Without entering into the details of this discussion, it is important to note that the Thousand survived the battle mostly intact. The survival of the Thousand is juxtaposed by Thucydides to the fate of the Mantineans, who were assaulted alongside the Thousand by the victorious right wing of the Spartan army. "Many of the Mantineans perished," says Thucydides, "but the bulk of the picked body of the Argives made good their escape" (καὶ τῶν μὲν Μαντινέων καὶ πλείους διεφθάρησαν, τῶν δὲ Ἀργείων λογάδων τὸ πολὺ ἐσώθη, 5.73.4). Donald Kagan comments: "It is hard to understand why of these two contingents fighting side by side one should have been almost annihilated and the other almost unharmed."[27] Accordingly, several scholars express the idea that "the Spartans were looking past the battle,"[28] sparing the oligarchic Thousand because they constituted the Spartan base of support in Argos, backing peace and alliance with Sparta.

After the lost battle and their questionable escape, how did the Thousand exonerate themselves and gain popularity? Their weapon seems to have been the myth of the battle of Champions.

---

[26] Woodhouse 1933, 84-5; Kagan 1962; Gillis 1963; see Bultrighini 1990, 136n239 for further references.
[27] Kagan 1981, 131.
[28] Hanson 2005, 159; Ruzé 2006, 270-271.

The relevant information comes from Diodorus' description of the battle of Mantinea. The salient feature of Diodorus' account in comparison with Thucydides' report is its exclusive focus on the fortunes of the Thousand in the battle, at the expense of all other actors. The Thousand are said to be the first troop at Mantinea who turned their opponents to flight (12.79.4). Diodorus is highly complimentary of the Thousand, proclaiming their superiority to the Spartans in "feats of courage" (ἀνδραγαθίαις, 12.79.6). However, eventually the Thousand are surrounded by the Spartan forces, who intend to slaughter them to a man. Diodorus emphasizes the comprehensiveness of the anticipated destruction: "to butcher all of them," "would kill all of them" (κατακόψειν ἅπαντας, πάντας ἂν ἀνεῖλεν, 12.79.6). The Thousand are saved only by an intervention of Agis' adviser, Pharax (12.79.6):

> Φάραξ [...] διεκελεύετο τοῖς λογάσι δοῦναι δίοδον, καὶ μὴ πρὸς ἀπεγνωκότας τὸ ζῆν διακινδυνεύοντας πεῖραν λαβεῖν ἀτυχούσης ἀρετῆς.

> Pharax [...] directed him to leave a way of escape for the picked men and not, by hazarding the issue against men who had given up all hope of life, to learn what valor is when abandoned by Fortune.

The Thousand are allowed to escape precisely because they are so ready to die, and because this readiness to die makes them lethal fighters. In other words, Pharax advises Agis to let the Thousand through because otherwise the mythical battle of Champions will ensue. The Thousand "out-Spartan" the Spartans themselves in their legendary capacity to embrace the beautiful death.

The conjunction of the laudatory rhetoric with the testimony that the Thousand were let through by the Spartans is extremely interesting. Together with the exclusive focus of Diodorus' narrative on the Thousand, these features suggest that Diodorus' tale may derive from the self-presentation of the Thousand, popularized in Argos after the battle.

5. Apollo Pythaeus: a countermove

The admiration for the Thousand soon bore fruit. The pro-Spartan oligarchic party now openly ventured to advertise the idea of peace with Sparta, hoping, as Thucydides reports, "first to make a treaty with the Lacedaemonians, to be followed by an alliance, and after this to fall upon the commons." (ἐβούλοντο δὲ πρῶτον σπονδὰς ποιήσαντες πρὸς τοὺς Λακεδαιμονίους αὖθις ὕστερον καὶ ξυμμαχίαν, καὶ οὕτως ἤδη τῷ δήμῳ ἐπιτίθεσθαι, 5.76.2). The plan was duly implemented. A few months after the battle of Mantinea, in the beginning of the winter of 418/417 BC, a Spartan envoy arrived in Argos, and after much discussion, the Argives accepted a peace treaty with Sparta (Thucydides 5.76.3); soon after, the oligarchic faction orchestrated a dissolution of the Argive alliance with the democratic regimes of Athens, Mantinea and Elis, and then Argos concluded an alliance with Sparta (5.78-9). The oligarchic coup, assisted by Sparta, followed at the end of the same winter (5.81).

Thucydides reports the terms of the treaty between Argos and Sparta after Mantinea. The treaty resolved the conflict between Argos and Epidaurus concerning the offerings to Apollo Pythaeus. However, as Simon Hornblower remarks, the terms of the agreement may be "the worst crux" in all of Thucydides.[29] The problematic sentence runs as follows (Thucydides 5.77.4):

> περὶ δὲ τῶ σιῶ σύματος, αἰ μὲν λῆν, τοῖς Ἐπιδαυρίοις ὅρκον δόμεν, <αἰ> δέ, αὐτὼς ὀμόσαι.
>
> As to the offering to the god, the Argives, if they wish, shall give an oath to the Epidaurians, but, if not, they shall swear it themselves.

The Doric dialect of the passage apparently created difficulties in the transmission of the text. The expression αἰ μὲν λῆν "if they wish" is Ahrens' emendation for ἐμενλῆν in the manuscripts; another emendation is an addition of αἰ before δέ. The whole structure of μὲν ... δέ... opposition thus has been restored. The presence of the emendation makes the interpretation less certain; however, perhaps the text in its emended form is not hopelessly obscure. My translation renders the Greek in the most straightforward manner, and thus differs from Richard Crawley's translation "the Argives shall impose an oath upon the Epidaurians." As Hornblower observes, "we cannot [...] get the sense 'the Epidaurians are to

---

[29] Hornblower 2008, 198.

swear' without emending τοῖς Ἐπιδαυρίοις to the accusative, τοὺς Ἐπιδαυρίους."[30] It seems to me that the impression of the garbled text in fact stems from our insufficient understanding of the situation which it describes. Let us clarify what we know or do not know about the terms of agreement, upon the assumption that the sentence is grammatically sound. The Argives are to swear to the Epidaurians — we do not know concerning what. The treaty provides an alternative suggestion: αὐτὼς ὀμόσαι (αὐτοὺς ὀμόσαι in the manuscripts). Gomme comments: "αὐτὼς, with ὀμόσαι, either marks a change of subject, or indicates that it was somehow noteworthy that this party, and not some other, should be swearing."[31] The contorted reading of τοῖς Ἐπιδαυρίοις ὅρκον δόμεν as "the Epidaurians are to swear" is an attempt to "save" the Argives to be the actors in the second part of the sentence; for if the Argives give oath to the Epidaurians, who are αὐτὼς? Perhaps the Spartans are. They are, after all, natural referents in a treaty between Sparta and Argos. There is a parallel from Thucydides (2.5.6): Θηβαῖοι μὲν ταῦτα λέγουσι καὶ ἐπομόσαι φασὶν αὐτούς: "This is the Theban account, and they add that the Plataians took an oath."[32] My interpretation that the Spartans are going to give an oath (we will presently discuss to whom and about what) is based on Diodorus' account (12.78.1), portraying the Spartans as directly involved in the conflict concerning the offerings to

---

[30] Hornblower 2008, 199.
[31] Gomme 1970, 137.
[32] Translation by Hornblower 1991, 242.

Apollo.³³ So, the general sense of the sentence is that the Argives (if they prefer) may give an oath to the Epidaurians; otherwise, the Spartans will swear.

Let us now attempt to establish the content of the oath. Another episode, described by Thucydides (5.42.1), provides an excellent typological parallel:

> ἐν δὲ τῷ χρόνῳ τούτῳ ᾧ οἱ Ἀργεῖοι ταῦτα ἔπρασσον, οἱ πρέσβεις τῶν Λακεδαιμονίων Ἀνδρομένης καὶ Φαίδιμος καὶ Ἀντιμενίδας, οὓς ἔδει τὸ Πάνακτον καὶ τοὺς ἄνδρας τοὺς παρὰ Βοιωτῶν παραλαβόντας Ἀθηναίοις ἀποδοῦναι, τὸ μὲν Πάνακτον ὑπὸ τῶν Βοιωτῶν αὐτῶν καθῃρημένον ηὗρον, ἐπὶ προφάσει ὡς ἦσάν ποτε Ἀθηναίοις καὶ Βοιωτοῖς ἐκ διαφορᾶς περὶ αὐτοῦ **ὅρκοι παλαιοὶ** μηδετέρους οἰκεῖν τὸ χωρίον, ἀλλὰ **κοινῇ νέμειν**,

> In the meantime, while the Argives were engaged in these negotiations, the Lacedaemonian ambassadors, Andromedes, Phaedimus, and Antimenidas, who were to receive the prisoners from the Boeotians and restore them and Panactum to the Athenians, found that the Boeotians had themselves razed Panactum, upon the plea that <u>oaths had been anciently exchanged</u> between their people and the Athenians, after a dispute on the subject, to the effect that neither should inhabit the place, but that they should <u>graze it in common</u>.³⁴

First of all, the placement of this passage in Thucydides' text is significant. It comes immediately after the description of the Argive proposal to the Spartans to replay the ritual

---

³³ Contrast Hornblower's conclusion of the discussion of Thucydides 5.77.4: "The only other conclusion we can reach, and it is not negligible, is that the Spartans felt able to dictate the solution to a religious dispute in which they themselves had no part." Hornblower 2008, 199. I note Kelly's comment on the favorable terms of the treaty offered by the Spartans to the Argives: "By its terms Argos and Sparta were to serve as equal partners in determining matters within the Peloponnesus." Kelly 1974, 98n73.

³⁴ On traditions associated with the conflict between the Athenians and the Boeotians over the territory around Panactum, see Vidal-Naquet 1986, 106–128; Daverio Rocchi 1988, 180–186; de Polignac 1995, 56–57.

battle over the Thyreatis (5.41). I believe that Thucydides placed the two passages adjacently because there is a thematic connection between them. The common theme is the use of the ancient disputes over border territories for contemporary political purposes. Let us now compare the Argive-Spartan treaty with the Boeotian claims. The Boeotians assert that their dispute with the Athenians about a border territory resulted in an ancient agreement (ὅρκοι παλαιοί) about this territory, stipulating that it should remain uninhabited and serve as common grazing land (κοινῇ νέμειν).[35] This description matches very well the reconstruction of the Archaic alliance of states around Apollo Pythaeus (see Chapter 3), whose authority was invoked in questions of the regulation of border territories. Specifically, the condition that the land around Panactum is supposed to remain common grazing territory recalls the difficult expression ὑπὲρ βοταμίων (Thucydides 5.53.1), employed in the Argive allegation that the Epidaurians neglected to send offerings to Apollo Pythaeus. Various explanations of the hapax *botamia* have been offered, one of the most frequent suggestions being that it should mean 'pasture-land.'[36] Jameson, in particular, proposes that the manuscript variant *parapotamia*

---

[35] On Panactum, see Kelly 1972; Ober 1985.

[36] Kowalzig 2007a, 147 and n51 with further references; Hornblower 2008, 141–142. On the importance of pasture land in the relations between neighboring cities, see Howe 2003; 2008, 77–97 and p. 84 on Panactum (Howe draws a parallel between this episode and the Lelantine War, as well as the conflict over the Thyreatis); Chandezon 2003, 331–390.

should refer to the plain of Iria, traversed by Bedheni river, between Epidaurus and Asine, a cattle-grazing territory.[37]

Thus, I believe that the treaty between the Argives and the Spartans arranged that the Argives were to exchange oaths with the Epidaurians concerning the territories overseen by Apollo Pythaeus, swearing that these territories would remain uninhabited common pasture land; alternatively, the Spartans were to exchange such oaths with the Argives. In the latter case, the object of the oaths should be the territory of Thyreatis. I have argued that the conflict, initiated by the Argive democrats concerning the offerings to Apollo Pythaeus resurrected the Archaic alliance between Argos, Epidaurus and Sparta as a pretext, justifying the war with Epidaurus. The treaty between Argos and Sparta picks up the theme, and proposes to revive the Archaic alliance between these cities in reality. Apollo Pythaeus has been returned to his aristocratic roots.

---

[37] Jameson 1994, 64n11. Another interesting point in the Boeotian-Athenian episode, providing a parallel for the Argive-Spartan treaty, is the mention of the destruction of the Athenian fort at Panactum by the Boeotians under the pretext that the land, according to the ancient oaths, should remain uninhabited. A clause of the Argive-Spartan treaty (Thucydides 5.77.2) specified that the Argives should destroyed a fort, which the Athenians built at Cape Heraeum near Epidaurus during the recent war between Epidaurus and Argos (5.75.6), and which was garrisoned by the Athenians together with the Argives and other allies. Perhaps this stipulation was ideologically connected with the regulation of the offerings to Apollo Pythaeus.

6. Waiting for the Gymnopaediae

Thucydides narrates that at the end of the winter of 418/417 BC, "The Lacedaemonians and Argives, each a thousand strong, [...] took the field together, and [...] uniting, put down the democracy at Argos and set up an oligarchy favorable to Lacedaemon" (καὶ Λακεδαιμόνιοι καὶ Ἀργεῖοι, χίλιοι ἑκάτεροι, ξυστρατεύσαντες [...] ξυναμφότεροι ἤδη καὶ τὸν ἐν Ἄργει δῆμον κατέλυσαν, καὶ ὀλιγαρχία ἐπιτηδεία τοῖς Λακεδαιμονίοις κατέστη, 5.81.2). However, the oligarchic regime in Argos was short-lived. After several months the Argive democrats were ready for a countercoup. Thucydides reports that the Argive *dêmos* waited for the moment of the Gymnopaediae in Sparta to attack the oligarchs (5.82.2).

Why did the democratic faction choose the Gymnopaediae as a moment for the attack? The usual answer is that the democrats hoped that the Spartans would be unwilling to suspend the festival in order to come to the oligarchs' aid. Indeed, Thucydides says that the Spartans did not respond for some time to the oligarchs' pleas for help; however, eventually they did postpone the Gymnopaediae and marched to Argos, only to learn in Tegea about the oligarchs' defeat, whereupon they refused to go any further and returned to Sparta to celebrate the Gymnopaediae (5.82.3). Barbara Kowalzig captures the irony of the situation: "The Spartans resume their dancing for Apollo Pythaieus at the Gymnopaidiai, as if... the Battle of Champions had only just been won."[38] The reluctance of the Spartans to come to the oligarchs' help brings to a close the story of the misalliance between the Spartans and the Argive oligarchs, and thematically harks back to the beginning of that story, the Spartan reaction to the Argive suggestion of reviving the battles for the Thyreatis: "Idiocy!" (μωρία, Thucydides 5.41.3).[39]

However, perhaps the Argive democrats had a further incentive to wait until the Gymnopaediae. As I have argued, the Archaic ritual battles took place in the framework of the Gymnopaediae for the Spartans. Given the earlier Argive proposal to the Spartans to replay the battle for the Thyreatis, it is possible that after the oligarchic coup the Thousand were planning to fight a ritual battle with the Spartans (conceivably with the one thousand Spartans who assisted in the coup). According to this conjecture, at the moment of the Spartan Gymnopaediae the Thousand may have left Argos for the preliminary part of the festival (but did not yet reach the Spartans in the Thyreatis). Interestingly, we have a description of a coup in Argos that resembles this hypothetical scenario. Aeneas Tacticus (17.2-4) narrates the following story:

> Ἑορτῆς γὰρ πανδήμου ἔξω τῆς πόλεως Ἀργείων γενομένης ἐξῆγον πομπὴν σὺν ὅπλοις τῶν ἐν τῇ ἡλικίᾳ· συχνοὶ δὲ τῶν ἐπιβουλευόντων καὶ αὐτοὶ παρεσκευάζοντο καὶ αὐτοῖς συνητοῦντο ὅπλα εἰς τὴν πομπήν. Καὶ <ὡς> ἐγένετο πρὸς τῷ ναῷ τε καὶ τῷ βωμῷ, οἱ μὲν πολλοὶ τὰ ὅπλα θέμενοι ἀπωτέρω τοῦ ναοῦ πρὸς τὰς εὐχάς τε καὶ τὸν βωμὸν

---

[38] Kowalzig 2007a, 179.
[39] On the possible ulterior motifs of the delay in the Spartan help to the Argive oligarchs, see Ruzé 2006, 271-272.

ὥρμησαν. Τῶν δὲ ἐπιβουλευόντων οἱ μὲν ἐπὶ τῶν ὅπλων ὑπέμειναν, οἱ δὲ ταῖς ἀρχαῖς τε καὶ τῶν πολιτῶν τοῖς προέχουσι παρέστησαν ἐν ταῖς εὐχαῖς, ἀνὴρ ἀνδρί, ἔχοντες ἐγχειρίδια. Καὶ τοὺς μὲν κατεβεβλήκεσαν, οἱ δὲ αὐτῶν εἰς τὴν πόλιν σὺν τοῖς ὅπλοις ἔσπευσαν. Ἕτεροι
δὲ τῶν συνεπιβουλευόντων ὑπομείναντες ἐν τῇ πόλει μετὰ τῶν προσαλισθέντων ὅπλων προκατέλαβον οὓς προσῆκε τόπους τῆς πόλεως, ὥστε δέξασθαι τῶν ἔξω οὓς ἐβούλοντο. Διὸ δεῖ <πρὸς> τὰς τοιαύτας ἐπιβουλὰς ἐν οὐδενὶ καιρῷ ἀφυλάκτως διακεῖσθαι.

At Argos a public festival took place outside the city, at which there was an armed procession of the men of military age; and a number of the conspirators made ready and joined in the demand for arms to carry in the procession. In the vicinity of the temple and the altar, most of the people piled their arms at some distance from the temple and went to the service of prayer at the altar; but among the conspirators some remained by the arms, while others, armed with daggers, took their places during the prayers next to the magistrates and most prominent citizens, each picking his man. After these had been struck down, some of them [of the conspirators] ran off with the arms to the city; while another party of conspirators, who had remained in the city, occupied points of vantage, armed with the extra weapons they had collected, so as to allow only those whom they wished to enter the city. At no time, therefore, should you neglect to be on your guard against such plots.

This account is usually connected to the oligarchic coup of 418/417;[40] however, there is no trace of the Spartan assistance mentioned by Thucydides (admittedly, the Spartans are also absent from Diodorus' description of the oligarchic coup).[41] Still, the association of the story with the democratic coup seems at least possible.

---

[40] Oldfather 1923, 91n1; Dain and Bon 1967, 126-127; Losada 1972, 95n2; David 1986, 120; Whitehead 1990, 146, with other references; Bultrighini 1990, 138; Sauzeau 2008, 12.
[41] Sauzeau 2008, 12n25 notes the absence of the Spartan allies. Bultrighini 1990, 138 assumes that the Argive procession in Aeneas' account is an armed procession to the Heraion; however, the oligarchic coup of 418/417 and the Heraea are incompatible, since the Heraea took place in

However, Aeneas' narrative is unlikely to be a veristic report of events. Polyaenus (1.23.2) tells the same story about the beginning of Polycrates' tyranny on Samos: an armed procession occurs before a public sacrifice to Hera, and the conspirators are Polycrates and his brothers Syloson and Pantognostus. When the sacrifice starts, most people deposit their weapons at the altar. Polycrates' brothers kill the unarmed men at prayer, while Polycrates occupies the citadel. The only difference between this story and Aeneas' narrative is that the motif of gathering the weapons so as to arm the supporters is absent. Aristotle reports another variant, starring Peisistratus (*Athenian Constitution* 15.4–5):

> παρεῖλε δὲ τοῦ δήμου τὰ ὅπλα τόνδε τὸν τρόπον. ἐξοπλασίαν ἐν τῷ Θησείῳ ποιησάμενος ἐκκλησιάζειν ἐπεχείρει, καὶ χρόνον προσηγόρευεν μικρόν, οὐ φασκόντων δὲ κατακούειν, ἐκέλευσεν αὐτοὺς προσαναβῆναι πρὸς τὸ πρόπυλον τῆς ἀκροπόλεως, ἵνα γεγωνῇ μᾶλλον. ἐν ᾧ δ' ἐκεῖνος διέτριβε δημηγορῶν, ἀνελόντες οἱ ἐπὶ τούτῳ τεταγμένοι τὰ ὅπλα, καὶ κατακλείσαντες εἰς τὰ πλησίον οἰκήματα τοῦ Θησείου, διεσήμηναν ἐλθόντες πρὸς τὸν Πεισίστρατον. ὁ δὲ ἐπεὶ τὸν ἄλλον λόγον ἐπετέλεσεν, εἶπε καὶ περὶ τῶν ὅπλων τὸ γεγονός, ὡς οὐ χρὴ θαυμάζειν οὐδ' ἀθυμεῖν, ἀλλ' ἀπελθόντας ἐπὶ τῶν ἰδίων εἶναι, τῶν δὲ κοινῶν αὐτὸς ἐπιμελήσεσθαι πάντων.

The way in which he disarmed the people was this: he held an armed muster at the Temple of Theseus, and began to hold an Assembly, but he lowered his voice a little, and when they said they could not hear him, he told them to come up to the forecourt of the Acropolis, in order that his voice might carry better; and while he used up time in making a speech, the men told off for this purpose gathered up the arms, locked them up in the neighboring buildings of the Temple of Theseus, and came and informed Peisistratus. He, when he had finished the rest of his speech, told his audience not to be

---

the summer, while the coup occurred in the winter. Interestingly, Scheid and Svenbro (1996, 31, 77) tentatively equate the Heraea with the Endymatia (the festival during which the ritual battles took place in the Archaic period, according to my suggestion).

surprised at what had happened about their arms, and not to be dismayed, but to go away and occupy themselves with their private affairs, while he would attend to all public business.

We can also remember the Argive story of Archinus (Polyaenus 3.8), which I analyzed in Chapter 5. In all these examples the seizure of the citizens' armor is a trope for depriving them of their civic agency (Aristotle's Pesistratus spells this idea out). However, the motif of the reuse of the confiscated armor for arming the supporters of the coup does not seem to occur in the stories about the Archaic tyrants; on the basis of the story of Archinus I infer that this motif is specific to the hostile descriptions of the democratic coups. On this reasoning, Aeneas' story, featuring the redistribution of the armor by the conspirators, should describe a democratic takeover as perceived by the oligarchs.

However, if we accept that Aeneas' story relates to the democratic coup of 417 BC, what do we learn about its real course of events? Not much, since the conspirators' seizure of the gathered arms and the sacrilegious killings of men at prayer are certainly topoi. The only detail that is perhaps realistic is the information about the public festival outside the city.

Thus, we have an oblique indication that during the democratic coup some of the Argive oligarchs were away from Argos, participating in a festival, and that this festival coincided with the Spartan Gymnopaediae. One last strange little piece of the puzzle comes from Thucydides (5.80.3), who, immediately before describing the oligarchic coup in Argos, narrates the following story about the Argive attempt to make the Athenians evacuate the fort near Epidaurus (as stipulated in the Argive-Spartan treaty):

> ἔπεμψαν δὲ καὶ παρὰ τοὺς Ἀθηναίους οἱ Ἀργεῖοι πρέσβεις, τὸ ἐξ Ἐπιδαύρου τεῖχος κελεύοντες ἐκλιπεῖν. οἱ δ' ὁρῶντες ὀλίγοι πρὸς πλείους ὄντες τοὺς ξυμφύλακας, ἔπεμψαν Δημοσθένη τοὺς σφετέρους ἐξάξοντα. ὁ δὲ ἀφικόμενος καὶ ἀγῶνά τινα πρόφασιν γυμνικὸν ἔξω τοῦ φρουρίου ποιήσας, ὡς ἐξῆλθε τὸ ἄλλο φρούριον, ἀπέκλησε τὰς πύλας· καὶ ὕστερον Ἐπιδαυρίοις ἀνανεωσάμενοι τὰς σπονδὰς αὐτοὶ οἱ Ἀθηναῖοι ἀπέδοσαν τὸ τείχισμα.

> ...the Argives, besides, sent ambassadors to the Athenians, bidding them evacuate the fort at Epidaurus. The Athenians, seeing their own men outnumbered by the rest of the garrison, sent Demosthenes to bring them out. The general, under color of a gymnastic contest, which he arranged on his arrival, got the rest of the garrison out of the place and shut the gates behind them. Afterwards the Athenians renewed their treaty with the Epidaurians, and by themselves gave up the fortress.

Simon Hornblower remarks that Thucydides "is both generous with detail to an uncharacteristic degree about this small episode, but also allusive, compressed, and hard to understand."[42] The point of Thucydides' inclusion of the story is uncertain — unless, conceivably, the Athenian joke serves as an uncanny prefiguration of the democratic coup in Argos. The troops whom Demosthenes lured out of the fort must have been Argive;[43] these Argives, unable to withstand the temptation of a gymnastic contest, seem an apt parody of the Argive oligarchs, who were to be similarly locked out of their city — while perhaps on their

---

[42] Hornblower 2008, 205. Rood 1998, 107-108 notes that this is one of only two occurrences of *agôn gumnikos* in Thucydides.
[43] Hornblower 2008, 206.

way to a ritual battle.

7. Bryas, *hubris* and memories of the past

At the conclusion of this exploration, let us consider, as a coda, one more text recounting the story of the Argive one thousand. Pausanias narrates the following story apropos the statue of Zeus Meilichius that he saw in Argos (Pausanias 2.20.1–2):

> ἄγαλμά ἐστι καθήμενον Διὸς Μειλιχίου, λίθου λευκοῦ, Πολυκλείτου δὲ ἔργον. ποιηθῆναι δὲ ἐπυνθανόμην αὐτὸ ἐπ' αἰτίᾳ τοιαύτῃ. Λακεδαιμονίοις πολεμεῖν πρὸς Ἀργείους ἀρξαμένοις οὐδεμία ἦν ἔτι ἀπαλλαγή, πρὶν ἢ Φίλιππος σφᾶς ἠνάγκασεν ὁ Ἀμύντου μένειν ἐπὶ τοῖς καθεστηκόσιν ἐξ ἀρχῆς ὅροις τῆς χώρας. τὸν δὲ ἔμπροσθεν χρόνον οἱ Λακεδαιμόνιοι μηδὲν ἔξω Πελοποννήσου περιεργαζόμενοι τῆς Ἀργείας ἀεί τι ἀπετέμνοντο, ἢ οἱ Ἀργεῖοι τετραμμένων πρὸς πόλεμον ἐκείνων ὑπερόριον ἐν τῷ τοιούτῳ καὶ αὐτοί σφισιν ἐνέκειντο.
> προηγμένου δὲ ἀμφοτέροις ἐς ἄκρον τοῦ μίσους ἔδοξεν Ἀργείοις λογάδας τρέφειν χιλίους· ἡγεμὼν δὲ ἐτέτακτο ἐπ' αὐτοῖς Βρύας Ἀργεῖος, ὃς ἄλλα τε ἐς ἄνδρας ὕβρισε τοῦ δήμου καὶ παρθένον κομιζομένην παρὰ τὸν νυμφίον ᾔσχυνεν ἀφελόμενος τοὺς ἄγοντας. ἐπιλαβούσης δὲ τῆς νυκτὸς τυφλοῖ τὸν Βρύαντα ἡ παῖς φυλάξασα ὑπνωμένον· φωραθεῖσα δὲ ὡς ἐπέσχεν ἡμέρα, κατέφυγεν ἱκέτις ἐς τὸν δῆμον. οὐ προεμένων δὲ αὐτὴν τιμωρήσασθαι τοῖς χιλίοις καὶ ἀπὸ τούτου προαχθέντων ἐς μάχην ἀμφοτέρων, κρατοῦσιν οἱ τοῦ δήμου, κρατήσαντες δὲ οὐδένα ὑπὸ τοῦ θυμοῦ τῶν ἐναντίων ἔλιπον. ὕστερον δὲ ἄλλα τε ἐπηγάγοντο καθάρσια ὡς ἐπὶ αἵματι ἐμφυλίῳ καὶ ἄγαλμα ἀνέθηκαν Μειλιχίου Διός.

> ... you come to a seated image of Zeus Meilichius, made of white marble by Polycleitus. I discovered that it was made for the following reason. Ever since the Lacedaemonians began to make war upon the Argives there was no cessation of hostilities until Philip, the son of Amyntas, forced them to stay within the original boundaries of their territories. Before this, if the Lacedaemonians were not engaged on some business

outside the Peloponnesus, they were always trying to annex a piece of Argive territory; or if they were busied with a war beyond their borders it was the turn of the Argives to retaliate. When the hatred of both sides was at its height, the Argives resolved to maintain a thousand picked men. The commander appointed over them was the Argive Bryas. His general behavior to the men of the people was violent, and a maiden who was being taken to the bridegroom he seized from those who were escorting her and ravished. When night came on, the girl waited until he was asleep and put out his eyes. Detected in the morning, she took refuge as a suppliant with the people. When they did not give her up to the Thousand for punishment both sides took up arms; the people won the day, and in their anger left none of their opponents alive. Subsequently they had recourse to purifications for shedding kindred blood; among other things they dedicated an image of Zeus Meilichius.

Pausanias' tale is not embedded in any chronological framework; however, the confrontation between the *dêmos* and the Thousand almost certainly should be identified with the democratic countercoup against the rule of the Thousand, described by Thucydides and Diodorus. The dating of Polycleitus, the sculptor who made the image of Zeus Meilichius, corroborates this identification.

However, the most striking feature of the passage is a radical flattening of the historical record. The confrontation between Argos and Sparta lacks any historical specificity; the only elements that are left are the timeless hatred between Argos and Sparta and the Thousand who are the embodiment of that hatred.

The Thousand are set in opposition with the *dêmos*; however, the antagonism is moral and not social. Pierre Sauzeau has recently analyzed Pausanias' narrative about Bryas and the Thousand, observing an affinity between this corps and the mythical hybristic warriors such as the Phlegyae.[44] Bryas' conduct brings us back full circle to the *hubris* of the Bronze Generation, featured in the myth of the Lelantine War; however, now the same characterization is applied to a commander of historical elite forces. Elsewhere Pausanias gives an account of an Attic cult of Zeus Meilichius. He comments that the altar was a place of Theseus' purification, after he had killed Sinis, "the Ravager," who was his relative (Pausanias 1.37.4).[45] The historical Thousand, who were intended to participate in the ritual battles, become assimilated with the primeval wrongdoers. The death of the whole Thousand at the hands of the Argive *dêmos* resembles the myth of destruction of the lawless community of Asine. The story of the destruction of the Thousand functions as an aetiology of the creation of the statue of Zeus Meilichius. We see new myths emerging from old rituals, and new elements of cult attached to the myths.

---

[44] Sauzeau 2008, 10.
[45] Bultrighini 1990, 141.

Conclusion

Border between Myth and Ritual

> *I felt the collapse of time — as if I was there. I kept thinking I was my greatgrandfather.*
> Rodney Sweeney, on reenacting Pickett's charge

1. Old frontiers

The histories of the border disputes between Eretria and Chalcis and between Argos and Sparta show prominent similarities in the Archaic period: in both cases the participants of ritual battles for border territories belonged to the social class of *hippeis*. Ritual battles were an aristocratic tradition.

Another similarity is that the institution of ritual battles in both cases was associated with the myth of a destroyed city, that is, Euboea-Chalcis and Asine. The myth of the destruction of an excessively belligerent city recalls Crisa and the Delphic Amphictyony.[1]

The contrast between mythical total destruction and the controlled violence of ritual battles brings us to the question that I have asked in the introduction: what is the relation between the ritual battles and the hoplite ideal of agonistic warfare? The war of total

---

[1] Van Wees 1986, 302n76 cites the alliances in the Lelantine War and the Delphic Amphictyony as exceptionally early symmachies.

annihilation is the "evil twin" of the hoplite ideal;[2] both are cultural constructs. The habitat of the wars of total destruction is myth; the hoplite ideal, as it has been long recognized, shows conspicuous ritual traits. I would like to suggest that the true opposition of an unmitigated assault, as the result of which everybody dies, is a confrontation led according to strict rules, in which nobody dies; that is, a ritual battle. Thus, I propose that the ritual battles were the focal expression of the hoplite ideal.[3] They provided a behavioral model that was to a lesser or greater extent adopted in less ritualized confrontations.

The relation between ritual and myth — between restrained and unrestrained violence — is made more intricate by the fact that ritual battles reenacted mythical destructive confrontations. The reenactment provided the aristocratic participants with a powerful link to the legendary past.[4] However, the past also was a dangerous place, characterized by pre-civilized savagery. The ritual reenactments of catastrophic mythical battles show a dialectical attitude to the past: they reinforce the significance of the conflict myth in the identities of the warring sides, and at the same time emphasize the distance between the past and the present,

---

[2] See Ellinger 1993, 337.
[3] Compare Singor's suggestion (2009, 595, 599) that the rise of hoplite fighting was an aristocratic phenomenon, influenced by heroic notions expressed in Archaic poetry.
[4] On the construction and utilization of the mythical past in the Archaic period see especially Nagy [1979] 1999; Snodgrass 1981, 68–78; Morris 1988; Antonaccio 1995.

between the shattering devastation of the myth and the strictly controlled aggression of the ritual.[5]

Interestingly, the dark aspect of the past, prominent in the Euboean myth of the bronze-clad Curetes, is greatly attenuated in the myth of the battle of Champions. The Spartan ideal of the beautiful death shows no ambivalence toward the three hundred at Thyrea: the Champions' conduct is presented as the highest standard for emulation. In Hesiodic terms, the Champions resemble the Generation of Heroes, rather than the Bronze Men. I connect this presentation of the Champions with the Spartan modification of the myth of confrontation over the Thyreatis in the wake of the wide-ranging reforms that converted the aristocratic class of *hippeis* into an elite corps.

The later histories of the border confrontations over the Lelantine Plain and the Thyreatis diverge. In both cases, toward the end of the sixth century the border territory that earlier had been ritually contested was annexed by one state;[6] however, the identity of the occupying state makes a difference. In the case of the Thyreatis, it was Sparta; in the case of the Lelantine Plain, Athens. The ritual confrontation between Eretria and Chalcis in the

---

[5] On the connection between the mythical catastrophe and the regularity of ritual, see Nagy 1990b, 4. The association between the wars of total destruction and Artemis, observed by Ellinger, is paralleled by the connection between this goddess and the ritual battles. In the ritual battles, Artemis oversees the young men's encounter with dangers of the past in the marginal space of the borderland.

[6] See Singor 2009, 599–601.

Archaic period was not followed by a real conflict between the two *poleis*. In the case of Argos and Sparta, the genuine later hostilities were integrated with the myth-ritual complex of fighting over the Thyreatis. An analysis of Plutarch's passage, criticizing Herodotus' presentation of the events of the Persian Wars (*On the Malice of Herodotus* 868e), can further illuminate the differences between the two pairs of states:

> Τὸ γὰρ τῆς ἔχθρας γελοῖόν ἐστιν· οὔτε γὰρ Αἰγινήτας ἐκώλυσεν ἡ πρὸς Ἀθηναίους διαφορὰ καὶ Χαλκιδεῖς ἡ πρὸς Ἐρετριέας καὶ Κορινθίους ἡ πρὸς Μεγαρέας τῇ Ἑλλάδι συμμαχεῖν·

> For what he alleges of their hatreds is ridiculous. For neither did the difference between the Aeginetans and the Athenians, nor that between the Chalcidians and the Eretrians, nor yet that between the Corinthians and the Megarians, hinder them from fighting together for Greece.

The preceding investigation helps us see more clearly both the strong points and the faults of Plutarch's assertion. It is apparent from Plutarch's reference to the Megarian "spear-friends," or from his description of the *agôn* in which it befell Cleomachus to die, that he was familiar with the phenomenon of ritual battles. Accordingly, it is likely that the three pairs of cities listed by Plutarch engaged in a ritualized strife, accompanied by a real amity, in the Archaic period. It has been already proposed that there existed an entente between Aegina and

Peisistratid Athens,[7] and Herodotus' description of the "ancient enmity" (ἔχθρης παλαιῆς, 5.81.2) between Athens and Aegina shows signs of cultic integration between the two states.[8]

However, in insisting that these traditional confrontations did not play any role in the participation of states in the Persian wars, Plutarch entirely sidesteps the transformations of the ritual hostilities into real ones at the end of the Archaic period. The pair of cities conspicuously absent from Plutarch's list is Sparta and Argos, the ritual confrontation between whom had already turned into real antagonism by the time of the Persian Wars. According to the Argive version of events, reported by Herodotus, Argos' neutrality in the Persian wars was caused precisely by Cleomenes' assault at Sepeia (7.148–149).

Plutarch also disregards the seriousness of hostilities between Aegina and Athens in the period before and during the Persian wars. These hostilities were accompanied by a violent strife between the Aeginetan oligarchic and democratic factions, in which Athens supported the democrats.[9] The motif of the ancient enmity between Athens and Aegina, which beforehand had been probably motivating a ritual strife, was picked up by the Aeginetan oligarchs in their struggle with post-Peisistratid Athens.[10] The emphasis on the lack of

---

[7] Nagy 2011b, 78, with reference to Figueira 1993.
[8] Herodotus 5.85.2.
[9] Herodotus 6.49–50, 73, 91. See Chapter 5, Section 1.
[10] Αἰγινῆται δὲ εὐδαιμονίῃ τε μεγάλῃ ἐπαερθέντες καὶ ἔχθρης παλαιῆς ἀναμνησθέντες ἐχούσης ἐς Ἀθηναίους, τότε Θηβαίων δεηθέντων πόλεμον ἀκήρυκτον Ἀθηναίοισι ἐπέφερον· "The

conventions, expressed by Herodotus' description of the war between Athens and Aegina as a herald-less war (πόλεμον ἀκήρυκτον, 5.81.2), resembles the unbounded quality of Cleomenes' attack, and makes particular sense if viewed against the background of an earlier regulated and ritualized confrontation. In the case of the Aeginetan oligarchs, as in the case of the Argive democrats in the 460s, the myth of confrontation with the neighboring city was adapted for new political and ideological purposes.

2. The rest of the Greeks

I began this study by considering Thucydides' statement that the ancient war between Eretria and Chalcis caused the Greek world to divide into two camps (1.15.3). The only explicitly attested pair of cities thus divided is Samos and Miletus. Herodotus (5.99.1) reports that the Eretrians sent ships to aid Miletus during the Ionian Revolt because the Milesians had earlier helped them in the war against the Chalcidians, who were supported by the Samians. A concluding brief glance at this part of Greece will serve several purposes, giving some

---

Aeginetans, both elated by their present prosperity and mindful of their ancient enmity toward the Athenians, now responded to the Theban request by waging a herald-less war against the Athenians." Herodotus 5.81.2.

indications about the nature of the Archaic division into two camps, rehearsing the themes that we have encountered, and offering prospects for further research.

In his recent exploration of the history and geography of the Maeander Valley, Peter Thonemann describes a long-running border dispute between Samos and Priene as follows:

> The island of Samos, [...] lying off the Asiatic coast north of Mt Mycale, had long-standing claims to territory in or overlooking the Maeander delta plain. One particular dispute between Samos and Priene over a stretch of land on Mt. Mycale seems to have been particularly bitter. The conflict concerned territorially underdefined but economically precious marginal resources, the region known as Batinetis ('brambles') and Dryoussa ('oak-woods') on Mt Mycale. Both states agreed that this land had originally formed part of the territory of Melia, destroyed in the late eighth or early seventh century BC; the dispute seems to have run more or less continuously from the seventh to the late second century BC.[11]

Plutarch transmits the following tradition about the confrontation between Samos and Priene (*Greek Questions* 20):

> Σάμιοι καὶ Πριηνεῖς πολεμοῦντες ἀλλήλοις, τὰ μὲν ἄλλα **μετρίως** ἐβλάπτοντο καὶ ἔβλαπτον, μάχης δὲ μεγάλης γενομένης, χιλίους Σαμίων οἱ Πριηνεῖς ἀπέκτειναν.
>
> When the Samians and the Prienians were at war with each other, on the other occasions they suffered injuries and inflicted injuries <u>to a moderate degree only</u>; but when a great battle took place, the people of Priene slew one thousand Samians.

The familiar juxtaposition of the restrained violence and the all-out annihilation suggests that we are again dealing with ritual and mythical counterparts of the confrontation. Indeed, Thonemann concludes that "the emphasis should lie on the *normality* of warfare between

---

[11] Thonemann 2011, 28.

Priene and Samos over the territory on Mt Mycale,"[12] and cites Graham Shipley's earlier remark that "for young Samian hoplites, it may have been almost a *rite de passage* to fight in defence of the Peraia."[13]

The traditional confrontation between Samos and Priene also involved Miletus. Plutarch continues in the passage that I have just quoted (*Greek Questions* 20):

> ἑβδόμῳ δ'ὕστερον ἔτει Μιλησίοις συμβαλόντες παρὰ τὴν καλουμένην δρῦν τοὺς ἀρίστους ὁμοῦ τι καὶ πρώτους ἀπέβαλον τῶν πολιτῶν.
>
> Six years later they [the Prienians] engaged the Milesians at a place called the Oak, and lost practically all the best and the foremost of their citizens.[14]

We further learn that the city of Melia was jointly destroyed for its arrogance (*adrogantiam*) by Miletus, Samos, Priene and other cities constituting the Ionian League (Vitruvius *On Architecture* 4.1.4).[15] The League also established a sanctuary called the Panionium, dedicated to Heliconian Poseidon (Herodotus 1.148), on the territory that had previously belonged to Melia.[16]

The myth of the destroyed Melia, whose territory served both as the common sanctuary and as the object of dispute for the cities belonging to the Ionian League, provides

---

[12] Thonemann 2011, 29.
[13] Shipley 1987, 35.
[14] The same information is given by Aristotle in the *Samian Constitution* (F 576 ap. Zenobius 6.12).
[15] Singor 2009, 586.
[16] Asheri, Lloyd, and Corcella 2007, 178, with further references.

another parallel for the myths about the destruction of Asine and Euboea-Chalcis, which we have discussed.

The cities of Samos and Miletus also supply a beautiful illustration of the role of the contested territory in the identity of the opposing cities. Thonemann notes that "the most popular of all the nominal elements in the archaic onomastics of Miletus was the name of the river Maeander, present in the form Mandr- or -mandros in around a seventh of *all* personal names attested at Miletus before 500 BC," and that in Samos the Maeander-names were nearly as popular.[17] Thonemann connects the popularity of these names with his observation that the lower Maeander plain functioned "as an agreed *locus* of ritualized military display for the cities of Miletus, Priene, Magnesia, Samos and even for the seventh-century Lydian kingdom itself."[18] Importantly, when Aristotle speaks about the ancient wars between neighbors, in which the elites used horses, he cites as an example Eretria and Chalcis, and also the Magnesians on the Maeander (*Politics* 1289b):

> ἐχρῶντο δὲ πρὸς τοὺς πολέμους ἵπποις πρὸς τοὺς ἀστυγείτονας οἷον Ἐρετριεῖς καὶ Χαλκιδεῖς καὶ Μάγνητες οἱ ἐπὶ Μαιάνδρῳ καὶ τῶν ἄλλων πολλοὶ περὶ τὴν Ἀσίαν·

---

[17] Thonemann 2011, 27, 29. Thonemann 2006.
[18] Thonemann 2011, 29, 27. Thonemann compares the role of the lower Maeander flood plain with that of the Thyreatis.

...and they used to use horses for their wars against their neighbors, as for instance did the Eretrians and Chalcidians and the people of Magnesia on the Maeander and many of the other Asiatic peoples.[19]

Finally, the confrontation between Samos and Miletus also had a continuation in the fifth century. Thucydides (1.115.2) reports that in 446 BC a war between oligarchic Samos and democratic Miletus took place:

> ἕκτῳ δὲ ἔτει Σαμίοις καὶ Μιλησίοις πόλεμος ἐγένετο περὶ Πριήνης, καὶ οἱ Μιλήσιοι ἐλασσούμενοι τῷ πολέμῳ παρ' Ἀθηναίους ἐλθόντες κατεβόων τῶν Σαμίων. ξυνεπελάβοντο δὲ καὶ ἐξ αὐτῆς τῆς Σάμου ἄνδρες ἰδιῶται νεωτερίσαι βουλόμενοι τὴν πολιτείαν.
>
> In the sixth year of the truce, war broke out between the Samians and Milesians about Priene. Worsted in the war, the Milesians came to Athens with loud complaints against the Samians. In this they were joined by certain private persons from Samos itself, who wished to revolutionize the government.

Thus, we again witness the traditional confrontation invoked in a struggle involving the oligarchic-democratic division.[20] Athens interfered and set up a democracy on Samos. However, this change of the regime was soon followed by a counter-revolution on Samos. Thucydides narrates that after the Samian oligarchs came to power, they managed to gain the

---

[19] Trans. by H. Rackham.

[20] Perhaps the explanation of the Eretrian assistance to Miletus as a repayment for the earlier help against Chalcis, reported by Herodotus, can be also construed as a takeover of the aristocratic tradition of the Lelantine War by the democratic regime. At the point of the Ionian revolt when Eretria sent its ships, Aristagoras already established *isonomia* in Miletus, according to Herodotus (5.37.2); Eretria also probably was a democracy (Knoepfler 1998, 105; cf. Walker 2004, 236–262).

support of the *dêmos*, and revolted from Athens. Their first step after that was to launch an expedition against Miletus (Thucydides 1.115.3-5). The ancient confrontations between neighboring cities keep being transformed according to the needs of the moment.

www.ingramcontent.com/pod-product-compliance
Lightning Source LLC
LaVergne TN
LVHW011927070526
838202LV00054B/4516